Writing the Self

Writing the Self

Diaries, Memoirs, and the History of the Self

Peter Heehs

BLOOMSBURY

NEW YORK • LONDON • NEW DELHI • SYDNEY

Bloomsbury Academic

An imprint of Bloomsbury Publishing Plc

175 Fifth Avenue	50 Bedford Square
New York	London
NY 10010	WC1B 3DP
USA	UK

www.bloomsbury.com

First published 2013

Library of Congress Cataloging-in-Publication Data
Heehs, Peter.
Writing the self : diaries, memoirs, and the history of the self / Peter Heehs.
p. cm.
Includes bibliographical references and index.
ISBN 978-1-4411-6802-3 (hardcover : alk. paper)–ISBN 978-1-4411-6828-3 (pbk.
: alk. paper) 1. Self in literature. 2. Self (Philosophy)–History. 3. Autobiography in
literature. 4. Soul in literature. I. Title.
PN56.S46H44 2013
809'.93384–dc23
2012035414

ISBN: HB: 978-1-4411-6802-3
PB: 978-1-4411-6828-3
ePub: 978-1-4411-5344-9
ePDF: 978-1-4411-2815-7

Typeset by Fakenham Prepress Solutions, Fakenham, Norfolk NR21 8NN
Printed and bound in the United States of America

Contents

1

The Self and History

I know that I exist; the question is, what is this "I" that I know?
 – René Descartes

All of us feel we are different than everybody else. We see the world through our own eyes, hear it with our own ears, touch it with our own hands. We have our own thoughts and feelings that we can share with other people but that no one experiences exactly as we do. We decide to do one thing and not another, take credit for our successes and feel the sting of our failures. The multitude of thoughts, feelings, sense impressions, impulses, and actions that make up our day-to-day lives seem to belong to a single someone. We feel that we were this someone in the past and will remain the same someone in the future. We have changed, of course, and will continue to change, but there is something that seems constant through it all. We call this our "I," our personal identity, our self.

Nothing could be more intimate to us than this self. It is not just close to us, it *is* all we are. We do not have to look for it. It is right here. Or so it seems. But perhaps it's not so simple. For if we try to grasp our self, it is always just out of reach. We see, hear, and touch particular things, but can't see who is seeing, hear who is hearing, touch who is touching. We have what seem to be our own thoughts and feelings, but don't know where they come from and can't always make them go away. We decide to do something but can't say what pushed us to action and don't always do what we decide to do. Our self, which to our immediate perception is the surest of all things, is at the same time the hardest to pin down.

Despite its elusiveness, the self is something we take for granted and we have a pretty good idea of what we mean when we speak about it. We assume most adults have similar ideas, though when we talk to people from different cultures, or who were brought up in different circumstances, or belong to the other gender, or are considerably older or younger, we are sometimes surprised to find how odd their ideas of selfhood are. And when we read about people who dwell in distant lands or who lived in the distant past, we have reason to wonder whether our idea of the self is the only one possible.

To avoid possible confusion it will be good to make a distinction between the instinctive sense of self that humans have always had and the concept of self that is a product of thought and reflection. The sociologist Marcel Mauss had something like this in mind when he wrote that "there was never a human being who lacked the sense not just of the body but also of a combined mental and physical individuality," but that this sense was not the same as "the idea or concept that humans of various periods have created out of it."[1] According to Mauss, the concept developed over time, eventually becoming the conscious self with which we are familiar. The rudimentary sense of self of our earliest human ancestors survives in us in the feeling that we possess a particular body, are focal points of particular sense-impressions and initiators of particular actions. Zoologists tell us that some of these traits are present in primates and cetaceans, developmental psychologists say that they emerge in children at an early age, but neither dolphins nor babies have a developed idea of self and it is highly unlikely that prehistoric humans did. Historians and social scientists differ as to when this idea emerged in Europe, but most believe it did not assume its current form before the sixteenth century.

Many people will find it strange to speak of a history of the self or even the history of the concept of the self. This is because our ideas about the subject are colored by the belief that there is something eternal and immutable in us that is our essential self. Many religions have a version of this belief: Hinduism speaks of the *atman*, Christianity of the soul. Even people who reject the doctrines of these and other religions are influenced by the idea of an essential inner substance, which has left its traces in our languages and cultural practices. Think of words like "soulful," "selfish," and "substantial." Whether the soul (or *atman* or self) actually exists is a question this book does not go into. It is a work of history, not philosophy or theology. But even if the soul or *atman* is eternal, the terms "soul" and "*atman*" have histories. Neither is present in the earliest texts of the religion in question; both underwent considerable development across the centuries. Believers are entitled to think that there is an immortal essence that is correctly described by certain passages of certain texts (the Upanishads, the Bible, Plotinus's *Enneads,* etc.). Historians are obliged to point out that both believers and non-believers have had different ideas on the subject at different times. It follows – at least for the non-dogmatic – that no particular idea can be considered final.

When we look at what people have written about the self in different historical periods, we see that the prevailing ideas have changed dramatically over the years. Beliefs that were current in prehistoric cultures are all but inconceivable today; beliefs that many of us hold today would have been thought madness a century or two ago.

One of the main components of the modern idea of the self is interiority or inwardness, the feeling that there is a personal inner space that we alone have access to. All of us distinguish between things that happen inside – thoughts, feelings, impulses – and things that happen outside us in the world. It is all but impossible for us to imagine a sane adult who lacked this sense. But many scholars think that people in antiquity – the men and women of the Homeric age, for example – did not have inner lives.[2] Historians of the self differ as to when the inner sense, as we understand it today, finally emerged, but it certainly was present in Augustine of Hippo (354–430 CE), whose works are filled with admonitions like "Do not go abroad. Return within yourself. In the inward man dwells truth."[3] If Augustine had jumped into a time machine and gone back a millennium and a half to give this advice to the warriors before Troy, they would have stared at him in blank incomprehension. If on the other hand he had gone forward to 1581 and happened upon a copy of Michel de Montaigne's *Essays*, he would have been happy to read: "Everyone looks in front of him; as for me, I look inside of me." "This guy has the right idea," Augustine would have thought, although he would have been puzzled by the next sentence: "I have no business but with myself."[4] For Augustine, to be concerned with one's separate self was to turn away from God, the light of truth and creator of the soul. If he had gone forward another century or so in the hope that people had got things right, he would have been disappointed if he came upon this passage in John's Locke's *Essay Concerning Human Understanding*: "methinks, the understanding is not much unlike a closet wholly shut from light, with only some little openings left, to let in external visible resemblances, or ideas of things without."[5] For Augustine the inner realms were expansive halls, not closets fitted out with peepholes. "It's getting worse and worse," he would have thought, "I hope that people a couple of centuries ahead will have returned to their senses." But if he had landed in 1890 and picked up a copy of Friedrich Nietzsche's *Genealogy of Morality*, he would have been flabbergasted to read: "All instincts which are not discharged outwardly *turn inwards* – this is what I call the *internalization* of man: with it there now evolves in man what will later be called his 'soul.'"[6] No one could have blamed him if after reading this Augustine had jumped back into his time machine and gone back to the fifth century as fast as he could.

It is clear from this story that geniuses of different periods have held vastly different views about the nature of the self. But they did not arrive at their views entirely on their own. It was a cumulative process. Montaigne, Locke, and Nietzsche were aware of their predecessors' beliefs, incorporating them into their own or reacting against them. Yet the process was not linear, a predictable movement in a single direction. Nietzsche's body-based self was, in a way, an attempt to recover the spontaneous physicality of the Homeric age; but there was no way a nineteenth century European could get back to the days before the reflective mind. Nietzsche despised the Christian doctrines that Augustine helped to codify and looked down on the Enlightenment mentality that Locke helped to create, but he owed more to Christianity and the Enlightenment than he would have liked to admit.

The cumulative nature of the development of the idea of the self is what makes it possible to speak of its having a history. It also helps explain why in writing about this history I confine myself mostly to Western sources. Until recently, the histories of the idea of the self in the West and East have had little to do with one another. Augustine was influenced by Manichaeism, an Eastern religion, but his conception of the self was a synthesis of Neoplatonic and Christian ideas. Locke knew nothing about Asian ways of thought; he drew on – and reacted against – Christian doctrine, Cartesian rationality, and other trends that were current when he wrote. Nietzsche had a few vague notions about Buddhism but he was a master of the Western tradition from Homer to Schopenhauer. In tracing the lines of the history of the self, I take advantage of the cumulative experience of the West to bring coherence to the story.

There is one great problem with this approach. The modern Western idea of selfhood is not typical of ideas prevalent in other parts of the world. As anthropologist Clifford Geertz wrote in 1974: "The Western conception of the person as a bounded, unique, more or less integrated motivational and cognitive universe, a dynamic centre of awareness, emotion, judgment, and action, organized into a distinctive whole and set contrastively both against other such wholes and against a social and natural background is, however incorrigible it may seem to us, a rather peculiar idea within the context of the world's cultures."[7] People living in traditional cultures in Asia, Africa, Latin America, Australasia – virtually everywhere except Europe and North America – don't see the self like this. It would take dozens of pages to give even a summary account of the major differences between the modern Western and traditional non-Western views of selfhood; it is enough for the moment to say that people in traditional cultures give much more importance to social cohesiveness, much less to individual autonomy. In this respect, modern Westerners differ not only from traditional people in the present, but also from people in all known cultures before the European Renaissance. In recognition of these differences, I discuss a number of Asian thinkers and writers in Chapters 2, 3 and 12, and deal with the special case of the Japanese poetic diary in the last section of the present chapter. But I give most of my attention to the development of the Western idea of the self from the sixteenth century to the present.

Giving a Name to the Self: Terminology and Disciplines

The long history of the idea of the self is reflected in the terminology used in writing and speaking about it. For centuries, the word *soul* or its equivalent in other languages was the term of choice. The Greek *psyche* originally meant "breath," "life," "spirit" but later was applied to the soul or immaterial part of ourselves as distinguished from the body. The Latin *anima*, originally "breath," "passion," "living being," underwent a similar development. These two words dominated discussions of the subject in Europe until the seventeenth century, when new ways of thinking spawned a host of new terms or new uses of older terms: *mind, self, consciousness, person, identity, personal identity*. In the eighteenth and nineteenth centuries, philosophers introduced new words in their increasingly technical discussions: *subject, subjectivity, ego*. All twelve of these terms are still in use in English. In what follows, I will use *self* as my normal word but refer to the others when the context requires it.

The changes in the terminology used to discuss the self reflect changes in the disciplines that have concerned themselves with the question. At first, it was priests and other religious specialists who laid down the correct views about the human soul and its relationship with the superhuman. The rise of philosophical enquiry made it possible for creative minds to formulate conceptions that were less constrained by theological dogmas. The result has been a gradual abandonment of the idea of a freestanding *essential* soul, created by God, separate from the body, and able to survive bodily death, and the development of approaches that held that the self was in some measure *constructed* by social or psychological processes. The rise of psychology and the social sciences during the nineteenth century brought such constructivist theories to the forefront. This shift was accelerated during the twentieth century by the rise of physiological approaches, in which the construction of the self is viewed as a biological process.

Over the centuries the focus of those studying the self has moved from intangible essences such as the soul toward positive entities such as society, the body, and the brain. But the older ways of thinking are still alive. I will therefore make use of the writings of theologians and philosophers along with those of psychologists, sociologists, anthropologists, and physical scientists as I trace the development of the idea of the self in history. But my main source materials will be literary: diaries, memoirs, and other first-person documents in which gifted individuals gave expression to themselves and to their ideas about the self. I present both types of material chronologically to illustrate the development of the idea of the self over time. The book thus consists of two interwoven narratives: a history of the concepts of self and self-consciousness, and a history of self-expression as illustrated by first-person writing.

Giving Voice to the "I": Memoir, Autobiography, Diary

First-person genres are of special interest in the study of the self because they are, or at least profess to be, immediate self-expression. It is natural to think, along with sociologist Alain Girard, that "among all written texts, it is those in the first person that tell us most about the image of the self."[8] Note however that Girard spoke of the image of the self and not the thing itself. Contemporary critics of first-person writings agree that the narrators of diaries and memoirs are personae and not persons, images projected by the writers with future readers – themselves or others – in mind. Some critics go further, suggesting that first-person writings are *tools* of self-construction: not just accounts of what happened but ways of molding the stuff of the past into models of what the writers wish to be. To such critics, writing an account of one's life is an act of self-creation.[9]

Memoir, autobiography, and diary are separate genres though there is a certain amount of overlap between them. A memoir, as I use the term, is a retrospective narrative about a portion of the writer's life. An autobiography is a long memoir, covering most of the subject's life up to the time of writing. A diary is a document in which the writer records his or her experiences, thoughts and feelings shortly after they happen, in discreet entries, often dated. Diaries differ from memoirs in not being retrospective and in not having an explicit plot. They are written from day to day, with the present as a moving vantage point and without any knowledge of the future. But the distinction between diary and memoir is not absolute: many diaries became the bases of memoirs, many memoirs have passages that read like diary entries.

Diaries and memoirs are important sources for biographers and historians because they provide first-hand accounts of public and private events and offer privileged access to the personality of the writers. But only a naïve historian would take every statement in a diary or memoir at face value. It is hard for us to be honest with ourselves, harder to be frank with others, still harder to write the truth as we have seen it and preserve what we have written. No one has spoken of this with more perception than the novelist Fyodor Dostoyevsky. As the narrator of his *Notes from Underground* begins to write his memoir, he remarks: "There are things in every man's past that he won't admit except to his most intimate friends. There are other things that he won't admit even to his friends but only to himself – and only in strictest confidence. But there are things, too, that a man won't dare to admit even to himself, and every decent man has quite an accumulation of such things." Eighty years later, George Orwell wrote: "Autobiography is only to be trusted when it reveals something disgraceful."[10] By this standard, Jean-Jacques Rousseau's *Confessions*, the prototypical modern memoir, ought to be regarded as trustworthy, since it contains many things that eighteenth-century readers found scandalous. But historians agree that much of what Rousseau wrote was untrue. More recently, memoirists of the "misery lit" subgenre have vied in their efforts to reveal the most humiliating details of their lives, but the result has not been trustworthy memoirs. Many such books have fictional scenes; others are complete fabrications.

First-person speech is among the earliest forms of linguistic expression and remains one of the most prevalent. In both British and American English, "I" is the eleventh most frequently used word.[11] Even the least egoistical among us says it dozens of times a day, and neither we nor those who hear us have any doubt about the meaning of the word. Saying and writing "I" seems so natural that it comes as some surprise to learn that first-person genres are relative newcomers in literary history. Roman philosophers such as Seneca and Marcus Aurelius used literary letters to frame accounts of their day, but the first important memoir in the Western world was Augustine's *Confessions*, written in 397–398 CE. After that there was a gap of more than a thousand years before people in Europe began to write personal histories again. In English, the first example was *The Book of Margery Kempe* (1436), in Spanish, the *Life* of Teresa of Avila (1562–5). The memoir flourished in seventeenth-century England in such works as John Bunyan's *Grace Abounding to the Chief of Sinners* and George Fox's misnamed *Journal*. A century later it was given a surprising new turn by Rousseau in his *Confessions*. Since then, the secular memoir and autobiography have become established literary forms in the literatures of Europe and the Americas and, more recently, of Asia and Africa.

Even more than the memoir, the diary has been, in the words of critic Susan Sontag, an "exemplary instrument in the career of consciousness."[12] Diaries as we know them today did not appear in Europe before the sixteenth century but they were preceded by other sorts of verbal recording devices. The Greeks had *hypomnemata*, wax tablets on which they jotted down things they wanted to remember: ideas, quotations, things said or observed. The practice of using tablets as aides-mémoires continued for hundreds of years. Anthony the Great (c. 251–356) advised the serious monk to note down "his actions and the movements of his soul" as a means of preventing sin. Three hundred years later, a Middle Eastern abbot required novices to attach small tablets to their belts to write down their passing thoughts, the better to report them to their superiors.[13] Even after paper was introduced in Europe, the use of tablets lingered on. When Hamlet learns of his uncle's villainy, he cries out: "My tables [tablets]! Meet it is I set it down."[14]

By the time that Shakespeare wrote that line, paper was sufficiently inexpensive to become part of everyday life. Account books became necessary tools of trade and soon accountants were making notations that had nothing to do with commerce. One French Protestant merchant of the seventeenth century set down the details of his family life and local political events in a commercial ledger. A century later, a French notary used the first part of his account book for details of his practical life, the other for a coded narrative of his amorous conquests.[15] The leap from the account book to the personal diary took place somewhat earlier in England. By the end of the sixteenth century, scores of English Puritans were keeping their daily accounts with God on paper manuscripts. Around the same time, government official Samuel Pepys wrote one of the first and still one of the greatest personal diaries, noting down details about his work, his finances, his home life, his amusements, and his affairs, not to mention public events, such as the coronation of Charles II.

The primary aim of early diarists was to record what they observed, thought, and did. As the genre developed, people began to use their diaries for subjective expression as well as objective documentation. Along with self-expression came self-reflection, and along with self-reflection the desire for self-improvement. As the scholar Roger North observed in the seventeenth century, for a man to keep a diary was a useful "check upon all his exorbitancies," since, "being set down they would stain his reputation." Two hundred years later, Swiss philosopher Henri-Frédéric Amiel wrote toward the end of his 17,000-page *Journal*, "the chief utility of the personal diary is to restore wholeness of mind and equilibrium of consciousness, that is to say, inner health."[16] His remark could have been taken as a watchword by the millions who have tried using diaries as parts of self-improvement programs. More recently, the Web has made it possible for bloggers to upload their observations, confessions, and harangues a moment after writing them.

Smartphones and tablet computers are currently the last word in verbal communication, but the psychological impulse behind first-person writing has changed little since the age of styli and wax tablets. Autobiographers, memoirists, diarists, bloggers, and users of social networks share the urge to express themselves or to create themselves through writing. All belong to what might be called the fellowship of the first person, and whether they know it or not they owe a great deal to their predecessors. Augustine's *Confessions* served as the template for all later spiritual memoirs; Rousseau's *Confessions* reworked the conventions of the genre, and in turn became the model for the hundreds of confessional memoirs that crowd the bookstores today. Montaigne used what he learned from Seneca and other Romans to create a new literary form, the essay, and his style of self-expression has influenced all later French writers, along with hundreds from other countries. It would be difficult to overstate his importance to Descartes, Pascal, Rousseau, Emerson, Nietzsche, Milner, or Gide, to speak only of writers featured in this book. Diarists too were influenced by their predecessors, especially after 1887, when personal diaries began to appear in print. Writers and public figures saw the genre's possibilities and began to write diaries that were intended from the start for publication.

The Diary in Japan

None of the diarists mentioned above had any influence on Ennin, Abutsu-ni, Matsuo Basho or other contributors to the oldest continuous tradition of diary writing in the world, the *nikki bungaku* ("diary literature") of Japan. The earliest examples of *nikki* date from the eighth century, predating the Western diary by 800 years. Written in Chinese on the model of official court chronicles, they cover current events, the weather, and so forth, but reveal almost nothing about the lives of the diarists. In the early ninth century, the Buddhist monk Ennin kept a dated diary of his voyage to and residence in China. Only once did he let his emotions show, when he quoted from a letter he had written to an official begging him for food. About a hundred years later, Ki no Tsurayuki began the tradition of the Japanese literary diary with his *Tosa Nikki*, a record of a journey from Tosa Province to Kyoto told from the perspective of a fictitious female narrator. A master of the *waka* form of poetry, Tsurayuki interspersed his narrative with poems, establishing a convention that would characterize the *nikki* for the next thousand years.

As the *nikki* developed, it became more a literary form, less a factual document. Some authors wrote their "diaries" years after the event, avoided dated entries, and introduced fictional characters. Still, it remained a deeply personal genre, especially in the hands of women. *The Gossamer Years*, written in the middle of the tenth century by a court lady known as the Mother of Michitsuna is, in the words of critic Donald Keene, "the self-portrait of a woman of intense emotions." Disappointed in her marriage, she was forced to conclude: "unhappiness was part of my inescapable destiny, determined from former lives, and must be accepted as such."[17] Two centuries later, a young woman named Abutsu-ni recorded the pain of a demeaning and hopeless love affair in *Fitful Slumbers*. "It brings no comfort, I know, to brood over things," she began, "but I have become accustomed on sleepless nights to leave my door ajar and wait for the moon to rise, hoping to make it my companion."[18] Her honesty in describing her torment gives the work an emotional verisimilitude that transcends the *nikki*'s stylized form.

In the centuries that followed, many women wrote personal diaries that were intensely subjective but doubtfully factual, while many men wrote diaries filled with facts but lacking in subjectivity. The two currents came together in the work of Matsuo Basho (1644–94), the preeminent master of the *nikki*. Basho already was famous as a haiku writer when, at the age of forty, he set out on the first of four journeys he would commemorate in his poetic diaries. Though based on the events of his wanderings, they were far from being documentary accounts. He revised them for months after he returned home, introducing a lot of fictional material. His artful prose and poetry make a world come alive but tell us very little about himself. Self-revelation was not his aim. When he wrote about the beauty of the landscape, the loneliness of the traveler, and the ineluctable passage of time, he wanted his remarks to have a universal resonance. "It was a great pleasure," he wrote in *The Records of a Travel-worn Satchel*,

> to see the marvellous beauties of nature, rare scenes in the mountains or along the coast, or to visit the sites of temporary abodes of ancient sages where they had spent secluded lives, or better still, to meet people who had entirely devoted themselves to the search for artistic truth. Since I had nowhere permanent to stay, I had no interest whatever in keeping treasures, and since I was empty-handed, I had no fear of being robbed on the way.[19]

The translation of Basho's diaries from which this passage comes was published in 1967. When the Catholic monk and diarist Thomas Merton read it, he was – as he wrote in his own diary – "completely shattered." Basho's book gave him "a whole new (old) view of my own life. … Deeply moving in every kind of way."[20] At that moment, the *nikki* ceased to be an isolated literary tradition and Basho became a member of the now transcultural fellowship of the first person.

The Soul from Animism to Monotheism

Are you not aware, I [Socrates] said, that the soul of man is immortal and imperishable?
He [Glaucon] looked at me in astonishment, and said: No, by heaven: And are you really prepared to maintain this?

– Plato

Did humans have an idea of self in the Paleolithic age? If we were to base ourselves on the evidence of caveman novels, we would have to say yes, since people in such tales are pretty much like us, with the exception of fashion and lifestyle choices. If we were to go by the findings of ethnologists who study modern hunter-gatherer societies we would be inclined to say no, since they tell us that people in such societies see themselves as members of clans defined by their social roles and not as autonomous individuals. But this does not necessarily prove that prehistoric hunter-gatherers had no sense of "me" and "mine." Canadian philosopher Charles Taylor resorted to his own version of caveman fiction in order to make this point: "In those days when a paleolithic hunting group was closing in on a mammoth, when the plan went awry and the beast was lunging towards hunter A," it is probable that "something similar to the thought 'Now I'm for it' crossed A's mind. And when at the last moment, the terrifying animal lurched to the left and crushed B instead, a sense of relief mingled with grief for poor B is what A experienced. In other words," Taylor concluded, "the members of the group must have had very much the same sense that we would in their place."[1] But this "sense" was not a developed idea of self; it was more like what Mauss was thinking of when he wrote of the sense of "a combined physical and mental individuality."

We have to be careful when we try to figure out what our prehistoric ancestors were like because the world we live in is overlaid with concepts that they knew nothing about. Even ethnologists view the cultures they study through the lens of their scholarly minds. Still, archeological evidence together with ethnological data gives us a certain amount of insight into early human life. The belief in some form of survival after death was almost universal. The return of dead relatives in dreams lent support to the idea that their spirits continued to exist. Even the world of the living was populated by spirits: they dwelt in humans, animals, plants, physical features (rocks, rivers), and natural phenomena (lightning, rain). British anthropologist Edward Tylor gave the name "animism" to this belief that the life-principle is omnipresent, and asserted that primitive humans were animists.

In animistic societies, shamans – specialists in the lore of spirits – played an important role. They entered into contact with the spirit-world by means of trance-induced visions. Granted special powers by their spirit-guides, they attracted good fortune, averted evil fortune, healed the sick, read omens, and divined the future. Shamans held a special place within their clans, deferred to and looked after by the rest. But like all other members of primitive societies, they were not so much persons as personages in the drama of the group.

The invention of agriculture during the Neolithic period paved the way for the development of urban civilizations in the Middle East, South Asia, and China. We know a lot about life in ancient Mesopotamia and Egypt because both had advanced writing systems. At the top of their elaborate social structures were kings who were also the heads of their polytheistic religions. The priesthood presided over rituals that guaranteed the continuance of the orderly rhythms of life. People in both cultures had sophisticated ideas about the soul and its survival. Mesopotamians believed that there were two souls – the "dream soul" and the "ghost" or "body spirit" – that departed from the body at death. Priests performed special ceremonies to help this process along.[2] The religion of ancient Egypt is famous for the elaborate steps taken to insure postmortem survival. The bodies of the pharaohs and other important figures were embalmed and placed in tombs filled with goods that were needed in the afterlife. The soul was fivefold; the part known as the *ka* was what left the body at the time of death.

The Axial Age: Doctrines of Self and No-Self

Around 3200 years ago, the production of iron opened the way to rapid advances in technology, including tools for agriculture and warfare. New forms of social and cultural life emerged in the centuries that followed. Between 800 and 200 BCE, the seeds of modern religion and philosophy were sown in China, India, Iran, the Middle East, and Europe. The pivotal importance of these developments has led some historians to refer to this period as the Axial Age.

The religions of ancient Mesopotamia and Egypt were centered on the king and his priests. During the Axial Age the focus began to shift to the general population, in particular the rising commercial classes. Solitary religious teachers addressed themselves to aristocrats, merchants, and even common people. They challenged established orthodoxies with teachings that emphasized general human values and concerns. A statement in the Analects of Confucius, "What I do not wish men to do to me, I also wish not to do to men," is echoed by a phrase in the Biblical book of Leviticus: "you shall love your neighbor as yourself."[3]

In India the sages whose teachings are preserved in the Upanishads developed a philosophical synthesis based upon, but going beyond, the sacrificial religion of the earlier Vedas. The most notable doctrine of the Upanishads is that of the *atman* or individual self, which is one with the universal spirit or *brahman*. Like the Greek *psyche* and the Latin *anima*, the word *atman* derived from a verb meaning "to breathe," demonstrating its connection with the vital force; but the sages of the Upanishads viewed the *atman* as a substantial, non-material entity that existed independently of the body. Thinkers in India also developed the idea of the *ahankara* or individual ego, a construct that had to be exceeded before one could experience the essential self.

The teachings of the Upanishads were well established in the plains of the Ganges by the sixth and fifth centuries BCE, when there was a enormous outburst of innovative thinking and spiritual practice. Among the wandering teachers who challenged established norms was Vardhamana or Mahavira, the founder of the Jain religion. According to Mahavira, every *jiva*, living being or soul, is naturally bound but potentially free. Embodied souls come into contact with lifeless substance through the influx of *karma* ("action"), which is viewed as a fine form of matter. By means of individual effort, including the avoidance of injury to others, souls shake off the pollution of karma and attain liberation.

The teachings of Siddhartha Gautama, known as the Buddha or Enlightened One, have much in common with those of Mahavira, who is thought to have been the Buddha's older contemporary. Both teachers laid stress on the need of liberation from the cycle of *karma* and rebirth and insisted on the necessity of individual effort without the intervention of priests. Both called for a life of abnegation, although the Buddha, unlike Mahavira, condemned extreme asceticism. But the two differed greatly in their view of the self or soul. Mahavira, like the Upanishadic sages, accepted the idea; the Buddha denied it. There was, he said, no permanent self, just a constantly changing flux of consciousness. He told his disciples: "All consciousness should be seen as it actually is with proper wisdom thus: 'This is not mine, this I am not, this is not my self.'"[4]

At roughly the same time that Mahavira and the Buddha were preaching in India, the philosophico-religious traditions of China were taking shape.

Confucianism, formulated by Kong Fuzi or Confucius (551–479 BCE), laid stress on virtues such as humaneness, altruism, justice, and sincerity, and on the importance of regulated social relations. Daoism, based on the teachings of the legendary sage Laozi, stressed humility and moderation as means of achieving harmony with the universe. Neither tradition produced a systematic body of thought about the self but the teachings of Zhuangzi, a fourth-century BCE Daoist, argued against the social self implicit in Confucian writings. Daoism is therefore said by some to contain a doctrine of no-self comparable to that of Buddhism. In Zhuangzi's Daoism, as in philosophical Buddhism, "the 'self' is something that is constructed by the mind."[5]

The philosophical tradition of the Greeks dates back to the sixth century BCE. The earliest thinkers, such as Thales and Anaximander, gave most of their attention to the physical world and its ultimate basis. Philosophical interest in the human being did not begin until around 500 BCE, when Heraclitus of Ephesus pondered the question of personal identity. Less than a century later, Socrates (c. 469–399 BCE) made human concerns the focus of his philosophy. Asked a pedantic question about a mythological story, he replied: "I've not yet succeeded in obeying the Delphic injunction to 'know myself,' and it seems to me absurd to consider problems about other beings while I am still in ignorance about my own nature."[6] Since then the famous counsel "Know thyself" has been associated with him. Socrates's student Plato (424/423–348/347 BCE) was the first Greek thinker to formulate a theory of the soul as part of a comprehensive theory of the world. In the *Phaedo* he presented a dualistic view: the body and the soul are distinct, and the soul, being immaterial, is immortal. This was a new and surprising view of the *psyche*, which in earlier Greek thought was not regarded as an immortal essence. In *The Republic,* Plato wrote that the soul consisted of three parts: the rational soul or intellect, the spirited soul or will, and the appetitive soul or desire. The function of the intellect was to control desire with the help of the will. This model helped him account for psychological conflict, a recurrent problem in the history of the idea of the self. Aristotle (384–322 BCE), Plato's most famous student, altered his teacher's model of the tripartite *psyche*, writing in *On the Soul* that there was a vegetative soul, possessed by all living things, concerned with nutrition and growth; an animal soul, possessed by animals and humans, concerned with locomotion; and a rational soul, which humans possessed in proportion to their wisdom. But Aristotle, unlike Plato, did not see the soul as separate from the body. Rather it was, in the words of scholar Hendrik Lorenz, "a system of abilities possessed and manifested by animate bodies of suitable structure."[7]

The teachers of the schools of Hellenistic philosophy, which flourished after the death of Aristotle, were less concerned than he and Plato with system building. Their aim was to show the way to achieve the good life. To Epicurus (341–270 BCE) the soul, like everything else, was composed of material atoms, and would share the fate of all material things. The problem was not death, which could not be avoided, but the fear of death. Stoics such as Zeno of Citium (c. 334–c. 262 BCE) believed in a sort of postmortem survival but felt that the aim of life was to cultivate calm and indifference to poverty, pain, and death. The Stoic and Epicurean schools exerted great influence on the moral tone of the Roman Empire. The Roman Epicurean Lucretius (c. 99–c. 55 BCE) wrote that there was nothing to fear in death since "one who no longer is cannot suffer, or differ in any way from one who has never been born, when once this mortal life has been usurped by death the immortal."[8] The Stoic philosopher and statesman Seneca (c. 4 BCE–65 CE) recommended daily self-reflection in order to discover "that which does not each day pass more and more under the control of some power which cannot be withstood." This was the soul, which was "upright, good, and great. What else could you call such a soul than a god dwelling as a guest in a human body?"[9] But this soul was not an essential entity, as it was in Plato. Rather it was something that was constituted by personal effort.

Platonism persisted into the Roman period, but it took a new form in the teachings of Plotinus (c. 205–270 CE) and his followers. Born in Egypt, Plotinus studied in Alexandria and joined a military campaign to Persia in order to investigate Eastern philosophy. At the age of forty he settled in Rome, where he taught what became known as Neoplatonism. Plotinus divided the higher or intelligible world into three: the One, Intelligence, and the Soul. Below these is the sensible or material world. The soul is immaterial, substantial, and immortal. Its highest part is in a constant state of contemplation and identical with what it contemplates; when, however, "we look outside at what we are fashioned from, we are ignorant of our being one." But "if anyone could turn, either by themselves or by a lucky tug of Athena, they would see God and themselves and all things."[10] Plotinus's mystical philosophy would have a lasting influence on the monotheistic religions that had risen or would rise in western Asia: Judaism, Christianity, and Islam.

The Worship of One God

The monotheistic religions had such a huge influence on all aspects of Western culture, including the idea of the self, that it will be useful to trace their rise. There were hints of monotheism in the religions of ancient

Mesopotamia and Egypt. Marduk, the patron deity of Babylon, became the chief of all the gods of Mesopotamia when Babylon expanded militarily and politically under the king and lawgiver Hammurabi (eighteenth century BCE). Eventually the other gods in the pantheon became not just his subordinates but aspects of himself; still, Marduk was not recognized as the solitary god. During a brief period in the fourteenth century BCE the pharaoh Akhenaten replaced traditional Egyptian polytheism with a new form of worship centered on the solar deity Aten. This cult was eradicated after Akhenaten's death, but a distant memory of Aten's and Marduk's uniqueness may have influenced the people of Israel when they reformulated their religion during the Axial Age.

Yahweh, the one god of the Israelites, rose to prominence in a polytheistic environment. Originally he was typical Iron Age god, a god of war. Between 640 and 610 BCE, Josiah, the king of Judah, imposed the exclusive worship of Yahweh on his people, outlawing all other cults. Within a hundred years came catastrophe: the defeat of Judah, the destruction of the Temple, and the exile in Babylon. During the harsh years of the Babylonian Captivity, the Israelites acquired a new destiny. Yahweh told them, in the words of the prophet Isaiah: "I will give you as a light to the nations, that my salvation may reach to the end of the earth."[11] Yahweh was not just the one god of the Israelites; he was the one and only God, and the Israelites were his chosen people.

The religion of the Israelites went through further changes in the centuries that followed. They returned to their homeland but in the first century BCE the region became part of the Roman Empire. There followed a period of political oppression during which a number of charismatic teachers appeared, among them Jesus of Nazareth. During his brief ministry, Jesus gave special importance to what he called the Kingdom of God. Scholars debate what exactly he meant by this phrase, but two things seem indisputable. First, the coming of the kingdom would be the fulfillment of ancient prophecy. Second, it would come very soon. "The time is fulfilled," he told the Galileans, "and the Kingdom of God has come near; repent, and believe in the good news."[12]

In the older books of the Hebrew Bible, there was little speculation about the soul, and no suggestion that the soul was essentially different from the body. Likewise in the books making up the New Testament there is no mention of an immaterial soul that exists independently of the body. Certain that the Kingdom of God was near, Jesus had little to say about the afterlife. This question became more important after his crucifixion. Those who believed in his gospel were promised resurrection after death, which meant the restoration of life to the physical body. The idea of a disembodied, immaterial soul first entered Christian doctrine in the works of theologians who were familiar with Greek philosophy. Justin Martyr (103–165) was attracted by Plato's idea of the soul but knew it would be wrong to think that "the soul is immortal, but the body mortal, and incapable of being revived." The correct view, he wrote, was that body, soul, and spirit would all be saved.[13] The idea that the body itself would survive gave rise to philosophical conundrums. Athenagoras (c. 133–190) was led to speculate on the resurrection prospects of humans who had been eaten by animals who were later eaten by humans.

Roman philosophers were puzzled by all the attention that Christians gave to the body. To Epictetus (55–135), a Greek Stoic who taught in Rome, the human being was just "a little wisp of soul carrying a corpse."[14] Who would want to be encumbered with an unclean corpse for all eternity? Christians and Roman philosophers clearly had very different ideas about the aim of life. Christians were willing to abandon present pleasure to gain a postmortem reward. The Stoics and Epicureans sought the good life *while living* through self-examination and self-discipline. "Everyone hurries his life on and suffers from a yearning for the future and a weariness of the present," wrote Seneca in *On the Shortness of Life*. "But he who bestows all of his time on his own needs, who plans out every day as if it were his last, neither longs for nor fears the morrow."[15]

The letters of Seneca and the emperor Marcus Aurelius (121–180) are among the earliest documents in Western literature that consider the human being from a first-person perspective. A letter from Marcus to his teacher Fronto gives a detailed accounting of the day's activities, in the spirit of Stoic self-examination:

> From five A.M. till nine, I spent the time partly reading some of Cato's *Agriculture*, partly in writing not quite such wretched stuff, by heavens, as yesterday. … After easing my throat I went off to my father and attended him at a sacrifice. Then we went to luncheon. What do you think we ate? A wee bit of bread, though I saw others devouring beans, onions, and herrings full of roe. We then worked hard at grape-gathering, and had a good sweat, and were merry and, as the poet says, "still left some clusters hanging high as gleanings of the vintage." After six-o'clock we came home.[16]

Stoicism encouraged personal self-reflection; but it was a Christian who wrote the first comprehensive first-person study of the self. This was Augustine, whose intellectual and spiritual memoir marked the start of a new era in the history of self-consciousness.

The Invention of the Inner Self: Augustine of Hippo

In 397 Aurelius Augustinus had been serving as the bishop of Hippo, in what is now northeastern Algeria, for around two years. Converted to Christianity a decade earlier after a search that had taken him from Roman philosophy to Manichaeism to Neoplatonism to Catholicism, and from Africa to Italy and back, he hoped to settle down to a life of contemplation and writing. Instead he had been ordained a priest and asked to oversee the affairs of his congregation. His verbal skills, honed as a student and teacher of rhetoric, found outlet in sermons against heretics and unbelievers. His elevation to bishop at the age of forty-one burdened him with more official duties. He was harassed by "schismatic attacks on his ecclesiastic authority" and "politically motivated rumors about his sensational past."[17]

At this difficult moment, Augustine began work on what he would later call "My confessions, in thirteen books." As a student of Latin literature, he was familiar with the tradition of exemplary biographies of political and military figures, of which Plutarch's *Lives* was the supreme example. As a Christian, he had internalized the Biblical accounts of Jesus's life and the history of the early church as recorded in the letters of Paul the Apostle. He drew on these models as he worked on his *Confessions*, but he differed from his predecessors by placing himself front and center and making the struggles of his own mind and heart the crux of his story.

Augustine began with an account of his childhood and youth, interweaving the events of his early years with theological reflections and paeans of thanksgiving to God. After listing his mental and moral characteristics, he added: "But every one of these qualities are gifts of my God: I did not give them to myself. They are good qualities, and their totality is my self." Turning to his adolescence, he recalled the "foulnesses and carnal corruptions" he fell into, treating his youthful adventures with remarkable candor. "I prayed you for chastity," he wrote, "and said: 'Grant me chastity and continence, but not yet.'" At the age of seventeen, he went to the city of Carthage to continue his education. All around him "hissed a cauldron of illicit loves."[18] Eventually he paired up with a woman he loved and stayed with her for the next fifteen years.

Intellectually Augustine was drawn to Manichaeism, a Persian religion that had spread through the Roman Empire. Manichaeism taught a rigid dualism: God, powerful but not omnipotent, is the author of all good while Satan is the source of all evil. The human soul is a battleground where light and darkness compete, but humans are not responsible for the outcome. Rather it is "the Creator and orderer of the heaven and stars" who is responsible for a person's fate.[19] In 373 he returned to his hometown and opened a grammar school. Two years later, he went back to Carthage and set himself up as a teacher of rhetoric. His brilliance won him students, but he remained intellectually and spiritually dissatisfied.

After nine years of teaching at Carthage, Augustine decided to open a school in Rome. The ancient city disappointed him, but he met a powerful figure who offered him the coveted position of professor of rhetoric in Milan, the capital of the Empire. His mistress was now a social liability, so he sent her back to Carthage and agreed to marry a girl his mother found for him. As she was underage, he took a new mistress to tide things over. Intellectually, too, he was in an unsettled state. The teachings of the Manicheans had ceased to appeal and for a while he accepted a form of philosophical skepticism; but he also read the Neoplatonists. By them, he wrote in the *Confessions*, "I was admonished to return into myself. With you [God] as my guide I entered into my innermost citadel ... and with my soul's eye, such as it was, saw above that same eye of my soul the immutable light higher than my mind."[20] Later, prompted by his mother and Ambrose, the bishop of Milan, he undertook a study of Christian writings. His intellectual agitation left him in a state of uncertainty, which he described in one of the most vivid accounts of psychological conflict in Western literature:

> What is the cause of this monstrous situation? ... The mind commands the body and is instantly obeyed. The mind commands itself and meets resistance. ... The mind orders the mind to will. The recipient of the order is itself, yet it does not perform it. ... We are dealing with a morbid condition of the mind which, when it is lifted up by the truth, does not unreservedly rise to it but is weighted down by habit. So there are two wills. Neither of them is complete, and what is present in the one is lacking in the other.[21]

The conflict came to a head one day in a garden in Milan, when "a profound self-examination had dredged up a heap" of misery. In torment, he threw himself down on the ground and wept uncontrollably. Just then he heard a child's voice chanting, "Pick up and read, pick up and read." Taking this to be a command from God, he opened Paul's *Epistle to the Romans* and read: "Not in riots and drunken parties, not in eroticism and indecencies, not in strife and rivalry, but put on the Lord Jesus Christ and make no provision for the flesh in its lusts." Augustine "neither wished nor needed to read further." He accepted Christianity as his religion.[22]

Augustine brought the narrative portion of the *Confessions* to a close with an account of his baptism by Ambrose and the death of his mother as they were on their way back to Africa. The last four books consist of philo-sophical and theological reflection. "The profit derived from confessing my past I have seen and spoken about," he began, but many also were interested in "what I now am at this time." In particular, they wanted "to learn about my inner self." This gave him an opening for a philosophical treatment of the self, one of the first in Western literature. The self, he explained, consists of memory. As a psychological faculty, memory is that which "preserves in distinct particulars and general categories all the perceptions which have penetrated, each by its own route of entry." But it is also an inner *place*, a "vast hall" in which the "I" can carry out actions, such as distinguishing lilies from violets, or wine from honey, without smelling or tasting anything. In this inner space, Augustine wrote, "I meet myself and recall what I am, what I have done, and when and where and how I was affected when I did it." It is a vast expanse, comparable to "broad plains and caves and caverns," it is "a power of profound and infinite multiplicity. This," Augustine concluded, "is mind, this is I myself."[23]

Many of the images that Augustine used seem obvious, even hackneyed. But this is like saying that Shakespeare's characters speak in clichés. To Augustine's contemporaries his descriptions of inner space were anything but familiar. According to philosopher Phillip Cary, "people in the pre-Augustinian era of Western culture did not find it at all obvious that the self, along with its acts of knowing and remembering, should be conceived as a kind of inner eye looking at an inner object in an inner space." The Neoplatonists spoke of an inner domain, but this was identical for every soul. Augustine's inner space was private, "belonging only to a particular individual soul."[24] He arrived at this idea by combining the separate soul of Christianity, which was part of God's creation, with the eternal and uncreated soul of the Neoplatonists. Taking his station in the Neoplatonic "innermost citadel," he looked above and saw God and realized that He was not only "more inward than my most inward part" but also "higher than the highest element within me."[25] In this way he escaped from his separate innerness without having to think, like a Neoplatonist, that the soul was divine in its own nature. Modern readers are likely to think that this was all theological hair-splitting with no relevance to people who are interested in the self but are neither Neoplatonists nor Christians. But there is general agreement among intellectual historians that Augustine's discovery or "invention" of the private inner self was not only a revolutionary break with the past but an opening to still more radical changes in the future.

Along with the sense of private innerness, Augustine gave Western thought a powerful description of the roots of mental conflict. "Whoever does not want to fear, let him probe his inmost self," he wrote in a late sermon. "Reach into the farthest corner of your heart. Examine it then with care: see there, whether a poisoned vein of the wasting love of the world still does not pulse."[26] When the youthful Augustine carried out this exercise, he found himself in the "morbid condition" of being torn by opposing selves, "and the self which willed to serve [God] was identical with the self which was unwilling. ... So I was in conflict with myself and was dissociated from myself."[27] This idea of psychological conflict was of course not new. It is found in early Greek literature and was given classic expression by the Roman poet Ovid:

> I see the better way, and approve it; I follow the worse.[28]

But, in the words of American psychologist William James, "Augustine's psychological genius has given an account of the trouble of having a divided self which has never been surpassed."[29]

In 410, when Augustine was fifty-five, Rome was sacked by the Visigoths. Twenty years later he died in Hippo while Vandals were besieging the city. In 476 the last emperor of the Western Roman Empire was deposed. The Early Middle Ages, sometimes known as the Dark Ages, began. With the collapse of the Empire, the political, commercial, and educational institutions that had fostered the cultural life of Western Europe went into decline. Trade was confined to the immediate region; classical learning was all but forgotten. For most people, sheer survival was difficult enough.

The Pride of Saying "I": Chandrakirti and Shantideva

While Western Europe was sinking into darkness, India was entering a period of stability, prosperity, and cultural efflorescence. The Gupta Dynasty (320–550) and the empire of Harsha Vardhana (606–647) are remembered as the apogee of India's classical age, famous for its poets, artists, philosophers, and mathematicians. Harsha himself is said to have written three Sanskrit plays and he was a generous patron of scholarship and literature. During his reign, the Buddhist university of Nalanda became a magnet for scholars from all parts of India as well as China and other countries. According to tradition, the philosophers Chandrakirti and Shantideva studied and taught at Nalanda.

Among the questions Chandrakirti (c. 600–c. 650 CE) grappled with was the nature of the self. The Buddha, as we have seen, maintained that there was no permanent *atman* or essential self. This doctrine proved hard to reconcile with another Buddhist tenet: the law of karma and the associated idea of rebirth. If there is no self, what is it that bears the burden of karma from life to life? Generations of Buddhist thinkers struggled with this riddle. Some suggested that there was a "person," distinct from the self, that was a center of agency and responsibility; but this idea did not catch on.

Chandrakirti solved the problem by saying that there was no permanent self but that a nominal or conventional self arose "in dependence on the aggregates" of mind and body.[30]

Chandrakirti belonged to the Madhyamaka school of Mahayana Buddhism, which tried to steer a middle course between the belief that beings and things exist in their own right and that nothing at all exists. Much of the literature of Madhyamaka is forbiddingly technical and difficult. An exception is Shantideva's *The Way of the Bodhisattva* (early eighth century). A masterful dialectician, Shantideva picked apart the arguments of rival philosophical schools and his analysis has been picked apart by scholars ever since; but he also wrote movingly and in the first person about his strivings and speculations on the nature of the self.

In the second chapter of *The Way of the Bodhisattva*, Shantideva made his confession to the divine powers:

> All the evil I, a sinner, have committed,
> The sin that clings to me through many evil deeds;
> All the frightful things that I have caused to be,
> I openly declare to you, the teachers of the world.

As a follower of Mahayana, he made a solemn vow to dedicate himself to the welfare of all beings, as the great Bodhisattvas had done. But a few pages later he realized how absurd it was for one like him to make such a vow:

> When I pledged myself to free from their affliction
> Beings who abide in every region,
> Stretching to the limits of the sky,
> I myself was subject to the same afflictions.

"To speak like this was clear insanity," he admitted; but he resolved to go forward with renewed vigor, making the salvation of all creatures his "all-consuming passion."

Like his predecessor Chandrakirti, but in more personal terms, Shantideva insisted that there was no self-existent ego:

> The source of sorrow is the pride of saying "I,"
> Fostered and increased by false belief in self.
> To this you may say that there's no redress,
> But meditation on no-self will be the supreme way.

In his chapter on meditation he showed how a human could achieve self-mastery:

> Relinquishing all other aspirations,

Focusing myself on one intent alone,
I'll strive to still my mind,
And, calming it, to bring it to subjection.

As for the body, it was an "insupportable and unclean form." Why, he asked, "do I regard it as my 'I,' my 'self'?" But once he was able to shake off physical attachment, he would make his body an instrument, putting it to use "for the benefit of beings."[31]

There are interesting parallels between Shantideva's and Augustine's written testaments. Both began by confessing their sins and vowing to work as servants of the Divine. Both saw that the "I" was a fabrication, the mind unreliable, the body a stumbling block. But they dealt with the problem of the self in very different ways: Augustine by affirming an essential soul that was a creation of God, Shantideva by accepting the Buddha's teaching that the ultimate truth was no-self.

Mystical Visions: Hildegard of Bingen

In Western Europe, the Dark Ages lasted till the early eighth century, when things began to change for the better. By the late eleventh century, Christian scholars such as Anselm of Canterbury were applying reason to dogma, helping to inaugurate scholastic philosophy. In 1088 the University of Bologna was founded; the universities of Paris and Oxford followed soon after. Meanwhile, in politics, the kingdoms of England and France began to consolidate. Western European rulers, long put on the defensive by invading Vikings, Magyars, and Saracens, felt confident enough to launch the First Crusade in 1096. Three years later, the Crusaders stormed and captured Jerusalem.

Into this awakening world, Hildegard of Bingen (1098–1179) was born. Looking back in old age on her career as a visionary, she wrote to the monk Guibert of Gembloux:

From my infancy, when my bones and nerves and veins were as yet imperfect, I have always enjoyed the gift of this vision in my soul, up to the present time, when I am now more than seventy years old. Indeed my spirit, when God wills, ascends aloft to the heights of the firmament and to the changing aspects of different climes and spreads itself through diverse peoples though they are in far-off regions and places remote from me. And as I see things in this way I perceive them in the changing clouds and other creatures. And I do not hear them with my bodily ears, nor with the thoughts of my heart, nor do I perceive them

through a combination of my five senses, but ever in my soul, with my
external eyes open, so that I never suffer debilitating ecstasy.

The medieval church was wary of mysticism, particularly ecstatic mysticism.
None of the Fathers of the Church had based their claims to authority on
mystical insight. When Augustine explored the "vast hall" of his memory, he
did so as a reasoning being, and he was quick to quote scripture to support
his conclusions. Hildegard had a different approach:

> I retain the memory of whatever I see or learn in such vision for a long
> time, so that whatever I once see or hear I remember. And I see and
> hear and know at one and the same time; and in a flash that which I
> learn, I know.[32]

During her life, Hildegard had a number of run-ins with ecclesiastical
authorities. But she managed to walk a fine line between the mystic's self-
assurance and the renunciate's self-abnegation, and this generally kept her
out of trouble.

Hildegard was born in a small town in what is now southwest Germany.
When she was eight, her parents took her to a convent and placed her in the
hands of the abbess, an anchoress named Jutta. Walled off from the world,
Hildegard received little education. Jutta died in 1136, and Hildegard took
over as abbess. Now thirty-eight, she could reasonably expect to live out her
days in the isolation of her convent; but this was not what happened. She
had, from an early age, been subject to mystical visions. These became more
powerful as she grew. "When I was twenty-four years and seven months
old," she told the author of her *Life*, "I saw an extremely strong, sparkling,
fiery light coming from the open heavens. It pierced my brain, my heart
and my breast through and through like a flame which did not burn." As
a result, "suddenly I had an insight into the meaning and interpretation of
the psalter, the Gospel and the other Catholic writings of the Old and New
Testaments."[33]

In 1141, five years after she became abbess, Hildegard began to work on
a book in which she recorded a series of visions, which later was published
as *Scivias* or "Know the Ways." Written from the first-person point of view,
Scivias tells of a heavenly voice that spoke to her, describes the visions
that the voice commanded her to relate, and records the commentary on
the visions that the voice provided. One chapter, "The Ejection of Lucifer
from Heaven and the Fall of Adam and Eve," begins: "Then I saw as it were
a very great number of clearly defined living lamps, which taking on that
fiery brilliance, thus attained a most serene splendor." The voice explained
that the living lamps represented "the great army of supernal spirits shining

in blessed life" while the fiery brilliance indicated that "they put on the vigilance of divine love, while the others embraced the torpor of ignorance in not wishing to know God." When Lucifer "looked upon his beauty and considered his powerful strength he discovered pride," and desired to imitate God himself. Then "the zeal of the Lord, extending itself in fiery blackness, cast him down with all his followers, so that they were made to smolder instead of shine."[34]

Hildegard seems to have noted the substance of her visions on wax tablets at tremendous speed. Later she sat with a secretary who helped her express what she had seen and heard in proper Latin. The manuscript was illustrated with exquisite miniatures that may have been prepared with Hildegard's help. Looking at the illustrations and reading the texts, some critics have speculated that Hildegard's visions were the product of an ocular or neurological disorder. There is enough evidence of physical and psychological suffering in her life to lend plausibility to such theories, but they do not explain the beauty and significance of her work. A better way of looking on her literary output – which included nine books, seventy poems, seventy-two songs, and more than a hundred letters – would be to see it as the creative expression of a multifaceted genius. Along with writing, Hildegard excelled in music (her works are still performed) and she made important contributions to botany. Few women in the medieval world had such a lasting impact on the world around them. Before her death in 1179, she had corresponded with popes and emperors, established her own convent, and preached throughout western Germany.

Unveiling Inner Secrets: Ruzbihan Baqli

In the twelfth century, while Western Europe was just recovering its lost greatness, the Islamic world was approaching a peak of political, artistic, and intellectual glory. Founded in the seventh century by the prophet Muhammad, Islam spread rapidly by means of conquest and persuasion from its Arabian homeland to Afghanistan in the east and Spain in the west. Fiercely monotheistic, Islam recognizes the prophets of Judaism and Christianity, but insists that Muhammad received the final word of God in the form of the verses of the Quran. These are the basis of Islamic belief and practice; next in importance are *hadith* – narratives of Muhammad's words and deeds – which are used as tools to help understand the Quran and Islamic law.

The Quran is its own authority. A *hadith* is accompanied by an *isnad* or chain of transmission, which documents the route it took from the time of Muhammad to the present. This practice of tracking the provenance of *hadith* gave a fillip to the writing of history in Islamic lands, and also influenced the development of first-person literature. The earliest Muslim chronicle dates from the eighth century. The earliest personal diary from a country other than Japan was written in Baghdad around 1068. Its contents are varied – anecdotes, obituaries, miracles, poetry, dreams and their interpretation – but they tell us little about the writer, Ibn Banna. Still, his diary provides a valuable glimpse into the social and theological life of eleventh-century Iraq.[35]

In 1128 – sixty years after Ibn Banna began his diary, and twenty-two years after Hildegard first entered her convent – the Sufi visionary Ruzbihan Baqli was born in southern Persia. Like Hildegard, he was subject to visions from his early youth. Once, when he was fifteen, he heard a voice "from the hidden world, and it was said to me, 'you are a prophet.'" Ruzbihan was puzzled. He thought: "I have heard from my parents that 'There is no prophet after Muhammad,' so how can I be a prophet, when I eat and drink, answer the call of nature, and have private parts." Time passed, but the voices and visions continued. Ruzbihan became "lost in passionate love" for God. Giving up his work as a greengrocer, he went to the desert, where "great ecstasies and hidden visitations happened every day."[36]

Ruzbihan became a member of the mystic brotherhood known as the Sufis and began to meditate and chant in the Sufi way. Later he dropped his formal practice but he continued to receive revelations or "unveilings." Around 1181, when he was fifty-three, he began to write an account of the revelations he had been granted, partly in the form of a memoir, partly as a diary. *The Unveiling of Secrets,* as Ruzbihan's book is called, is probably the first text in the Islamic world in which a mystic recorded his visions and experiences from the standpoint of the "I."

Ruzbihan began many passages of *The Unveiling of Secrets* with "I saw" – just as Hildegard did in many of the chapters of *Scivias*. But Ruzbihan's visions, unlike his Christian contemporary's, often exceeded the bounds of scriptural orthodoxy:

> There I saw the Truth (glory be to him), approaching me as if he wished to bequeath me himself and caress me. When I saw him, my conscience boiled with longings for him, but I did not draw near him, because of his great majesty. ... Then he manifested his hand, and I saw something in his hand like a tiny ant, and I did not know what that was. He said, "This is the throne, the footstool, the heavens, the earth, the nadir, and the zenith."[37]

Truth is one of the names of God. To describe God in human form contravenes one of the cardinal tenets of Islam. Possibly to mollify the orthodox, Ruzbihan put a Quranic quotation and an appropriate *hadith* immediately after this passage. Elsewhere he explained that God told him: "I made a likeness of my beauty in your eye, so you would be familiar with me and love me."[38]

Not only did Ruzbihan write from the standpoint of the self, he also grappled with the problems of selfhood:

> Then I was annihilated of all my attributes, and I descended to the world of the angelic realm. ... Then I went to the fields of pre-eternity intoxicated and raving. ... Here I was beloved of God most high. ... Then he bestowed on me his attributes, and he made me assume his essence. Then I saw myself as though I were he, and I remembered nothing but myself. I halted at that point and descended from lordship to servanthood. Then I desired the station of passionate love until I saw myself in the abode of majesty.[39]

Scholar Carl W. Ernst argues that passages like this have to be accepted as expressions of mystical experience but at the same time viewed "as literary texts" that conform to the conventions of the "rhetoric of sainthood," which encouraged overstatement as a sign of closeness to God.[40] Ernst's comments are a reminder that the literature of the self never stands apart from its historical and cultural context.

There are comparatively few discussions of the self in Sufi literature because Sufis aspire for the experience of *fana*, in which the self is annihilated in the realization of God. But, as Ernst explains, in *fana* "the self is not destroyed in any final or absolute sense, but it is completely dependent for its identity on the measured manifestation of the Attributes, while an excess of divine presence overwhelms and scatters the self for the time being."[41] This helps us understand allusions to the states of non-being and non-self in Sufi literature, as in this passage from Ruzbihan's contemporary Farid ud-Din Attar: "Ride the steed of non-being to the place where nothing is ... until at last thou shalt reach the world where thou art lost altogether to Self."[42]

No Sufi developed a theory of the self or no-self to compare with those of Plato, Augustine, or Shantideva. The most interesting speculations in the Islamic world on the nature of the self during the eleventh and twelfth centuries were the work of philosophers. The Persian polymath Ibn Sina or Avicenna (c. 980–1037) devised an interesting thought experiment to show that the soul was not logically dependent on the body. Imagine, he wrote, that an adult human came into existence floating in the air without any sensory contacts. This "floating man" would still have self-consciousness. Ibn Rushd or Averroes (1126–98), an Andalusian authority on law, medicine, and philosophy who lived at the same time as Ruzbihan, tried to integrate Aristotelian metaphysics with Islamic theology. He proposed that mind is composed of three intellects, called the material, agent, and speculative intellects. The first two are immortal and impersonal, indeed there is only one material and one agent intellect for the entire human race. The speculative intellect is distinct in each person. It dies with the body, so there can be no individual survival of death.

This chapter has covered, in less than twenty pages, more than three thousand years of the history of the idea of the self. A few developments stand out. The conceptions of the self and soul that were formulated by philosophers during the Axial Age were taken up by theologians of various religions, who adapted them in ways appropriate to their dogmas. The early Jewish Bible had no concept of the soul as distinct from the physical body; this idea entered Judaism during the Talmudic period (c. 70–500 CE), especially after Jewish thinkers were exposed to the ideas of Neoplatonism. The same influence encouraged some of the fathers of the Church, notably Augustine, to formulate a distinctively Christian concept of the soul. Later, Islamic thinkers drew on Jewish, Christian, and Greek sources to develop ideas that were present in the Quran. Millions of people throughout the world accept some version of the teachings about the soul put forward by these religions. Millions of others are influenced by the concepts of no-self developed by Buddhist thinkers and present also in Daoism, Sufism, and other mystical traditions. These two opposing views, one positive, one negative, recur throughout the history of the self-concept.

Exercising the Soul and Mind

Meditation is a powerful and full study for anyone who knows how to examine and exercise himself vigorously: I would rather fashion my mind than furnish it.

– Michel de Montaigne

The works of Avicenna, Averroes, and other Islamic thinkers helped introduce the study of Aristotle to the universities of Western Europe. Up to the early thirteenth century, Augustine's Christianized Platonism had held the field. Now there were two sources of authority and this made it harder to settle sticky points such as whether the rational soul was a form of the body or an independent substance or both. Albertus Magnus (c. 1206–80) tried to have it both ways: "When we consider the soul according to itself, we shall agree with Plato," the German bishop wrote, but "when we consider it in accordance with the animation it gives to the body, we shall agree with Aristotle."[1] Later in the thirteenth century, the matter was decided in favor of Aristotle. Thomas Aquinas (1225–74), an Italian theologian, forged a synthesis of Christian doctrine and Aristotelian philosophy that became the intellectual framework of Western Christian belief. In regard to the soul, his position was complex. On the one hand he rejected Platonic dualism: the soul and body together make up one substance. On the other he held that the soul or intellect is incorporeal. He resolved the apparent contradiction by saying that the soul, without the body, is not a complete substance: it needs the body to exercise its faculties.

By the end of the fourteenth century, as scholastic debate became more and more lifeless, religious specialists turned back to the early church fathers and to the practices of the monastic orders. Throughout Europe, hundreds of monasteries harbored thousands of monks and nuns, most belonging to ancient orders with written rules of conduct. There were also individual recluses – anchorites and anchoresses – who remained enclosed in solitary cells, often attached to churches. Communities were happy to maintain these people, whose prayers and penances were to the benefit of all. One such recluse was an Englishwoman known, after the church where she stayed, as Julian of Norwich (c. 1342–c. 1416). In 1373, when she was around thirty, Julian fell gravely ill. As she prayed and prepared herself for death, she received a series of sixteen "showings" or inner revelations. She survived and a few years later wrote a brief account of the showings, followed by a more extensive account. Formally "unlettered," she dictated or wrote these reports in Middle English and not Latin. The result, *Revelations of Divine Love*, is the earliest surviving book in English by a woman. The viewpoint is first person, the style unaffected and earthy, the substance mystically insightful:

> And in this vision he [God] showed me a little thing, the size of a hazelnut, lying in the palm of my hand, and to my mind's eye it was as round as any ball. I looked at it and thought, "What can this be?" And the answer came to me, "It is all that is made." ... In this little thing I saw three attributes: the first is that God made it, the second is that he loves it, the third is that God cares for it. But what does that mean to me?[2]

One of Julian's showings had to do with the soul and its relation to the body. "I saw quite certainly that our essential being is in God," she wrote, "and I also saw that God is in our sensory being." All human faculties are gifts from God: "he, dwelling in us, has enclosed these gifts within himself until such time as we have grown and matured, our soul with our body and our body with our soul, neither of them receiving help from the other, until by the operation of nature we achieve our full stature." God "is nearer to us than our own soul, for he is the ground on which our soul stands."[3] The language, whether Julian knew it or not, was Aristotelian; but her first-person standpoint and experiential assurance give the *Revelations* an authority that is lacking in the scholastic discourse of the time.

When she was around seventy, Julian had a visitor: a slightly mad mother of fourteen named Margery Kempe (born c. 1373), who had decided, at the age of forty, to take a vow of chastity and to travel far and wide to meet religiously minded people. On a trip to Norwich, she heard of Dame Julian and went to see her. Margery was in the habit of telling people "about the grace, that God had put into her soul," and the "wonderful revelations" that she had received in order "to find out if there were any deception in them." Julian told her "to be obedient to the will of our Lord and fulfil with all her might whatever he put into her soul, if it were not against the worship of God and the profit of her fellow Christians." She added: "A double man in soul is always unstable and unsteadfast in all his ways. He that is forever doubting is like the wave of the sea which is moved and borne about with the wind, and that man is not likely to receive the gifts of God."[4] Margery included an account of this meeting when she dictated her memoirs years later. This book, known simply as *The Book of Margery Kempe*, is the first autobiography in English by anyone, woman or man. Margery employed the third person, referring to herself as "this creature," in an attempt to project a self-effacing humility she clearly did not possess. Her account, long and somewhat tedious, dealt mostly with her travels in the Holy Land, Italy, Spain, and Germany. She emerges from it as a distinct if not always likeable personality. To use a word that had not yet been invented, she comes down to us as one of the first *individuals* of medieval England.

Humanism and Individualism: The Renaissance in Italy

In the early nineteenth century, European historians decided that they needed a term for the cultural and social changes that began in Florence around 1400 and later spread throughout Europe, which seemed to mark the end of the medieval world and the beginning of the modern. The word they coined, the Renaissance, referred at first to the rebirth of classical letters but later was extended to cover the fields of art, science, and life in general.

Medieval clerics had some knowledge of Roman philosophy, mathematics, and natural history, but from the middle of the fifteenth century scholars in Italy turned their attention to Greek and Latin literature, oratory, and history. They held up the great creators of Athens and Rome as cultural paragons rivaling in importance the Apostles and Fathers of the Church. The best minds of the age turned from Christianity's other-worldly compulsions toward the possibilities and accomplishments of the human being in the world. Florentine scholar Giannozzo Manetti (1396–1459) defended the dignity of man against papal assertions of human imperfection. A generation later, Giovanni Pico della Mirandola (1463–94) brought humanism to the forefront of Italian thought. A multifaceted scholar, Pico studied Latin, Greek, Hebrew, and Arabic at Padua and scholastic philosophy in Paris. He ended up compiling nine hundred theses on religion, philosophy, and science which he proposed to defend in public debate in Rome. Before he could, church authorities denounced seven of them as unorthodox and six as doubtful. When Pico tried to defend himself, the pope condemned all nine hundred, and Pico had to flee to France.

Pico's preface to his theses, *Oration on the Dignity of Man*, is a celebration of human possibilities. He has God, the Great Artisan, declare to Adam, the primeval man:

I have placed you at the very center of the world, so that from that vantage point you may with greater ease glance round about you on all that the world contains. We have made you a creature neither of heaven nor of earth, neither mortal nor immortal, in order that you may, as the free and proud shaper of your own being, fashion yourself in the form you may prefer. It will be in your power to descend to the lower, brutish forms of life; you will be able, through your own decision, to rise again to the superior orders whose life is divine.[5]

Pico's *Oration*, often called the manifesto of Renaissance humanism, was also an early articulation of Renaissance individualism. During the Middle Ages, according to nineteenth-century Swiss historian Jacob Burckhardt, "man was conscious of himself only as a member of a race, people, party, family, or corporation – only through some general category." But in Renaissance Italy, "man became a spiritual *individual*," and "recognized himself as such."[6] More recent writers, for example Stephen Greenblatt, have questioned some of Burckhardt's conclusions; but even Greenblatt concedes that the social conditions of fourteenth-century Italy "fostered a radical change in consciousness." People "were cut off from established forms of identity and forced by their relation to power to fashion a new sense of themselves and their world."[7]

The changes in the way Renaissance people viewed the world is evident in the art of the period. The invention of perspective allowed painters to present spatial relations in a realistic manner. Portraitists depicted their subjects as specific, recognizable persons and not as idealized types. Renaissance literature displayed a remarkable increase in the subjective point of view. The artist Benvenuto Cellini (1500–71) wrote an autobiography in which he showed both the creative and the violent sides of his nature. To Burckhardt this book, while not introspective, "describes the whole man – not always willingly – with marvelous truth and completeness."[8]

Righteousness and Reform: Martin Luther

In 1519 a German monk named Martin Luther (1483–1546) sat in the tower of his monastery wrestling with a passage from Paul's *Epistle to the Romans*. What, he thought, did the apostle mean by the "justice of God"? According to Luther's teachers, the phrase meant the power to punish sinners and the unjust. But why did God threaten miserable sinners like Luther "with his justice and his wrath"? Terrified at the prospect of damnation, he meditated night and day on Paul's words. Finally he realized that they had to be read along with another Biblical phrase: "The just person lives by faith." God justifies sinners – declares them to be righteous – through an act of grace that is merited by faith alone. When he understood this, Luther wrote, "all at once I felt that I had been born again and entered into paradise itself through open gates." He saw "the whole of Scripture in a different light," and came to love the words "justice of God" as vehemently as he had hated them before.[9]

Luther wrote this account of his conversion toward the end of a tumultuous life that saw him defy the Catholic Church and the Holy Roman Empire and lead Europe into a era of theological, political, and social turmoil. It all started even before his experience in the tower. In 1517, the obstreperous monk formulated ninety-five theses and nailed them to the door of the church of Wittenberg. Most of them had to do with the sale of "indulgences," which were said to grant freedom from punishment for sin and had become an important source of income for the Church. Luther also published a number of pamphlets criticizing this and other practices. He became such a nuisance that in 1520 Pope Leo X issued an edict condemning forty-one errors in his writings. The next year, Emperor Charles V, the most powerful monarch of the day, summoned Luther before an assembly where he was asked to retract his errors. He refused. Seeing this as defiance of established authority, the pope excommunicated him and the emperor declared him an outlaw.

At the root of Luther's differences with the Church was his conviction that salvation comes by faith alone and not through "works," pious acts performed under the direction of priests or other specialists. To Luther, all baptized Christians were priests who had their own relationship with God. Truth resided in the Bible alone, so believers had to study it themselves. This was impossible for most, because the only available text of the Bible was in Latin. Luther therefore translated the New Testament into German; others made translations into other languages. The recently invented printing press made it possible to distribute Bibles and other religious texts to large numbers of people. Literacy grew, debate flourished, people soon began to think that they could formulate their own ideas about matters relating to God and the soul.

The changes set in motion by Luther and others led to the religious, political, social, and cultural upheaval known as the Protestant Reformation. Most of the Christians of northern Europe became members of denominations that rejected the authority of the Roman Catholic Church. The rulers of kingdoms and principalities weighed the political benefits of supporting the Protestants or remaining faithful to Rome. A period of warfare began that went on in one place or another for more than a hundred years. During this period the middle classes grew in power, laying the foundation for a mercantile economy that developed into modern capitalism. Along with these outward changes came a radical alteration in the way people looked at themselves and the world. It became normal for people to examine their own consciences, and many expressed their thoughts and feelings in memoirs and other first-person genres. This was true even of people who remained faithful to the old Catholic order.

The Counter-Reformation: Ignatius of Loyola and Teresa of Avila

Ignatius of Loyola (1491–1556) is often compared with Martin Luther. Both became leaders of their respective faiths, one defending and the other attacking the Church of Rome. Both were gifted and self-confident; both acted on their convictions with vigor; and both arrived at their convictions as the result of conversion experiences, though the circumstances differed greatly. Luther saw the light after years of solitary study, Ignatius while recovering from injuries sustained when he was hit by a cannonball.

Born to the nobility of the Basque country of Spain, Ignatius served as a knight until 1521, when he was injured during the battle of Pamplona. During his convalescence, he read religious books and decided to dedicate himself to the Church. Hanging up his sword before an image of the Virgin Mary, he retired to a cave near the Catalonian town of Manresa. His conversion happened here. Years later, he told an associate that "a single hour of meditation at Manresa had taught him more truths about heavenly things than all the teachings of all the doctors put together could have taught him."[10]

In 1524, after a trip to the Holy Land, Ignatius settled in Barcelona. Here he wrote the first draft of a system of spiritual practices that he developed during his isolation in Manresa. As he explained to the scribe of his third-person life history, these practices at first were just "some things which he used to observe in his soul and find useful for himself." Later he thought they might prove useful to others and therefore wrote them down.[11] He called them *exercitia spiritualia*, spiritual exercises or practices, defining them as ways "of examining one's conscience, of meditating, contemplating, praying vocally and mentally, and other spiritual activities."[12] Ignatius's immediate inspiration was the devotional practices of late Medieval Europe, in particular those of the *devotio moderna* movement, remembered primarily through *The Imitation of Christ*, a spiritual manual by Thomas à Kempis (d. 1471). But the practice of self-discipline by means of psychological exercises went back at least as far as Stoicism. The Greek and Roman Stoics practiced self-cultivation to achieve the good life on earth. Ignatius was interested in "the overcoming of self" to gain a heavenly reward. Central to this effort was "the ordering of one's life on the basis of a decision made in freedom from any ill-ordered attachment."[13] He called this freedom from attachment "indifference" (*ser indiferente*). Indifference was important to the Stoics as well, but they saw it as a way to attain freedom from earthly pain and the fear of death. For Ignatius it was a way to achieve salvation by dedicating oneself to Christ.

Ignatius's *Exercises* are meditations on points of Christian doctrine: sin, the life of Jesus, his death and resurrection. As such they are of limited interest to those who are not Christians, though they contain much of psychological value. In one section, he presented a group of rules "by which to perceive and understand to some extent the various movements produced in the soul: the good that they may be accepted and the bad that they may be rejected." One of these rules deals with "desolation," that is "darkness and disturbance in the soul, attraction towards what is low and of the earth, anxiety arising from various agitations and temptations." To combat this state – what we would now call depression – Ignatius recommended remaining in "an attitude of patience, for patience is opposed to the annoyances that come upon one; one should keep in mind that consolation will soon come."[14] Such advice could be helpful to people from any cultural background.

Ignatius went to Paris for study in 1534. For years he had been thinking of founding an order of militant monks to combat clerical disobedience in Europe and to take the Gospel to newly discovered lands. While in Paris, he collected a group of six men who joined him in taking vows of poverty, chastity, and obedience. Six years later the nascent order was recognized as the Society of Jesus. As general of the order, Ignatius spent much of his time working on its rules and constitution. His "rules to follow in view of the true attitude of mind that we ought to maintain within the Church militant" are notable for their insistence on unthinking obedience to the dictates of the Church. Rule 13 has become notorious: "To maintain a right mind in all things we must always maintain that the white I see, I shall believe to be black, if the hierarchical Church so stipulates."[15]

In 1544 and 1545, while working on his order's constitution, Ignatius jotted down some of his thoughts and feelings in a notebook. At first his interests were practical: the pros and cons of a proposed financial arrangement for the order's churches. Then he began to make brief notations on the state of his mind and heart. The first entry (February 2, 1544) was divided between inner and outer concerns:

> Great devotion during mass, with tears, with increased trust in Our Lady, and more inclined both then and during the whole day to choose complete poverty [for the proposed churches].[16]

Later entries were longer and more concerned with the writer's inner states:

> During the customary [morning] prayer, much helped by grace and
> devotion: if there was clarity, there was even more light, and evidence of
> some warmth. For my part, I found it all too easy to attend to any and
> every thought. I rose still helped by that grace. … Suddenly the tears
> streamed down my face, I broke into sobs, and felt a love so intense that
> it seemed to unite me excessively close to Their own love, a thing full
> of light and sweetness. That intense visitation and love seemed quite
> remarkable and to surpass other visitations.[17]

After a month, the entries became briefer, dealing mostly with the presence
or absence of tears at mass. But there were also references to deeper spiritual
experiences, for example: "Several times I had the vision of the Divine
Being in the form of a circle."[18] Finally, after a week of noting either "tears"
or "no tears," Ignatius abandoned the notebook. Published after his death
as *Spiritual Diary*, it is one of the earliest personal diaries, and the earliest
surviving spiritual diary, kept by a European. It is remarkable as a record
of psychological observations with an accent on religious feelings. But it
was also an instrument of self-discipline. By keeping an account of the
movements of his mind and heart, Ignatius was attempting to bring them
under control.

The founding of the Society of Jesus in 1540 is seen by historians as one
of the first expressions of the Counter-Reformation, the attempt by Catholic
Europe to stem the tide of Protestantism. Five years later the pope convoked
a council in northern Italy to reaffirm church doctrine in the face of the
attacks of Luther and other reformers. After eighteen years, the council was
closed without granting any concessions to the heretics who now controlled
half of Europe. Justification by faith alone was rejected: works, and the
priesthood, had an important role to play. The written Bible could not be
considered the sole authority: there were also the traditions of the Church.
Still, institutional Catholicism began to make some attempts to clean up its
act. In this it was helped by some remarkable individuals, notably Teresa of
Avila (1515–82).

Born in central Spain when Ignatius was still a soldier and Luther still a
monk, Teresa lived through the early years of the Reformation but knew little
of what was going on in Germany, Switzerland, and England. She entered a
convent at the age of twenty-one, and passed the next twenty years in "strife
and contention between converse with God and the society of the world."
It wasn't until she reached the age of forty that her spiritual efforts began
to bear fruit. Around this time someone gave her a copy of Augustine's
Confessions. As she read, she seemed to see herself. When she came to the

account of his conversion in the garden, it seemed to her "exactly as if the Lord had spoken to me."[19]

Teresa wrote these lines in *The Life of Saint Teresa of Avila by Herself,* the first notable spiritual autobiography since Augustine's. Begun around 1558 at the request of her confessor, the *Life* is at once a work of psychological penetration and a classic of Spanish literature. The prose is vivid, conversational, and direct, treating with equal clarity the problems of setting up convents and the crises of the spiritual life. Famous for its descriptions of the four levels of "prayer" or spiritual experience, the *Life* deals also with the nuts and bolts of daily practice. Aspirants should persist even if they are "engaged in a thousand revolving thoughts and distractions, as I used to be," she wrote. "It is very important at the beginning, when we embark on prayer, not to be frightened by our own thoughts. You may take my word for this; I know it by experience."[20]

Teresa's confessor encouraged her to write her memoirs because the intensity of her practice and the depth of her experiences had brought her under the scrutiny of church authorities. At the same time, she was trying to found a reformed convent meant to correct the laxity of those she had known. This brought her into conflict with powerful men who resented her activism. She was savvy enough, given the prejudices of the age, to speak of herself as a "weak and wicked woman," but she also knew how to garner the support of influential people, and was so effective in getting things done that people called her "a virile woman" and "a manly soul."[21] Before she died at the age of sixty-seven, she had founded a total of sixteen convents and assisted in the foundation of several cloisters for men. Seven years after her death, theologians for the Inquisition demanded that her books be burned. They failed in this attempt, and in 1622 she was canonized a saint.

What Do I Know?: Michel de Montaigne

The women and men discussed above did their psychological exploration under the aegis of the Church. Organized religion still held a virtual monopoly on the study of the soul. Its nature was defined by church-approved theologians, who cited unquestionable scripture. The thoughts of Catholics were subject to the scrutiny of a confessor, their acts to discipline by priests. Those who tried to strike out on their own were condemned by Church authorities. Even future saints such as Ignatius and Teresa had to defend themselves against accusations that they were not quite orthodox. The revival of classical learning provided a new set of authorities for scholars to read and emulate, but they had to move carefully as they opened new fields of study. The priest and astronomer Nicolaus Copernicus (1473–1543) waited till the year of his death to publish his heliocentric theory of the solar system and his book was prefaced with a note explaining that he did not seek to displace the geocentric model. Giordano Bruno (1548–1600), an Italian friar and philosopher, endorsed Copernicus's theory and espoused a view of God and the world that was regarded as pantheistic. For this he was burned at the stake.

Michel Eyquem de Montaigne (1533–92) lived and died a devout Catholic, but his pioneering research into the human condition owed little to the Bible or fathers of the Church. His masters were the Roman poets, playwrights, historians, and philosophers, whom he quoted aptly and copiously in his works. But his insights into the nature of mind came mostly from the study of his own. In a country torn by sectarian conflict, he managed to win the respect of Protestants as well as Catholics. His perilous position between the two factions may have helped him develop his skeptical outlook and his sense of irony. "After all," he once wrote, "it is putting a very high price on one's conjectures to have a man roasted alive because of them."[22]

Michel was the son of Pierre Eyquem, a merchant whose grandfather had been named first lord of Montaigne, an estate near Bordeaux. Something of a scholar, Pierre engaged a tutor for his son while he was still quite young. The tutor spoke no French so Michel grew up speaking Latin. After completing his literary and legal studies, he was appointed to the Parlement of Bordeaux and later spent some time at the court of Charles IX in Paris. After his father's death he returned to Montaigne, of which he was now the lord. Now thirty-eight and "weary of the servitude of the court and of public employments," he decided to pass the remainder of his life in study and reflection.[23]

Montaigne read and reflected but did not find the tranquility he hoped for. In fact, as he wrote a short while later, "when I retired to my home," resolved to spend the rest of his life in seclusion, "it seemed to me I could do my mind no greater favor than to let it entertain itself in full idleness." But he found to his surprise that "like a runaway horse" it gave "itself a hundred times more trouble than it took for others," producing "many chimeras and fantastic monsters, one after another, without order or purpose." This habit of mind is something encountered by everyone who tries to engage in self-study. When it happened to Teresa, she commended herself to God. When it happened to Montaigne, he put his chimeras and monsters into writing so that he would be able to "contemplate their ineptitude and strangeness at my pleasure."[24]

This was the beginning of Montaigne's *essais* – attempts – to observe and understand himself. Each *essai* – "essay" in English – began as a consideration of a chosen subject but quickly became a rambling record of whatever came to his mind. This was (to use a modern cliché) a new literary departure. The classical writers remained always within the boundaries of oration, epistle, or poem. They knew where they were going and they got there without too many detours. For Montaigne the detours became more important than the destination. "It is a thorny undertaking, and more so than it seems, to follow a movement so wandering as that of our mind, to penetrate the opaque depths of its innermost folds, to pick out and immobilize the innumerable flutterings that agitate it," he wrote. He had heard of "only two or three ancients" who had opened this road, and their works had not survived. To him it was "a new and extraordinary amusement."[25]

These quotations are from the essay called *De l'exercitation*, usually translated into English as "On Practice." *Exercitation* is the French form of the Latin *exercitatio*, "training," "discipline," "exercise." Ignatius used the Latin term for his book of spiritual practices, but his approach differed greatly from Montaigne's. Ignatius's exercises are prescribed meditations on the life and death of Christ. They are arranged in a fixed order and practiced under the direction of a priest. Montaigne's essays are rambling divagations touching many different subjects but in the end focused on the rambler, Montaigne himself. "I want to be seen here in my single, natural, ordinary fashion, without striving or artifice," he told his readers in his Preface, "I am myself the matter of my book."[26]

Among Christians, to think and write about oneself was regarded as self-indulgent vanity. Montaigne anticipated this objection and brushed it aside. Self-study produced vanity only "in those who touch themselves no more than superficially," becoming intoxicated with a limited self-knowledge. Those who looked deeply into themselves soon learned that whatever good qualities they might possess were balanced by weaknesses and defects. Of course, few people had the courage to look deeply into themselves: "Because Socrates alone had seriously digested the precept of his god – to know himself – and because by that study he had come to despise himself, he alone was deemed worthy of the name *wise*," wrote Montaigne. He did not imagine he was a great man like Socrates; rather he was "a man of the common sort." Even so, he felt that writing about himself might have some utility: "You can tie up all moral philosophy with a common and private life just as well as with a life of richer stuff," he said, because every man and woman bore the stamp of the human condition.[27]

Before Montaigne came along, self-depiction was the privilege of the few. One day he watched while the king of France was presented with a portrait the king of Sicily had drawn of himself. "Why," he wondered, "is it not permissible in the same way for each man to portray himself with the pen, as he portrayed himself with a pencil?"[28] He granted himself this permission. Like anyone trying something new, he was often dissatisfied with the results. His "daydream of meddling with writing," he wrote once to a friend, was a "stupid enterprise."[29] But as he pushed on, he became convinced that it was worth the effort: "It is many years now that I have had only myself as object of my thoughts, that I have been examining and studying only myself," he wrote in a late essay, "and if I study anything else, it is in order promptly to apply it to myself, or rather within myself. ... There is no description equal in difficulty, or certainly in usefulness, to the description of oneself."[30] But what he was doing was not mere description; it was also an act of self-creation. Modeling the personage in the book on himself, he had, he wrote, "to fashion and compose myself so often to bring myself out, that the model itself has to some extent grown firm and taken shape. Painting myself for others, I have painted my inward self with colors clearer than my original ones. I have no more made my book than my book has made me."[31]

It took Montaigne a number of years to realize his subject was himself. His earliest essays, written under the influence of Stoicism, treat such topics as "To Philosophize is to Learn to Die." An epigram from that essay – "The constant work of your life is to build death" – is striking but hardly original.[32] Later he turned from Stoicism to Skepticism, taking as his motto the words of the philosopher Sextus Empiricus: "What do I know?" His greatest achievement during this period was the essay "Apology for Raymond Sebond," in which he defended the work of a Spanish theologian by saying, in effect, that his philosophy was no better and no worse than anyone else's. When dealing with questions of practical life, philosophers turned round in circles. Centuries of debate had ended in an "infinite confusion of opinions." Logic was no help, since "no reason can be established without another reason," and so "we go retreating back to infinity." Ordinary people were no better off; the best that could be said of them was that they were "in agreement about nothing."[33] The result was universal uncertainty. If people did not learn about themselves, there was nothing that they *could* learn. They therefore should engage in self-enquiry. The first result might be skepticism; but increasing self-knowledge would lead to greater understanding and a greater capacity to make the most of life.

This theme comes out strongly in Montaigne's last essay, "Of Experience." He remained as skeptical as ever about the ability of reason to arrive at universal truths: "The inference that we try to draw from the resemblance of events is uncertain, because they are always dissimilar; there is no quality so universal in this aspect of things as diversity and variety." Philosophers and theologians were just fooling themselves when they thought they had formulated absolute truths about the world and God. "They want to get out of themselves and escape from the man. That is madness: instead of changing into angels, they change into beasts." In writing this passage he may have been thinking about the slaughtering of Protestants by Catholics and of Catholics by Protestants in France. He had no time for this sort of fanaticism. He turned his scrutiny on himself because "in the experience I have of myself I find enough to make me wise, if I were a good scholar." This was the most fruitful form of study: "To compose our character is our duty, not to compose books. ... Our great and glorious masterpiece is to live appropriately." He concluded his book on this positive note: "It is an absolute perfection and virtually divine to know how to enjoy our being rightfully."[34]

Montaigne did not formulate a philosophy of self because he was suspicious of any attempt to reduce the flux of life to a formula. "I do not portray being," he wrote. "I portray passing."[35] Nevertheless, he has had a lasting effect on the history of the idea of the self. The two most important French philosophers of self in the next century, René Descartes and Blaise Pascal, took Montaigne's *Essays* as their starting point. Subsequent philosophers – Rousseau, Emerson, Nietzsche and many others – acknowledged (or tried to conceal) their debt to him. Montaigne also had a lasting impact on the development of autobiography and other forms of first-person writing. In the words of scholar Donald M. Frame, the *Essays* "is by no means the first autobiography, if we may loosely call it that; but certainly never before, and rarely if ever since, has a man been portrayed with such clinical care and detachment, and at the same time with such humor and urbanity."[36]

Montaigne wrote his essays in his own hand while sitting at his own desk. Sixteenth-century writers were the first to be able to do this. The production of cheap paper had an enormous impact on the growth of the written word and writing had an enormous impact on the growth of self-consciousness. "By separating the knower from the known," wrote literary scholar Walter Ong, writing made possible an "increasingly articulate introspectivity, opening the psyche as never before not only to the external objective world quite distinct from itself but also to the interior self against whom the objective world is set."[37] Montaigne certainly was a master of introspectivity, but he also had an eye for the objective world, and during one period, at least, he used writing to help him hone his vision. Between 1580 and 1582, he kept a diary of his travels in Switzerland, Germany, Austria, and Italy. He set forth with two things in mind: to visit spas and other resorts to get relief from the pain of kidney stones, and to see Italy, the home of the classical culture he so admired. His entries show an unfaltering interest in the local people and customs, often combined with penetrating reflections on European life. One Wednesday in Baden, the landlord served them fish. Montaigne asked him why. The man replied that the people of the town "ate fish on Wednesdays [as well as Fridays] for religious reasons." This confirmed what Montaigne had already concluded: "that those here who hold to the Catholic religion are much more strict and devout because they are surrounded by the contrary faith."[38] Passages like this help to explain why he has been called the first social scientist. Like a modern anthropologist doing his fieldwork, he tried to blend in with the natives. Although traveling with a retinue, he avoided "making himself noticeable by some mannerism at variance with the taste of those who saw him," falling in line "with the ways of the place where he happens to be."[39]

The diary shows that Montaigne was interested in just about everything: machinery, table manners, dress, religions, food, architecture, and people of all sorts and stations. He never failed to remark on the beauty, or lack of it, of the women in the places he passed through. At a church in Sterzing he tried to chat up a girl by addressing her in Latin. (It didn't work.) Seven months later, in Italy, he "gave a dance for the peasant girls, and danced in it myself so as not to appear too reserved."[40] (One imagines he enjoyed himself as well.) In cities like Florence he found the women disappointing. Even the most famous of those "who let themselves be seen by anyone who wants," were, he thought, "nothing exceptional." His opinion of Tuscan social relations was more favorable: "Free nations do not have the same distinction between people's ranks as do the others; and even those of the lowest class have something lordly in their manner."[41] While in Italy he received a letter informing him that he had been elected mayor of Bordeaux, and by November 1581 he was back in France. During the years that remained to him he fulfilled his duties with distinction, and also revised and enlarged the *Essays*. He met his death peacefully, in the bosom of the Church but with an indifference worthy of a Stoic, in 1592.

During his lifetime Montaigne was admired more as a statesman than as an author. The *Essays* were looked on as an up-to-date version of classical Skepticism. Readers did not begin to appreciate his radical self-analysis until the eighteenth century, when Rousseau and others made it fashionable for people to write about themselves. Since then, many critics and countless readers have been willing to grant what Montaigne said about himself: "No man ever penetrated more deeply into his material, or plucked its limbs and consequence cleaner, or reached more accurately and fully the goal that he had set for his work."[42]

The Sufi's "I": Mughal and Ottoman Memoirs and Diaries

The Europe of Luther, Ignatius, and Montaigne was troubled by war and political instability, which for a while cancelled out the economic and cultural gains of the Renaissance. During the same years the empires of western and southern Asia were scaling peaks of political power and cultural achievement. The Ottoman Empire touched its zenith during the reign of Suleiman the Magnificent (1494–1566), while Akbar the Great (1542–1605) extended the rule of the Mughal Empire over what is now Afghanistan, Pakistan, and northern India. During this epoch, a Mughal emperor pioneered the Muslim autobiography, while Indian and Ottoman Sufis chronicled their inner and outer lives in memoirs and diaries.

Zahir ad-Din Muhammad Babur (1483–1530), the founder of the Mughal Dynasty, was descended on his father's side from Timur (Tamerlane) and on his mother's from Genghis Khan. Despite this illustrious heritage, he was a relatively small player in Turko-Mongol politics when he succeeded his father as ruler of Fergana, in present-day Uzbekistan, at the age of twelve. Two years later he led an expedition that captured Samarkand but soon lost it and Fergana as well. Regathering his forces, he occupied Kabul, making it a base for future conquests. Eventually moving south, he subdued the Delhi Sultanate, becoming ruler of an extensive empire.

Babur was a talented writer as well as a successful commander. Though well versed in Persian, the language of the elite, he turned to his mother tongue, Chagatai Turkish, when he began to write his memoirs. Covering his life from the moment of his accession to the year before his death, his book, the *Baburnama*, was the first autobiography in the Muslim world. Like Cellini's *Life*, which it preceded by thirty years, it traces the story of a man of action who had a rich artistic life. Much of the book is devoted to his military exploits, recounted in vivid detail. There was no Geneva Convention in those days, as his account of the aftermath of the Battle of Khanwa shows: "There were piles of the slain [on the battlefield], and towers of skulls were erected." He continued his description of the scene in verse:

> Many mountains of bodies were created, and on every mountain running streams of blood. / From the lances of the splendid ranks the fighters fled into mountain and plain.[43]

This son of the steppes took poetry-writing seriously. During a dark period in Tashkent, he wrote the following lines:

> No one remembers anyone in tribulation. / No one gladdens anyone in

exile. / In this exile my heart has not been gladdened. / No one can be comforted at all in exile.

After completing this quatrain, he showed it to the local khan hoping for some tips in "the technicalities of poetry." A short while later, he composed his first *ghazal*:

Other than my own soul I never found a faithful friend. / Other than my own heart I never found a confidant.[44]

Medieval Turkish and Persian poetry is highly conventional, filled with beautiful slave-boys and goblets of wine. Babur's treatments of such subjects carry conviction because he presented them as episodes in the story of his life. "May no one be so distraught and devastated by love as I," he wrote of a boy he met in the bazaar, "May no beloved be so pitiless and careless as you." Although a pious Muslim (and at least formally a Sufi initiate) he enjoyed getting drunk and wasn't shy about admitting it. He also didn't hesitate to depict himself in moments of doubt or fear. His purpose, he wrote, was not "to compliment myself: I have simply set down exactly what happened."[45] This claim to be telling the truth as it happened is the autobiographer's trademark and the skill with which Babar made good the claim rendered him one of the most memorable figures of his age.

Babur's great-great-grandson Shah Jahan (1592–1666) ruled over an empire that stretched from Kabul to central India. Its magnificence was epitomized by the Taj Mahal, the tomb he built for his third wife Mumtaz Mahal. Mumtaz bore him fourteen children, of whom the eldest to survive into adulthood were Jahanara Begum (1614–81) and Dara Shikoh (1615–59). Both left behind autobiographical writings that gave expression to their Sufi convictions. The development of first-person writing in Islamic literature was everywhere associated with Sufism, in part because Sufis were more likely than most to have access to the written word. But there were psychological reasons as well. As critic Derin Terzioglu explained: "Central to the Sufi quest for God was the view that one can only know God if one knows oneself. This was in fact an ancient idea that went back to the Delphic oracle 'Know yourself,' and had been reworked into the Islamic tradition in the form of the hadith, 'One who knows oneself knows one's Lord.'"[46]

Sufism entered India during the thirteenth century, and by the time of Shah Jahan most of the Sufi orders were represented. His daughter Jahanara was drawn by the teachings of Khwaja Moinuddin Chisthi and wrote a biography of him in Persian. In an appendix to this work she gave an account of her visit to the master's tomb in 1643. "Know that, after the performance of religious duties, requirements, and the recitation of the holy

Qur'an," she began, "this weak woman who hopes for salvation regards no action as nobler than the remembrance of the spiritual states and stations of the revered saints." Entering the shrine barefoot and kissing the ground, she circumambulated the tomb seven times, "sweeping it with my eyelashes, and making the sweet-smelling dust of that place the mascara of my eyes." Thereupon "a marvelous spiritual state and mystical experience befell this annihilated one, which cannot rightly be written."[47] Similar in tone to the memoirs of Margery Kempe, Jahanara's account tells us less about herself as an individual than of the ideal of Sufi submissiveness she tried to emulate.

Like his sister, crown prince Dara Shikoh made conventional hagiography a vehicle for personal observations. His *Hasanat-ul-'Arifin* or Aphorisms of the Saints consists of sayings and anecdotes of holy men he had met or learned of. "All these sayings are mine," he claimed, "for they are in accordance with the greatest of all aphorisms – the Truth." One of his informants was Baba Lal, a Hindu *sannyasi* he met in 1653. The Baba told him that there were four types of spiritual leaders, the greatest of which was "like a candle, which is capable of illuminating a hundred thousand candles." This inspired Dara to compose a quatrain:

> The Gnostic endows you with illumination – body and soul:
> A barren thorny mound he transforms into a rose garden.
> The Perfect leads you out of the erroneous path –
> A candle illuminates a thousand candles![48]

Dara's interest in Hindu philosophy caused him to commission a Persian translation of the *Upanishads*, which he regarded as "the source and the fountain-head of the ocean of Unity, in conformity with the holy *Qur'an* and even a commentary thereon."[49] His liberal approach to religion did not help him when he was captured by his brother Aurangzeb while the two were contending for the throne. Aurangzeb had Dara declared an apostate, and ordered his execution.

The Mughal Empire that Babur founded flourished until the early eighteenth century. In the West, the Ottoman Empire began to decline a century earlier. During this period Sufi writers in the empire's Turkish heartland used first-person writings to help them fix their place in an unstable society. Seyyid Hasan, a dervish of Istanbul, kept a diary during the 1660s in which he wrote a great deal about the people he met and the food he ate, but never described his activities as a preacher or even mentioned his name. His purpose, in the words of critic Cemal Kafadar, was not to give expression to his individual self but to map out "the labyrinthine network of companionship" spun by himself and those around him.[50] Two decades later, the Anatolian master Niyazi-i Misri (1618–94) used his diary to record the

events of his inward as well as his outward life. In his account of his persecution at the hands of Kadizadeli fundamentalists, the dominant mood was
fear. As if to compensate, he wrote of his spiritual life in highly exalted terms,
presenting himself, in one passage, as Adam, the perfect man, at whose right
hand stood the pure asking for illumination and advice, while at his left stood
bandits clamoring for ignorance and insanity. The grandiosity of this picture
may be explained, at least in part, by the Islamic "rhetoric of sainthood" that
goes back to Ruzbihan and beyond. Finding himself in dire circumstances,
Misri used the conventions of this "old topos in Sufi literature" to make sense
"of a world that increasingly seemed fractured and in flux."[51]

Between the fifteenth and seventeenth centuries, a few individuals in
Europe and Asia expressed themselves in first-person writings that gave
evidence of a heightened sense of self. For some – Luther, Ignatius, Teresa,
the Sufis of India and Turkey – the self-expression took a form consistent
with religious beliefs, though these beliefs were under stress. For others
– Pico della Mirandola, Montaigne – the push to self-discovery followed
the forms of ancient literature, though it often went beyond the classical
models. For others – Cellini, Babur, Basho – art and poetry were the tools
that opened the gates of self-expression. At the time these writers and their
writings were exceptional. In the centuries that followed, diaries, memoirs,
and other sorts of first-person writing became well-established genres.

Self-Examination

*Now began I afresh to give myself up to a serious examination after my
state and condition for the future, and of my evidences for that blessed
world to come.*

– John Bunyan

Sometime around May 1534 – a year after Montaigne was born and sixteen
years after Luther nailed his Ninety-Five Theses to the door of the church
of Wittenberg – a young French lawyer named Jehan Cauvin had a sudden
change of heart. For some time he had been committed to the reform of the
Church, but he was still, as he later wrote, "addicted to the superstitions of
the papacy." Then

> God subdued and made teachable a heart which, for my age, was far
> too hardened in such matters. Having received some foretaste and
> knowledge of true piety, I was inflamed with such great desire to profit
> by it that, although I did not give up my other studies, I worked only
> slackly at them. ... Before the year was out, all those who had some
> desire for true doctrine ranged themselves around me to learn, although
> I was hardly more than a beginner myself.[1]

This was the start of a ministry that would change the history of France
and eventually the whole Western world. Within two years, John Calvin (as
he is known in English) had renounced his church income, taken refuge
in Switzerland, and published the enormously influential *Institutes of the
Christian Religion*. In this treatise he wrote of the absolute sovereignty of
God, who has predestined the elect to salvation and the rest to eternal
damnation. This harsh doctrine, far from encouraging fatalism, drove those
who accepted it to inner examination and outward activism. Self-scrutiny
was necessary because "the heart of man has so many recesses of vanity, and
so many retreats of falsehood, and is so enveloped with fraudulent hypocrisy,
that it frequently deceives" itself. Every true Christian had to examine
his or her conscience in order to root out this hypocrisy and cultivate a

living faith in Christ. Salvation came by faith alone but there was also "a necessary connection between faith and good works"; though when God sends us "back to our own works," he "promises life to us only if we find it in ourselves."[2]

For those who are not Protestant Christians, the verbal contortions of Calvin and Luther when they talk about faith and works are often hard to understand. Even if their arguments are accepted, a conundrum remains: if salvation comes by faith alone, why should a person do anything at all – particularly if his or her salvation or damnation is preordained by God? Luther had a lively correspondence on this subject with Desiderius Erasmus, the greatest Christian humanist of the day. Erasmus proposed a compromise solution: the push toward the attainment of salvation was due only to God's grace, but the human will nevertheless had "a certain place in the unfolding of the act." Luther would have none of this. If "nothing can take place but according to [God's] will," then humans (along with angels and animals) quite simply had no free will. It followed that "the first care of every Christian ought to be to lay aside all reliance on works, and strengthen his faith alone more and more, and by it grow in the knowledge, not of works, but of Christ Jesus."[3] This left the conundrum unanswered, as did Calvin's treatment of the question: "God saves whom he will of his mere good pleasure" without regard to works. The psychological consequences of this were clear: "they who know not themselves to be God's peculiar people will be tortured with continual anxiety."[4]

Modern historians and sociologists have focused on this anxiety while trying to figure out what made sixteenth and seventeenth century Calvinists tick. Certainly they feared damnation, which meant an eternity of suffering in hell. Just as certainly they longed for salvation without knowing whether they were among the elect and aware there was nothing they could do to improve their odds. The only way they could deal with the resulting anxiety was to look for what Calvin called proofs of the indwelling of the spirit and signs of divine election. Self-scrutiny might provide them with evidences that they were guided by the Spirit, while the performance of good works was the surest sign that they were among the elect. The early twentieth-century sociologist Max Weber tried to explain this to non-Calvinists. "However useless good works might be as a means of attaining salvation," he wrote, "they are [for the Calvinist] indispensable as a sign of election. They are the technical means, not of purchasing salvation, but of getting rid of the fear of damnation."[5] This was part of Weber's theory that the "worldly asceticism" of Calvinists, Pietists, and others gave rise to a "Protestant ethic" that encouraged disciplined activity and eventually helped in the development of capitalism. Other sociologists have questioned Weber's thesis, but few reject his conclusion: Calvinists, while remaining deeply religious, felt authorized to engage in secular activities and to reap their rewards. Paradoxically, a religion that taught the fruitlessness of works impelled its adherents toward secular exertions.

A Staff to Hold Me Up: English Puritan Diaries

England became Protestant not because an anguished monk or lawyer examined his conscience but because a thwarted king wanted a divorce. Henry VIII broke with Rome and became head of the Church of England in 1534, though it was not until 1563 that the Church adopted reforms that made it largely Calvinist in belief. The result did not please everyone. Many believers wanted increased "purification" from residual Catholic practices. These Puritans, as they became known, sometimes found themselves in conflict with the established Church. Others, known as Dissenters, founded separate denominations that often were persecuted by church and civil authorities. Contentions between religious groups, together with a mass of other social, political, and economic developments, made the history of sixteenth- and seventeenth-century England a welter of uncertainty and conflict, culminating in the Civil War (1642–51).

During this troubled period, English Protestants had special reason to scrutinize their feelings, thoughts, and actions. Finding no comfort in the course of outer events, they looked within for signs of God's working. Many began and ended their days with periods of self-examination. Putting their good works and sins in the balance, they anxiously looked for signs of divine election. Catholics had it easier. By confessing their sins periodically to a priest, they gained some relief from anxiety because the priest could grant them absolution on the authority of Christ. The Protestant rejection of priestly mediation left believers to their own devices. They turned for help to the Bible, which began to appear in printed translations in the 1520s and 1530s. As literacy became more general, many turned to another literary helper, the diary, which for some took the place of the Catholic priest.

In the private pages of their diaries, Puritans could confess their sins directly to God. The very act of writing granted a sort of absolution. They also could enter into covenants – solemn agreements – with their Creator. Among Catholics only specialists – monks, nuns, priests, and so forth – could take solemn vows that bound them to the religious life. Calvinism extended this privilege to lay men and women, who solemnized private vows in a spirit of great seriousness. Janet Hamilton, a seventeenth-century Englishwoman, renewed hers every four years. Once she began: "Lord, thou knowest my former engagements which passed betwixt my soul and thee, when I entered into covenant with thee (to my soul's great comfort) in the sweet castle of Blackness, I giving myself up unto thee ... and to our noble work of Reformation." She hoped that her contract might "be as a staff to hold me up from staggering on the dark mountains."[6] A century earlier Richard Rogers, one of the first Puritan diarists, wrote of his desire to renew his covenant and to make it more firm in order

> to come nearer to the practice of godliness and oftener to have our conversation in heaven, our minds seldomer and more lightly upon the things of this life, to give to our selves less liberty in the secretest and smallest provocation to evil, and to endeavor after a more continual watch from thing to thing that as much as might be we might walk with the Lord for the time of our abiding here below.[7]

Rogers's desire for self-knowledge is movingly expressed in a diary entry from October 1587. After reviewing his moral progress and thanking God for his mercy, he expressed the desire "to know mine own heart better, where I know that much is to be gotten in understanding of it, and to be acquainted with the diverse corners of it and what sin I am most in danger of and what diligence and means I use against any sin and how I go under any affliction."[8]

Rogers was thirty-six when he wrote this entry, well known throughout East Anglia as a preacher. His sermons projected a calm authority; his diary reveals his inner anguish. It was a constant struggle, he wrote in 1589, for him to keep his sinful tendencies in check, "to force my self, through God's goodness, to come out of this slavery" to laxity and greed.[9]

Rogers's obsession with his weaknesses and sins is typical of Puritan writings. Nowhere is this more evident than in the diary of his younger contemporary, Samuel Ward, a preacher remembered mainly as one of the translators of the King James Bible. The earliest entries in Ward's diary consist almost entirely of lists of sins, for example:

> Mine idleness in not rising to prayers. My little care of God in the morning and thinking on him. My desire of vain glory, when we were gathering herbs with Mr. Downam, whereby I might see how prone when occasion is given *superbire* [to be proud]. My careless hearing at Mr. Newhouse's catechising.

and (two days later):

> My overmuch quipping and desire of praise thereby. My negligence in my calling. My forgetfulness in noting my sins.

He made up for the last-named lapse a few days later:

> My negligence is not calling upon God before I went to the Chapel, and
> the little desire I had there to call on God, and my drowsiness in God's
> service. My sins even through the whole day, being Sunday: 1. My negli-
> gence aforesaid, 2. My hearing of the sermon without that sense which
> I should have had.

And so on down to

> 12. In not going to evening prayers, 13. In supping liberally, never
> remembering our poor brethren, 14. In not taking order to give the
> poor women somewhat at 7 o'clock, 15. My dullness in stirring of my
> brother to Christian meditations, 16. My want of affections in hearing
> the sermons repeated, 17. My sluggishness in prayer, and thus sin I daily
> against thee, O Lord.[10]

This is the sort of thing that has given "Puritanism" a bad name, wrote
historian Margo Todd. The word came to signify something "rigid, narrow,
and quaintly absurd in design," upon which we moderns "look down with
complacency."[11] When we approach the Puritan mind, Todd insisted, we
have to project ourselves into the world of sixteenth-century Calvinists. But
this is not easy for people of the present century to do. We are far more likely
to attend a weekend workshop on self-love than to emulate the Puritans'
self-abasement.

The sincerity of Ward's endeavor is clear in his efforts at self-scrutiny,
which were modeled on Augustine's. But he never made the turn toward
inner discovery that comes out clearly in the *Confessions*. Ward examined his
self chiefly to chronicle its failings, as in an entry of 1595, where he noted: "I
could not get out of my self" any "good meditations against pride."[12] Rogers
wrote similarly: "I would to God when I cannot presently [i.e. immediately]
recover my self, yet that I might go about it little by little, and so mark the
strength of sin in my self when I shall see how hardly [i.e. with what diffi-
culty] my heart is brought to yield."[13]

Ironically the rise of self-consciousness among Puritans expressed itself
chiefly in the form of self-flagellation. This comes out explicitly in *A Journal
or Diary of a Thankful Christian*, a self-help guidebook that became a
bestseller when it was published in 1656. The keeping of a journal, wrote the
book's author,

> especially if we look often into it, and read it over will be a noteable
> means to increase in us that self-abasement & abhorrency of spirit that
> is most acceptable in the sight of God. ... Oh! how will the serious

survey of such a Journal abase the soul before the Lord! Such a course would very much help our faith.[14]

Self-abasement is the flip side of self-affirmation, which also came to the forefront during the Elizabethan age. A term was needed for the thing that was being affirmed and toward the end of the sixteenth century the noun "self" broke loose from reflexive pronouns like "myself" (or "my self" as Rogers and Ward wrote). But it took nearly a century for the word to assume its modern sense. Shakespeare, who examined what we now call self-consciousness in *Hamlet* and other plays, occasionally used the noun "self," as in this passage from *Julius Caesar*:

> I cannot tell what you and other men
> Think of this life; but for my single self,
> I had as lief not be as live to be
> In awe of such a thing as I myself.[15]

But he never used it in its modern philosophical sense. His contemporary Edmund Spenser came closer when he wrote, in the second book of the *Faerie Queene*:

> That is our Self, whom though we do not see,
> Yet each doth in him self it well perceive to be.[16]

A half-century later, the metaphysical poet Thomas Traherne wrote clearly of the self as an independent entity:

> A secret self I had enclosed within,
> That was not bounded with my clothes or skin,
> Or terminated with my sight, the sphere
> Of which was bounded with the Heavens here.[17]

Edifying Narratives: John Bunyan and George Fox

The intense self-scrutiny that found an outlet in Elizabethan diaries was given a more public form in spiritual memoirs. Narratives of conversion were stock elements of Protestant profession and teaching, and from the mid-seventeenth century many of them were consigned to print. The most influential were *Grace Abounding to the Chief of Sinners* by John Bunyan and *The Journal of George Fox*. The authors of both books were preachers formed by the printed word, so it was natural for them to turn to printed books to tell the story of their redemptive journeys.

Bunyan was born to poor parents in Bedfordshire in 1628. At sixteen he joined the Parliamentary Army, composed mainly of Puritans and Dissenters, in their war against the Royalists, who supported the established church and in some cases leaned toward Catholicism. After the Parliamentarian victory in 1647, Bunyan left the army and resumed his work as wandering tinker. In *Grace Abounding*, he depicts himself as a rowdy and profane young man. (This is in line with the model of the spiritual memoir created by Augustine, in which an incorrigible sinner is redeemed by the grace of God.) One day, while he was playing on the village green, "a voice did suddenly dart from heaven into my soul, which said, Wilt thou leave thy sins and go to heaven, or have thy sins and go to hell?"[18] This marked the beginning of a long period of doubt, depression, and occasional joy as he struggled to find an answer to the question that tormented him: Was he among those destined to be saved? He took up the study of the Bible, but this led to further doubts. In regard to the question of his election,

> I found at this time, that though I was in a flame to find the way to heaven and glory, and though nothing could beat me off from this, yet this question did so offend and discourage me, that I was, especially at some times, as if the very strength of my body also had been taken away by the force and power thereof. This scripture [*Romans* 9:16] did also seem to me to trample upon all my desires, "It is not of him that willeth, nor of him that runneth, but of God that sheweth mercy."

He realized that unless God "had voluntarily chosen me to be a vessel of mercy, though I should desire, and long and labour until my heart did break, no good could come of it." Again and again he asked himself: "How can you tell that you are elected? And what if you should not? How then?"[19]

Despite the pitfalls of scriptural interpretation, Bunyan searched through the Bible for guidance. He also was helped by manuals of devotion and by Luther's commentary on the epistles of Saint Paul. But sometimes the necessary guidance came from within. At crucial moments on his journey, he was helped by words that "darted in upon me" or "fell upon my soul," for example: "My grace is sufficient," "Thy righteousness is in heaven," "I must go to Jesus."[20] He looked for Biblical confirmation of these phrases that seemed to sound in his heart, but he was certainly going beyond the formula "by scripture alone" when he heeded his inner voice.

Bunyan became a Baptist preacher and his outspokenness put him at odds with the authorities, particularly after the monarchy was restored in 1660. The next year he was imprisoned after he declared that he would not stop preaching. While in jail he wrote *Grace Abounding* and his masterwork, *Pilgrim's Progress*, a first-person allegory in which he presents his inner qualities and the forces of the outside world as characters. The protagonist, Christian, is a pilgrim bound from the ordinary life (the City of Destruction) to heaven (the Celestial City). He is helped by Faithful, Hopeful, and others he meets along the way, and hindered by Mr. Worldly Wiseman, Ignorance, and others including the devil Apollyon. From time to time Evangelist (the Gospels) meets him and gives him guidance and encouragement. "In every city bonds and afflictions abide in you; and therefore you cannot expect that you should go long on your pilgrimage without them," Evangelist tells Christian and Faithful before they enter Vanity Fair, "But be you faithful unto death, and the King will give you a crown of life."[21] Critics agree that Bunyan drew on the personal journey sketched already in *Grace Abounding* while writing *Pilgrim's Progress*. In so doing, he helped create the English novel. Within fifty years, Daniel Defoe had published the fictional memoirs *Robinson Crusoe* and *Moll Flanders*. Other first-person novels, such as *Pamela* and *Gulliver's Travels*, soon followed. All these works, from the apparently factual to the obviously fantastic, have in common the theme of personal self-formation.

In 1643, about a year before Bunyan joined the Parliamentary Army, an apprentice shoemaker and shepherd named George Fox left his birthplace in the Midlands and took to the road. Deeply religious but unsatisfied by the clergymen he encountered, he wandered for several years, often "in great trouble" of mind. During this period, as he later recorded in his *Journal* (which was not a diary but a memoir), "I fasted much, walked abroad in solitary places many days, and often took my Bible, and sat in hollow trees and lonesome places till night came on; and frequently in the night walked mournfully about by myself." He had already "forsaken the priests" of the established religion. Now he "left the separate preachers also, and those esteemed the most experienced people; for I saw there was none among them all that could speak to my condition." Eventually he gave up hope of finding anyone who could help him. Then in his solitude he "heard a voice which said, 'There is one, even Christ Jesus, that can speak to thy condition,'" and his heart leapt for joy. He now realized "why there was none upon the earth that could speak to my condition, namely, that I might give Him all the glory" so that "Jesus Christ might have the pre-eminence who enlightens, and gives grace, and faith, and power. Thus when God doth work, who shall hinder it? and *this I knew experimentally* [i.e. through inner experience]."[22]

Fox was still not free from "troubles, trials, and temptations" but now he could see their nature clearly. When the light appeared, he was able to distinguish what was "out of the light," namely, "darkness, death, temptations, the unrighteous, the ungodly."[23] Eventually God showed him

> that every man was enlightened by the divine Light of Christ, and I
> saw it shine through all; and that they that believed in it came out of

condemnation to the Light of life, and became the children of it. ... This I saw in the pure openings of the Light without the help of any man; neither did I then know where to find it in the Scriptures; though afterwards, searching the Scriptures, I found it.[24]

The enlightenment of all by the "divine Light of Christ" became Fox's central tenet. No outward teaching, not even the Bible, could take precedence over the inner light. When he spoke to the men and women who had begun to gather around him, he was impelled to direct them "to that inward Light, Spirit, and Grace, by which all might know their salvation and their way to God; even that Divine Spirit which would lead them into all truth, and which I infallibly knew would never deceive any."[25]

Fox's followers called themselves Children of Light, then Friends of the Truth, and finally just Friends. Others called them Quakers because Fox told his oppressors to "tremble at the word of the Lord."[26] The Quakers' teachings were radical even by the standards of seventeenth-century England, where Anabaptists and Ranters and Muggletonians competed for adherents with the established church. John Bunyan, a Baptist, occasionally heard voices that "darted in upon me," but his teachings were based solidly on the Bible. To Fox, all scripture was of secondary importance to the Light of Christ within. The religious and civil authorities found this disconcerting and imprisoned him a number of times on different charges. During one spell in jail, he dictated his *Journal* to his son-in-law. Edited and published after his death, it is a curious document. Many of the experiences Fox recorded are luminously mystical. Others are so weird that even the philosopher Josiah Royce, a sympathetic observer, conceded that they were "pathological." But Royce also believed that "Fox possessed a consciousness of the presence of the divine which was a central feature" of the Inner Light, "which he believed to be the most precious possession of all believers."[27]

The Protestant revolution began in the early sixteenth century when Luther insisted that all Christians needed to approach God on their own, without the mediation of priests. In questions of belief and behavior, the only authority was the Bible. It did not follow that people at once became free to do and think whatever they wanted. Luther, Calvin, and other Protestant leaders were just as rigid as Catholics on points of doctrine. But once it became possible for people to think they could arrive at their own interpretation of the Bible, authorities found it difficult to limit the scope of individual inspiration. It took less than 150 years to get from Luther's priesthood of all believers to George Fox's Inner Light, and the rate of change continued to increase. Nevertheless, most rank-and-file Christians in Europe and America remained deeply conservative.

A City on the Hill: The Puritan Diary in New England

George Fox crossed the Atlantic in 1671 and spent two years touring the English colonies. Less than a century after the first settlements, America was home to a variety of religious denominations: Virginia was Anglican, Massachusetts primarily Puritan, Rhode Island a place for Baptists, Quakers, and others who did not fit in elsewhere.

Many New England colonists, fleeing persecution in England, regarded themselves as elected by God to establish his kingdom in the New World. The Pilgrims of Plymouth drew up a covenant in 1620 by which they constituted themselves "a civil body politic" for "the glory of God, and advancement of the Christian faith." Ten years later John Winthrop exhorted his fellow Puritans: "We are entered into covenant with Him [God] for this work. … We must consider that we shall be as a city upon a hill. The eyes of all people are upon us."[28] Winthrop kept a diary during his years as governor of the Massachusetts Bay Colony. As a Calvinist, he could not imagine that this would help him gain salvation: "God will have mercy on whom he will have mercy," he wrote, and "there was never any holy meditation, prayer, or action that I had a hand in, that received any worth or furtherance from me or anything that was mine."[29] But as an anxious believer, he hoped for a taste of grace while examining himself in his diary.

To establish a perfect commonwealth, it was necessary get rid of anyone who didn't toe the Puritan line. Anne Hutchinson, at first orthodox and dutiful, perturbed the elders when she began "to set forth her own stuff." Asked to investigate, Winthrop found that she affirmed "the indwelling of the person of the Holy Ghost, and of union with Christ," putting "immediate witness" (inner experience) before reliance on grace. In addition, declared John Cotton (the minister Hutchinson had followed to New England), her faith was not based on "public ministry" (that is, sermons by people like Cotton) but "by private meditations, or revelations only."[30] This was almost as bad as heeding the Inner Light. In 1638 Hutchinson was tried, convicted of blasphemy, excommunicated, and banished from Massachusetts.

Thomas Shepard, one of Hutchinson's prosecutors, insisted that tolerance of other religions was "the foundation of all other errors and abominations in the churches of God." In his diary, he wrote disapprovingly that many Christians wanted "to have joy and peace alway"; to him "temptations, fears, and wrestlings" also were good. His first-person writings – the diary and an autobiography – give ample evidence of such struggles. Both are filled with the sort of self-accusation that is typical of Puritan writings, for example: "In prayer I saw my heart very vile, filled with nothing but evil, nay, mind and mouth and life, and void of God."[31] But there are also passages showing that he was capable of sophisticated self-observation:

> I saw if my mind acted it spun nothing but deceit and delusion; if my will and affections acted, nothing but dead works. O how do I need Christ to live in me! Yet I saw if a man hath eyes and life he will not lean on another to lead him and carry him as when he wants both; so here. I saw the Lord made me live by faith by making me feel a want of both, to distrust myself and trust more unto the Lord.[32]

Shepard had occasional moments of assurance, but these were followed by uncertainty. One morning he "saw that Christ had not only made a general offer of himself but particular 1) by letting me feel my emptiness, 2) by making me feel his sweetness." But still he could not find "a full, clear, and settled evidence of his [Christ's] favor. I did not hear him speak peace to my soul, and I saw this was a matter of great mourning." Wavering of this sort seems to have been a normal result of Calvinist self-scrutiny. As a historian of the period wrote, Puritans who were justified by faith were "taken from the rack of fear only to be strapped to the wheel of doubt."[33]

Michael Wigglesworth, a minister who wrote the bestselling poem *The Day of Doom*, was even more obsessed than Shepard by sin and self-hatred. "Ah Lord," he wrote in his diary in June 1653, "I am vile and poor, and sinful, helpless in my self." He was especially bothered by the sin of pride, which he felt "still again and again abounding," together with "self-admiration, though destroying my self daily." This sentence epitomizes the struggle between Wigglesworth's true (religious) self and the false (sinful) self that sought to destroy it. Their conflict drove him to intense self-hatred. "I loathe my self," he wrote after experiencing a "filthy dream," "and could even take vengeance of my self for these abominations."[34]

Self-examination within the framework of Calvinist belief took a deep psychological toll. Thoughts of suicide were common. Susanna Anthony of Rhode Island wrote that her heart was "a sink of sin, more loathsome than the most offensive carrion that swarms with hateful vermin!" She was "strongly beset to lay violent hands on myself, verily fearing, if I lived, I should be a most blasphemous wretch." Yet for some Puritans "confronting the ugliness of sin helped them gain a greater appreciation of God's 'astonishing' grace," as historian Catherine Brekus wrote. Shepard lamented that he was "nothing else but a mass of sin," but he also was open to redeeming experience: "The Lord suddenly appeared and let me see there was strength in him to succor me, wisdom to guide, mercy in him to pity, spirit to quicken, Christ to satisfy, and so I saw all my good was there, as all evil was in myself."[35]

It was hard for men and women of ordinary flesh and blood to maintain the self-surveillance demanded of seventeenth-century Puritans. Many men who came of age in the second half of the century, for example Jeremiah Dummer and Samuel Sewall, abandoned their theological studies and went into business. The language of the counting house sometimes found its way into Dummer's diary:

> I considered how very accurate I and others endeavour to be in stating in our books of merchandise an account of profit and loss, by which we may at any time know, whether we improve or decline in our worldly estate; and yet how careless most men are and my self especially in the vastly superior concerns of the soul so as to keep no account of the growth of grace or corruption, that 'tis very hard to tell on which side the balance lies. ... Why then should I not then at least with equal justice keep a diary wherein to enter all the mercies of God (which are goods not given, but only entrusted to me) that I may make suitable returns in the course of my life?

Dummer, who led a busy life in England as an agent of the colonial government, never abandoned his interest in the "concerns of the soul": "My life is still running on," he wrote when he was around thirty, "the years roll swiftly over my head, and will never return; yesterday will never come back; and thus Death is advancing apace towards me, and I in the meanwhile am doing nothing for God, nothing for my soul, nothing for eternity." But he was drawn by the alluring life of London and was honest enough to write about this openly: "This day I was at the House of Lords to hear a trial; and before it began I was entertained with a sight of all the great female beauties of the Court which pleased me to that degree that I thought I could have gazed on them forever." His subsequent reflections on the superficiality of beauty – "if you take the finest woman in the world and strip off the epidermis, you'll see that the horror of her aspect will fright away the beholders" – carry less conviction than his admission that he could have gazed upon their unflayed bodies forever.[36] During his later years, a historian wrote, Dummer "slipped slowly and regretfully down into the wider, sunnier world," shedding "his Puritan conscience slowly and fearfully, with many a hindward look at the wrathful God."[37]

Dummer's contemporary Samuel Sewall underwent a similar transformation. In his middle years he was enough of a hardliner to serve as an assistant magistrate in the Salem witchcraft trials. Later he mellowed out. By 1711 his practice of religion had become what it is for most people in all places and times: a mixture of moral edification and socializing:

Went and heard Mr. Bridge, and Dr. Cotton Mather pray and preach, at the said Dr's house. Mr. Bridge's text was about God's lifting up a standard, when enemy breaks in as a flood. Dr. Mather's, the whole world lies in wickedness. Had cake and butter and cheese, with good drinks, before parting.[38]

By the beginning of the eighteenth century the edge of Calvinist self-scrutiny had been dulled by a healthy interest in the things of everyday life.

The Unequalled Self: Samuel Pepys

In England the excesses of Puritanism reached their peak during the Interregnum (1649–60) and declined rapidly after the restoration of Charles II. Most people were glad to see the last of the Parliamentarians and their holier-than-thou posturing. Quakerism and Baptism fell into disfavor, and there was dancing around maypoles (which had been banned by the Puritans) when the Anglican Church was reestablished. Theaters reopened and people flocked to see plays in which the female roles were for the first time played by women. This was a thrill to young professionals like Samuel Pepys, who wrote in his diary after seeing Nell Gwyn, the celebrated actress and mistress of the king: "So great performance of a comical part was never, I believe, in the world" before Nell's presentation. When later he saw her standing outside her room "in her smock sleeves and bodice, looking upon one," he had to admit "she seemed a mighty pretty creature."[39] Clearly we are in a different world than that of Fox and Bunyan (both of whom were still alive).

Pepys was a naval administrator and man about town, who for nine years kept a record of his life and times in a marvelously detailed diary. It is an important source for historians of the period, containing first-hand accounts of many important events, such as the Great Fire of 1666. But his accounts rise above mere chronicle. Here is part of his description of the Fire:

So I down to the water-side, and there got a boat and through bridge, and there saw a lamentable fire. … Everybody endeavouring to remove their goods, and flinging into the river or bringing them into lighters [barges] that layoff; poor people staying in their houses as long as till the very fire touched them, and then running into boats, or clambering from one pair of stairs by the water-side to another. And among other things, the poor pigeons, I perceive, were loth to leave their houses, but hovered about the windows and balconies till they were, some of them burned, their wings, and fell down.[40]

To notice and record the fate of the pigeons in the midst of the general destruction is proof that Pepys had the eye of a born writer. By trusting in the value of his personal impressions, he turned reportage into art.

The same justness of observation comes out in Pepys's descriptions of his day-to-day life, and it is these that make the diary a significant document in the history of the self. He examined his actions, thoughts, and emotions with as much diligence as his Puritan contemporaries but without their anguish at not measuring up to an unattainable ideal. If he acted badly, he set it down frankly without undue moralizing. This sincerity made the diary "a miracle among human books," in the opinion of Robert Louis Stevenson. "Whether he did ill or well, he was still his own unequalled self; still that entrancing *ego* of whom alone he cared to write."[41]

Stevenson cited a passage of the diary in which Pepys wrote of an argument he had with his wife Elisabeth. It happened in the morning of January 9, 1663. After telling him how much she lacked company during the day, Elisabeth took out a letter she had written to him earlier that he had refused to read:

> She now read it, and it was so piquant, and wrote in English, and most of it true, of the retiredness of her life, and how unpleasant it was; that being wrote in English, and so in danger of being met with and read by others, I was vexed at it, and desired her and then commanded her to tear it. When she desired to be excused it, I forced it from her, and tore it, and withal took her other bundle of papers from her, and leapt out of the bed and in my shirt clapped them into the pocket of my breeches, that she might not get them from me, and having got on my stockings and breeches and gown, I pulled them out one by one and tore them all before her face, though it went against my heart to do it, she crying and desiring me not to do it, but such was my passion and trouble to see the letters of my love to her, and my Will wherein I had given her all I have in the world, when I went to sea with my Lord Sandwich, to be joined with a paper of so much disgrace to me and dishonour, if it should have been found by any body. Having torn them all, saving a bond of my uncle Robert's, which she hath long had in her hands, and our marriage license, and the first letter that ever I sent her when I was her servant [i.e., suitor], I took up the pieces and carried them into my chamber, and there, after many disputes with myself whether I should burn them or no, and having picked up, the pieces of the paper she read to-day, and of my Will which I tore, I burnt all the rest, and so went out to my office troubled in mind.[42]

This may be the most honest account of an outburst of anger ever written. Pepys began by admitting that he became vexed knowing well that his wife was in the right. He did not think of her feelings but only the shame he would have felt if her letter got into the wrong hands. He described his destruction of the papers as it happened, not omitting the ridiculous detail of his leaping out of bed in his nightshirt and trying to get dressed while appropriating the papers and carrying on the argument. He made no attempt to justify his actions or to draw a moral lesson from them. Most amazingly, he recorded the whole shameful scene for himself and perhaps for others to read even thought the spark that set it off was his fear of being shamed.

In 1663 Pepys was well on the way to becoming one of the most admired and powerful civil servants of his day. He recorded the outward signs of his rise with the undisguised pride of a child. After returning from a Sunday visit to Lord Montague, he wrote:

> I consider the manner of my going hither, with a coach and four horses and servants and a woman with us, and coming hither being so much made of, and used with that state, and then going to Windsor and being shewn all that we were there, and had wherewith to give every body something for their pains, and then going home, and all in fine weather and no fears nor cares upon me, I do think myself obliged to think myself happy.[43]

At the same time, he felt compelled to record the small and often inglorious details of his existence. "The greatness of his life was open, yet he longed to communicate its smallness also," Stevenson wrote of Pepys. "Being in many ways a very ordinary person, he has yet placed himself before the public eye with such a fulness and such an intimacy of detail as might be envied by a genius like Montaigne."[44]

Pepys had no explicit or even implicit theory of the self. The ego he was entranced with was simply Samuel Pepys: Surveyor-General of the Victualling, fellow of the Royal Society, husband, adulterer, bon vivant, friend – an amalgam of his social identities. He never plumbed the depths of his soul as Montaigne and Augustine did. Nor did he engage in the tormented self-examination of a Luther or Ward. When he wrote about his mind, it was not to speculate about its workings but simply to record its status, and he rated its status in respect to his outward life:

> My mind is now in a wonderful condition of quiet and content, more than ever in all my life, since my minding the business of my office, which I have done most constantly; and I find it to be the very effect of my late oaths against wine and plays, which, if God please, I will keep

constant in, for now my business is a delight to me, and brings me great credit, and my purse increases too.[45]

The mental contentment, noted in passing, was the result of his efficiency at work and the satisfaction it brought him in itself and through appreciation by others. It had nothing to do with Stoic equanimity or Christian discipline. His Protestantism was entirely conventional and he never anguished over his backslidings, which he recorded with as much fidelity as incidents at the office. Once he and Elisabeth had a falling out when she found him *in flagrante* with a maidservant. He did all that he could to pacify his wife, making copious pledges and declarations of love; but when she told him later that she had dismissed the maid, he noted that the news "troubled me, and the truth is, I have a good mind to have the maidenhead of this girl," which he "should not doubt to have" if given the chance.[46] Such inconsistency is common enough among human beings. What is remarkable about Pepys is that he recorded it so candidly, without trying to excuse or justify his failings.

The Truth of Matter of Fact: Robert Hooke

It is interesting to compare Pepys's quasi-scientific diary with the notebooks of the scientist Robert Hooke, who was his contemporary. The scientific method, developed by Francis Bacon and others in the early part of the century, put a premium on dispassionate observation and logical classification in order to discover similarities and differences that would permit a reasoned judgment of cause and effect. With this in mind, natural philosophers (as scientists were then called) made use of what we would now call laboratory notebooks to record their observations. Hooke kept such notebooks for years; but unlike most other scientists of his time and ours he included himself among the phenomena he observed. He began his notebook of 1672 to record meteorological data in order to help him make comparisons "requisite for the raising axioms, whereby the cause or laws of weather may be found out." This was pure Baconian science. But he also made notations about his activities, expenses, health, and so forth:

10 Mar.   [Sign of mercury] fell from 170 to 185. Most day clear but cold. Sometimes windy from the South. [Drawing of moon] apoginum. It grew cloudy about 4, [Mercury] falling still.   I told Cox how to make reflex glasses by silver and hinted to him working them by pointing. Howett brought me £10 from Br. John Hooke. News of 3 empty Dutch ships taken by the Monmouth.

He recorded his observations about the weather and himself with the same objectivity. A quarter-century later, he decided to write an autobiography, in which he would include "as many remarkable passages, as I can now remember or collect out of such memorials [i.e., memoranda] as I have kept in writing, or are in the registers of the Royal Society; together with all my inventions, experiments, discoveries, discourses, etc. which I have made, the time when, the manner how, and means by which, with the success and effect of them." So much one would expect from a brilliant, ambitious, and often cantankerous scientist. But he also planned to include information on "the state of my health, my employments and studies, my good and bad fortune, my friends and enemies, etc." All of it – scientific discoveries, the state of his health, his disputes with other scientists – would be "the truth of matter of fact, so far as I can be informed by my memorials or my own memory, which rule I resolve not to transgress."[47]

It is unfortunate that Hooke did not get very far with his projected autobiography. It would have been an invaluable source for historians of the period, helping them situate Hooke's contributions to physics, chemistry, technology, architecture, and other fields. But it would also have been an example of the application of the scientific method to the study of the human being. Hooke's objective in all his work was "to examine, and to record, the things themselves as they appear."[48] This might be taken as the watchword of the philosophers, scientists, and mathematicians who laid the groundwork for the modern study of the human being before and during Hooke's lifetime. Some of the most important of these thinkers are discussed in the next chapter.

Reasons of the Mind and Heart

I am, then, in the strict sense only a thing that thinks; that is, I am a mind, or intelligence, or intellect, or reason.

– René Descartes

The heart has its reasons which reason itself does not know.

– Blaise Pascal

The Reformation helped make the self an autonomous subject and an object of individual study, but this was not its intention. The self of Luther and Calvin was one that sought its own effacement. Luther wrote that the man who "totally despairs in himself, chooses nothing for himself" was "nearest unto grace." Calvin wrote: "No man can arrive at the true knowledge of himself, without having first contemplated the divine character, and then descended to the consideration of his own." He would then find that his nature was made up of "unrighteousness, turpitude, folly, and impurity."[1] This self-abhorrence and drive for extinction may have been liberating for a handful of men and women, but when it was imposed on whole communities the results were disastrous. Some Puritans, for example Susanna Anthony and Michael Wigglesworth, seem to have been borderline psychotics, while the persecutions and mob violence in Calvinist Geneva and New England were as bad as anything in Catholic France and Spain. Still, the habits of self-scrutiny and self-reliance that were encouraged by the doctrines of "faith alone," "scripture alone," and "the priesthood of all believers" helped bring about a fundamental change in the way European people looked on themselves.

The leaders of the Reformation and Counter-Reformation had no love for the intellectual and artistic innovations of the Renaissance but they were unable to stifle the new ways of thought completely. By the middle of the seventeenth century, many men and a few women were contributing to the experimental study of the world that came to be called science. The Church watched over these developments nervously and, when necessary, stepped in to suppress them. The Italian Galileo Galilei made fundamental discoveries in astronomy, physics, and other fields; but when he endorsed Copernicus's heliocentric theory in a book of 1632, he was convicted of heresy. Mindful of the fate of his countryman Bruno a generation earlier, he recanted and passed the remainder of his life under house arrest.

I Am Thinking, Therefore I Exist: René Descartes

When news of Galileo's trial reached the Netherlands, the French mathematician and philosopher René Descartes paid it special attention. For the last four years he had been working on a treatise called *The World*, a sort of early modern "theory of everything." Heliocentrism was vital to his calculations. "If it is false," he wrote to a friend, "so are all the foundations of my Philosophy, since they clearly demonstrate this motion [of the earth around the sun]." It was impossible for him to omit this part of his theory "without rendering the remainder completely defective." He therefore preferred to suppress *The World* "rather than publish it in a mutilated version."[2] The treatise did not see the light until a decade after his death.

Descartes was born in a small town in central France in 1596. Sent to a Catholic school, he excelled in mathematics, but also "pored over all the unusual and strange books that I could lay my hands on." At length he became dissatisfied. The systems of the ancients seemed to him "palaces which were built on mere sand." The whole of philosophy, after centuries of theorizing, was mired in uncertainty: "there was no point in it which was not still under dispute, and consequently doubtful." Abandoning his studies, he traveled around Europe and met different sorts of people, but he "found nothing in them to reassure me, and I noticed as much diversity among them as I had earlier done among the opinions of philosophers." The best he could say about his reading and travels was that they helped him to free himself "little by little from many errors which can dim our natural light and even make us less able to listen to reason." At length, after studying countless books in libraries as well as "the book of the world," he resolved "to study my own self, and to use all the powers of my mind to choose the path I should follow."[3]

There are many similarities between Descartes's intellectual journey and that of Montaigne a half-century earlier. Both absorbed all the philosophy and science available to them but realized that these did not lead to certainty. Neither accepted the pat answers of theology. As a result, both were left in doubt about the nature of the world. Each decided that the only way out of the impasse was to make a study of himself. But at this point, their paths diverged sharply. Montaigne gave his attention to the very contingent reality of one particular person: Michel de Montaigne. Descartes took himself as an example of the logical category "human being" and tried to make this the basis of a universal theory. Montaigne's methods were those of the psychologist and anthropologist, Descartes's those of the mathematician and logician.

Montaigne's *Essays* was one of the "unusual and strange books" that Descartes read, and it troubled him greatly. For him and other seventeenth-century readers, the core of Montaigne's work was its skepticism. The essayist showed that neither the evidence of the senses nor the workings of reason could be relied on and that no traditional authority had all the answers. The only thing philosophers agreed on was that "the sovereign good consists in tranquility of soul and body." The best way to attain this was to admit that the mind was incapable of absolute truth.[4] Such a conclusion was possible for Montaigne the humanist but not for Descartes the mathematician. He wanted utter certitude, and he thought that he could find it.

In 1618 Descartes enlisted as a gentleman soldier in the army of a Dutch prince. When he could, he studied mathematics and thought about how he could apply it to his search. In the spring of 1619 he wrote to a friend that he planned to construct "a completely new science by which all questions that can be raised by any sort of quantity, either continuous or discrete, may be solved by a general method."[5] That winter his unit was billeted in the German town of Ulm. He didn't have very much to do and passed his days in reflection. On November 10, comfortably ensconced in a well-heated room, he had an intellectual revelation. All the answers he was searching for appeared to him in a flash of light. He went to bed still keyed up with the thrill of his discovery. While he slept, he had three dreams. In the first he was assailed by phantoms and buffeted by winds. Disturbed, he woke but went to sleep again. In the second he heard a clap of thunder. This woke him, and he saw sparks flying around the room. In the third he came upon a dictionary and then an anthology of Latin poetry. He opened it and read the line: "What path shall I take in life?" A stranger appeared and cited another verse. Descartes wanted to show him the poem he had found, but at this point the book and stranger disappeared, and he woke up.

Descartes believed that his dreams were of supernatural origin. He understood the first two to be warnings about his past, the third a prophecy about his future. It seemed to him that he had been specially chosen to bring about the unification of all the sciences by means of reason, but he did not broadcast his intentions to the world. "Like actors who go masked lest some inappropriate emotion appear on their faces," he wrote in a private notebook, "so will I, as I enter into the public world (*mundi theatrum*) where I was previously a spectator, go covered up."[6]

Descartes continued his travels and his studies. After a decade on the move, he settled down in the Dutch Republic and began working on *The World*. Setting it aside after Galileo's trial, he looked around for another way of presenting his findings. In 1637 he published three scientific treatises, on optics, meteorology, and geometry, prefacing them with a methodological statement called *Discourse on the Method of Rightly Conducting the Reason and Seeking Truth in the Sciences*. Now regarded as one of the indispensable works of Western philosophy, the *Discourse* is also a primary text in the first-person approach to the study of the self.

In the first part of the *Discourse*, cited above on page 66, Descartes sketched his intellectual formation. In part two he explained how he hit upon the elements of his method. Looking back over everything he had learned, he selected three disciplines – geometrical analysis, algebra, and logic – that "seemed as if they ought to contribute something to my goal." He was certainly no slouch in the first two disciplines: the coordinate system named after him is still used in laboratories and classrooms. But he realized that both geometry and algebra were restricted in application, dealing only "with very abstract matters which seem utterly useless" in larger inquiries. As for logic, it was only useful for explaining "to someone else that which one already knows," and besides included so many different precepts that it was hard to figure out which were useful and which were not. Still, he thought that these three disciplines could form the basis of a new method that would keep their advantages while getting rid of their defects. First, however, he had to cut down the number of precepts. It seemed to him that four were enough: "The first was to never accept anything as true which I could not accept as obviously true"; the second, "to divide each of the problems I was examining in as many parts as I could" to facilitate its solution. The third was "to develop my thoughts in order," starting from the simplest and moving to the most complex. Finally, he had to properly report his findings: "to make my enumerations so complete and my reviews so general that I could be assured that I had not omitted anything."[7] These precepts would be the basis of his method.

In obedience to the first precept, Descartes had to "reject as absolutely false anything about which I could imagine the slightest doubt, so that I could see if there would not remain after all that something in my belief which could be called absolutely certain." He knew he could not trust sense data, since "our senses sometimes trick us." He knew that it was possible for anyone, even himself, to make mistakes in geometry and logic, so he decided to reject "as false all the reasonings that I had considered as valid demonstrations." He realized that thought in general was unreliable and so was obliged to consider all he had ever thought as "no more true than the illusions in my [ordinary] dreams." Then he paused:

> I immediately realized that, though I wanted to think that everything was false, it was necessary that the "me" who was doing the thinking was something; and noticing that this truth – I think, therefore I am – was so certain and sure that all the wildest suppositions of skeptics could not shake it, I judged that I could unhesitatingly accept it as the first principle of the philosophy for which I was seeking.

It was possible for him to imagine that he had no body or even that there was no world, but he could never imagine he did not exist. The very fact that he doubted the existence of other things proved that he, the doubter, did exist. Further, he "realized that I was a substance whose essence, or nature, is nothing but thought." It followed that "this self, that is to say, the soul, through which I am what I am, is entirely separate from the body ... so that even if I did not have a body, my soul would continue to be all that it is."[8]

Descartes's pronouncement "I think, therefore I am" – a better translation might be "I am thinking, therefore I exist" – is one of the most celebrated statements in philosophy. It is so inseparably connected with his name that it is easy to overlook the fact that it was not original to him. Aristotle and Augustine and Aquinas all made similar statements. What is important about Descartes's use of the idea is that he made it the first principle of his philosophy, the starting point for his attempt to bring mathematical rigor to the study of the human being, the world, and God. The skepticism of Sextus Empiricus and Montaigne had put this enterprise in danger. To get off to a good start, he had to latch on to something that could never be doubted. He found this in his own existence and from the certainty of his existence he proceeded to demonstrate the existence of God and the world. This represented a tremendous shift from the approaches of classical and medieval philosophy. For the first time in the history of Western thought, a subjective fact – the existence of the enquirer – became the foundation of all forms of knowledge, including even the knowledge of God.

When someone pointed out to Descartes that his argument had been anticipated by Augustine, he concurred but noted that his predecessor had used it as part of a theological demonstration, while he used it "to show that this I which is thinking is an immaterial substance with no bodily element."[9] The absolute distinction between the thinker and the material world was fundamental to Descartes's philosophy, and it has had a huge impact on the way modern humans think and act. Descartes developed his ideas on this subject in *Meditations on First Philosophy*, a book written in Latin (since it was meant for the academic world) and published in 1641. In the sixth meditation, Descartes wrote that there are two completely different sorts of substance: *res extensa* or extended substance, which is body, and *res cogitans* or thinking substance, which is soul or mind. (He was the first person to use mind – *mens* in Latin – as the equivalent of *anima* or soul.) The two substances are governed by completely different laws: body is subject to physical necessity, mind is endowed with free will. Matter in general and bodies in particular are mechanical; there is nothing spiritual about them. (Animals, who do not possess souls, are just clocklike machines, with no subjective life.) All this is very neat and clear, but it leaves an enormous problem: How do mind and matter interact? How does the pain of a pinprick register in the mind? How does a mental command to reach for something cause our arm to move? According to Descartes, such interactions are regulated by the pineal gland, which is located in the middle of the head. Almost no one found this satisfactory, and the problem of the relationship between mind and matter remained. More than three hundred seventy years later, philosophers and scientists are still debating the issue, with no resolution in sight.

Descartes's stated purpose in writing the *Meditations* was to prove that God exists and that the soul is immortal. He never got around to the soul's immortality but he devoted two chapters to proofs of God's existence. One of them runs something like this: I have an idea of God, the perfect being. If I can form an idea of perfection, there must be something that is the source of that perfection. The idea of God is something so perfect that I could never have arrived at it myself. It follows that only the existence of God can account for the perfection present in my idea of God. Few found this argument convincing but many were impressed by Descartes's methods, and in time some discovered that it was possible to make use of the methods without bothering themselves about God. By trying to develop a scientific approach to the question of God's existence, Descartes inadvertently gave scientists the tools they needed to do without Him. In addition, by insisting on the distinctness of mind (or soul) and matter (or body), he made it possible for scientists to investigate matter without reference to the soul. Eventually this made it possible for people to doubt the soul's very existence.

The Self is Hateful: Blaise Pascal

In 1639 Descartes was asked his opinion of an essay on conic sections by a sixteen-year-old prodigy named Blaise Pascal. Descartes said he was unimpressed: it was just an extension of the work of his colleague Gérard

Desargues. Pascal acknowledged his debt to Desargues, but his work was in fact quite original. It is still known to mathematicians as Pascal's theorem. Eight years later, when the young man's eminence was unquestioned, he and the author of *Meditations on First Philosophy* got together to discuss the theory of the vacuum. Descartes asked to be kept informed of Pascal's experimental results.

As a scientist and mathematician, Pascal was phenomenally prolific. He developed the first mechanical calculator, an ancestor of the modern computer. He did pioneering practical and theoretical work on atmospheric pressure, made major contributions to geometry, and helped lay the foundations of the calculus of probabilities. In addition, he wrote on scientific method and the philosophy of mathematics. But he is also remembered as a mystic, a Catholic apologist, and a theorist of the self.

In 1646 Pascal's family came in touch with members of a movement within Catholicism known as Jansenism. Similar to Calvinism in the stress it laid on grace and predestination and in its ascetic morality, Jansenism was attacked as heretical by Jesuits (members of Ignatius of Loyola's Society of Jesus) and other hardliners. Despite or perhaps because of this, Pascal found himself attracted to the movement. Abandoning his research, he began to write on religious subjects, but after a few years was drawn back to science. Then during the night of November 23–24, 1654, he had a mystical experience. He wrote about it immediately afterwards:

> From about half past ten at night until about half past midnight,
> FIRE.
> GOD of Abraham, GOD of Isaac, GOD of Jacob
> not of the philosophers and of the learned.
> Certitude. Certitude. Feeling. Joy. Peace.
> GOD of Jesus Christ.
> My God and your God.
> Your GOD will be my God.
> Forgetfulness of the world and of everything, except GOD.

What follows marks a lapse from mystical consciousness to Christian apologetics: "He is only found by the ways taught in the Gospel." This is interrupted by "Joy, joy, joy, tears of joy," then a realization that the epiphany was over: "I have departed from him"; "My God, will you leave me?"; "Let me not be separated from him forever." There is a final return to religious discourse – "He is only kept securely by the ways taught in the Gospel" – and then a closing prayer: "May I not forget your words. Amen."[10]

The intensity of the experience must have been shattering but Pascal kept it to himself. He did however put two copies of his account into a sort of amulet he had sewn into his coat. Discovered after his death, the text eventually was published under the name *Pascal's Memorial*. It is a precious document in the history of first-person writing, one of the few accounts of a mystical experience that was set down in the heat of the moment and not retrospectively. While the experience lasted, Pascal was absorbed in the light of the Divine. The certitude he found in the warmth of that light was a far cry from the intellectual certainty that Descartes and other philosophers arrived at through the use of reason. Their God, the God "of the philosophers and the learned," was a pale shadow of the "Fire" that Pascal lived in for a privileged moment. But as he fell back to the ordinary consciousness, he himself slipped into the theology of "the ways taught in the Gospel." In the years that followed, he developed his argumentative powers and placed them at the service of the Church.

From January 1655 Pascal began to spend much of his time at the convent of Port-Royal of Paris, which was the center of Jansenist activity in France. Later the same year he began working on the polemical writings known as *Lettres provinciales* (Provincial Letters), in which he attacked the beliefs and methods of the Jesuits and supported the Jansenist position on "efficacious grace." To Jansenists, their position was a return to that of Augustine; to the Jesuits and others, it came close to Calvinism. The theological issues, gripping to many in seventeenth-century France, are of little interest today. What is of lasting importance in the *Lettres* is their style, a combination of eloquence, wit, irony, and humor that helped set the tone of modern French prose. An example is his observation on brevity in expression: "I have made this letter longer than usual, only because I have not had the time to make it shorter."[11]

At the time he was writing the *Lettres provinciales*, Pascal was planning an "Apology of the Christian Religion," which he left incomplete at the time of his death. The fragments that survive were published seven years later as *Pensées* (Thoughts). A mixture of psychological observation and theological disputation, the *Pensées* insist that every man and woman has to make an existential choice, which Pascal saw in terms of belief or non-belief in God:

> Let us therefore examine this point, and say: God is, or is not. But towards which side will we lean? Reason cannot decide anything. There is an infinite chaos separating us. At the far end of the infinite distance a game is being played and the coin will come down heads or tails. How will you wager?[12]

Pascal the mathematician, using the terms of statistical analysis, tried to show that it is in our interest to bet on God. If God exists, we have everything to gain; if God does not exist, there is nothing to lose. "Pascal's Wager," as it is called, has been discussed for centuries and has not convinced many who were not already sure of God's existence. More important than the argument were the author's assumptions: first, reason cannot decide the matter; second, people have to make a choice, they cannot have it both ways.

Pascal laid stress on the necessity of choice because for the first time since the Hellenistic period it had become possible for a thinking person to doubt the existence of God. The spirit of skepticism was abroad, conspicuously in the *Essays* of Montaigne. Pascal was dismissive of his predecessor but he took him seriously enough to allude to the *Essays* dozens of times in the *Pensées*, admitting "It is not in Montaigne but in myself that I find everything I see there." He was especially troubled by Montaigne's attitude toward the self. "What a foolish project he had to paint his own portrait!" he complained. To Montaigne, the self was endlessly fascinating. To Pascal, "The self is hateful."[13]

Writing as a philosopher, Pascal agreed with Descartes that "my self consists in my thinking." But he did not equate this self with the immortal soul: "I who think would never have existed if my mother had been killed before my soul had been created. So I am not a necessary being." In another passage he cast doubt on the very idea of the self. After showing that it consisted neither of physical nor mental qualities, he asked: "Where is the self, then, if it is neither in the body nor in the soul? And how can you love the body or the soul except for its qualities, which do not make up the self, since they are perishable?"[14] Using Montaignian doubt to arrive at faith, Pascal sometimes found himself stranded between the two. Using the mind-body dualism of Descartes to clarify the nature of the self, he sometimes lost track of it altogether.

Self as a Forensic Term: John Locke

Descartes died in 1650, Pascal in 1662. By that time all educated Europe was trying to come to terms with Descartes's rationalism and his soul–body dualism. During the second half of the seventeenth century, Baruch de Spinoza and Gottfried Leibniz pushed rationalism in new directions. Spinoza insisted there is only one entity, God or Nature, and thus no individual beings. The human soul is a modification of infinite thought, the human body a modification of infinite extension, but neither has independent existence. Leibniz also rejected dualism but did so by saying that the world consists of an infinity of immaterial entities in harmony with one another and reflecting the same universe. The philosophies of these men became influential on the Continent but less so in Britain, where thinkers since Bacon had been reluctant to build systems filled with immaterial entities. To Thomas Hobbes reality consisted of bodies and motion. The identity of a thing depended on the continuance of motion: "as long as that motion remains, it will be the same *individual* thing," just as a human being "will be always the same, whose actions and thoughts all proceed from the same beginning of motion." An act of generation produces a single human just as a fountain produces a single river "whether the same water, or other water, or something else than water" flows between its banks.[15] What mattered was the motion, not the stuff that was moving. In this way, Hobbes freed himself from the substance-based theories of self that had prevailed since antiquity. A generation later, his countryman John Locke went further with this idea.

It is said that Hobbes had a custom-made staff with compartments for pen and inkhorn. When an idea came to him while he was out walking, he would stop and jot it down in a notebook. Locke also was inventive when it came to information technology. He developed a "new method of making commonplace-books" – a sort of seventeenth-century spreadsheet – to help him organize his ideas.[16] When he traveled, he carried a more conventional pocket diary. The entries he made during a trip to France are filled with quantitative data, for example:

> Here [at Nîmes] we saw an amphitheater of very large stones, an admirable structure, if we consider that it hath stood ever since the Romans' time and built without any mortar. At the entrance, which is under an arch, the wall is 17 of my paces thick. Ascending up a pair of stairs we came to a walk round in which there is, towards the outside from whence the light comes, 60 arches in the whole circumference, the space of each arch being 11 of my paces, so that the whole circumference is 660 of my steps in a circle.[17]

He brought the same scientific spirit to his study of the human mind.

Locke was born to Puritan parents in Somerset in 1632. At Oxford he tired quickly of the Latin classics but read Descartes and other modern philosophers with enthusiasm. He eventually earned a degree in medicine and entered the service of the Earl of Shaftsbury. It was at Shaftsbury's London residence in 1671 that Locke conceived the idea underlying his *Essay Concerning Human Understanding*. He and some friends were talking philosophy when they "found themselves quickly at a stand, by the diffi-culties that rose on every side." After struggling unsuccessfully to clear up their doubts, it occurred to Locke "that we took a wrong course; and that before we set ourselves upon inquiries of that nature, it was necessary to examine our own abilities, and see what objects our understandings were, or were not, fitted to deal with."[18] In other words, to understand any topic of mental inquiry, one had first to understand the mind.

Locke did not aspire to be a system-builder; he would content himself "to be employed as an under-labourer in clearing the ground a little, and removing some of the rubbish that lies in the way to knowledge." He went about this work as a solitary individual relying on the results of his own self-study. "I have not made it my business either to quit or follow any authority," he insisted, "Truth has been my only aim; and wherever that has appeared to lead, my thoughts have impartially followed."[19] He pursued this work over the next two decades, finally publishing his results in 1690.

In the Book One of the *Essay* Locke dealt with what he thought was the biggest bit of "rubbish" in the way of a right understanding of the mind, the theory of innate ideas. Going back as far as Plato and endorsed by Descartes, this theory holds that there are certain ideas such as the truths of geometry, of ethics and of God that are inborn in the human mind and the basis of all knowledge. Descartes wrote that he was "certain that I can have no knowledge of what is outside me except by means of the ideas I have within me."[20] Locke held the opposite view: sensory knowledge was the basis of all knowledge. He denied that there were any innate ideas, basing his denial in part on the observation that there are no universally accepted beliefs on any subject and no universally accepted principles of conduct.

In Book Two he turned to the question of where our ideas come from if they are not inborn:

> Let us then suppose the mind to be, as we say, white paper, void of all characters, without any ideas: – How comes it to be furnished? Whence comes it by that vast store which the busy and boundless fancy of man has painted on it with an almost endless variety? Whence has it all the materials of reason and knowledge? To this I answer, in one word, from *experience*.[21]

The mind is a blank sheet – others used the phrase *tabula rasa* or blank slate – that sensory experience writes on. Once recorded, sense impressions can be acted on by mental reflection; this produces the multitude of ideas that we possess. It followed that truth is not a fixed quantity given by God but something to be found by each individual by means of personal effort. This had social consequences. Individuals were not obliged to accept the status quo; they could improve their lot. For this a proper education, in which the child was exposed to the most helpful impressions, was essential. On these and related assumptions Locke built his political philosophy, which became the basis of modern liberalism.

The nature of the human being was an important part of Locke's theory, but he did not go into this in detail until he added a chapter called "Of Identity and Diversity" to the second edition of the *Essay*. This contains some of the most influential thoughts about consciousness, the self, and personal identity ever written. (Locke was the first English writer to use these terms systematically in philosophical discourse.) "Consciousness," he wrote, "unites substances, material or spiritual, with the same personality [i.e., personhood]." Whether or not consciousness was associated with "one individual immaterial substance" was debatable, but everyone had to admit "that there is something that is himself, that he is concerned for, and would have happy; that this self has existed in a continued duration more than one instant, and therefore it is possible may exist, as it has done, months and years to come."[22] This self is something that persists over time and its persistence is the result of continued consciousness and not enduring substance.

Another name for this self, Locke wrote, was "person." He made a distinction between man, the human being, and person, "a thinking intelligent being, that has reason and reflection, and can consider itself as itself, the same thinking thing, in different times and places." A person is identical in itself as well as over time. In establishing what a person was, Locke appealed to moral necessity. Self or person, he wrote, "is a forensic term [that is, a term having to do with law], appropriating actions and their merit; and so belongs only to intelligent agents, capable of a law, and happiness, and misery." Consciousness is what makes the self "concerned and accountable" for past actions.[23]

Locke's theory of the self is as remarkable for what it did not say as for what it said. He nowhere affirmed the existence of an immaterial substance or soul. He wrote rather: "Self depends on consciousness, not on substance. Self is that conscious thinking thing, – whatever substance made up of, (whether spiritual or material, simple or compounded, it matters not) – which is sensible or conscious of pleasure and pain, capable of happiness or misery, and so is concerned for itself, as far as that consciousness extends." The question of the substantial soul, over which people had agonized for millennia, simply didn't matter. What was important was the persistence of consciousness, because consciousness provided a mechanism for moral responsibility. When the Day of Judgment came, the Lord's sentence would "be justified by the consciousness all persons shall have" without regard to the substance, if any, that consciousness was linked to.[24]

Locke was a pious Christian, but when it came to writing philosophy he was almost as unconcerned about the God of Christianity as about the nature of the soul. "Our reason," he wrote, "leads us to the knowledge of this certain and evident truth, – That there is an eternal, most powerful, and most knowing Being; which whether any one will please to call God, it matters not."[25] This was not the sort of thing to give comfort to pious readers who hoped to find evidences of God in Locke's *Essay*. Some complained that his arguments opened the door to atheism. He certainly intended no such thing, but it is true that it is just a step from his God that doesn't matter to eighteenth-century Deism, which reduced God to a mere creative principle that takes no interest in the created universe.

The Justice and Reasonableness of God: Jonathan Edwards

The unintended erosion of religious conviction produced by the works of Descartes, Locke, and others had little effect on the majority of Christian believers. In Britain and its colonies, the Church – Anglican, Puritan or Independent – still overshadowed the lives of villages and towns, though the strenuous religiosity of the early part of the century gave way to a more relaxed routine, making it possible for men like Dummer and Sewall to abandon the Church for secular pursuits. The Puritan spirit remained strong, however, as can be seen in the diary of Joseph Moody, a New Englander born in 1700. Anxious about salvation and overcome by the sense of sin, he brooded over his lack of a true conversion experience and the insistence of his sexual urges. "This morning I got up pretty late," he wrote in 1722. "I defiled myself, though wide awake. Where will my unbridled lust lead me? I have promised myself now for a year and a half that I would seek after God, but now I am perhaps farther away from him than ever before."[26] Jonathan Edwards, born three years after Moody, was haunted like him by Calvinist anxieties but was able to find comfort in a personal relation with God that was buttressed by philosophical reasoning.

The son and grandson of Puritan ministers, Edwards entered the Collegiate School (later Yale College) when he was just thirteen. Along with theology, he studied philosophy and the natural sciences, undergoing the influence of Locke's *Essay* and the works of Isaac Newton and other scientists. While at college Edwards had a decisive experience that he wrote about later in a posthumously published text known as the *Personal Narrative*. The work begins as a typical conversion story on the pattern of Augustine and Bunyan. A period of childhood innocence was followed by a fall: "I entirely lost all those affections and delights ... and returned like a dog to his vomit, and went on in ways of sin." A time of intense struggle ensued, much of it centered on the question of the sovereignty of God. From his childhood, he had been troubled by the Calvinistic doctrine that God chose "whom he would" for eternal life, rejecting the rest and "leaving them eternally to perish, and be everlastingly tormented in hell." Echoing the sentiments of virtually all non-Calvinists, he admitted that this "used to appear like a horrible doctrine to me." His conversion consisted of "a wonderful alteration in my mind" by which he became convinced that the doctrine was true. He was unable either then or for a long time afterwards to explain how the change came about but could only say that "my reason apprehended the justice and reasonableness" of the belief.[27]

This conviction deepened into another: he came to feel that far from being "horrible," the doctrine of unconditional election and damnation was "an exceeding pleasant, bright and sweet doctrine." This "*delightful* conviction" (as he called it) seems to have been rooted not in ethical reasoning but in experiences he had after his conversion. Walking alone in the Connecticut countryside, he "found, from time to time, an inward sweetness, that used, as it were, to carry me away in my contemplations." This gave him

> a calm, sweet abstraction of soul from all the concerns of this world; and a kind of vision, or fixed ideas and imaginations, of being alone in the mountains, or some solitary wilderness, far from all mankind, sweetly conversing with Christ, and wrapt and swallowed up in God. The sense I had of divine things, would often of a sudden as it were, kindle up a sweet burning in my heart; an ardor of my soul, that I know not how to express.[28]

A hundred years later, similar mystical experiences would turn another New England thinker, Ralph Waldo Emerson, away from institutional religion. This was not an option for Edwards. Filled with "a burning desire to be in everything a complete Christian," he became a minister and is better known today for the hair-raising sermon "Sinners in the Hands of an Angry God" than for the inward sweetness he felt when swallowed up in God.[29]

In 1722 and 1723 the young Edwards kept a diary. He began with a set of "Resolutions" that are very much in the spirit of earlier Puritan covenants. The first begins: "Resolved, that I will do whatsoever I think to be most to God's glory, and my own good, profit and pleasure." Five months later, after reaching Resolution 35, he began to make notes on his progress. Asking himself why he questioned God's favor, he provided five answers, including, "I do not feel the Christian graces sensibly enough, particularly faith. I fear they are only such hypocritical outside affections, which wicked men may feel, as well as others. They do not seem to be sufficiently inward, full, sincere, entire and hearty." The same self-questioning and self-observation continued over the next eight months. He tried hard to keep the resolutions,

"But alas! how soon do I decay. O how weak, how infirm, how unable to do anything of myself." A few days later he found himself "overwhelmed with melancholy." Three days more and he fell "exceedingly low in the weekly account." Familiar with the sort of commonplace books that had been popularized by Locke and others, he decided "to make an alphabet [alphabetical compilation] of these resolutions and remarks, that I may be able to educe them on proper occasions, suitable to the condition I am in, and the duty I am engaged in."[30] The sincerity of his effort is obvious but the strain of self-scrutiny was difficult to maintain, and he abandoned the diary in September 1723, fourteen months after his first resolutions.

Edwards was as hard on others as he was on himself. As a minister he preached the doctrine of God's sovereignty and the emptiness of the human being in uncompromising terms. "Man should not glory in himself, but alone in God," he told his parishioners. "So much as the dependence of the creature is on God, so much the greater does the creature's emptiness in himself appear to be: and so much the greater the creature's emptiness, so much the greater must the fullness of the being be who supplies him." There was no place at all for self-affirmation. The human being "should be emptied of himself, that he should be sensible that he is 'wretched, and miserable, and poor, and blind, and naked.'" Only in self-abasement could men and women find salvation.[31]

From his pulpit in Northampton, Massachusetts, Edwards preached sermons that so upset the people of the town that much ordinary business was suspended. Hundreds joined his church; hundreds of others throughout New England were caught up in a general enthusiasm. This was the start of America's First Great Awakening but the results were not all happy. Some of those who listened to revivalist sermons suffered fits of hysteria. Others, convinced of their inevitable damnation, committed suicide. By 1740 the movement cooled down considerably. It was around this time that Edwards wrote the *Personal Narrative*, in which he looked back on his conversion and the years that followed. This autobiographical exercise helped him discover and clarify "his sense of personal identity," wrote religious scholar David L. Weddle. "In the process of discovering God," he "found himself."[32]

Edwards ended his narrative on a humble note: "I have vastly a greater sense, of my universal, exceeding dependence on God's grace and strength, and mere good pleasure, of late, than I used formerly to have; and have experienced more of an abhorrence of my own righteousness." At the same time he had "constant sense of the absolute sovereignty of God, and a delight in that sovereignty."[33] Anxious to share the joy of his conviction with his congregation, he attempted to rekindle the embers of revival. Finding his listeners unresponsive, he resorted to dramatic imagery: "The God that holds you over the pit of hell, much as one holds a spider, or some loathsome insect, over the fire, abhors you, and is dreadfully provoked," he cried in his "Angry God" sermon of 1741. "O sinner! Consider the fearful danger you are in."[34] The sense of God's sovereignty that gave delight to Edwards produced nightmares in his parishioners. The revival movement continued for a few years more but in the end it became too much for the community. In 1650 Edwards's congregation dismissed him. Eight years later he died.

Seventeenth-century philosophy, the period of Descartes and Locke, is sometimes called the Age of Reason. It marked the beginning of that great shifting of the foundations of European thought known as the Enlightenment. At the beginning of the century, the human was defined in terms of God, and revealed scripture was the supreme authority. The soul was viewed as a created substance subject to God's judgment. By the end of the century, in the minds of many thinkers, the situation was reversed. God was conceived of in terms of humanity and reason was regarded as an indispensable arbiter. The soul or self was seen as a subject of philosophical inquiry rather than theological pronouncement. The religious establishment was still well entrenched, but from now on it had to fight an increasingly desperate battle against the forces of enlightenment. Pascal and Edwards are sometimes seen as bridges between the worlds of revelation and reason. In the eighteenth century it became more and more difficult for people to feel they were at home in both domains.

6

The Soul Dethroned

The soul, as far as we can conceive it, is nothing but a system or train of different perceptions ... all united together, but without any perfect simplicity or identity.

– David Hume

The English term "the Enlightenment" was not used as a label for eighteenth-century thought before the middle of the nineteenth century; but this does not mean that eighteenth-century men and women were unaware of the distinctiveness of their era. In 1784 Immanuel Kant, for many the exemplary Enlightenment figure, was asked to provide an answer to the question: "What is enlightenment?" He didn't waste time getting to the point. "Enlightenment is man's emergence from his self-imposed immaturity," he began,

> Immaturity is the inability to use one's understanding without guidance from another. This immaturity is self-imposed when its cause lies not in lack of understanding, but in lack of resolve and courage to use it without guidance from another. *Sapere Aude!* [Dare to know!] "Have courage to use your own understanding!" – that is the motto of enlightenment.

Most people, Kant went on, were unable to think for themselves, but the few that were should throw off the yoke of immaturity and show others how to do the same. For this all they needed was freedom. People should refuse to bind themselves to unalterable symbols of authority, for that would "preclude forever all further enlightenment of the human race." If they lacked moral courage, they could put off enlightenment for a while, but to renounce it utterly would be "to violate and trample" their "divine rights." Thus in answer to the question, "Do we presently live in an enlightened age?" Kant's answer was: "No, but we do live in an age of enlightenment."[1]

Freedom to act under the direction of reason rather than the coercion of authorities was one of the great themes of Enlightenment thought. If humanity was to escape from its immaturity, those in authority had "to leave everyone free to use his own reason in all matters of conscience."[2] Since the time of Copernicus, the disciplined use of reason had brought about an enormous increase in scientific knowledge. Inspired by the pioneers

of astronomy, physics, and chemistry, eighteenth-century moral philosophers sought to apply the scientific method to the study of the soul and
society, laying the groundwork for the disciplines we now call sociology
and psychology. Their works provided a secular alternative to the ethical
teachings of Christianity. It became possible to believe in the goodness and
perfectibility of human nature, to reject original sin and predestination.
Most philosophers remained convinced Christians but they stopped taking
interest in tired theological exercises such as proofs of the existence of God.
During the course of the century it became possible for the first time in
European history to openly profess atheism.

Intellectual historians regard the Enlightenment as a critical moment in
the history of the self. By 1700, writes Charles Taylor, "something recog-
nizably like the modern self is in process of constitution." The autonomous
individual that was taking form had, in Taylor's view, three main components: the "self-responsible independence" brought to the forefront by
Locke, the "recognized particularity" epitomized by Montaigne, and the
"individualism of personal commitment" that was a child of Protestantism.[3]
As the century progressed, these strands intertwined, becoming something
new and strange. Those who participated in these developments found it
necessary to employ a new set of terms. Most philosophers dropped "soul" as
being overburdened with theological connotations. The seventeenth-century
terms "self" and "personal identity" entered general use, and two new terms,
"the ego" and "the subject," came into currency as philosophical discussions
took an increasingly technical turn.

Personal Identity is Fictitious: David Hume

In 1776, the year of his death, Scottish philosopher David Hume wrote an
autobiographical sketch. "It is difficult for a man to speak long of himself
without vanity," he began, "therefore, I shall be short." He added that it might
"be thought an instance of vanity that I pretend at all to write my life," but
given his importance in the history of Western philosophy, one may pardon
the vanity, if any, and regret that the account was not longer. He began by
speaking of his birth in a respectable but impecunious family of Edinburgh
in 1711. He did well at school and university and "was seized very early with
a passion for literature." This distracted him from his legal studies, which
he abandoned in 1734. Finding the commercial life "totally unsuitable," he
crossed over to France where he continued his reading and wrote his first
book, *A Treatise of Human Nature*. Back in Britain, he published the *Treatise*,
convinced it would be an immediate success. He was mortified when it "fell

dead-born from the press, without reaching such distinction, as even to excite a murmur among the zealots."⁴ It took the zealots a number of years to see what the *Treatise* represented.

Hume had received a Christian upbringing but his reading of Locke and other philosophers shattered his religious beliefs. During his teens, he tried to find a new ground of certitude, recording his efforts in a notebook he later destroyed. "It began," he recalled in 1751, "with an anxious search after arguments, to confirm the common opinion: doubts stole in, dissipated, returned, were again dissipated, returned again; and it was a perpetual struggle of a restless imagination against inclination, perhaps against reason."⁵ Eventually he realized that this sort of enquiry led inevitably to skepticism. One doubt engendered another, which engendered another, till at last nothing remained of what he had taken for granted. "Let our first belief be never so strong," he noted in the *Treatise*, "it must infallibly perish by passing through so many new examinations, of which each diminishes somewhat of its force and vigour." Eventually there would be "a total extinction of belief and evidence," which would make it possible to look at existence in a completely new way.⁶

The *Treatise* is now regarded as a key text of European thought and a landmark in the history of the idea of the self. Hume called it "an attempt to introduce the experimental method of reasoning into moral subjects."⁷ By "experimental" he meant based on experience rather than abstract reasoning. He thus situated himself in the empirical line of philosophy, the line of Bacon, Hobbes, and Locke, as opposed to the rationalism of Descartes and his followers. It was necessary for philosophers to search for general principles, but they could never "go beyond experience; and any hypothesis, that pretends to discover the ultimate original qualities of human nature" had to be rejected. He made the human being the center of his study because all fields of knowledge, even mathematics, science, and religion, were related to human nature, and "however wide any of them may seem to run from it, they still return back by one passage or another."⁸

Despite his insistence on the necessity of empirical observation, Hume took up some pretty abstract topics in the first three parts of the *Treatise*: the nature of ideas, of space and time, of knowledge and probability. He then turned to examine the philosophy of the skeptics, and found it deeply troubling. Skeptical doubt, "both with respect to reason and the senses, is a malady, which can never be radically cured," he observed. It arises naturally "from a profound and intense reflection" on philosophical subjects, and increases "the farther we carry our reflections." One ended up doubting the existence of "an external and internal world"; the only ways to avoid this were carelessness and inattention.⁹ Hume was anything but careless and inattentive, and when he turned to the nature of personal identity, he gave his skepticism full rein.

"There are some philosophers who imagine we are every moment intimately conscious of what we call our SELF," he began. These philosophers – he might have added "along with the rest of humanity" – feel the self's "existence and its continuance in existence; and are certain, beyond the evidence of a demonstration, both of its perfect identity and simplicity [i.e., wholeness]." Hume was not so sure:

> For my part, when I enter most intimately into what I call myself, I always stumble on some particular perception or other, of heat or cold, light or shade, love or hatred, pain or pleasure. I never can catch myself at any time without a perception, and never can observe any thing but the perception. When my perceptions are removed for any time, as by sound sleep; so long am I insensible of myself, and may truly be said not to exist.

He allowed that others might have different ideas but added that if anyone did have "a different notion of himself, I must confess I can reason no longer with him. … He may, perhaps, perceive something simple and continued, which he calls himself; though I am certain there is no such principle in me."[10]

This is one of the most remarkable examples of first-person writing about the idea of the self in the English language, and one of the most quoted passages in Western philosophy. For all that, it is a statement that has few, if any, Western antecedents, though it does have a remarkable kinship with Eastern thought. The Buddha, about whom Hume knew nothing, insisted two thousand years earlier that what we call the self is just a heap or bundle of perceptions, feelings, and mental events, which do not constitute an abiding entity. Hume, remarkably, used the same image when he explained how the process worked. The mind, he wrote, is "nothing but a bundle or collection of different perceptions, which succeed each other with an inconceivable rapidity, and are in a perpetual flux and movement. … There is properly no simplicity in it [the mind] at one time, nor identity in different; whatever natural propension we may have to imagine that simplicity and identity." He concluded: "The identity, which we ascribe to the mind of man, is only a fictitious one."[11]

Hume's "bundle theory" of self was much criticized by his contemporaries and is still argued over by philosophers, cognitive scientists, and psychologists. One problem with it is the nature of the "I" that enters into intimate contact with "what I call myself." Hume seems to be assuming the existence of the entity he denies. In apparent reference to this problem, he made a

distinction between "personal identity, as it regards our thought or imagination, and as it regards our passions or the concern we take in ourselves,"
that is, between the mental sense of personal identity and the practical sense
of identity that all humans, himself not excepted, feel as they go about their
lives.[12] This helped him think about the question of personal identity but he
was never satisfied with his conclusions. In an appendix to the *Treatise*, he
admitted that after reading over the section on personal identity, he found
himself "involved in such a labyrinth, that, I must confess, I neither know
how to correct my former opinions, nor how to render them consistent."[13]
But he never renounced his belief that the self lacked structural and temporal
identity. In an abstract to the *Treatise* published in 1740, he asserted against
Descartes that the soul was just a sequence of perceptions such as "heat
and cold, love and anger, thoughts and sensations," but that the resulting
amalgam was neither substantial nor always the same.[14]

In the second book of the *Treatise*, Hume dealt with the passions or, as we
would now say, the emotions. Since at least the time of Plato, most philosophers had said that the passions had to be controlled by reason. Hume, in his
contrarian way, said the opposite: "Reason is, and ought only to be the slave
of the passions, and can never pretend to any other office [i.e., function] than
to serve and obey them." Without the passions, there would be nothing to
motivate action, for "reason alone can never be a motive to any action of the
will."[15] After discussing the question of the passions at length, Hume turned
his attention to morality, concluding that what constituted vice and virtue
could never be demonstrated rationally. There were thus no grounds for
claiming that any set of moral standards was eternal and immutable. After
presenting his arguments on this subject, he added a personal observation:

> In every system of morality, which I have hitherto met with, I have
> always remarked, that the author proceeds for some time in the ordinary
> way of reasoning, and establishes the being of a God, or makes obser-
> vations concerning human affairs; when of a sudden I am surprized to
> find, that instead of the usual copulations of propositions, *is*, and *is not*,
> I meet with no proposition that is not connected with an *ought*, or an
> *ought not*.[16]

Those who made the change from propositions with *is* (e.g. a father is a male
parent) to propositions with *ought* (e.g. you ought to respect your parents)
never explained their reasons for doing so. God and his commandments just
leaped into the picture and stayed there.

Hume recovered quickly from his disappointment over the failure of
the *Treatise*. He retired to the country, where he continued his studies and
writing. In the early 1740s he published a collection of essays, after which

he applied for a university post in Edinburgh. He was turned down when local clergymen petitioned against him. A few years in the service of well-placed Englishmen brought him some measure of financial stability. He then resumed his writing, producing two books in which he presented the ideas of the *Treatise* in a more accessible style, and also began work on his monumental *History of England*. Around this time he wrote, but did not publish, two works on religious themes. In *Dialogues Concerning Natural Religion* he showed the weakness of the supposed proofs of God's existence, in particular the argument from design. In "On the Immortality of the Soul" he showed the insufficiency of the metaphysical, moral, and physical arguments for the soul's immortality, concluding, ironically, that only "divine revelation" (in which he did not believe) could "ascertain this great and important truth."[17]

Hume was always noted for his calm demeanor, which he retained even after being stricken by cancer in his sixty-fourth year. "His temper, indeed, seemed to be more happily balanced, if I may be allowed such an expression, than that perhaps of any other man I have ever known," wrote his friend Adam Smith, the philosopher and economist, in a note on Hume's last illness. "I have always considered him … as approaching as nearly to the idea of a perfectly wise and virtuous man, as perhaps the nature of human frailty will permit."[18]

To Change the Common Way of Thinking: Denis Diderot and the *Encyclopédie*

Between 1763 and 1766 Hume held diplomatic posts in Paris, where he was warmly received by "men and women of all ranks and stations." There was, he later remarked, "a real satisfaction in living at Paris, from the great number of sensible, knowing, and polite company with which that city abounds above all places in the universe."[19] In the mid-1760s, the most remarkable group of people in the French capital were those associated with the *Encyclopédie*, a multivolume "Systematic Dictionary of the Sciences, Arts and Crafts" published between 1751 and 1772. Despite the name, it was much more than a simple reference work. According to its principal editor, Denis Diderot, its aim was to "change the common way of thinking."[20] The contributors included the greatest thinkers of the French Enlightenment: Diderot, d'Alembert, Voltaire, Rousseau, Montesquieu, d'Holbach, Condillac, along with many others. The articles – in the end around 75,000 – covered all fields of human knowledge. They were arranged under three heads: Memory,

Reason, and Imagination. It did not escape the notice of the clergy that the "Science of God" was placed under Reason as a sub-discipline of Philosophy, and that Natural and Revealed Theology were bracketed with the Science of Good and Evil Spirits.[21]

The *Encyclopédie* broadened the scope of learning by including many articles on science, technology, and the trades. It expanded the ranks of the learned by appealing not only to the traditional privileged classes but also to the growing bourgeoisie. In so doing, it played a significant role in one of the most important social trends of the eighteenth century: the transfer of knowledge and knowledge-based power from the clergy and nobility to the people. It held up the individual as the primary agent of social change, and named reason as the individual's primary tool. "The finest privilege of our reason," Diderot wrote, "consists in not believing anything by the impulsion of a blind and mechanical instinct." The philosopher was obliged to trample underfoot "prejudice, tradition, venerability, universal assent, authority – in a word, everything that overawes the crowd."[22]

The great redoubts of authority and venerability in eighteenth-century France were the monarchy and the Catholic Church. Diderot's attitude toward them is encapsulated in his famous (but usually misquoted) dithyramb:

> And his hands will twist the entrails of the priest
> Into a cord for strangling the kings.[23]

Still, he avoided giving offence to those in power and cultivated friendships with men and women at court who admired his intellect and industry. This was not enough to prevent officials from making things difficult for him. In 1759 the Attorney General of Paris put a ban on the publication and sale of the *Encyclopédie* on the grounds that its writers were trying to destroy religion by promoting materialism, moral corruption, and the spirit of independence. The project had to move underground, though the volumes continued to appear.

Some claimed that the *Encyclopédie* promoted atheism. Strictly speaking this was untrue: the articles on atheists and atheism, written by clergymen, condemned them in very strong terms. But the *Encyclopédie* did champion religious tolerance, and tolerance challenged the monopoly of the Catholic Church on religious and ethical matters, leaving the door open to unbelief. Diderot himself never claimed to be an atheist; to him it did not matter whether God existed or not. Most other Enlightenment figures in France and America regarded themselves as Deists, believing that God created the world but took no further interest in it, but some members of Diderot's circle openly called themselves atheists, notably Paul-Henri Thiry, the Baron d'Holbach, who presented a full-blown materialism in his *System of Nature*

(1770). "Man," he wrote (in the gender-specific language of his time), was an entirely physical being, and should "cease to search outside of the world he lives in, for [immaterial] beings that provide him with a happiness which nature refuses him." By studying nature, he could master its laws, unveil "its energy and the immutable way it acts" and apply "his discovery to his own felicity."[24] This was the most openly Epicurean view of life since Lucretius's *De rerum natura*.

And Who Are You?: The Self in the Eighteenth Century Novel

Along with articles, criticism, essays, and plays, Diderot wrote novels and was a theorist of this new literary genre. In a piece of 1762 addressed to the English novelist Samuel Richardson, he declared: "Whether we wish it or not, we play a part in your works, we intervene in the conversation, we give it approval and blame, we feel admiration, irritation and indignation." Human experience was enlarged: "In the space of a few hours I had been through a host of situations which the longest life can scarcely provide in its whole course." And since Richardson's characters were drawn from actual life and not the worlds of chivalry and romance, "the passions he portrays are those I feel within me."[25]

Richardson cast his spell over readers like Diderot by framing his novels as collections of letters and diary entries written by his characters. The immediacy of the first-person presentation brought the story to life more vividly than narrative or drama. "The hearts of the writers [that is, the characters] must be supposed to be wholly engaged in their subjects," Richardson explained in the preface to *Clarissa*, "so that they abound not only with critical situations, but with what may be called instantaneous descriptions and reflections." Lovelace, the villain of the novel, put it more forcefully: "I have time for a few lines," he wrote to a friend just before setting a trap for Clarissa, "and I love to write to the moment."[26] The last phrase has been used by generations of critics to describe Richardson's methods. By allowing his characters to reveal their thoughts and motives in their own unguarded words, he helped his readers delve into the minds of others, observing men and women in the process of self-formation.

Pamela, or Virtue Rewarded (1740), Richardson's first novel, is the improbable story of a servant-girl's journey across the lines of the English caste system. Pursued by Mr. B., a dissolute country squire, Pamela tries to ward off his attentions by pointing out the social gulf between them; yet she is not ashamed to be what she is. In one scene, B. dresses her up in finery and then pretends to mistake her for an imaginary sister in order to steal a kiss:

> "Why," said he, "you are very pretty, child: I would not be so free with your *sister*, you may believe; but I must kiss *you*."
> "O sir," said I, as much surprized as vexed, "I am Pamela. Indeed I am Pamela, *her own self!*"

Pamela is not overawed by B.'s rank and insists he live up to the supposed ideals of his class. In the midst of another seduction scene, she cries out angrily: "Let me alone! I *will* tell you, if you were a king, and insulted me as you have done, that you have forgotten to act like a gentleman." Carried off to his Lincolnshire estate, she is so harassed by her captors that she contemplates suicide, but then remembers the teachings of the church. To take her life in a fit of despondency would be to commit an unpardonable sin. Stepping back from the brink, she thanks God that she has "been delivered from a worse enemy – *Myself!*"[27]

By depicting his heroine as a model of self-reliance, Richardson made her a mouthpiece for the Lockean ideas that were molding English intellectual life. Readers of *Pamela* got the message: inner values are more important than outward status, rationally guided sentiment more powerful than social rules. They were gratified when Pamela is released from her confinement and when B., recognizing her sincerity and intelligence, asks her to be his wife. When a friend compliments him on his pretty bride, B. replies: "I told you before, that her fine person made me a lover; but it was her mind, that made me an husband."[28] In the novel's sequel, Pamela herself is a student of Locke, referring to the philosopher's theories as she and her husband plan the upbringing of their son. "The noble doctrine of *independence*," she writes, "should be early instilled" into his mind.[29]

For all his interest in Locke's ideas, Richardson was not a philosophical writer. He wanted his books to provide entertainment as well as instruction, but people flocked to buy them because they were page-turners, not sugar-coated sermons. Later novelists such as John Cleland, Henry Fielding, and Horace Walpole felt less obliged than Richardson to provide moral uplift: Cleland's *Memoirs of a Woman of Pleasure* (1748) was the first erotic novel in English, Fielding's *Tom Jones* (1749) the first great comic novel in the language, Walpole's *The Castle of Otranto* (1761) the original gothic tale. All these books explored their characters' inner states while recounting their outer adventures. Meanwhile the didactic novel of sentiment that Richardson helped create took new forms as it spread to different countries. The best-selling book of the eighteenth century, Rousseau's *Julie, or The New Heloise* (1761), was modeled on Richardson's *Clarissa* and dealt with many of the same themes: sincerity, rational sentiment, the constricting effects of society, the importance of personal independence.

As the novel developed, it became self-reflexive. In Laurence Sterne's *The Life and Opinions of Tristram Shandy, Gentleman* (1759–67), the eponymous protagonist sets out to tell his story but never gets very far on account of his "digressive and progressive" manner of proceeding. He condemns the result as "vile" but notes also that "digressions, incontestably, are the sunshine; – they are the life, the soul of reading!" Eighty pages later he decides it is time to write an "Author's Preface," in which he explains what is wrong with contemporary theories of the mind: "That wit and judgment in this world never go together; inasmuch as they are two operations differing from each other as wide of east from west – So, says Locke – so are farting and hiccupping, say I." Locke, in his *Essay*, said that the association of ideas was akin to madness because it interfered with the proper operation of reason. Sterne made it clear, in a parody of learned writing, that wit (which comes from unexpected associations) and judgment (which is based on reason) are equally necessary for a properly equipped mind:

> The great gifts and endowments both of wit and judgment, with everything which usually goes along with them – such as memory, fancy, genius, eloquence, quick parts, and what not, may this precious moment, without stint or measure, let or hindrance, be poured down warm as each of us could bear it – scum and sediment and all (for I would not have a drop lost) into the several receptacles, cells, cellules, domiciles, dormitories, refectories, and spare places of our brains.[30]

Sterne's book is both a defense of wit and the associations that make it possible and a witty example of association gone wild. The proper way to start a book, he wrote after reaching Volume 8, Chapter 2, is to "begin with writing the first sentence – and trusting to Almighty God for the second." As for snaring that second sentence, he wrote, "I wish you saw me half-starting out of my chair, with what confidence, as I grasp the elbow of it, I look up – catching the idea, even sometimes before it half-way reaches me – "[31] Descartes, Locke, and Hume believed that the study of the mind was the best way to arrive at an understanding of the self and world. Digressive novelists like Sterne and Diderot (whose *Jacques le fataliste* was written on the model of *Tristram*) showed that the mind did not always allow itself to be studied, and that the self was even more mysterious. Sterne approached this subject in his usual roundabout way. When a postal commissary delivers a bill to Tristram, he expresses surprise:

– Upon what account? said I. – 'Tis upon the part of the king, replied the commissary, heaving up both his shoulders –
– My good friend, quoth I – as sure as I am I – and you are you –
– And who are you? said he. – Don't puzzle me; said I.[32]

Tristram Shandy, a fictional autobiography, was published when biography and autobiography were becoming recognized genres in English. Samuel Johnson's *Lives of the Poets* appeared in 1779–81, James Boswell's *Life of Samuel Johnson* in 1791. Benjamin Franklin began work on his memoirs in 1771, Edward Gibbon undertook his in 1789. Most earlier memoirs had been written by religious specialists on the model of Augustine's *Confessions*. Now men of literature used the Augustinian template for narratives of secular redemption that often involved a break with religion. By impishly naming his memoirs the *Confessions*, Rousseau lifted himself up to Augustine's level and at the same time asserted his difference.

As fictional and non-fictional narratives developed in tandem, novelists and autobiographers began to learn each other's tricks. Novelists often claimed to be editors of their characters' letters, diaries, or memoirs. Memoirists plotted their narratives like novels, treating their books as well as their lives as works in progress. Such memoirs should be read, according to one critic of the genre, "not as expressions of a previously held self-conception but as actively constructing a self-conception through the creation of life-narratives."[33]

A Little Speculation on the Human Mind: James Boswell

By the end of the eighteenth century, the practice of keeping diaries was widespread in British society, so much so that it found its way into fiction. Lemuel Gulliver had a notebook in his pocket when he landed on Lilliput. Robinson Crusoe kept a diary until he ran out of ink. Crusoe's creator Daniel Defoe published a fictionalized *Journal of the Plague Year* in 1722. Fifty-five years later, the first diary novel appeared. It has remained a popular subgenre ever since. Actual people who kept diaries during the century included preachers, lawyers, merchants, soldiers, sailors, doctors, and a good number of writers. Twenty-two-year-old James Boswell, filled with "an ardent desire for literary fame," started a journal just before he left Scotland for London in 1762.[34] He began on an imitative note: "The ancient philosopher certainly gave a wise counsel when he said, 'Know thyself.' For surely this knowledge is of all the most important." But then he made the project his own: "I have therefore determined to keep a daily journal in which I shall set down my various sentiments and my various conduct, which will be not only useful but very agreeable." The journal will "give me a habit of application and improve me in expression; and knowing that I am to record my transactions will make me more careful to do well."[35]

Boswell was raised in a strict Presbyterian family; his mother, as he noted in an autobiographical sketch, "was one of that sect which believes that to be saved, each individual must experience a strong conversion." These Calvinist roots are apparent in his yearning for the "habit of application" and the desire "to do well." He sprinkled his journal with good resolutions, in the manner of a Rogers or Edwards: "Be reserved and calm, and sustain a consistent character," he wrote in 1763. "It will please you when high, and when low it will be a sure comfort." He studied himself with the sharpness of a Ward or Wigglesworth, but he did so as a young man about town and not as a strait-laced puritan. If he went to church, it was more to look at the ladies than listen to the sermon, and if he did listen, his mind often wandered. "I went to St James's Church and heard service and a good sermon on 'By what means shall a young man learn to order his ways,'" he wrote one evening. He then reflected on his thoughts during the sermon: "What a curious, inconsistent thing is the mind of man! In the midst of divine service I was laying plans for having women, and yet I had the most sincere feelings of religion."[36]

Like his older contemporary Sterne, Boswell was a vernacular psychologist who treated himself as his own chief subject. His account of a secret assignation with an actress was honest, insightful, and hilarious. He headed it, "A little speculation on the human mind":

> For here was I, a young man full of vigour and vivacity, the favourite lover of a handsome actress and going [to her room while her landlady was at church] to enjoy the full possession of my warmest wishes. And yet melancholy threw a cloud over my mind. I could relish nothing. I felt dispirited and languid. I approached Louisa with a kind of uneasy tremor. I sat down. I toyed with her. Yet I was not inspired by Venus. I felt rather a delicate sensation of love than a violent amorous inclination for her. … I sweated almost with anxiety, which made me worse. She behaved extremely well; did not seem to remember the occasion of our meeting at all. I told her I was very dull. Said she, "People cannot always command their spirits". The time of church was almost elapsed when I began to feel that I was still a man. I fanned the flame by pressing her alabaster breasts and kissing her delicious lips. I then barred the door of her dining-room, led her all fluttering into her bedchamber, and was just making a triumphal entry when we heard her landlady coming up.[37]

Boswell was not an introspective man; his eyes were always turned to the world outside. The streets, churches, brothels, and learned societies of London provided him with entertainment and matter for his journal, but as he watched the outer spectacle he kept track of an inner one as well. Hume had described the mind as "a kind of theatre, where several perceptions successively make their appearance; pass, re-pass, glide away, and mingle in an infinite variety of postures and situations."[38] One part of Boswell watched this drama while another was playing different roles in the comedy of life. One morning in Turin he had a mortifying exchange with a young lady, after which he went out in his carriage. Suddenly he "saw a crowd running to the execution of a thief." He leaped out of the carriage and hurried to the gallows. The criminal was standing on a ladder while a priest "held a crucifix before his face. He was tossed over, and hung with his face uncovered, which was hideous." Boswell "stood fixed in attention to this spectacle, thinking that the feelings of horror might destroy those of chagrin. But so thoroughly was my mind possessed by the feverish agitation that I did not feel in the smallest degree from the execution." A little later, he "went into a church and kneeled with great devotion before an altar splendidly lighted up. Here then I felt three successive scenes: raging love – gloomy horror – grand devotion. The horror indeed I only *should* have felt."[39]

The role that Boswell liked to play best was conversation partner with the great. His self-critical remarks on one of his performances reveal his foppishness and vanity but also his journalistic skills:

> I had as my guests Mr Samuel Johnson, Dr Goldsmith [and three others]. I was well dressed and in excellent spirits, neither muddy nor flashy. I sat with much secret pride, thinking of my having such a company with me. I behaved with ease and propriety, and did not attempt at all to show away; but gently assisted conversation by those little arts which make people throw out their sentiments with ease and freedom.[40]

These "arts" worked well with Dr. Johnson, drawing out many of the classic remarks that fill *The Life of Samuel Johnson*. When the author advised him to keep a journal, Boswell was glad to be able to say that he did so already, filling it "with all sorts of little incidents." Johnson replied, "there is nothing too little for so little a creature as man. It is by studying little things that we attain the great knowledge of having as little misery and as much happiness as possible."[41]

Boswell's accounts of Johnson's words and deeds are justly famous but none of them compare in gravitas to his description of the last days of Hume. Boswell found the philosopher "placid and even cheerful" as he approached his end. The young man cautiously introduced the topic of immortality.

Hume replied that he thought it "a most unreasonable fancy that we should exist forever." His own coming annihilation did not bother him in the least, "no more than the thought that he had not been [before his birth], as Lucretius observes." Boswell, a conventional believer, was filled with "a degree of horror, mixed with a sort of wild, strange, hurrying recollection of my excellent mother's pious instructions" and other bits of religious consolation. He regained some measure of composure from one of Hume's remarks: "If there were a future state, Mr Boswell, I think I could give as good an account of my life as most people."[42]

A Copernican Revolution: Immanuel Kant

When David Hume died, Immanuel Kant was a fifty-two-year-old professor at the provincial Prussian university of Königsberg. He later wrote that it was Hume who "many years ago first interrupted my dogmatic slumber, and gave my investigations in the field of speculative philosophy quite a new direction."[43] Until then, Kant had been a rationalist in the tradition of Leibniz. All rationalists – Descartes, Spinoza, Leibniz and their followers – sought certainty through knowledge obtained by reasoning from self-evident axioms. Their rivals, the empiricists – Locke, Hume and others – maintained that knowledge comes from experience, that is, from sense-observations and inferences based on them. Hume precipitated a crisis by showing that empiricism, pushed to its extreme, ends up in a denial of everything we take for granted: matter, cause and effect, the mind, the self. This leaves no basis for the application of reason in science or in philosophy. He also argued that belief in God and the immortal soul was based on nothing better than the authority of scripture.

Kant was impressed, and troubled, by Hume's arguments but not willing to accept his conclusions. A pious Christian, he wanted to find a way to justify belief in God and morality. A talented scientist, he wanted to show that it was possible to increase knowledge by applying reason to empirical data. He came to see that to achieve these ends he had to introduce a new approach to philosophy, one that would incorporate the strengths of rationalism and empiricism and go beyond them.

Kant was made a full professor in 1770. In his inaugural dissertation, he hinted at the direction his thoughts were taking when he wrote, against the rationalists, that sensation is a valid source of knowledge, though such knowledge is confined to "phenomena" or appearances. He also wrote, against the empiricists, of a "pure intuition" of the forms of time and space, and of certain concepts of "pure intellect," such as possibility, existence, and necessity.[44] These ideal things, he explained in a letter to a colleague, "contain the conditions of all phenomena and empirical judgments." He said in the same letter that he had arrived at a concept that he did "not fear ever to be obliged to alter, though I may have to widen it." This concept would allow him to test the viability of all metaphysical questions.[45]

Kant published virtually nothing over the next decade. Finally in 1781 he brought out the *Critique of Pure Reason*, in which he presented the ideas he had been working on at enormous length. Routinely considered one of the greatest works of philosophy ever written, the *Critique* is also one of the most difficult. But Kant's ideas about the self (not to mention knowledge, ethics, art, and a multitude of other topics) have influenced all subsequent philosophers and, through them, many people with no interest in phenomena, pure intellect, or metaphysics in general.

In the *Critique* Kant wrote a great deal about the "I" or ego, but he did not do so in the first person. Like Locke, and unlike Montaigne and Sterne, he felt that nothing good could come out of personal reflections. In a work published a few years after the *Critique*, he distinguished "noticing oneself" from "*observing* oneself": the former was part of the philosopher's task, the latter might "deliver material for a diary" but could easily lead to madness. It was all right to attend to the thoughts that one summoned into one's mind but not to write "an inner history of the *involuntary* course of one's thoughts and feelings." This was, he said, "the most direct path to illuminism or even terrorism."[46] The *Critique* is a landmark in the theoretical study of the self but contains little in the way of self-observation.

Before looking at what Kant wrote about the self, it is necessary to get an idea, however inadequate, of some of the main ideas of his philosophy. A good place to start is the Preface to the second edition of the *Critique*:

> Hitherto it has been assumed that all our knowledge must conform to objects. But all attempts to extend our knowledge of objects by establishing something in regard to them *a priori*, by means of concepts, have, on this assumption, ended in failure. We must therefore make trial whether we may not have more success in the tasks of metaphysics, if we suppose that objects must conform to our knowledge.[47]

We normally think that things just exist and we obtain knowledge of them through our senses. Rationalist philosophers tried to extend this knowledge by reasoning on the basis of things regarded as self-evidently true, such as God or the soul. For reasons that Kant explained at great detail in the *Critique*, this approach has not worked and never will work. He therefore reversed our usual way of looking at experience. Our minds do not passively register what exists in the world, he said, the world is in a sense constructed by forms and concepts inherent in our minds. In the same Preface, he suggested that this reversal was as revolutionary as Copernicus's reversal of the relative positions of the sun and earth. By giving mind a role in the creation of the world, Kant turned philosophy inside out.

The forms that order the world are space and time, the concepts are the "categories" of quantity (e.g. unity), quality (e.g. reality), relation (e.g. causality), and modality (e.g. possibility). Through these the mind synthesizes or puts together the world accessible to our senses, which Kant called the phenomenal world. But what about things as they actually are, before they are acted upon by space, time, and the categories? Kant said that such "things-in-themselves" are simply unknowable. They belong to the "noumenal" world, which is beyond the reach of the senses and mind.

Just as there is a phenomenal world and a noumenal world, so there is a phenomenal self and noumenal self. The first is our ordinary day-to-day self. It is part of the phenomenal world and therefore subject to necessity, like billiard balls and stars. The noumenal self is free, but its freedom cannot be proved theoretically. It is however of great importance for leading an ethical life. Along with the phenomenal and noumenal self, Kant spoke of the "transcendental unity of apperception." Here is how he describes it: "In the transcendental synthesis of the manifold of representations in general, and therefore in the synthetic original unity of apperception, I am conscious of myself, not as I appear to myself, nor as I am in myself, but only that I am."[48] Even philosophers find that difficult. What Kant was trying to say is that there is a silent "I think" behind every operation of the mind. This provides a "unity of apperception" that is required for coherent experience. The underlying "I" is the "logical subject" of all experience, but it is not a thing. Kant devoted a whole section of the *Critique* to getting rid of the false arguments by which people try to show that the self or soul is a unitary substance or person. I may, he wrote, "think myself on behalf of a possible experience, at the same time abstracting from all actual experience"; yet it would be wrong to conclude "that I can be conscious of my existence even apart from experience and its empirical conditions."[49] It is impossible to show that there is a substance in me, a transcendental self or soul, that exists in its own right.

Kant the man believed that God and the soul existed; Kant the philosopher maintained that it was impossible to demonstrate their existence. His purpose in writing the *Critique* was to point up the limitations of reason in order to make room for faith. But by the time of his death in 1804, it looked to many as if God and the soul had become casualties of enlightenment.

Rousseau and Romanticism

The philosophers, far from ridding me of my vain doubts, only multiplied the doubts that tormented me. ... So I chose another guide and said, "Let me follow the inner light; it will not lead me so far astray as others have done, or if it does it will be my own fault."

– Jean-Jacques Rousseau

Immanuel Kant was a man of regular habits. It is said that he missed his evening walk only once, when he was absorbed in reading Jean-Jacques Rousseau's *Émile*. In a note jotted down after he finished Rousseau's treatise, he said that he had always felt "a consuming thirst for knowledge," but that there was a time when he "despised the people, who knew nothing." He continued: "Rousseau corrected me in this. This blinding prejudice disappeared and I learned to honor man. I would find myself more useless than the common laborer if I did not believe that this attitude of mine [as an inquirer] can give worth to all others in establishing the rights of man."[1]

Rousseau stands with Kant as one of the greatest philosophers of the eighteenth century but the two could hardly have been more different. Kant, a phlegmatic product of the German university system, led a cerebral life remarkable for its lack of incident. Rousseau, a self-educated, mercurial citizen of Geneva, preached the gospel of sensibility to all of Europe and was alternately celebrated and condemned for his audacity. Kant was the intellectual zenith of the Enlightenment, Rousseau the bridge between the Enlightenment and Romanticism. These two movements – one seeking universal principles, the other encouraging individual self-expression – together laid the groundwork for the modern Western self.

The critique of the Enlightenment took shape while the Enlightenment was underway, and several major counter-Enlightenment figures had their feet in both worlds. Rousseau was a contributor to the *Encyclopédie* and many of his writings bear the stamp of Enlightenment rationality, but his first published work was a refutation of the Enlightenment belief that the development of the arts and sciences would lead to an improved human society. Emanuel Swedenborg made important contributions to metallurgy and physiology before turning from scientific rationality to visionary spirituality. Johann Georg Hamann, like his friend Kant, was influenced by

Hume, but in the end he returned to devotional Christianity and became an inspiration to the writers of the *Sturm und Drang* movement, a precursor of literary Romanticism. Overall, the eighteenth century, generally looked on as the high-water mark of Enlightenment rationality, was shot through with contrary tendencies that anticipated the anti-Enlightenment trends of the nineteenth and twentieth.

The Feeling of Existence: Jean-Jacques Rousseau

After a unconventional upbringing in Switzerland, Italy, and France, the thirty-year-old Rousseau arrived in Paris in 1742. Under his arm was a treatise on music that he planned to present to the Academy of Sciences, which published it the next year. He fell in with Diderot, and a few years later wrote a number of articles on music for the *Encyclopédie*. Then in August 1749 he read an announcement that the Academy of Dijon was offering a prize for the best essay on the subject: "Whether the reestablishment of the sciences and arts have contributed to the purification of morals." He described his reaction years later:

> If anything was ever like a sudden inspiration it was the impulse that surged up in me as I read that. Suddenly I felt my mind dazzled by a thousand lights; crowds of lively ideas presented themselves at once, with a force and confusion that threw me into an inexpressible trouble. … Oh, Sir, if ever I could have written even the quarter of what I saw and felt under that tree … in what simple terms would I have demonstrated that man is naturally good, and that it is through these institutions alone that men become bad.[2]

What he retained from that intellectual illumination became the substance of three of his most influential writings, the *Discourse on the Sciences and Arts* (which won the prize at Dijon), the *Discourse on Inequality* (1755), and *Émile* (1762). The key idea – that the human being is good by nature but corrupted by social institutions – pervades all his writings, and these writings helped to inspire not only the Romantic movement in literature and art but also the politics of the French Revolution and utopian socialism.

When the *Discourse on the Sciences and Arts* was published in 1750, Rousseau became the toast of Paris. His opera *The Village Soothsayer* was performed before King Louis XV and Madame de Pompadour. He published the article on Political Economy in the *Encyclopédie*. He corresponded with Voltaire, who condemned his *Discourses* as advocating a retreat from civilization. He began a relationship with the young noblewoman Sophie d'Houdetot, who became his inspiration for the heroine of *Julie, or The New Heloise*. The immense success of that novel, published in 1761, made him famous throughout Europe, the continent's first celebrity author. Then in the spring of 1762 he published two major works, *The Social Contract* and *Émile*. Both were banned, *Émile* was publicly burned, and Rousseau took refuge in Switzerland.

Émile, or On Education is a treatise on social and educational theory in the form of a novel. Its central idea is that a suitable education would make it possible for the innately good human being to exist in society without being corrupted. Every child moves through a series of fixed developmental stages and a different sort of education is required for each stage. In book one, which deals with the young child, Rousseau lays stress on the importance of sincerity and self-expression: "To be something, to be oneself, and always at one with oneself, one must act as one speaks. One must be decisive about what course to take and must follow that course with vigour and persistence." Society tries to throttle the urge for self-expression: "Civil man is born, lives, and dies in slavery. At his birth the infant is bound up in swaddling clothes; at his death he is nailed down in his coffin."[3] Rousseau was ahead of his time in urging mothers to breast-feed their babies and to avoid restricting their movements with swaddling clothes. Book two deals with the growing child's interactions with the world. "Man is very strong when he is content to be what he is," Rousseau insists; "he is very weak when he wants to elevate himself above humanity."[4] He introduces an idea that is fundamental to his understanding of the self: the distinction between *amour de soi* (love of self) and *amour-propre* (self-love). The first is the natural desire for one's own well-being, the second is the socially induced urge to enjoy special consideration from others. Book three, covering the period of late childhood, deals with occupational training. Toward the end of the book, Rousseau asserts: "Here our child is ready to cease being a child and to return to his own individuality. ... We have made him an active and thinking being. In order to make him a man, it remains for us to make him a lovable and sensitive being, that is to perfect reason by sentiment."[5] This training of the sentiments is the subject of book four. Rousseau returns to the distinction between *amour de soi* and *amour-propre*, showing that the latter is the source of personal dissatisfaction and social unrest: "*Amour de soi*, which concerns only ourselves, is content when our true needs are satisfied; but *amour-propre*, which makes comparisons, is never satisfied and never can be." *Amour-propre* not only "prefers ourselves to others" but "requires also that others prefer us to themselves, which is impossible."[6]

Rousseau considered religious instruction to be part of the training of the sentiments, and introduced a country priest from Savoy to present his ideas on the subject. The "Profession of Faith of a Savoyard Vicar" occupies about half of the fourth book of *Émile*, and is the most famous part of the treatise. It is also the part that caused the book to be burned in Catholic Paris and Calvinist Geneva and forced Rousseau to flee from France to Switzerland and from Switzerland to England. He claimed to have been surprised by the violent reaction. After all, he was just trying to defend a form of religion from the attacks of the deists and atheists of Paris. But the natural religion he proposed did away with all but a shadow of the Christian God. It was a religion of inner sentiment in which the voice in the heart takes precedence over scriptural revelation and priestly mediation.

God exists, the vicar proclaims, and to prove it he offers a version of the theological argument from design:

> Let us compare the special ends, the means, the ordered relations of every kind, then let us listen to the inner voice of feeling; what healthy mind can reject its evidence? Unless the eyes are blinded by prejudices, can they fail to see that the visible order of the universe proclaims a supreme intelligence?

True knowledge of God comes from the inner consciousness and not from reasoned arguments. Similarly, true rules of conduct are founded on conscience, "the voice of the soul":

> Conscience! Conscience! Divine instinct, immortal voice from heaven; sure guide for a creature ignorant and finite indeed, yet intelligent and free; infallible judge of good and evil, making man like to God!

Conscience is what we need to proceed safely through life. Religious doctrines, which are human inventions, cannot help us: "Their revelations do but degrade God, by investing him with passions like our own. ... Instead of bringing peace upon earth, they bring fire and sword." People have to learn how to awaken the voice of the soul. For that to be possible, "we must remove the trembling supports on which they think they rest." This means, though the vicar does not say it openly, that we have to dismantle organized religion.[7]

David Hume was not surprised to learn that Rousseau got into trouble over *Émile*. "He had not had the precaution to throw any veil over his sentiments," he wrote in a letter to a friend, "and as he scorns to dissemble his contempt of established opinions, he could not wonder that all the zealots were up in arms against him."[8] Hume found the Genevan's writings admirable, though sometimes extravagant and verbose. When he heard that Rousseau had been chased from the village where he had been living by a stone-throwing mob incited by the local pastor, he invited him to stay in

England. Rousseau agreed, and in January 1764 the two went to London. They did not hit it off very well. Hume was surprised to find that Rousseau had "a hankering after the Bible, and is indeed little better than a Christian in a way of his own." He had read little, seen little, reflected little, "and has not indeed much knowledge: He has only felt, during the whole course of his life; and in this respect, his sensibility rises to a pitch beyond what I have seen any example of."[9] By this time Rousseau's extreme sensitivity, aggravated by years of persecution, had pushed him to the brink of madness. After breaking violently with his benefactor Hume, he returned to France in 1767.

Two years earlier, while still in Switzerland, Rousseau began to write a defense of himself and his work in the form of an autobiography. Completed in 1770, but not published until after his death, the *Confessions* is viewed by many as Rousseau's most important book, and is unquestionably a watershed in the history of the self. The opening lines show he was aware he was breaking new ground: "I am resolved on an undertaking that has no model and will have no imitator. I want to show my fellow-men a man in all the truth of nature; and this man is to be myself." Here and elsewhere, he insists on his uniqueness: "I am not made like any that I have seen; I venture to believe that I was not made like any that exist." His confession, he says, will be utterly sincere; when he stands book in hand before God at the final judgment, he will be able to say: "I have shown myself as I was, contemptible and vile when that is how I was, good, generous, sublime when that is how I was; I have disclosed my innermost self as you alone know it to be."[10]

Before Rousseau, most autobiographies were written by religious figures – Augustine, Teresa, Bunyan, and others – to show how they were lifted from a life of sin and confusion by the grace of God. Rousseau is at pains to show that he had always been good even while doing things he later understood to be shameful. He reveals that he once blamed a servant-girl for a petty theft he had committed, causing her to lose her job. This "atrocious deed," he tells the reader, has "lain unalleviated" on his conscience ever since and was one of the reasons he decided to write his book. Having made a clean breast of it, he finds a way to exculpate himself ("it was my fondness for her that was the cause"), and concludes by saying that the incident has "had the good effect of preserving me for the rest of my life from any inclination towards crime," because the impression of this, the only crime he ever committed, has remained with him ever since. Elsewhere he says that he has "always laughed at the false naivety of Montaigne, who, while pretending to confess his faults, is very careful to give himself only loveable ones," but he does precisely this whenever he reveals a fault of his own. His theatrical confessions seem to have been necessary to make him feel that he was doing what he wanted to do: "to make my mind, as it were, transparent to the reader." For this, he had "to display it from every angle, to show it in every light, and to ensure that there is no movement taking place within it that he [the reader] does not observe, so that he may be able to judge for himself what principle it is that produces such effects."[11]

Historians have discovered that the *Confessions* contains many misstatements of fact. Rousseau himself did not guarantee the accuracy of every detail, but insisted he had been faithful to "the chain of feelings that have marked the successive stages of my being." The book, he said, was "the history of my soul." To write it, all he had to do was "look inside myself."[12] It is this interiority that has made the *Confessions* so influential, the initiator of a new sort of personal writing. The best way to approach it, writes scholar Nicholas Dent, is to "see in it Rousseau's carving out a fresh form for self-understanding and assessing the meaning of a life to take." Through his "lengthy discussions of his feelings, the vagaries and inflections of his moods, in the dissection of his motives," he shows "the absolute centrality of the life of one's inner being to the substance and significance of a human existence."[13] Every writer of an autobiography or memoir since the *Confessions* was published has been indebted, directly or indirectly, to Rousseau. He certainly was wrong in thinking it would "have no imitator," as the current vogue of confessional memoirs shows; but none of the imitations have had a fraction of the impact of the original.

In 1770 Rousseau returned to Paris, where he earned his livelihood copying music. He wrote on botany, on music, on Polish politics, and also began a curious set of dialogues entitled *Rousseau Judge of Jean-Jacques*, in which he defended himself against his real and imagined enemies. The main speakers are "Rousseau," the writer's public persona, and a "Frenchman" representing unenlightened public opinion. "Rousseau" later pays a visit to "Jean-Jacques," the writer himself, and finds him to be candid, honest, and incapable of wrongdoing. "Nothing inspires as much courage as the testimony of an upright heart, which draws from the purity of its intentions the audacity to state aloud and without fear the judgments dictated solely by love of justice and truth," declares "Rousseau." "But at the same time, nothing exposes someone to so many dangers and risks coming from clever enemies as this same audacity."[14]

In the dialogues, Rousseau wrote eloquently on some of his major themes, such as innocence corrupted by social institutions and the difference between love of self and self-love. But he also gave evidence of delusional thinking, which manifested itself dramatically in 1776, when he tried to place the manuscript of the dialogues on the high altar of the Cathedral of Notre Dame. Later the same year he began his final work, a series of reflections called *Reveries of the Solitary Walker*. The book, which he identified as "an appendix to my *Confessions*," was meant "to give an account of the successive variations of my soul." He would observe himself scientifically, taking "the barometer readings of my soul" and keeping a meticulous record of the results without trying "to reduce them to a system." His enterprise, he said, was similar to Montaigne's though his motives were "entirely different": Montaigne "wrote his essays only for others to read," he would write for himself alone.[15]

In the *Reveries* Rousseau looks back on some key moments of his life, trying to find some answer to the question "who am I?" Most memorable are his reflections on a brief and happy stay he had on the Island of Saint-Pierre in Switzerland:

> If there is a state where the soul can find a resting-place secure enough to establish itself and concentrate its entire being there ... where the present runs on indefinitely but this duration goes unnoticed, with no sign of the passing of time, and no other feeling of deprivation or enjoyment, pleasure or pain, desire or fear than the simple feeling of existence, a feeling that fills our soul entirely, as long as this state lasts, we can call ourselves happy, not with a poor, incomplete and relative happiness such as we find in the pleasures of life, but with a sufficient, complete and perfect happiness which leaves no emptiness to be filled in the soul.

The source of such happiness is "nothing external to us, nothing apart from ourselves and our own existence." Unfriendly people could and did chase him away from his island sanctuary, but they could not prevent him "from being transported there every day on the wings of imagination."[16]

Rousseau died suddenly in 1778. His body was placed in a shrine in the village of Ermenonville but sixteen years later was transferred to the Panthéon in Paris, where it lies with other heroes of the French republic. His influence on the thinkers of the revolutionary generation will be discussed in the next chapter. His influence on Western culture in general is impossible to measure because it is so pervasive. His "presence is ubiquitous," wrote scholar Allan Bloom; he "did not produce an ism of his own, but he did provide the authentically modern perspective."[17]

Dreams of a Spirit-Seer: Emanuel Swedenborg

Science was central to the Enlightenment project. From the mid-sixteenth century, many of the leading minds of Europe sought intellectual certainty by finding regularities in the physical world, establishing them by experiment, and stating them in mathematical form. During the seventeenth and eighteenth centuries, this approach was extended to the study of the self. Descartes made the thinking human being the starting point for philosophical enquiry. Locke in his *Essay* and Hume in his *Treatise* assumed that an understanding of the mind must precede any attempt to understand other things. Hume ended up doubting that it was possible to arrive at certain knowledge of the self and indeed of much that we normally take for granted. This put the Enlightenment project in peril. Kant attempted to salvage it by distinguishing between the world of appearances (the phenomenal world) and the world as it is in itself (the noumenal world). Humans could never have knowledge of noumenal entities such as God, freedom, or the immortal soul, but they could and should have faith that they exist.

Most eighteenth-century scientists observed a distinction between empirical studies and religious beliefs well before Kant wrote about phenomena and noumena. By and large, they held traditional ideas about the soul and God, but they didn't let this get in the way of their empirical investigations. A few tried to find ways to bring the certainties of science into the study of non-physical matters. Newton, for example, wrote more on alchemy and biblical interpretation than on physics and mathematics. Another scientist whose investigations took him beyond the material world was Emanuel Swedenborg, a Swedish polymath and mystic. After making important contributions to metallurgy and crystallography, he turned his attention to the animal kingdom and did significant work in anatomy and physiology. Eventually he became interested in the great unsolved problem of the relationship between the soul and body.

In 1743 Swedenborg took a leave of absence from his work at the Bureau of Mines and went to the Netherlands to publish his treatise *The Animal Kingdom* and to do some research. As usual on his travels, he kept a diary. Early entries were about towns passed through and sights seen. Then, toward the beginning of 1744, he began to record his dreams and reflect on his states of mind. When he reached The Hague, he "found that the impulse and ambition for my work had passed away," along with his "inclination towards women," which had always been his "chief passion." His dream records became long and detailed. One night, it seemed to him that "I was first united to others by what was sinful, and then that I was enveloped by strange and indescribable circumvolutions"; later he felt that "everything was in response to my thoughts, yet in such a manner that there was a life and a glory in the whole of it that I cannot in the least describe, for it was all heavenly. … In short, I was in heaven, and I heard a speech that no human tongue can utter, nor can anyone describe the glory and bliss of that life."[18]

From then on, his visits to heaven become habitual, and he made it his chief task to describe the glory of "the whole."

Reflecting on the experiences he was having, Swedenborg developed a sort of devotional psychology:

> When a person is in such a state as not to possess a love that centers upon self but upon the common good, which on earth or in the moral world represents love in the spiritual world, and all this is not for the sake of self or of society but for the sake of Christ, who is love itself and the center, then one is in the right state.

Will and mind contend with spirit for control of the person:

> I have also observed that our whole will, which we have inherited and which is ruled by the body and introduces thoughts into the mind, is opposed to the spirit. For this reason, there is continual strife, and there is no way for us to unite ourselves with the spirit, which by grace is with us."[19]

The only way out of such conflict was contrition for one's sins and surrender to God.

Swedenborg continued to write in his diary until October 1744. The upshot of his half-year's self-examination was a decision to abandon his scientific studies and to explore the inner worlds that had been opened to him. Between 1747 and 1756 he produced an enormous treatise on things human and divine called *Arcana Coelestia* (Heavenly Mysteries). Written in the form of a commentary on the first two books of the Bible, *Arcana Coelestia* was founded on his personal experiences. For him the study of the spirit world was as empirical as psychology or mineralogy:

> I am well aware that many will say that no one can possibly speak with spirits and angels so long as he lives in the body; and many will say that it is all fancy, others that I relate such things in order to gain credence, and others will make other objections. But by all this I am not deterred, for I have seen, I have heard, I have felt.[20]

The master key to Swedenborg's spiritual writings is his theory of correspondences. This assumes that the stories of the Bible correspond to inner truths, and also that there are correspondences between body and mind, earth and heaven, and so forth. As he explained it in *Heaven and Hell*, his most famous work, "The whole natural world corresponds to the spiritual world, and not merely the natural world in general, but also every particular of it." This opened the way to a sophisticated understanding of religious doctrines in terms of human psychology: "Evil in man is hell in him, for it is the same thing whether you say evil or hell. And since man is the cause of his own evil he is led into hell, not by the Lord but by himself." [21]

By the 1760s Swedenborg's name was well known throughout Europe. Part of his celebrity came from reports that he possessed the gift of supernatural knowledge. Once while in Gothenburg he became aware that a fire had broken out in Stockholm, two hundred fifty miles away. He spoke to people at a dinner party about it, and what he told them was confirmed when news of the fire reached Gothenburg two days later. Hearing of this incident, Immanuel Kant's interest was piqued and he made some inquiries, after which he wrote that the reports seemed to him "to have the greatest weight of proof," placing "the assertion respecting Swedenborg's extraordinary gift beyond all possibility of doubt." [22] Later however, after reading *Arcana Coelestia*, he published a book entitled *Dreams of a Spirit-Seer* in which he dismissed Swedenborg's claims to have direct knowledge of the spiritual worlds. Other famous writers have taken him more seriously, among them William Blake, Honoré de Balzac, Charles Baudelaire, and William Butler Yeats. Some of his admirers found his revelatory books a modern restatement of esoteric doctrines such as Neoplatonism and the Kabbalah. But to Ralph Waldo Emerson, a onetime admirer who in the end rejected the Swedish sage, his brilliance was dimmed by his reversion to outdated religious forms. "The genius of Swedenborg," he wrote, "wasted itself in the endeavor to reanimate and conserve what had already arrived at its natural term." Swedenborg failed because he attached himself "to the Christian symbol, instead of to the moral sentiment, which carries innumerable christianities, humanities, divinities, in its bosom." [23]

Each Human Being has His Own Measure: Hamann, Herder, Goethe

Swedenborg was not the only mid-eighteeenth century thinker who turned from the perceived aridity of Enlightenment philosophy back to the "Christian symbol." The period was notable for evangelical movements such as Pietism and Methodism that sought to bring personal devotion back to the forefront of Protestant observance. Evangelicals valued Biblical study, diary-writing and conversion narratives as much as the Puritans, and these practices spread through Germany and Scandinavia along with Pietism. Swedenborg's visions and his account of them in the *Dream Diary* may be viewed, historically, as a renewal and transformation of the Pietistic teachings he had been exposed to in his childhood. When he wrote in his diary, after his dream-visions of 1744, "The only thing is to humble oneself to the grace of Christ, in all humility to ask for no more than that," he was giving classic expression to Pietistic belief.[24]

Another writer touched by Pietistism was the Prussian Johann Georg Hamann. Born in Königsberg in 1730 (six years after Kant was born in the same city), he studied theology, philosophy, and law, and then went into business. In 1758 he found himself in London after a failed diplomatic mission. Not wishing to return to Prussia, he enjoyed a life of dissipation until he ran out of money and friends. Filled with a sense of "emptiness and darkness and wilderness," he picked up the Bible and went through it from cover to cover. As he read, he jotted down his thoughts and feelings in a diary and later expanded these notes into a memoir. "On the evening of 31 March," he wrote in the memoir:

> I read the fifth chapter of Deuteronomy, and fell into deep thought. ... I felt my heart throb, I heard a voice sigh in its depths. ... All at once I felt my heart swell, and pour out in tears, and I could no longer – I could no longer conceal from my God that I was the fratricide, the murderer of his only begotten Son. The Spirit of God went on ... to reveal to me more and more the mystery of the divine love.

Hamann saw that there are two parallel systems of symbols that transmit the divine revelation: "God has revealed himself to man in nature and in His word," he wrote in his diary. "Both revelations [the Book of Nature and the Book of Scripture] explain and support each other and cannot contradict each other."[25] The similarity between this parallelism and the correspondences of Swedenborg (about whom Hamann knew nothing at the time) is striking.

After his conversion, Hamann set himself against the intellectualism of the Enlightenment, which he felt was not up to the task of interpreting the dual revelation. "God condescended as much as He could to man's disposition and ideas, even to his prejudices and weakness," he wrote. Yet humans, who foolishly imagined that the divine Word ought to be in "consonance with the taste of the age in which they live," mocked a revelation they could not fathom.[26] To understand divine teachings people had to be ready to abandon ordinary logic. "Daily at home I have the experience that one must always contradict oneself from two viewpoints," Hamann wrote in a letter to a friend. "*Our knowledge is piecemeal,*" and any attempt to eliminate contradictions leads to dogmas of the pure reason.[27]

Hamann's works were considered obscure even by his contemporaries, yet he had great influence on German philosophers and writers and, through them, on the intellectual history of Europe. In philosophy, his most important disciple was Johann Gottfried von Herder. Born near Königsberg

in 1744, Herder studied under Kant but was drawn to the enigmatic
Hamann, from whom he learned to distrust philosophical system-builders.
Nations and cultures were irreducibly individual, he said; the right model
for philosophical investigation was not science, which sought universal
truths, but history, which celebrated individual differences. In this Herder
went against the Enlightenment dogma that there is one unvarying human
nature. Hume had written in his *Enquiry Concerning Human Understanding*:
"Mankind are so much the same, in all times and places, that history informs
us of nothing new or strange in this particular."[28] Herder disagreed with this
idea. People from different periods and cultures vary in significant ways, and
this is good because each culture has a specific role to play in the organic
whole. Further, each individual differs from all the others. "A human soul is
an individual in the realm of minds," Herder wrote, "it senses in accordance
with an individual formation, and thinks in accordance with the strength
of its mental organs." He added: "If, then, our philosophers do not yet so
frequently attempt this cognition of individual minds, another person
has more opportunity and duty for this: the *historian*."[29] Herder's writings
marked the beginning of the historicist approach to the study of the human
being and also provided a philosophical basis for nineteenth- and twentieth-
century nationalism.

One of the first writers to be influenced by Herder was Johann Wolfgang
von Goethe. The two men met in 1770 when Goethe was a well-regarded
but conventional young poet and Herder a slightly older critic. Four years
later, Goethe published *The Sorrows of Young Werther*, a Rousseau-inspired
novel that became an overnight sensation and launched the literary
movement known as *Sturm und Drang* (Storm and Stress), which featured
heroes in tragic revolt against the conventions of society. *Sturm und Drang*
marked the public beginning of a new way of looking at the individual.
As Herder put it: "Each human being has his own measure, as it were an
accord peculiar to him of all his feelings to each other."[30] Everyone has
to find that inner accord through a process of self-discovery and self-
formation that was the work of an entire lifetime. This idea became the
template for the *Bildungsroman* or novel of formation of which Goethe's
Apprenticeship of Wilhelm Meister was the first great example. In it Goethe
has the eponymous hero declare: "Even as a youth I had the vague desire
and intention to develop myself fully, myself as I am." Despite society's
hindrances, "I still have the same intention"; regardless of the consequences,
"I must stake out my own path."[31]

What Am I to Call My Self?: The Romantic Movement in England

The *Sturm und Drang* movement lasted little more than a decade, but it gave a decisive turn to German literature. By the end of the eighteenth century one of its offspring, literary Romanticism, had come of age in England. Romanticism eventually became a far-flung movement affecting literature, art, music, philosophy, politics, and everyday life throughout Europe and the Americas. It will not be possible to examine all these developments here, but we will look briefly at the effect literary Romanticism had on the Western conception of the self.

English literary Romanticism is usually said to date from the publication of *Lyrical Ballads* by William Wordsworth and Samuel Taylor Coleridge in 1798, but it was anticipated by earlier poets, such as William Cowper, Robert Burns, and William Blake, who favored informal diction in their descriptions of nature and the life of ordinary people. Blake later moved on to a more convoluted style in his prophetic books, where he developed an esoteric cosmology similar to Swedenborg's. He read the Swedish sage as a young man but later mocked him in *The Marriage of Heaven and Hell*. Still, Swedenborg's influence is evident even in that work:

> Man has no Body distinct from his Soul for that calld Body is a portion
> of Soul discernd by the five Senses. the chief inlets of Soul in this age.[32]

In Blake's mythology, the universe as we know it is the result of a "fall into Division," which will be followed by a "Resurrection to Unity." In the poem *Milton*, Blake explains that division is brought about by Selfhood, which tries "to impose an immutable and thus false identity on the individual."[33] In the poem's second book, the Seven Angels tell Milton that he must go within himself to discover what is permanent and what transitory in his being:

> Judge then of thy Own Self: thy Eternal Lineaments explore
> What is Eternal & what Changeable? & what Annihilable!

Later Milton speaks:

> The Negation must be destroyd to redeem the Contraries
> The Negation is the Specter; the Reasoning Power in Man
> This is a false Body: an Incrustation over my Immortal
> Spirit; a Selfhood, which must be put off & annihilated alway
> To cleanse the Face of my Spirit by Self-examination …
> To cast off Bacon, Locke & Newton from Albions covering
> To take off his filthy garments, & clothe him with Imagination.[34]

Many of Blake's themes – the fall into division, the labor of self-discovery, the eternal spirit and the separate individual, the superiority of imagination to reason – have parallels in Christian thought, but in Blake there is always a difference. His "fall," for example, corresponds to the Biblical fall of man but excludes original sin.

The Christian antecedents of Romanticism are more clearly visible in the works of Blake's younger contemporary Coleridge. In an early poem, he speaks of the separate self as "a sordid solitary thing," which wanders through the world

> Feeling himself, his own low Self the whole:
> When he by sacred sympathy might make
> The whole ONE SELF! SELF, that no alien knows!

He concludes that the return to the undivided self is the Messiah's "destin'd victory."[35]

The conflict between the higher and lower self had been a mainstay of Christian discourse from the time of Augustine. Coleridge returned to this theme again and again. In December 1829, he wrote in a diary notebook:

> The Question, *What* within the sphere of my inward immediate Consciousness am I [to] call my *Self* ...
> May the answer be – this is the very mark & character of thy state that thou art to determine this for thyself? ... Dare I claim the Law and Light of the Spirit as *me*? No! Dare I call the appetites & passions & animal fancy *me*? No – for then I must despair.

The only solution was to search within, for "we cannot believe aught of God but what we find in ourselves."[36] All this has obvious affinities with Augustinian self-scrutiny, but Coleridge highlighted the then-novel idea that it is the "very mark" of human life for every self to determine what it is. He wrote in a similar vein in a letter of 1818 that Nature had "two great Ends": "Individualization, or apparent detachment from Nature," and "the re-union with Nature as the apex of Individualization – the birth of the *Soul*, the Ego or conscious Self, into the Spirit."[37]

This same idea – that the self is in some sense its own creator – was formulated independently by another Romantic poet, John Keats, in a letter of 1818:

> The common cognomen of this world among the misguided and super-stitious is "a vale of tears" from which we are to be redeemed by a certain arbitrary interposition of God and taken to Heaven – What a little circumscribed straightened notion! Call the world if you please "The

vale of Soul-making." ... There may be intelligences or sparks of the divinity in millions – but they are not Souls till they acquire identities, till each one is personally itself. ... How then are these sparks which are God to have identity given them – so as ever to possess a bliss peculiar to each one's individual existence? How, but by the medium of a world like this? This point I sincerely wish to consider because I think it a grander system of salvation than the Christian religion – or rather it is a system of Spirit-creation.[38]

For Keats, the striving and pain of self-creation was linked to his vocation as a poet. "Poesy alone can tell her dreams," he wrote in *The Fall of Hyperion* (1819); all humans had "days of joy and pain," but

Only the dreamer venoms all his days,
Bearing more woe than all his sins deserve.[39]

To Keats, as to Blake, Coleridge, and the other English Romantics, the poet had a special destiny, evoked memorably by Percy Bysshe Shelley in his *Defence of Poetry*. The greatest poets of the age, Shelley wrote, "measure the circumference and sound the depths of human nature with a comprehensive and all-penetrating spirit." Because they seek to reframe the relationship between the individual and society, they are nothing less than "the unacknowledged legislators of the world."[40]

No English Romantic poet took his vocation more seriously than William Wordsworth. In the autobiographical poem *The Recluse* he wrote of "an internal brightness" that had been granted to him, something "that must not pass away" before it had fully expressed itself:

Something within which yet is shared by none,
Not even the nearest to me and most dear,
Something which power and effort may impart;
I would impart it, I would spread it wide.[41]

Wordsworth never completed *The Recluse* but he did leave behind what was meant to be the first of its three parts, a "poem on the growth of my own Mind" that was published after his death as *The Prelude*.[42] In this enormous work he sketched the defining incidents of his inner life, moments known only to him that made him what he was. Of his childhood he wrote:

Fair seed-time had my soul, and I grew up
Fostered alike by beauty and by fear. ...
Dust as we are, the immortal spirit grows
Like harmony in music; there is a dark
Inscrutable workmanship that reconciles

Discordant elements, makes them cling together
In one society.

In another passage he addressed the "Wisdom and Spirit of the universe":

Thou Soul, that art the eternity of thought,
That givest to forms and images a breath
And everlasting motion, not in vain
By day or star-light, thus from my first dawn
Of childhood didst thou intertwine for me
The passions that build up our human soul.[43]

The Prelude is the supreme autobiographical poem in English. It is also the first great example in the language of the narrative of *Bildung* that Goethe initiated with *The Apprenticeship of Wilhelm Meister*. Other examples soon followed: Lord Byron's *Childe Harold's Pilgrimage* and Coleridge's *Biographia Literaria* come immediately to mind. Before long every significant work of literature, art, and music was, as Susan Sontag put it, "a first-person performance."[44] The drama was sometimes turbulent (Byron's *Don Juan*, Géricault's *Raft of the Medusa*, Beethoven's *Eroica Symphony*), sometimes tranquil (Keats's odes, Constable's landscapes, Schubert's lieder), but all such works had a signature characteristic: individual expressiveness. Before the nineteenth century, the artist was looked on as a talented craftsperson. The Romantic artist stood forth as a creative genius.

The expressive individualism of the Romantic era was not the prerogative of the genius alone. Increasingly it became the norm for all men and women who enjoyed some measure of economic self-sufficiency. It was, and remains, "a tremendously influential idea," wrote philosopher Charles Taylor, who called it "one of the cornerstones of modern culture. So much so that we barely notice it, and we find it hard to accept that it is such a recent idea in human history and would have been incomprehensible in earlier times."[45] Other intellectual historians gave equal importance to the Romantic revolution. Isaiah Berlin considered it one of the three main turning points in the history of Western civilization, not just a modification of artistic or behavioral norms, but "a radical change in the entire conceptual framework." Before Romanticism, it was taken for granted that human nature, human values, human interests were fixed quantities. The Romantic creators showed that this was not so. Human beings could change their natures, decide their values, determine their aims.[46] This altered the whole idea of what constituted a self and radically changed the relationship between self and society. And because the individual could no longer be constrained by established social norms, the results were often explosive. It is no coincidence that the Romantic era in literature coincided with a period of unprecedented political revolution.

Revolution and Reaction

Now that we are free, we must again become strong; we should view the human will as constituting the self and as all-powerful over physical nature.

– Benjamin Constant

To the English Romantic writers, and thousands of others throughout Europe, the French Revolution promised not just political change but a wholesale transformation of life. "A visionary world seemed to open upon those who were just entering it," wrote the poet Robert Southey. "Old things seemed passing away, and nothing was dreamt of but the regeneration of the human race."[1] When the young Wordsworth landed in Calais in July 1790, a year after the storming of the Bastille, he was caught up in the general enthusiasm:

> But Europe at that time was thrilled with joy,
> France standing on the top of golden hours,
> And human nature seeming born again.[2]

The next year, in *The French Revolution*, Blake prophesied a time when "the happy earth" would "sing in its course," and "The mild peaceable nations be opened to heav'n."[3] Later, after the Reign of Terror and the wars that followed, the English poets and countless others became disheartened. "I wish you would write a poem," Coleridge wrote to Wordsworth in 1799, "addressed to those, who, in consequence of the complete failure of the French Revolution, have thrown up all hopes of the amelioration of mankind." But many still felt that the ideals of the Revolution would set the tone for the coming century. It remained, wrote Shelley to Byron in 1816, "the master theme of the epoch in which we live."[4]

Europe experienced more political, social, and cultural change during the twenty-six years between the start of the Revolution and the final defeat of Napoleon in 1815 than it had during the previous two centuries. Freedom, equality and popular sovereignty were no longer mere ideals but principles enshrined in the *Declaration of the Rights of Man and of the Citizen*. "Men are born and remain free and equal in rights," this document begins, subverting norms accepted since the beginning of human society. Another article, "The principle of all sovereignty resides essentially in the nation," put an end, in principle, to the divine right of kings, which had prevailed in one form or another since the time of the pharaohs. "Law is the expression of the general will" – not the whims of monarchs or nobles. "No one shall be disquieted on account of his opinions, including his religious views" – a big change from the intolerance still current both in Catholic and Protestant countries.[5]

The ideals announced in the *Declaration* did not spring fully formed from the minds of its authors. The freedoms enjoyed by individual men and women had been on the increase since the Renaissance. The Reformation successfully challenged the authority of the Catholic Church, the Enlightenment made it possible to escape dogma through the use of reason. Rousseau, Kant, and others contested the idea that humans are inherently evil, a belief often used to justify the existing social order. Rousseau wrote that humans were naturally good but were spoiled by civil society. In *The Social Contract*, his main work of political theory, he theorized that governments came to being when people entered into a voluntary compact with one another. "The problem," he wrote, was "to find a form of association … in which each, while uniting himself with all, may still obey himself alone, and remain as free as before." Entering into the social contract, "each of us puts his person and all his power in common under the supreme direction of the general will, and, in our corporate capacity, we receive each member as an indivisible part of the whole."[6] This whole was the "Sovereign," which gave expression to the "general will," formulating its own laws as required. Government, which was often confused with the Sovereign, was simply "an intermediate body set up between the subjects and the Sovereign, to secure their mutual correspondence, charged with the execution of the laws and the maintenance of liberty, both civil and political."[7] It is hard for us today to see how radical this was when *The Social Contract* was published. Two hundred fifty years of imperfect democracy have familiarized all of us with the ideas of popular sovereignty and individual freedom. In 1762 France was an absolute monarchy. The king derived his right to rule from God. In principle his subjects enjoyed only as much freedom as he chose to grant them. Rousseau turned the whole thing upside down. The people, born free, are the sovereign power; they delegate executive power to the government, which may or may not be headed by a king. It is no wonder that *The Social Contract* was banned in France immediately after its publication.

Neglected after Rousseau's death, *The Social Contract* was rediscovered in 1789 by theorists of the Revolution. The passages quoted above from the *Declaration of the Rights of Man* – "Men are born and remain free," "The principle of all sovereignty resides essentially in the nation," "Law is the expression of the general will" – echo passages in Rousseau's treatise.

People of all factions, from the moderate Girondists to the extreme Jacobins, had catchphrases from his writings ready to hand to justify their divergent positions. Whether Rousseau himself would have supported these positions is hard to say. He certainly would have cringed from the carnage presided over by the Jacobin Maximilien Robespierre, who was a close reader of his works and who wrote of him: "Divine man, you taught me to know myself."[8]

Rousseau is often called one of the fathers of the Revolution, though some doubt whether the title is deserved. One cannot deny his intellectual impact on Robespierre, the Abbé Sieyès, Jean-Paul Marat, Jacques-Pierre Brissot, and many other revolutionary leaders, or his appeal as a cultural icon to people who never read his books; but his actual influence on the events of 1789–1799 is harder to pin down. Historian Gordon H. McNeil may have got it right when he wrote: "Instead of Rousseau making the Revolution," it might be better to say "the Revolution made Rousseau, or at least his reputation as a political philosopher."[9]

The Study of Myself: Pierre Maine de Biran

In his first-person note on Rousseau, Robespierre singled out the *Confessions*, "that free and courageous emanation of the purest soul," as the most significant of the writings that helped him know himself and "appreciate the dignity" of his nature.[10] For him, as for most post-revolutionary thinkers, Rousseau the explorer of the inner self was of more lasting interest than Rousseau the social theorist. In the years that followed, the *Confessions* became the main inspiration for a new sort of French literature, the personal diary or *journal intime*. The first great practitioner of this genre was the philosopher François-Pierre-Gonthier Maine de Biran.

A few months before his death in 1824, Biran looked back with a certain amount of complacency on more than thirty years of self-study:

> It is quite a long time now that I have been involved in the study of man, or rather the study of myself; and at the end of an already long life, I can truthfully say that no other man has seen or *watched himself go by* as I have, even though I have been concerned most with those affairs that normally draw men out of themselves. I remember that even from my childhood I marveled at the sense of my existence; already I was led, as if by instinct, to look within in order to know how it was possible that I could be alive and be myself.[11]

Biran passed his childhood on his family's estate in southwest France. After completing his education, he was appointed to the king's bodyguard, and was present at Versailles in October 1789 when a mob broke into the palace and forced the king and queen to return to Paris. Back on his estate, he studied mathematics and philosophy, read Rousseau, took walks, and engaged in reflection. In 1794 he began a personal diary with the idea of bringing some scientific order to his musings. In this he followed the example of Montaigne, whose essays were meant to tame the "monsters" that beset him when he retired to *his* estate two hundred years earlier. But the literary form that Biran took up was new to France. The English, American, and German diary was an expression of Calvinist and Lutheran self-scrutiny, but this was not encouraged in Catholic countries where priestly mediation and private confession were the norm. French Catholics who engaged in personal intro-spection ran the risk of being condemned as Quietists, as were the mystic Jeanne Guynon and her clerical defender François Fénelon, the author of *The Inner Life*. Biran found Fénelon uplifting, Montaigne intriguing, Pascal and Rousseau inspiring, but neither Fénelon's treatises nor Montaigne's essays nor Pascal's *Pensées* nor Rousseau's *Confessions* provided him with the literary model he needed. He turned instead to the daily journal, hitherto used in France primarily for practical purposes, and transformed it into a repository for his inmost feelings and thoughts. "Today," he began under the date May 27, 1794,

> I had an experience too beautiful, too remarkable by its rarity ever to be forgotten. I was walking by myself a few minutes before sundown. The weather was perfect; spring was at its freshest and most brilliant; the whole world was clothed in that charm which can be felt by the soul, but not described in words. All that struck my senses filled my heart with a mysterious, sad sweetness. The tears stood in my eyes. Ravishment succeeded ravishment. If I could perpetuate this state, what would be lacking to my felicity? I should have found upon this earth the joys of heaven.[12]

We can only envy Biran his experience, particularly when we recall that he was writing during the Reign of Terror. Revolutionary leader Georges Danton was guillotined the previous month, Robespierre's turn would come in July. Biran made no mention of such events in his diary. His only aim, he wrote, was to achieve wisdom, and he had to do it on his own because there were no wisdom schools in France like those of ancient Rome. Besides, he doubted whether the indifference advocated by the Stoics could really lead to wisdom: "So long as you [he is addressing himself] remain in this state of indifference, so long as passion does not impel you to movement, you will languish in a life of obscurity." Aware he lacked the drive he needed, he gave himself a little pep talk: "Leave this peace, put your mental and physical instruments to violent use, throw yourself outward, choose an aim that will free your faculties from their numbness; become a man!"[13]

Biran then began to formulate the ideas that would rule his philosophical life. "What is this so-called activity of the soul?" he wrote. "It always seems to me that its state is determined by one or another state of the body." Such a thought was heretical in a philosophical environment defined by the rationalism of Descartes. Biran found some support for his ideas in the works of the French empiricist Étienne Bonnot de Condillac. Perhaps, Biran thought, he could "analyze the will as Condillac analyzed the understanding."[14] In his *Essay on the Origins of Human Knowledge* (1746), Condillac challenged Cartesian orthodoxy with an empiricism based on Locke's; but while Locke said that knowledge derived from sensation and also from sense-based reflection, Condillac insisted that *all* mental states were simply transformed sensations. Consciousness was an integrative power, letting us know that the perceptions that come in succession were ours, affecting "a being who is constantly the same *us*." Consciousness was the foundation of experience: without it "each moment of life would seem to be the first moment of our existence."[15]

Biran acknowledged his debt to Condillac in his first book, *The Influence of Habit on the Faculty of Thought* (1799); but he diverged from his predecessor in one important respect: he gave primary importance to the role of voluntary activity in the making of the self. "It is I who move or who *will* to move, and it again is I who am moved," he wrote. "Here are the two terms of the relation needed to ground the first simple judgment of personality: *I am*."[16] Descartes was famous for saying "I think, therefore I am." Biran countered: No, I *will*, therefore I am. It was willed physical effort meeting the resistance of the world that engendered the "I" of consciousness.

Reading Biran's diary thirty years after his death, the Swiss diarist Amiel noted sardonically: "Why does Maine de Biran make *will* the whole of man? Perhaps because he had too little will. A man esteems most highly what he himself lacks, and exaggerates what he longs to possess."[17] This is a bit unfair. While it is true that Biran spent most of his time on his estate, engaged in study, contemplation, and writing, he also took part in important events before, during, and after the Napoleonic era. In 1797 he was elected to the Council of Five Hundred, the lower house under the Directory. When that body was dissolved, he entered local politics and in 1805 was elected Deputy for Bergerac. He even became a member of a five-man commission charged with drafting a resolution asking for more personal freedom under the Empire. Napoleon denounced this commission but allowed Biran to return to his estate unharmed. Dictators were different in those days.

Despite such forays into public life, Biran was not a forceful personality. Irresolute in politics and inept in society, he let statesmen, society matrons, and even his sister push him around. He also was a terrible bore. A daughter of the Prefect of the Dordogne later recalled that when Biran came to dinner, he went on and on about the *moi* or self. She and her sister never forgot "that at every enunciation of this monosyllable, M. de Biran would forcefully press the tips of his extended, unseparated fingers against his chest, no doubt to affirm with greater emphasis the fact of his personality."[18]

The self was certainly the focus of Biran's intellectual and spiritual life. He reverted to the subject frequently in his diary but his explanations were often opaque. In the end, however, it was the experience of the self alone that established its existence. When a friend asked him what, after all, was this *moi* he was always taking about, Biran found he could not answer. That evening he wrote in his diary: "One has to situate oneself in the private point of view of consciousness. Then, when the unity that judges all phenomena while remaining unchanged is present, one sees the self, and one no longer has to ask what it is." This passage, from November 1817, makes it clear that he was moving toward mysticism even if he was not yet fully aware of it. He had begun to read books like *The Imitation of Christ*, and to introduce a religious coloring to his psychological observations. "What is this real state of our thinking and sensing being that is different from what we currently are aware of?" he wrote the same evening, "It is impossible for us to say, but God knows and sees."[19]

By December 1818, God had become a primary element in Biran's conception of self and world. He could distinguish, he wrote, three basic perspectives of self-consciousness. In the first, "I am nothing for me in myself"; I exist only in the eyes of others. In the second, "I separate myself from the outer world and judge it, but hold onto it as the object or term of all my mental operations." Finally, "I lose sight completely of the word outside and of myself, and the invisible world, God, is the object or goal of my thought." Turning his eyes, inevitably, to his personal existence, he concluded:

> In my best moods, up till now, I have been alone with myself. "Poor counsel wherein God hath no place," Fénelon says. The presence of God creates the way out of ourselves and that is what we need. But how can I reconcile this with my psychological doctrine of the *self*?"[20]

He eventually developed his idea of the three perspectives of self-consciousness into an elaborate theory of three "lives." There were, he wrote in his diary in September 1823, three principles in the human being, that is, "three lives and three orders of functioning." First was the life of sensation, which the human being shared with the animal. Second was human life properly speaking, which consisted of thought and volition. Finally there was "a superior nature, a third life" which makes us feel "that there is another happiness, another wisdom, another perfection, beyond the greatest human happiness." If he could properly analyze these three orders of functioning, "the result would be the most instructive and most complete treatise on *anthropology* ever written."[21] (At the time "anthropology" meant the study of human nature in general.) A short while later, he began his *New Essays on Anthropology*.

Up to the present, Biran wrote in the introduction to this book, philosophy had been concerned only with the life of sensations and the mind. The life of the spirit, the most important of man's three lives, had been "abandoned to the speculations of mysticism," though it, no less than the other two, was based "on facts of observation." But how was one to study these facts? Certainly, he wrote in his diary, "we must not limit ourselves to vain speculation." Spiritual experiences had to have causes, perhaps "purely subjective," perhaps "inherent in certain organic dispositions." To determine what these causes were was "the greatest and most difficult problem in the science of man." Here Biran was on the verge of establishing a true science of religion, but his Catholic training held him back. The data for his research had to be sought, he wrote, in "the code of the Christians, in all the words of Jesus Christ, as preserved in the Gospels." Speaking more like a missionary than a proto-William James, he wrote in his diary that Christianity alone "reveals to man a third life, superior to that of the sensibility and that of the human reason or will. No other system of philosophy has risen to that height."[22] In politics too Biran returned to his ancestral beliefs. After the Restoration of 1815, he reentered public life, becoming a champion of the resurrected monarchy.

Society is Too Powerful: Benjamin Constant

While Maine de Biran was using his diary to record his psychological observations and philosophical musings, his political adversary Benjamin Constant was using his to keep track of his convoluted personal life. These two pioneers of the French *journal intime* sometimes crossed paths in government assemblies and literary salons, but their diaries provide no evidence that they ever exchanged a word. Once, however, Biran recorded his impressions of Constant's novel *Adolphe*, which contained, he wrote, many "profound and subtle observations on the human heart." A good example is this reflection Constant gave to a friend of his tragic heroine, Ellénore:

The most passionate feeling is not capable of fighting the established order. Society is too powerful, it replicates itself in too many forms, it blends too much bitterness with love it has not sanctioned; it favours that tendency to inconstancy, and that impatient weariness, maladies of the soul, which sometimes suddenly seize on it in an intimate relationship.[23]

In his fiction, his politics, and his personal life, Constant was always preoccupied with freedom and with the power of society or other individuals to limit or deny it. In a famous passage written a year before his death, he said that he had always "defended the same principle: freedom in all things, in religion, philosophy, literature, industry and politics," adding, "And by freedom I mean the triumph of the individual both over an authority that would wish to govern by despotic means and over the masses who claim the right to make a minority subservient to a majority."[24]

It is likely that the circumstances of Constant's life helped nurture this yearning for freedom. Born in Lausanne in 1767, he grew up knowing the indignity of being ruled by another Swiss canton. His father, an army officer, was generally absent and always stern; his step-mother treated him badly. Most of the women he loved were older and imperious; they tormented him as he tormented them. The Revolution raised his hopes only to dash them when it began to devour its children. After the fall of Robespierre, he and his lover Germaine de Staël went to Paris and rose to prominence in enlightened political and literary circles. Becoming a French citizen, he served on Napoleon's advisory tribunal until the Emperor dismissed him for his outspokenness. Turning to theory, he worked on *The Principles of Politics,* one of the founding texts of liberalism, and wrote *Adolphe,* one of the greatest works of French Romanticism. After Napoleon's fall, he served as a deputy, becoming a forthright critic of the restored Bourbon monarchy. Yet this champion of freedom found freedom difficult to deal with in his own life. The words he put in the mouth of his alter ego Adolphe apply to him as well: "I was given complete freedom; and this freedom only made me the more impatient of the yoke that I appeared to have elected to bear."[25]

Constant's journals give evidence of psychological conflicts that make Adolphe look like a model of emotional health. His first journal, begun in 1803 when he was trying to decide between de Staël and another woman, took the form of a two-column cost-benefit analysis. This proved to be of little help in arriving at a decision: in such matters he always acted on impulse. In 1804 and 1805 he kept a regular record of his personal and intellectual life, with occasional reflections on his failure to impose order on the former. In April 1804, unable to shake a throng of unhappy thoughts, he wrote: "Have I then lost all power over myself? ... Is my destiny no longer in my own hands?" He concluded, "all I need in order to be happy is will," but this was the one thing he could never develop. A few days later he set down this remarkable piece of self-analysis: "What I have, even more than energy, is mobility. I have excellent qualities – pride, generosity, dedication – but I am not altogether an authentic person. There are two people in me, one of whom observes the other, knowing well that its convulsive movements must pass away."[26] In *Adolphe*, Constant has his hero explain the workings of this dual personality: "Almost always, in order to live at peace with ourselves, we disguise our failings and weaknesses, presenting them as expedients and schemes; this satisfies that part of us which, as it were, acts as spectator of the other."[27] Like Rousseau before him and Stendhal, Gide, and Sartre after, Constant used his fiction as well as his personal writings to develop a vernacular psychology.

At the end of 1804 – a year that saw him work diligently on a history of religion, meet Goethe, Schiller, and Herder in Weimar, continue his tumultuous relationship with de Staël, and become involved with two former mistresses, one of whom he eventually married – Constant reflected on the utility of his journal, which had become a friend he looked forward to meeting each evening, a discreet auditor he had developed "a sort of need" for:

When I began it I made it a rule to write down everything I experienced. I have kept to this rule as well as I could, but the habit of playing to the audience is so strong that I have not been able to keep to it completely. How strange is man, a being that can never be completely independent! Others are others, we can never make them *self*. ... Are others what I am? I do not know. ... Between us and that which is not us, there is an insurmountable barrier.

Still, he could not ignore the demands that others, de Staël in particular, made on him. "What a strange mania for isolation and independence has dominated my life," he wrote a few months later, "and by what even stranger weakness have I become of all men the most dependant on another and the least isolated!" His life became such a drama, the scenes so repetitive, that he began to use a number code for entries. Thus on June 30, 1805, a particularly bad day, he noted: "*Wrote to Mme de Staël, to Mme Dutertre. 12. 12. 2. Letter from Mme de Staël. 2. 2. 2. 2. 2. 2. 2. 2. 2. 2. 2. 2. 13 over 12. but 2 most certainly,*" where 12 = "love for Mme. Dutertre," 2 = "desire to break my eternal bond [with Mme. de Staël], which comes up so often," and 13 = "uncertainty about everything."[28] He eventually broke his "eternal bond" with de Staël, but he could not cut the bonds that tied him to society.

As Adolphe discovered, the social structure "weighs so heavily upon us, its hidden influence is so powerful, that it very soon shapes us into the universal mould."[29]

A Man at War with Society: Stendhal

Although hardly religious in the conventional sense of the term, Constant spent many years laboring on a book in which he traced the origin and evolution of the religious impulse. He began by saying that religion was an incontestable fact but was careful to distinguish institutional and personal religion. The only way to discover the true "religious sentiment" was "to descend into the depths of one's soul."[30] There is no sign in his diary that he ever attempted to do this, unless by "soul" he meant an amalgam of passion and thought; but he did write once that he was repelled by outright atheism and that he had a "religious corner," adding immediately that it was "all sentiment and vague emotion: it could not be reduced to a system."[31] Henri Beyle (Stendhal) was an early reader of Constant's book and he thought it was a waste of ink and paper. He told an acquaintance that "what the author called 'religious sentiment' does not exist by nature, that it is the result of indoctrination." People who profess to be religious make use of this sentiment or rather this appetite to satisfy their ambitions and desires.[32] Such is the role that "religious sentiment" plays in Stendhal's novels.

Stendhal fled his native Grenoble at the age of sixteen, ostensibly to study at the École Polytechnique but actually to find fame as a writer and satisfaction as a lover. Disappointed by Paris, he enlisted in the army and took part in Napoleon's Italian campaign. In Milan in 1801 he began to keep a diary, writing "the history of my life day by day" to prepare himself for what was to come. His literary ambition was boundless. Two months after his twentieth birthday he wrote that his goal was "to acquire the reputation of being the greatest French poet, not by intrigue, like Voltaire, but by truly earning it." A year later, with no fame in sight, he gave himself a bit of good advice: "To create sublime works, you must live only for your genius: form it, cultivate it, correct it."[33] For this, the journal was his primary instrument. He used it as a storehouse for things observed and felt, but also as a workshop of personality. As the nineteenth-century critic Jules Lemaître noted, Stendhal's diary "was no involuntary, casual outpouring," but a means for the writer "to modify himself, to fashion himself little by little in accordance with a predetermined aim." For Stendhal "to analyze himself was to act," for he was, above all, a man of action.[34]

In 1806 he joined the army again, serving in Germany, Austria, and Russia. In 1810, at the age of twenty-seven, he was appointed to the Council of State. Somehow he found time to write a book on Italian painting but unfortunately lost the manuscript during the Grand Army's retreat from Moscow. His diary entries during these years make him look like a sort of profane Puritan. He needed, he wrote in October 1808, to engage incessantly "in the examination of my consciousness: as a man who seeks to form his character, his manners, to instruct himself, to amuse himself, to learn the tricks of his trade."[35] After Napoleon's final defeat, he returned to Milan and applied himself to writing, eventually making a name for himself with critical works on painting and music. Expelled from Italy in 1821, he settled in Paris, frequenting the polite society he despised. His retrospective account of this period, *Memoirs of an Egotist*, traces the path of the sensitive but self-confident writer through the streets, salons, and bedrooms of the capital, and pillories the narrow-minded smugness and hypocrisy of France under the Restoration.

Stendhal's diary, which he worked on until 1823, is both a revelation and a concealment. Addressing himself to an imaginary future reader, he noted that it was meant to be "a mathematical and rigid report of my manner of being, neither too favorable or too unfavorable, but stating purely and severely what I believe to have taken place." It was, he continued, "a written part of my intimate consciousness and what is most worth while, what I have felt at the sound of music by Mozart, while reading Tasso, upon being awakened by a barrel organ, while giving my arm to my mistress of the moment, is not to be found here. Hence, I beseech you on bended knee not to make fun of me."[36] Three characteristics of his personality are visible in this short passage: extreme sensitivity, egocentricity, and a conflicted relationship with society. He called sensitivity his "defining trait," and was aware that it pushed him to excesses that others could not understand. When he loved, he wrote grandiloquently, his love was "too vast and too beautiful not to be ridiculed in society."[37] But when he was able to bridle it, this childish sensitivity became part of a mature self-scrutiny: "*Nosce te ipsum* [know thyself]," he wrote in 1811. "I believe with [the philosopher Destutt de] Tracy and the Greeks that this is the road to happiness." But for him the self was not a philosophical abstraction but rather a palpable sensation, felt always in relationship to others. If he wanted to be himself, he wrote, he should have "no project in society except that of making myself suffer there."[38] And suffer he did; the times seemed to demand it. "In the present order of society," he wrote in a letter to a friend, "lofty souls must almost always be unhappy, the more so in that they scorn the obstacle that stands in the way of their happiness."[39] Stendhal passed this destiny on to Julien Sorel, the hero of *The*

Red and the Black, who was, as the narrator of the novel puts it, "an unhappy man at war with the whole of society."[40]

Like Stendhal when he left Grenoble to seek his fortune, Julien is sensitive, intelligent, and inordinately ambitious. A carpenter's son, he is on the lookout for insults when he is employed by the mayor of his town. When the mayor's wife shows him genuine affection, he tells himself: "This woman cannot despise me any longer"; that being the case, "I ought to be stirred by her beauty; I owe it to myself to be her lover."[41] Later, when he is given a place in the house of a peer of the realm, he again foresees the worst: "I am going to be treated with the utmost contempt, and nothing will amuse me more. ... Yes, to cover with ridicule that odious being whom I call myself will amuse me."[42] Rousseau would have said that Julien had no love of self but an incredibly strong sense of self-love. This pushes him to seduce the peer's daughter, and soon he has been ennobled and given a commission in the army. But before he can enjoy his success, his first lover reveals his duplicity. Enraged, he returns to his hometown and shoots wildly at her. Put on trial for attempted murder, the two women in his life come to his aid, but he spoils his chances for acquittal by telling the jury that he deserves death for his crime, adding:

> Even were I less guilty, I see before me men who, without pausing to consider what pity may be due to my youth, will seek to punish in me and to discourage forever that class of young men who, born in an inferior station and in a sense burdened with poverty, have the good fortune to secure a sound education, and the audacity to mingle with what the pride of rich people calls society.[43]

This seals his fate. He goes to the guillotine unrepentant: "I have been ambitious," he tells himself, "I have no wish to reproach myself," for he had only acted in accordance with the spirit of the times.[44]

Between *The Red and the Black* and his other masterpiece, *The Charterhouse of Parma*, Stendhal worked on his most autobiographical novel, *Lucien Leuwen*, and two memoirs, *Memoirs of an Egotist* and *Life of Henry Brulard*. In all these works he is in search of his true "I," but as usual he found it hard to free the "I" from the grasp of society. The hero of *Lucien Leuwen* is from a rich family but is just as obsessed as Julien Sorel about his social position. "Am I in the middle of the list, or right at the end?" he wonders. After falling in love with a high-born widow, his self-questioning becomes acute. "In truth," he tells her, "I don't know what I am, and I would give a lot to anyone who could tell me."[45] Lucien's puzzlement was echoed by Stendhal himself in the first chapter of *Life of Henry Brulard*: "I'm going to be fifty, it's high time I knew myself. What have I been? What am I? The truth is, I'd be very hard put to say." As always with Stendhal, the answer is to be found by sorting out his relationships with others. In the end he decides that the history of his life is the history of his relationships with women. "What then have I been? I can't know. Of which friend can I ask that, however enlightened? Mr. di Fiori [a close friend] himself couldn't give me an opinion. To which friend have I ever said a word about my disappointments in love?"[46]

What is this "I": Delacroix, Vigny, Amiel

Stendhal yearned to be great and used his diary as a means to achieve this. He also preached his gospel of greatness to others. Eight years after the novelist's death in 1842, the painter Eugène Delacroix noted in his diary that Stendhal had once written to him: "Don't neglect anything that could *make you great.*"[47] Delacroix found this rather pathetic, yet he too was driven to use every waking hour to attain greatness in his chosen field. He began his diary in 1822, the year *The Barque of Dante*, his first major painting, was exhibited at the Paris Salon. His intention was to write "for himself alone; therefore I will, I hope, be true; I will become better by means of it." A quarter century later, he wrote in a similar vein: "Laziness is certainly the greatest obstacle to the development of our faculties. The 'Know thyself' is thus the fundamental axiom of every society in which each member will carry out his assigned role and fulfill it completely."[48] Interested in the progressive movements of his day, he had a more optimistic view of society than Stendhal; but he also stood for the dignity of the individual, thus echoing the Romantic writers of Germany and England. This passage of his diary recalls the critique of Enlightenment rationality of a Herder or Blake:

> Scientists and philosophers seem to be much less advanced than ordinary people, because they have not succeeded in proving that which they use for proof. I am a man. What is this *I?* What is *a man?* They spend half their lives putting things together bit by bit and going over all they have discovered; they spend the second half laying the foundations of an edifice that never rises from the ground.[49]

Literary Romanticism was a late arrival in France, despite the pioneering work of Rousseau. The Revolution and its aftershocks made it difficult for French writers to explore the new ideas coming out of Germany. Full-blown Romanticism did not really arrive until the late 1820s in the work of Victor Hugo and Alfred de Vigny. Both kept diaries, but Hugo's is simply a record of his literary, political, social, and sexual activities. He "never had the leisure to look into himself," observed the scholar Ernest Renan.[50] Vigny was the reverse. An introvert by nature, he became even more so when he retired to his estate in southwest France for the last twenty-five years of his life. He wrote nothing for publication, but read, reflected, and developed a highly introspective psychology. "Nothing in me suspends, stops or troubles this invincible inner *attention* of my mind to plumb, question, analyze what I do, what others do to me, what happens to me, what others say to me," he wrote in 1856. This self-examination brought him many insights, such as this one he headed "*Reverie – Examination of consciousness*": "I am so impressionable that the thing before me draws my attention with an intensity that is like a passion. At that moment, the past as well as the future efface themselves, leaving only the present moment." But though drawn to the contemplative life (he was one of the first Europeans to take a respectful interest in Buddhism), he never ceased to apply his insights to the problems of poetic expression, as in this passage from his diary:

> ON PURE THOUGHT. – Thought alone, pure Thought, the inner practice of ideas and their play among themselves, is a genuine happiness for me. ...

> What is important is to delight in the full possession of thought and in the anticipated view of the form and accomplished beauty of a sovereignly beautiful work.[51]

Such a work was "Pure Spirit," the last poem he wrote, which has a verve recalling the flights of Shelley and Wordsworth at the dawn of the Romantic era:

> Your reign has come, PURE SPIRIT, King of the World!
> When your azure wing surprised us in the night,
> Goddess of our conduct, marauding War
> Reigned over our forebears. Today it is THE WRIT,
> THE UNIVERSAL WRIT ... [52]

But by 1863, when this poem was written, the Romantic impulse had played itself out, not least in France, where "marauding War" was opening the way to the military disaster of 1870. A spirit of ironic detachment replaced the passionate engagement of the revolutionary years as well as the confident religiosity of the period before and after.

Henri-Frédéric Amiel began keeping a diary as a nineteen-year-old in 1838 and continued until a few days before his death in 1881. The result is not only the longest but also one of the most penetrating examples of the French *journal intime* – a 17,000-page journey from pious faith to philosophical uncertainty. Born in Geneva, Amiel inherited from his Calvinist forebears a religious temperament and the habit of self-examination. He began his odyssey as a rather conventional Christian: "There is but one thing needful," he wrote in 1848, "to possess God. All our senses, all our powers of mind and soul, all our external resources, are so many ways of approaching the divinity, so many modes of tasting and of adoring God. … Only be at peace with self, live in the presence of God, in communion with Him." He wrote this in Berlin, where he had gone to study philosophy. The Idealism of Fichte, Schelling, and Hegel soon colored his Calvinism: "The center of the universe," he wrote in 1852, "is still the self, the great *Ich* ["I"] of Fichte. The tameless liberty, the divine dignity of the individual spirit, expanding till it admits neither any limit nor anything foreign to itself, and conscious of a strength instinct with creative force."[53]

Amiel became a professor of philosophy in Geneva, publishing an occasional article as well as a few volumes of philosophical verse. His friends were disappointed that he did not produce more; unknown to them, he was putting the best of his literary energy into the diary. It was, he wrote in 1864, "my dialogue, my society, my companion, my confidant. It is also my consolation, my memory, my punching-bag, my echo, the reservoir of my intimate experiences, my psychological itinerary, my protection against intellectual rust, my reason for living, virtually the only useful thing I can leave behind me."[54] He wrote in it daily, sometimes several times a day, recording his impressions of the things around him, the books he read and passing events, but most of all his reflections on life and self.

The Calvinist imprint remained strong for many years. His work, he wrote in 1858, "consists in taming, subduing, evangelizing and *angelizing* the evil self; and in restoring harmony with the good self. Salvation lies in abandoning the evil self in principle and in taking refuge with the other, the divine self." But eventually he came to feel that the monotheistic religions, "founded upon an infantine cosmogony, and upon a chimerical history of humanity," were impotent in an age of science. He felt more at home with Buddhism and Hinduism and with the thought of his German contemporary Arthur Schopenhauer, who spoke to him by stressing "impersonality, objectivity, pure contemplation, the negation of will, calmness, and disinterestedness, an aesthetic study of the world, detachment from life, the renunciation of all desire, solitary meditation." The result of Amiel's own meditations was a phenomenology of self that was at the same time "a window opened upon the mystery of the world":

> I am a spectator, so to speak, of the molecular whirlwind which men call individual life; I am conscious of an incessant metamorphosis, an irresistible movement of existence, which is going on within me. I am

sensible of the flight, the revival, the modification, of all the atoms of my
being, all the particles of my river, all the radiations of my special force.

As death approached, he became more and more preoccupied with the
idea of self-abnegation as a way to greater self-consciousness. "Oh, for
escape from self, for something to stifle the importunate voice of want and
yearning!" he wrote in 1880; but the same year he had some overwhelming
experiences of pure selfhood: "Existence is reduced to the simplest form, the
most ethereal mode of being, that is, to pure self-consciousness. It is a state
of harmony, without tension and without disturbance, the dominical state
of the soul, perhaps the state which awaits it beyond the grave." In February
1881, three months before his death, he wrote that what remained to him
from his studies and contemplation was his "new phenomenology of mind,
an intuition of universal metamorphosis":

> All particular convictions, all definite principles, all clear-cut formulas
> and fixed ideas, are but prejudices, useful in practice, but still narrow-
> nesses of the mind. The absolute in detail is absurd and contradictory.
> … It is lawful to be *man*, but it is needful also to be *a* man, to be an
> individual.[55]

This "phenomenology" appealed to few of those who read Amiel's journal
when it was published after his death. His first readers were attracted mainly
by his style and originality. It was only years later that philosophical critics
became interested in his personal quest of self – or of no-self.

The introspective diaries of Amiel, Vigny, and Biran were not typical of
the French *journal intime* as it took shape during the nineteenth century.
The master theme of French writing during this period was the struggle of
men and woman to balance the need for personal freedom with the demands
of society. Rousseau sketched the outlines of this struggle in his memoirs,
novels, and treatises. Constant, Stendhal, and others filled in the details,
developing what one historian has called a characteristically French "model
of selfhood as a way to live independently within a society that infused its
spirit of domination into every personal and social relation."[56] No surprise
then that France was one of two countries where early nineteenth-century
scholars laid the groundwork for the scientific study of society. Henri de
Saint-Simon and Charles Fourier were major influences on Auguste Comte
and the other fathers of sociology, and their experiments in communal
living became the prototypes of later attempts at social planning. The other
country, or rather country-in-making, where philosophers and scholars
did pioneering work in the development of social theory was France's great
continental rival, Germany.

Idealism and Irrationalism

The self posits itself, *and by virtue of this mere self-assertion, it* exists;
and conversely, the self exists *and* posits *its own existence by virtue of*
merely existing.

– Johann Gottlieb Fichte

Damn and hell, I can abstract from everything but not from myself;
I can't even forget myself when I sleep.

– Søren Kierkegaard

Society became a subject of study only after the emergence of the self-conscious individual made society stand out as a recognizable entity. Before that it was just the water in which everybody swam. People have always been aware of their place in the social order but until the sixteenth century they rarely viewed this order as something that could be different from what it was. Kings were kings, aristocrats were aristocrats, priests were priests. The emergence of the individual during the Renaissance prepared the way for a radical rethinking of social relationships. Seventeenth- and eighteenth-century philosophers challenged assumptions that had been taken for granted since time immemorial. Locke, in his *Second Treatise on Civil Government*, affirmed that all people were "equal and independent" and that therefore "no one ought to harm another in his life, health, liberty, or possessions" – an idea taken up and transformed by Thomas Jefferson in the United States Declaration of Independence. Kant in his *Lectures on Ethics* wrote in a similar vein: "There is nothing more sacred in the wide world than the rights of others."[1] The idea that individual people, whatever their origin, had inalienable rights was something new in the history of the world, and it had explosive consequences during the revolutionary era. Even after the restoration of the monarchy in England and France, liberal thinkers such as Constant and John Stuart Mill kept the cult of the individual alive. At the other end of the spectrum, conservative thinkers such as Edmund Burke and Joseph de Maistre laid stress on the importance of existing political and social institutions at the expense of individual liberty.

In the states that were amalgamating themselves into the German nation, there were conservative as well as liberal tendencies, along with a strong thrust of cultural nationalism. These elements found their way into the social and political works of the three leading Idealist philosophers of the early nineteenth century: Johann Gottlieb Fichte, Friedrich Wilhelm Joseph Schelling, and Georg Wilhelm Friedrich Hegel. All three are better known for their metaphysical systems, but in these too the relationship between the individual and the collectivity, or the self and the Whole, played an important role. All of them wrote copiously on the "I" or subject but never from a first-person point of view. Their extreme impersonality and hyper-rationality pushed a number of writers of the next generation to stress the importance of personal responsibility and the limitations of reason.

The Individual is a Matter of Indifference: Fichte, Schelling, Hegel

Fichte and Schelling are now looked on primarily as bridges between two better-known philosophers, Kant and Hegel. As a young man, Fichte saw Kant in Königsberg and wrote a very Kantian essay that the master himself praised; but he later rejected one of the cornerstones of Kant's philosophy: the distinction between the phenomenal and noumenal worlds. There was no need, he said, to regard the world of phenomenal appearances as real and therefore no need to distinguish a separate noumenal world of things-in-themselves. There is only one world and one thing-in-itself, namely, the universal *Ich* or I, which brings itself into being by the act of self-knowledge. This left Fichte with the task of explaining how the material world and individual beings came into existence. He said, roughly speaking, that the I or Ego posits or puts itself forward in opposition to the Non-Ego. Ego and Non-Ego limit each other (if they didn't, they would cancel each other out). In opposition to the limited Non-Ego, the Ego posits empirical egos and the natural world. The result is the separate beings and things we experience from day to day.

Fichte's *Foundations of Natural Right* is almost as difficult as his metaphysical works, but it contains much of interest for the study of the history of the self, particularly the idea that self-consciousness is a social phenomenon. To posit itself as a self-conscious being, the rational being must posit itself "as an *individual*, as one among several rational beings that it assumes to exist outside itself." Free beings that mutually assume each another's existence have the option of living in community. "I must think of myself as necessarily in community with other human beings with whom nature has united me," Fichte wrote, "but I cannot do this without thinking of my freedom as limited through their freedom."[2] Descending from the rarified air of philosophical speculation, Fichte applied his communitarian ideas to the problem of German nationhood. He was an early supporter of the French Revolution and its ideals of liberty, equality, and fraternity but was opposed to Napoleon's seizing of German lands. Drawing on the idea of the nation-soul that had been developed by Herder and other Romantic thinkers, Fichte urged the German people to resist incorporation into a universal monarchy. "Only when each people, left to itself, develops and forms itself in accordance with its own peculiar quality," he said in a famous lecture, "and only when in every people each individual develops himself in accordance with that common quality, as well as in accordance with his own peculiar quality – then, and then only, does the manifestation of divinity appear in its true mirror as it ought to be." If nations allowed the qualities that make them distinctive to be diluted or worn away, the flatness that resulted "would bring about a separation from spiritual nature, and this in its turn will cause all men to be fused together in their uniform and collective destruction."[3]

Schelling began as an expositor of Fichte's philosophy but quickly moved beyond him. Fichte believed that the natural world lay outside the realm of philosophy. Schelling, who was fascinated by the latest scientific discoveries, wanted to bring metaphysics and science together. In his *System of Transcendental Philosophy*, published in 1800, he distinguished two approaches to knowledge: natural philosophy, which starts from the objective world and moves toward the Absolute, and transcendental philosophy, which starts from the Absolute and moves toward nature. Each system finds completeness when it "reverts back into its own principle." Thus "transcendental philosophy would be completed only if it could demonstrate this identity" – the identity between objective and subjective knowledge – "in its own principle (namely the self)."[4] Schelling went on in this early work to suggest that aesthetic knowledge and artistic creation were the only ways by which this identity could be established; but later in life he was drawn to Christian mysticism, and eventually became a defender of traditional Christian beliefs, such as the incarnation: "The self, as itself a personality, desires personality," he wrote in a late work, "it demands a Person who is outside of the world and above the universal, and who understands – a Heart that is like unto our own."[5]

In his philosophy of nature, Schelling proposed that Spirit moved toward complete self-consciousness through an evolutionary process. This progression, he wrote, was "the greatest and most marvellous drama, which only an infinite mind could have composed." So conceived, historical progress had to be viewed as a collective and not an individual phenomenon.

In the end, society would be reborn in the nation, and poetry, science, and religion would "find their objectivity in the spiritual and political unity of a people." The "ethical and religious totality" of the nation would be embodied in the state.[6]

We can take a breather here and highlight some of Fichte's and Schelling's main themes. As Idealist philosophers, both held that reality is fundamentally mental or spiritual. Both were influenced by Kant but rejected his idea of a noumenal world with unknowable things-in-themselves. Both believed that it is through self-knowledge that Ego or the Absolute brings itself and the world into being. Both affirmed that individual selves are associated with one another in communities or societies, which take political form as nations or states. These are expressions of the Absolute, and have a role to play in the Absolute's unfolding. All these ideas reappear, in altered form, in Hegel's all-encompassing system.

Hegel was a roommate of Schelling's at the University of Tübingen, and for some time they worked on similar lines. But Hegel came to think that Schelling's Absolute was too close to Kant's unknowable noumenal realm. The absolute Spirit does not transcend reality, he said; it is immanent in it and emerges as the result of "a long and laborious journey" from primitive sense-consciousness to absolute self-consciousness. This comes about in the process of Spirit's "positing itself, or in mediating with its own self its transitions from one state or position to the opposite."[7] This rather opaque passage, which unfortunately is typical of his style, relates to the famous Hegelian dialectic: an existing proposition or state of affairs engenders its own contradiction, which leads to the development of a new proposition or state of affairs, which overcomes that which came before while preserving what was valuable in it. This three-step process of thesis, antithesis, and synthesis (terms not used in this connection by Hegel himself) is also found in some of his predecessors. What is distinctive about Hegel's dialectic is that it is realized in the process of world history and applied to actual societies and institutions.

There have been, Hegel wrote in his *Philosophy of History*, three stages of the movement of Spirit through history: the Oriental world, the classical world, and the Germanic world. Orientals never attained to the knowledge "that Spirit – Man *as such* – is free." Therefore they were ruled by despots. Hegel believed that "the consciousness of Freedom first arose among the Greeks." They and later the Romans were free but they regarded only some of their fellows as equally free. Therefore they kept slaves and "their whole life and the maintenance of their splendid liberty, was implicated with the institution of slavery," while their freedom was transient and limited. "The first to attain the consciousness that man, as man, is free: that it is the *freedom* of Spirit which constitutes its essence" were, in Hegel's opinion, the Germanic nations. "This consciousness arose first in religion" – and by religion he meant Christianity – "but to introduce the principle into the various relations of the actual world, involves a more extensive problem than its simple implantation." When the process is complete, the freedom of all will find a home in the modern state. This was the aim of the historical dialectic, for "the History of the world is none other than the progress of the consciousness of Freedom."[8]

Hegel presented his ideas on the development of self-consciousness and the significance of world history in a number of works that are long, complex, and often impenetrable. We will confine ourselves here to a few points related to the idea of the self. First, self-consciousness in Hegel, even more than in Fichte, is a social phenomenon. We obtain self-consciousness by becoming aware of ourselves as objects of others' knowledge; others become conscious of themselves in the same way. The result is a struggle for recognition, which Hegel explained by means of the "master-bondsman" relationship. "Self-consciousness," he began, "exists in itself and for itself, in that, and by the fact that it exists for another self-consciousness; that is to say, it *is* only by being acknowledged or 'recognized.'" Two individual consciousnesses are linked in an unequal relation: one is the master, the other the bondsman. The master sees the bondsman as an object whose only role is production; but soon the master lapses into meaningless enjoyment, while the bondsman, by means of goal-directed activity, achieves self-knowledge and overcomes the master. Hegel concluded that "it is solely by risking life that freedom is obtained; only thus is it tried and proved that the essential nature of self-consciousness is not bare existence, is not the merely immediate form in which it at first makes its appearance, is not its mere absorption in the expanse of life. … The individual, who has not staked his life, may, no doubt, be recognized as a Person; but he has not attained the truth of this recognition as an independent self-consciousness."[9]

Hegel's dwelling on freedom might give the impression that he would have endorsed the self-sufficient individual of Locke, Jefferson, Constant, and others of the liberal tradition, or the organic individual of Goethe, Shelley, and other Romantic writers. He certainly would not have done so. The individual in Hegel is always subordinate to Spirit. It is Spirit that moves through history using transient individuals as its instruments. We have reached a time, Hegel wrote,

> when the universal nature of spiritual life has become so very much emphasized and strengthened, and the mere individual aspect has become, as it should be, correspondingly a matter of indifference, when,

too, that universal aspect holds, by the entire range of its substance, the full measure of the wealth it has built up, and lays claim to it all, the share in the total work of mind that falls to the activity of any particular individual can only be very small. Because this is so, the individual must all the more forget himself.[10]

Unfortunately, as Hegel explained in lectures given shortly before his death in 1831, at this crucial moment in the evolution of Spirit, people talked about virtue rather than putting it into practice and even looked for ways to avoid doing their duty. At the same time "the isolation of individuals from each other and from the Whole makes its appearance; their aggressive selfishness and vanity; their seeking personal advantage and consulting this at the expense of the State at large." To prevent this, God put a check on transient things and established "something inherently and independently durable," namely "the principle of thought, perception, reasoning, insight derived from rational grounds."[11] This principle will last forever, transient individuals will pass away.

Will as Irrational Impulse: Arthur Schopenhauer

Hegel believed that the history of philosophy and indeed of the world had reached its culmination in his system. Spirit, he wrote, had achieved full self-realization "as the result of its knowing itself to be absolute spirit." It manifested itself unconsciously in nature, "but in the State, in the deeds and life of History, as also of Art, it brings itself to pass with consciousness." He did not say so outright but left it to be understood that the subject of this absolute knowledge was none other than Georg Wilhelm Friedrich Hegel and that the state in question was the Prussian monarchy. It was thus with a certain amount of self-satisfaction that he declared at the end of his lectures on the history of philosophy that "a new epoch has arisen in the world" and that the evolution of spiritual forms was "concluded."[12]

Hegel enjoyed great celebrity during his lifetime and his philosophy remained influential well into the twentieth century, but he was not without his detractors. The most obstreperous and brilliant was Arthur Schopenhauer, who called Hegel's philosophy "a colossal piece of mystification which will yet provide posterity with an inexhaustible theme for laughter."[13] Schopenhauer's principal work, *The World as Will and Representation*, went completely unnoticed after its publication in 1818. Two years later he deliberately scheduled his lectures at the University of Berlin at the same hour as Hegel's. Practically no one showed up, and he abandoned the idea of pursuing an academic career.

Strongly influenced by Kant, Schopenhauer began *The World as Will and Representation* with the boldly Kantian assertion: "The world is my representation," that is, it exists only in reference to myself.[14] But Schopenhauer rejected Kant's idea that the noumenal world, the world of things-in-themselves, is unknowable. It is possible, he said, to lift the veil of phenomena and to see the underlying reality. This, the solitary thing-in-itself, is Will. By this Schopenhauer did not mean conscious volition, because Will is unconscious, an eternal purposeless striving that can never be satisfied. Individual acts have purposes, but "willing as a whole has no end in view." In the human being, it exists primarily in the form of the will-to-live, which manifests itself "as an untiring mechanism, as an irrational impulse, which does not have its sufficient ground or reason in the external world."[15] It is this that drives living beings to preserve themselves and reproduce. In the early nineteenth century, before Darwin and Freud, this idea was revolutionary.

According to Schopenhauer, our knowledge of Will comes to us through the medium of our bodies. Like other physical objects, bodies are representations. We know the body as "an object among objects" by means of the senses; but we also know it immediately as will. An act of will and a movement of the body "do not stand in the relation of cause and effect, but are one and the same thing." Stated otherwise, "the whole body is nothing but the objectified will, i.e., will that has become representation."[16] These ideas on body and will are similar to Maine de Biran's, though Schopenhauer (who never mentioned modern philosophers without disdain) was at pains to distance himself from Biran in the second volume of his treatise. His own ideas on these subjects were later picked up by Friedrich Nietzsche, who brought Vitalism to the forefront of Western philosophy just as Idealism was beginning to pale.

To Schopenhauer the world is a horrible place, and Will the cause of endless suffering. Human beings are capable of freeing themselves from the hold of this purposeless force but fail to do so because they are prey to a delusion that makes them see themselves and other objects as isolated things. He explained this *principium individuationis* or principle of individuation in an extended metaphor:

> Just as the boatman sits in his small boat, trusting his frail craft in a stormy sea that is boundless in every direction, rising and falling with the howling, mountainous waves, so in the midst of a world full of suffering and misery the individual man calmly sits, supported by and trusting the *principium individuationis*, or the way in which the individual knows things as phenomenon. ... His vanishing person, his extensionless present, his momentary gratification, these alone have reality for him.[17]

The only way out of the delusion of individuality and the suffering that goes along with it is to deny the will by means of knowledge "until at last in the individual case this knowledge is purified and enhanced by suffering itself." Then the individual

> sees through the form of the phenomenon, the *principium individu-ationis*; the egoism resting on this expires with it. The *motives* that were previously so powerful now lose their force, and instead of them, the complete knowledge of the real nature of the world, acting as a *quieter* of the will, produces resignation, the giving up not merely of life, but of the whole will-to-live itself.[18]

For most people, the best way to experience this quieting of the will is through aesthetic creation and appreciation. Artistic genius, Schopenhauer wrote, is the ability to see the timeless principle behind the individual form; this demands "a complete forgetting of our own person and of its relations and connexions." Stated otherwise, artistic genius is "the most complete *objectivity*, i.e., the objective tendency of the mind, as opposed to the subjective directed to our own person."[19] For those capable of such objectivity, the contemplation of works of genius gives them the only true pleasure they will ever experience. A more radical way of denying the will is through ascetic practices. Surprisingly for a confirmed atheist, Schopenhauer turned to the world's religious traditions for examples of such self-denial. By the time he published the later editions of *The World as Will and Representation*, he was aware of the similarities between his philosophy and certain forms of Hinduism and Buddhism. While he rejected their "myths and meaningless words," he agreed with the goal they proposed: self-extinction or absorption in the impersonal.[20] Despite all the differences between Schopenhauer and Hegel, they agreed on one important point: the individual is nothing.

What It Means to Live as a Human Being: Søren Kierkegaard

Reading Fichte or Schelling or Hegel on the I or Ego or Self, it sometimes seems as if they were unaware that they possessed such a thing themselves. It's all very well to talk about the Self positing itself, but what about the self that all conscious beings regard as the basis of their identity? It's fine to talk about the collective Self becoming aware of itself in History, but what about the individual choices that we have to make from day to day? These were the sort of questions Søren Kierkegaard asked himself while he was reading Schelling and Hegel at the University of Copenhagen during the early 1830s.

Kierkegaard had gone to the university to study theology with the idea of becoming a priest. He had absorbed from his father, a stern, depressive Lutheran, an acute sense of sin and suffering. The weight of this was so great that decades later he could write in his journal of "my life's dark background from the very earliest time; the anxiety with which my father filled my soul, his own terrible melancholy, the many things I cannot even note down in this respect." At one point the young Kierkegaard experienced what he called a psychological "earthquake" that pressed upon him "a new infallible law for the interpretation of all phenomena." He never explained what this "law" was but commented on it in terms of his roots: that his father's "great age was not a divine blessing but rather a curse," that his family's mental abilities "existed only for tearing us apart," and "the thought of my considerable mental talents was my only consolation, ideas my only joy, people of no consequence for me."[21]

Kierkegaard was a brilliant student and in an effort to shake off his melancholy he played the role of a witty bon vivant. But his inner discontent remained. One evening in 1836 he wrote in his journal: "I have just come back from a party where I was the life and soul. Witticisms flowed from my lips. Everyone laughed and admired me – but I left, yes, that dash should be as long as the radii of the earth's orbit —————— and wanted to shoot myself." But there were also moments of illumination, as in this entry of 1838: "There is an *indescribable joy* that is kindled in us just as inexplicably as the apostle's unmotivated exclamation: 'Rejoice, and again I say, Rejoice'. – Not a joy over this or that, but a full-bodied shout of the soul."[22]

Kierkegaard had begun to keep a journal, or rather to jot down his reflections, in 1833, when he was twenty. From the start he was concerned with the application of knowledge to life. "What I really need," he wrote in 1835, "is to be clear about *what I am to do*, not what I must know." He still saw his destiny in terms of religion – finding out "what the Deity really wants *me* to do" – but it was a very personal religion: "the thing is to find a truth which is truth *for me*, to find *the idea for which I am willing to live and die*." The death of his father in 1838 affected him to such an extent that he believed the aged man had "died *for* me, so that something might still come of me."[23] Reapplying himself to his theological studies, he graduated with honors in 1841. Although now able to enter the ministry, he never took a position in the Danish state church.

In 1837 Kierkegaard fell in love with a fourteen-year-old girl named Regine Olsen. In September 1840 he proposed to her and was accepted, but a year later he broke off the engagement. His reasons for doing so are not fully clear. In his journals, where he wrote of her repeatedly, he spoke of his unwillingness "to initiate her into terrible things," such as his relationship with his father, or to reveal "the eternal night brooding deep inside me."[24] Like much of what he wrote about Regine, this passage is overwrought, but it is certain that he took his decision deliberately and that it had much to do with his vocation as a writer. "Three cheers for the perils of life in service to the idea," he wrote in *Repetition, A Venture in Experimental Psychology*, which he published in 1843.[25] This book, about a man who proposed marriage but changed his mind, is an example of how Kierkegaard used autobiographical material in his literary works.

Kierkegaard published eleven books in 1844 and 1845. Among them are four of his masterpieces: *Either/Or, Fear and Trembling, Philosophical Fragments*, and *The Concept of Anxiety*. All of these, along with *Repetition*, appeared pseudonymously. Kierkegaard did it this way not so much to conceal his authorship as to try out different identities – something like a Web writer using different screen names. The philosophical background of all five works is the historical dialectic of Hegel. Kierkegaard admitted in his journal that he had "learned much" from the German philosopher, but he felt that anyone who has been tested in life "will find Hegel comical despite all his greatness." In particular, "all this nonsense about world-evolution now assuming a higher level" had to be rejected, because it "overlooks the significance of individuals in the race." Hegel's dialectic sought a both/and solution; Kierkegaard insisted that any real choice had to be either/or. There was no way to avoid risk and possible loss. As he explained later in his intellectual autobiography, when he was working on *Either/Or* he realized that "I could not possibly succeed in striking the comforting and secure *via media* in which most people pass their lives: I had either to cast myself into perdition and sensuality, or to chose the religious absolutely as the only thing." The question that was tormenting him was "how to become a Christian."[26] From a certain point of view, this wasn't a problem at all. As a Danish citizen he was automatically a member of the Danish Lutheran Church. Besides he had a Ph.D. in theology. But this was not enough for him. Christianity was built on a paradox: the incarnation of God in a human body. No amount of reasoning could help him or anyone else understand this. Those who aspired to become Christians had to take a leap of faith, and they had no way of knowing where they would land.

To be faced with a choice, Kierkegaard explained, is like standing on the edge of a cliff. The climber experiences a natural fear as a result of his exposed position but also an unfocused fear connected with the freedom of being able to choose to jump. Kierkegaard called such unfocused fear "anxiety," defining it as "freedom's actuality as the possibility of possibility."[27] It was only by confronting such anxiety that people could realize freedom.

At the end of 1845 Kierkegaard became the target of ad hominem attacks in a Copenhagen satirical review, to which he replied in his witty way. He seems to have relished the controversy but also to have been wounded by the attacks. In February 1846 he wrote in his journal that he was thinking of qualifying for the priesthood, since "it has long been clear to me that I ought not to continue as an author."[28] But continue he did. At the end of February, he published *Concluding Unscientific Postscript to Philosophical Fragments*, one of his most important philosophical works, in which he looked minutely at subjectivity, inwardness, and truth.

He began his discussion with the assertion "truth is subjectivity," brushing aside the assumption of most philosophers and scientists that there is such a thing as objective truth. He then offered the following definition: "*An objective uncertainty, held fast through appropriation with the most passionate inwardness, is the truth*, the highest truth there is for an *existing* person." Modern philosophers, with their claims of objective certainty, had forgotten "that the knower is an existing person." Their claims to stand outside the framework of lived experience were untenable. Modern men and women, on account of their unnecessary knowledge, had "entirely forgotten what it means to *exist* and what *inwardness* is." It might actually be better if this "superfluity of knowledge" could be removed so that "one could again come to know what it means to live as a human being."[29]

The *Postscript* is not an easy read; sometimes the author seems to go out of his way to make things difficult for the reader. In addition he does not confront several obvious objections to his ideas. Does he really want to sacrifice humanity's accumulated knowledge so that a few could learn what it means "to live as a human being"? (He evoked the image of the library of Alexandria in flames when he spoke of getting rid of the "superfluity of knowledge.") Is he simply restating, as a nineteenth-century Lutheran, the same arguments about the primacy of faith that Luther put forward three hundred years earlier? What is his take on the chaos that engulfed Europe when Luther's and Calvin's ideas about faith collided with those of the Catholic Church? Isn't he taking it for granted that his brand of Christianity was the only faith worth the leap? Even if such objections were valid, they would not negate the value of Kierkegaard's book, which remains interesting to modern readers because of its philosophical acuteness and psychological insight rather than its Christian apologetics.

Most of the works Kierkegaard published after 1846 were religious tracts, but he continued to explore the existential questions he had raised in his philosophical works. In his journal of 1847–51, he returned repeatedly to the question of "the single individual." This was, he wrote, "the category through which, in a religious respect, this age, history, the human race must pass." But it was precisely this category that "the self-willed race and the confused crowds" saw as the greatest threat to their well-being. He himself had been exposed to the fury of the mob during the controversy of 1846. He now regarded this as a blessing, since it gave him "time to learn inwardly." In regard to accusations that he was "causing young people to acquiesce in subjectivity," he wrote that it was necessary to counter the "phantoms of objectivity" that were driving people "to sacrifice individualities altogether." To the public the individual was nothing, though "in community the individual *is*; dialectically, the individual is crucial as the prior condition for forming a community." The thing that had to be fought was not the community but "the crowd."[30]

In 1849 Kierkegaard published his last great work, *The Sickness unto Death*. It was in this "Christian psychological exposition" that he dealt most directly with the idea of the self. His definition of the term has become notorious: "The self is a relation that relates itself to itself or is the relation's relating itself to itself in the relation; the self is not the relation but the relation's relating itself to itself."[31] It is hard to say how seriously he expected us to take this. It reads like a parody of the abstract definitions of self in the works of Fichte or Schelling. Nevertheless, he certainly took the problem of the self seriously, speaking of it in terms of faith and the opposite of faith, which is despair.

Despair can take three forms: being "in despair not to be conscious of having a self," being "in despair not to will to be oneself," and being "in despair to will to be oneself." In all three cases, despair is at root "the will to be rid of oneself." But the eternal does not permit this: "in spite of all his [a person's] despairing efforts, that [eternal] power is the stronger and forces him to be the self he does not want to be." Even if a person succeeds in escaping from the grip of despair, eternity "will make it manifest that his condition was despair" and prevent an escape into inauthentic existence. In the end "in relating itself to itself and in willing to be itself, the self rests transparently in the power that established it."[32] By facing despair, a person becomes an authentic self.

During the last years of his life, Kierkegaard waged war against the Danish state church, publishing dozens of articles and tracts against its errors. He wrote in his journal, "Any attempt directed at bringing about a Christian state, a Christian nation, is by its very nature un-Christian, anti-Christian," since it assumed that everyone in the state was a Christian, and this made it "so easy to be one."[33] To Kierkegaard, becoming a Christian was anything but easy: the process could only begin when a single individual took the leap of faith. He continued with his struggle against the church and the crowd until November 1855, when he died, apparently of a chronic disease, at the age of forty-two.

It took many years for Kierkegaard's works to be translated from Danish into other languages and still longer for them to be accepted as classics of philosophy and psychology. Ironically, his ideas have had their greatest impact among agnostics and atheists rather than Christians. Martin Heidegger, Jean-Paul Sartre, Albert Camus, and other twentieth-century philosophers were fascinated by his discussions of anxiety and freedom, subjectivity and the existing person, the single individual and the crowd. His influence on these writers has caused people to regard him as the first of the three nineteenth-century precursors of existentialism. The second was Fyodor Dostoyevsky.

The Freedom to be Irrational: Fyodor Dostoyevsky

Dostoyevsky, like Kierkegaard (about whom he knew nothing), was concerned with the question of freedom in an age when people had lost faith in religion and religious codes of conduct without knowing what to put in their place. Philosophers and scientists erected systems of thought that were supposed to provide a rational explanation for everything under the sun. But a growing number of people questioned the ability of reason to deal with the problems of life. Kierkegaard put such questionings in the mouths of some of his characters in works like *The Concept of Anxiety*. Dostoyevsky did the same in his novels. In *Notes from Underground*, the narrator declares: "I will admit that reason is a good thing. No argument about that. But reason is only reason, and it only satisfies man's rational requirements. Desire, on the other hand, is the manifestation of life itself – of all of life – and it encompasses everything from reason down to scratching oneself."[34]

Desire belongs to the realm of the unconscious, the irrational. It was Dostoyevsky's insight into the workings of this realm that made him one of the most perceptive novelists of all time. All of us do stupid things, but few of us observe our stupidity with the unflinching honesty of some of Dostoyevsky's characters. Who can forget the moment when Fyodor Karamazov, who has just made a fool of himself in front of his sons and Father Zosima, decides to go back for more? His state of mind, the narrator tells us, "could be described as follows: Since it was not in his power to regain their respect, why shouldn't he go on and disgrace himself altogether?" As he turns back, "he still did not know exactly what he was going to do, but he did know that he was no longer in full control of himself and that the least provocation could push him to the very limit, to some unspeakable abomination."[35] The results are hilarious and pitiable at the same time.

Fyodor Karamazov never reflected on his irrationality. The narrator of *Notes from Underground* did so interminably. In the first part of the novel, he subjects the reader to a first-person rant about himself, contemporary Russia, and the nineteenth century in general. Critics have shown that his concerns reflected Dostoyevsky's misgivings about the rationalistic utopianism of Nikolay Chernyshevsky and others. But as in all great fiction, the underlying themes surpass their historical context. The narrator feels nothing but scorn for people who think there are rational solutions for the problems of individual conduct and social organization: "What makes them think that man's will must be reasonable and in accordance with his own interests?" he asks. "All man actually needs is *independent* will, at all costs and whatever the consequences." He himself has often acted against his own best interests: the second part of the novel consists of a memoir in which he recounts a series of blunders he committed some time earlier. Attempting to justify his irrationality, he writes: "There is one instance when a man can wish upon himself, in full awareness, something harmful, stupid and even completely idiotic. He will do it in order to *establish his right* to wish for the most idiotic things and not to be obliged to have only sensible wishes." Even if the fulfillment of such wishes "harms us and goes against all the sensible conclusions of our reason about our interest," it "leaves us our most important, most treasured possession: our individuality." In Kierkegaard's works, the single individual asserts his or her freedom by confronting anxiety, forgetting about reason, and taking the leap of faith. The narrator of *Notes from Underground* shifts the terms around: people assert their individuality by putting their faith in themselves, turning their backs on reason, and using their freedom to plunge into irrationality. But this, he tells us in his closing statement, actually makes him better than us: "All I did was carry to the limit what you haven't dared to push even halfway – taking your cowardice for reasonableness, thus making yourselves feel better. So I may still turn out to be more *alive* than you in the end."[36]

Fyodor Karamozov certainly feels himself more alive than those around him and he satisfies his oversized lusts with gusto. So does his first son Dmitri – until their competing libidos bring about their mutual destruction. His second son, Ivan, has the same vital push, what he calls "the Karamazov drive – the vile earthly drive," but he broods about it in ways that his father and brother are incapable of.[37] This reflection makes him miserable, because he tries to use his reason to understand his irrational impulses. One thing is clear: even in him, the irrational drive to live, survive, and reproduce is stronger than the reflective mind. As he tells his youngest brother Alyosha: "I was thinking that even if I believed that life was pointless … even if I were completely overcome by the horrors of human despair – I would still want to live on: once I have started drinking from this cup, I won't put it down until I have emptied it to the last drop."[38] It is Ivan, torn between reason and irrationality, who is the author of the fable of the Grand Inquisitor, which stands as Dostoyevsky's boldest attempt to make sense of the questions of faith and freedom and the place of the individual in the universe.

After the Inquisition has tried and condemned Christ for disturbing the peace of Seville, the Grand Inquisitor comes to his cell to explain why the Church has to get rid of him. He frames his argument around the three temptations of Christ as related in the Gospels: that he should turn stones into bread to eat, that he should cast himself from a pinnacle to be saved by angels, and that he should worship the devil to gain the lordship of the earth. The Inquisitor tells Christ that he erred three times by resisting these temptations. His excuse for not turning the stones into bread was that he "did not want to deprive man of freedom," but did he not know that "man has no more pressing, agonizing need than the need to find someone to whom he can hand over as quickly as possible the gift of freedom with which the poor wretch comes into the world"? People do not want freedom, they want something to worship, in particular something "they can all worship *in common*." By refusing the second temptation, Christ denied his followers the comfort of an evident miracle, but did he really think, the Inquisitor asks, that people would "remain with God without recourse to miracles"? Christ rejected the lordship of the earth, but a thousand years later, the Church found it necessary to accept it, since without universal lordship, it would not have been possible for the Church to bring order to the world. "There are three forces, only three," the Inquisitor concludes, "that can capture all the conscience of these feeble, undisciplined creatures, so as to give them happiness," namely, "miracle, mystery and authority."[39] Ivan's fable ends ambiguously, but his point, and Dostoyevsky's, is clear. The rationality, freedom, and individuality that men and women had fought for in the eighteenth century had proved too difficult to bear. They still had to come to terms with irrationality, social bondage, and the crowd.

Dostoyevsky is widely regarded as one of the keenest observers of human psychology in Western literature. Friedrich Nietzsche and Sigmund Freud, both specialists in the irrational, esteemed him as the greatest among their predecessors. He was, Nietzsche wrote, "the only psychologist ... from whom I had something to learn; he ranks among the most beautiful strokes of fortune in my life, even more than my discovery of Stendhal."[40] But by the time Dostoyevsky's novels were published, the study of the mind and its conscious and unconscious processes was passing into the hands of specialists. The term "the unconscious" soon became common currency in the literature of psychology. Dostoyevsky declined to associate himself with this young, callow science, preferring the robes of the prophet. In one of his private notebooks he wrote: "I am called a psychologist, it's not true, I am only a realist in the highest sense, i.e. I depict all the depths of the human soul."[41]

The first half of the nineteenth century in Europe saw the development of two very different approaches to the problem of the self. The first was based on the belief that the human individual was just an ephemeral constituent of society. This came out prominently in the highly rational thought of the German Idealist philosophers, who made the "I" of which they spoke seem like a bloodless abstraction. The other was based on the sense, inherited from the Romantic writers, that rationality missed out on what made humans human, and that only an "existing person" (to use a phrase of Kierkegaard's) could fruitfully engage with the problems of existence. This second strain of thought took root also in the United States, where it assumed a form that was characteristically American.

The Individual and the Crowd

May I love and revere myself above all the gods that men have ever invented. May I never let the vestal fire go out in my recesses.

– Henry David Thoreau

In 1831 the French monarchy sent a young nobleman named Alexis de Tocqueville to the United States to study the country's penal system. After returning to France and submitting his report, Tocqueville wrote *Democracy in America*, a work of political theory that helped create the field of sociology. By examining the effect of democratic institutions on the thought and behavior of American men and women, Tocqueville threw new light on worldwide changes in the relationship between the individual and society. Novelists like Stendhal, W. M. Thackeray and Nathaniel Hawthorne were using these changes as the backdrop of their fiction; Tocqueville, along with Auguste Comte and later Karl Marx and Émile Durkheim, made them the focus of their research.

Tocqueville coined the term "individualism" to describe an attitude he found prevalent in America. Unlike simple selfishness, "a passionate and exaggerated love of self," individualism was "a mature and calm feeling, which disposes each member of the community to sever himself from the mass of his fellows and to draw apart with his family and his friends, so that after he has thus formed a little circle of his own, he willingly leaves society at large to itself."[1] It did not follow that individuals were able to form judgments by themselves. "In the United States," Tocqueville noted ironically, "the majority undertakes to supply a multitude of ready-made opinions for the use of individuals, who are thus relieved from the necessity of forming opinions of their own." Even religion held sway "much less as a doctrine of revelation than as a commonly received opinion."[2]

From the day of his arrival in New York, Tocqueville was struck by the pervasiveness and influence of religion in the United States. At that time the country was in the throes of the Second Great Awakening, and a massive flood of religious revival was spreading from the eastern seaboard to the western frontier. Unlike the First Great Awakening of the 1730s and 1740s, which Jonathan Edwards helped to launch, the second reached out to the unchurched masses, promising salvation to all who accepted God's grace, and planting millennial hopes in the minds of millions. The young Frenchman had never seen anything like it. In his country, conventional Catholicism was again on the rise (as Stendhal noted with scorn), but the ideals of the Enlightenment were still quite strong, particularly among the educated classes. As a member of this elite, Tocqueville had "almost always seen the spirit of religion and the spirit of freedom marching in opposite directions"; in America, he was surprised to find that religion and freedom "were intimately united and that they reigned in common over the same country."[3]

Tocqueville assumed that the primary purpose of religion was to prevent men and women from lapsing into selfishness by imposing social obligations on them. The dangers of self-absorption were particularly great in America, where the spirit of individualism reigned. In order to survive, religion cut a deal with democracy: "By respecting all democratic tendencies not absolutely contrary to herself and by making use of several of them for her own purposes, religion sustains a successful struggle with that spirit of individual independence which is her most dangerous opponent." He was amazed that the innumerable sects in the United States were "clothed with fewer forms, figures, and observances" than anywhere else in the world and also that worshippers cared little about doctrine.[4] He was particularly struck by a new denomination that flourished in Boston and other cities, "a sect," he wrote, "which is Christian only in name, the *Unitarians.*" He made it a point to meet William Ellery Channing, the leading Unitarian preacher. He told Channing he feared that if things went much further, people would be left without the religious basis that civilized life required. "Are you not afraid," he asked, "that by virtue of purifying" the forms of Christianity "you will end by making the substance disappear?" Channing replied that there was no reason to fear: "The human spirit has need of a positive religion, and why should it ever abandon the Christian religion? Its proofs fear nothing from the most serious examination of reason."[5]

Unitarians rejected the doctrine of the Trinity, holding that God was only one "person" and that Christ was an exemplary man and prophet but not a divine being. *All* humans shared "a kindred nature with God" and derived their knowledge of God's attributes and perfections from their own souls. "The divine attributes are first developed in ourselves, and thence transferred to our Creator," Channing said, reversing the traditional Christian position. In contrast to Calvinists who treated the Bible as the inerrant word of God, Unitarians used their minds to interpret it: "We reason about the Bible precisely as civilians do about the constitution under which we live," Channing wrote. He hit out at Calvinism for holding its adherents by means of fear. "A doctrine which contradicts our best ideas of goodness and justice," he said, "cannot come from the just and good God."[6] Religion in New England had come a long way since Edwards preached "Sinners in the Hands of an Angry God" three generations earlier. Unitarian ministers now held the pulpits of important New England churches, such as the Second Church of Boston. In 1829 a Harvard graduate named Ralph Waldo Emerson became the junior pastor of this church, but he soon found that even its humanized and rationalized Christianity was too constricting for his mind.

Self-Reliance and Self-Transcendence: Ralph Waldo Emerson

Emerson began to keep a journal when he was an undergraduate. In one of the earliest surviving entries, he wrote that he planned to note down "new thoughts (when they occur)" as well as "old ideas that partial but peculiar peepings at antiquity can furnish or furbish." For several years, old ideas outnumbered new ones by a wide margin. In April 1824, under the heading "Myself," he undertook a written self-examination similar to those of his Puritan ancestors. He found he lacked the "good-humoured independence and self-esteem which should mark the gentleman." This unfitted him for the professions of law or medicine but, he wrote, "in Divinity I hope to thrive. … My understanding venerates, and my heart loves that cause which is dear to God and man."[7]

Intellectually curious, Emerson allowed his mind to graze in pastures unknown to the average divinity student. He was familiar with Romantic writers such as Goethe, Wordsworth, and Coleridge, British philosophers such as Locke and Hume and, indirectly, Kant and the other German Idealists. He also had some knowledge of Swedenborg's writings, and was so moved by a translation of Montaigne's *Essays* that he felt "as if I had myself written the book, in some former life, so sincerely it spoke to my thought and experience."[8] In 1827 he jotted down a list of the "peculiarities of the present age," of which two are of special interest: "It is said to be the age of the first person singular." (Emerson, a master of first-person writing, was among of the first to see that the subjective turn was becoming aware of itself.) "Transcendentalism. Metaphysics and Ethics look inwards – and France produces Mad[ame] de Staël; England, Wordsworth; America, Sampson Reed; as well as Germany, Swedenborg."[9] Sampson Reed was an American Swedenborgian whose 1826 pamphlet *Observations on the Human Mind* was in Emerson's opinion "the best thing since Plato of Plato's kind."[10] His discussions with another American, the scholar Frederic Henry Hedge, familiarized him with the basic ideas of Kant, Fichte, and Schelling. He picked up from them the word "Transcendentalism," which later would be applied to the intellectual movement of which he was the leading figure.

Emerson preached at Boston's Second Church for only three years. In October 1832 he resigned his ministry and two months later departed for Europe, where he met Coleridge, Wordsworth, and the essayist Thomas Carlyle, and visited monuments, galleries, and museums. His journals of the period are filled with observations that mark a change in his outlook. One day at the Natural History Museum in Paris he was overwhelmed by "the inexhaustible riches of nature":

> Not a form so grotesque, so savage, nor so beautiful but is an expression of some property inherent in man the observer, – an occult relation between the very scorpions and man. I feel the centipede in me, – cayman, carp, eagle, and fox. I am moved by strange sympathies; I say continually "I will be a naturalist."[11]

Emerson delivered a few lectures on natural history after his return to America, but his approach to nature was always more poetic than scientific. One spring afternoon in 1834 he wandered through the woods of Mount Auburn cemetery in Cambridge, observing the plants and animals like a proper naturalist. Then, as he wrote in his journal, he

> found a sunny hollow where the east wind would not blow, and lay down against the side of a tree to most happy beholdings. At least I opened my eyes and let what would pass through them into the soul. I saw no more my relation, how near and petty, to Cambridge or Boston; I heeded no more what minute or hour our Massachusetts clocks might indicate – I saw only the noble earth on which I was born, with the great Star which warms and enlightens it. ... The pines glittered with their innumerable green needles in the light, and seemed to challenge me to read their riddle.[12]

He recorded a similar experience in his landmark essay *Nature*, published in 1836: "In the woods, we return to reason and faith. There I feel that nothing can befall me in life … which nature cannot repair. Standing on the bare ground, – my head bathed by the blithe air, and uplifted into infinite space, – all mean egotism vanishes. I become a transparent eye-ball; I am nothing; I see all; the currents of the Universal Being circulate through me; I am part or particle of God."[13] This often-cited passage sums up the relationship between the three main elements of Emerson's world-view, God, nature, and himself. From his point of view, the third was the most important. A couple of weeks before the Mount Auburn experience he noted in his journal: "The subject that needs most to be presented, developed, is the principle of Self-reliance." A few days later, he added: "All the mistakes I make arise from forsaking my own station and trying to see the object from another person's point of view." He had to avoid the impulse to justify his actions to others. "Absolve yourself to the universe," he told himself, "and, as God liveth, you shall ray out life and heat, – absolute good."[14]

These thoughts became the core of another celebrated essay, "Self-Reliance." "Nothing is at last sacred but the integrity of your own mind," he admonished his readers. "Absolve you to yourself, and you shall have the suffrage of the world." The enemy of self-reliance was conformity to the dictates of the crowd. "Whoso would be a man, must be a nonconformist," he insisted, "No law can be sacred to me but that of my nature." This was the spirit of individualism Tocqueville had noticed a decade earlier, calling it a danger to social cohesion. Emerson approached the question from the opposite point of view: "Society everywhere is in conspiracy against the manhood of every one of its members," he wrote. He was especially concerned about "the unintelligent brute force that lies at the bottom of society," which was becoming more and more rambunctious during the Jacksonian era. It was easy in such a world "to live after the world's opinion," just as it was "easy in solitude to live after our own; but the great man is he who in the midst of the crowd keeps with perfect sweetness the independence of solitude."[15]

Like other writers of whom we have spoken, Emerson was aware of an ongoing struggle between the free individual and the unthinking masses. In Germany and Denmark, Schopenhauer and Kierkegaard inveighed against "the crowd." In Britain, Carlyle battled against "the sphere of blind Custom."[16] In France, Stendhal pilloried the bourgeoisie while Tocqueville painted an unflattering portrait of the American provincial. Emerson took aim at the half-educated horde that wrote in the newspapers, voted in the elections, and packed the churches: "I believe man has been wronged; he has wronged himself," he said in his "American Scholar" lecture of 1837:

> He has almost lost the light that can lead him back to his prerogatives. Men are become of no account. Men in history, men in the world of to-day, are bugs, are spawn, and are called "the mass" and "the herd." In a century, in a millennium, one or two men; that is to say, – one or two approximations to the right state of every man. All the rest behold in the hero or the poet their own green and crude being, – ripened; yes, and are content to be less, so *that* may attain to its full stature.

To avoid becoming part of the celebrity-worshipping mob, scholars had to learn from nature, from books, and from action, but above all they had to learn to trust themselves, for "in self-trust, all the virtues are comprehended."[17]

The next year, Emerson extended these ideas in his "Divinity School Address." "Truly speaking," he said, "it is not instruction, but provocation, that I can receive from another soul. What he announces, I must find true in me, or wholly reject; and on his word, or as his second, be he who he may, I can accept nothing." Applying this rule to himself, Emerson saw that he had to reject most of the doctrines of Christianity. Jesus, a great prophet, in effect told men: "I am divine. Through me, God acts; through me, speaks. Would you see God, see me; or, see thee, when thou also thinkest as I now think." In other words, the true message of Jesus was that all human beings were divine in nature and potentially divine in action. "But," Emerson continued, "what a distortion did his doctrine and memory suffer in the same, in the next, and the following ages!" People transformed him into the only Son of God, saying "This was Jehovah come down out of heaven. I will kill you, if you say he was a man." The results have been disastrous: "The doctrine of the divine nature being forgotten, a sickness infects and dwarfs the constitution." Emerson admonished the students "to go alone; to refuse the good models, even those which are sacred in the imagination of men, and dare to love God without mediator or veil."[18] A predictable howl went up when the speech was published. The Princeton proto-fundamentalist Charles Hodge called Emerson "an infidel and an atheist," while the Harvard Unitarian Andrews Norton characterized his teachings as "the latest form of infidelity," striking "directly at the root of faith in Christianity."[19]

This marked the end of Emerson's engagement with conventional religion. He gave himself full freedom to experience and give expression to his personal religion, which was founded on his individual relationship with God. "The relations of the soul to the divine spirit are so pure that it is profane to seek to interpose helps," he wrote in "Self-Reliance." The highest truth "remains unsaid; probably cannot be said," but it had to do with something that transcended the separate individual, that involved "the resolution of all into the ever-blessed ONE." The self-gathered individual should "stun and astonish the intruding rabble of men and books and institutions, by a simple declaration of the divine fact" that "God is here within."[20]

Emerson's journal shows the growth of his religion from its Unitarian beginnings to its Transcendentalist culmination. In 1830 he wrote: "Every man makes his own religion, his own God," and God was nothing but "the most elevated conception of character that can be formed in the mind. It is the individual's own soul carried out to perfection." This was a radical conception for the early nineteenth century but in fact was fairly close to what Channing was saying at the time. Emerson had traveled a long way when he wrote in 1837:

> Who shall define to me an Individual? I behold with awe and delight many illustrations of the One Universal Mind. I see my being embedded in it; as a plant in the earth so I grow in God. I am only a form of him. He is the soul of me. I can even with a mountainous aspiring say, *I am God*, by transferring my *me* out of the flimsy and unclean precinct of my body, my fortunes, my private will, and meekly retiring upon the holy austerities of the Just and the Loving, upon the secret fountains of nature.

There are obvious echoes here of Platonism, Indian Vedanta, German Idealism, all of which formed part of Emerson's reading at the time. But there is also an original conception of the spiritual individual, founded on inner experience. In the same journal entry, he wrote: "A certain wandering light comes to me which I instantly perceive to be the cause of causes. It transcends all proving. It is itself the ground of being; and I see that it is not one, and I another, but this is the life of my life."[21] These ideas found their way into some of his most distinctive essays, such as "The Over-Soul":

> We live in succession, in division, in parts, in particles. Meantime within man is the soul of the whole; the wise silence; the universal beauty, to which every part and particle is equally related; the eternal *one*. And this deep power in which we exist and whose beatitude is all accessible to us, is not only self-sufficing and perfect in every hour, but the act of seeing and the thing seen, the seer and the spectacle, the subject and the object, are one. We see the world piece by piece, as the sun, the moon, the animal, the tree; but the whole, of which these are the shining parts, is the soul.[22]

Inner experience was always the basis of Emerson's personal religion. "This wide difference between my faith & other faith," he wrote in a notebook of 1841, was "that mine is some brief affecting experience which surprised me on the highway or in the market place ... & made me aware that I had played the fool with fools all this time, but that there was for me & for all, – law, and ineffable sweetness of childlike carriage – and I should never be fool more."[23] He did not label such experiences "mystical" or "superhuman," but viewed them as "the necessary or structural action of the human mind." Spiritual states were natural phenomena. "I hold that ecstasy will be found mechanical, if you please to say so," he noted in his journal; it was just "an example on a higher field of the same gentle gravitation by which rivers run."

He came to regard this naturalizing of the supernatural as the core of his mission. "In all my lectures," he wrote in 1840,

> I have taught one doctrine, namely, the infinitude of the private man. This the people accept readily enough, and even with loud commendation, as long as I call the lecture Art, or Politics, or Literature, or the Household; but the moment I call it Religion, they are shocked, though it be only the application of the same truth which they receive everywhere else, to a new class of facts.[24]

Emerson continued to lecture for the next quarter-century and maintained his journal until he was seventy-two. In a late entry, he summed up his intellectual life: "I told [Bronson] Alcott that every one of my expressions concerning 'God,' or the 'soul,' etc. is entitled to attention as testimony" – that is to say, a solemn affirmation of what he witnessed – "because it is independent, not calculated, not part of any system, but spontaneous, and the nearest word I could find to the thing."[25]

To Be What We Are: Henry David Thoreau

Emerson delivered "The American Scholar" as a commencement address to the Harvard graduating class that included Henry David Thoreau. It appears that Thoreau did not attend; he was never much for public celebrations.[26] Two months later, he had a private meeting with the author of *Nature*, a book he had read more than once. "What are you doing now?" Emerson asked him. "Do you keep a journal?" A few days later, Thoreau began one. "To be alone I find it necessary to escape the present. – I avoid myself," he wrote. "How could I be alone in the Roman emperor's chamber of mirrors? I seek a garret"[27] This was the start of a twenty-two year exercise in first-person writing that in many respects surpassed the model that inspired it.

Thoreau and Emerson remained friends until Thoreau's early death in 1862. They shared ideas throughout their association; the thoughts of one are often found in the journal of the other. "It is sometimes impossible," wrote their biographer Robert Richardson, "to say who took what from whom."[28] Emerson thought himself the majority partner in this intellectual commerce. "I am very familiar with all his thoughts," he wrote in 1841, "they are my own quite originally drest." At that point the internationally famous author may have been right in thinking that the unpublished twenty-four-year-old had "not yet told what that is which he was created to say."[29] But Thoreau developed a power of physical description and a grounding in the facts of nature that Emerson would never possess. In his first book, *A Week on the Concord and Merrimack Rivers*, which was based on journal entries, he offered a "sensualist" alternative to Emerson's Transcendentalism:

> We need pray for no higher heaven than the pure senses can furnish, a *purely* sensuous life. Our present senses are but the rudiments of what they are destined to become. … May we not *see* God? Are we to be put off and amused in this life, as it were with a mere allegory? Is not Nature, rightly read, that of which she is commonly taken to be the symbol merely?[30]

But Thoreau also was a poet and he did not want his writing to be limited to the recording of factual data. "Facts should only be as the frame to my pictures," he wrote in 1851, "they should be material to the mythology which I am writing … facts to tell who I am, and where I have been or what I have thought."[31] The "mythology" he was writing was the epic of a place on earth (Concord, Massachusetts), with its seasons and forests and ponds and living things, of whom one (Henry David Thoreau) was the observer and also part of what was being observed. Eventually observer and observed came together, as he identified himself with his surroundings.

Thoreau's journal was the place where he gathered the material for his epic. His published books – *A Week*, *Walden*, *The Maine Woods*, *Cape Cod* – were attempts to bring out the significance of this material and to communicate it to others. They contain some of his deepest thoughts and most striking descriptions but they are sometimes tendentious and often judgmental toward the other human beings he happened to come across. His attitude toward the people of Concord was similar to that of his contemporary Kierkegaard toward the people of Copenhagen. "The mass never comes up to the standard of its best member, but on the contrary degrades itself to a level with the lowest," Thoreau wrote in his journal, "Hence the mass is only another name for the mob." There is no doubt he considered himself one of the "best" and he had good reasons doing so, but his friends, Emerson included, felt he lacked the human sympathy needed in a great social critic. They may not have known that he was as harsh on himself as on others, at times almost Puritan in his self-abasement: "Now if there are any who think that I am vainglorious, that I set myself up above others and crow over their low estate," he wrote in February 1852, "let me tell them that I could tell a pitiful story respecting myself as well as them, if my spirits held out to do it; I could encourage them with a sufficient list of failures, and could flow as humbly as the very gutters themselves." He actually thought worse of himself than others did, "being better acquainted with the man." But finally it was nature and not himself or others that held his interest. "The mind that perceives clearly any natural beauty is in that instant withdrawn from human society," he noted in July of the same year. "The grandest picture in the world is the sunset sky. In your higher moods what man is there to meet?"[32]

Thoreau is justly renowned as a nature writer, excelling in description as well as evocation. When the two are equally balanced, the results are sometimes breathtaking: "A warm, cloudy, rain-threatening morning," he wrote in November 1857:

> About 10 A.M. a long flock of geese are going over from northeast to southwest, or parallel with the general direction of the coast and great mountain-ranges. The sonorous, quavering sounds of the geese are the voice of this cloudy air, – a sound that comes from directly between us and the sky, an aerial sound, and yet so distinct, heavy and sonorous, a clanking chain drawn through the heavy air. ... So they migrate, not flitting from hedge to hedge, but from latitude to latitude, from State to State, steering boldly out into the ocean of the air.

At other times the poet took over, as in this passage of 1852:

> The river is silvery, as it were plated and polished smooth, with the slightest possible tinge of gold, to-night. How beautiful the meanders of a river, thus revealed! How beautiful hills and vales, the whole surface of the earth a succession of these great cups, falling away from dry or rocky edges to gelid green meadows and water in the midst, where night already is setting in![33]

But sometimes the naturalist cancelled out the poet. One afternoon in 1856 he and Emerson went out to botanize. "Having found his flowers," Emerson wrote of his friend, "he drew out of his breast pocket his diary and read the names of all the plants that should bloom this day, May 20; whereof he keeps account as a banker when his notes fall due." Thoreau worried about this turn. "I fear," he wrote, "that the character of my knowledge is from year to year becoming more distinct and scientific; that, in exchange for views as wide as heaven's cope, I am being narrowed down to the field of the microscope." He managed to prevent conflict between the scientist and the poet by subordinating both to the philosopher. Asked by the secretary of the Association for the Advancement of Science for details about scholarly interests, he sent them something he thought they would understand but noted in his journal: "The fact is I am a mystic, a transcendentalist, and a natural philosopher [i.e., a scientist] to boot."[34]

Thoreau's transcendentalism was less idealistic, more grounded in physical reality, than that of Emerson, Hedge, Alcott and the other members of the Transcendental Club. Thoreau saw the bookish Emerson as being out of touch with the nitty-gritty of everyday life. "I doubt if Emerson could trundle a wheelbarrow through the streets, because it would be out of character," he wrote in 1852. "One needs to have a comprehensive character." Hawthorne, a sometime Concord neighbor, wrote in his journal this account of Thoreau's comprehensive personality:

> He is a keen and delicate observer of nature – a genuine observer – which, I suspect, is almost as rare a character as even an original poet; and Nature, in return for his love, seems to adopt him as her especial child, and shows him secrets which few others are allowed to witness. ...
>
> With all this he has more than a tincture of literature, – a deep and true taste for poetry, especially for the elder poets, and he is a good writer, – at least he has written a good article, a rambling disquisition on Natural History, in the last *Dial,* which, he says, was chiefly made up from journals of his own observations. ...
>
> After dinner. ... Mr. Thoreau and I walked up the bank of the river; and, at a certain point, he shouted for his boat. ... Mr. Thoreau managed the boat so perfectly, either with two paddles or with one, that it seemed instinct with his own will, and to require no physical effort to guide it.[35]

Hawthorne was one of many who were struck by the intimacy of Thoreau's relations with the physical world. Few philosophers before or after – Maine de Biran, Schopenhauer, Nietzsche, Merleau-Ponty, one or two others – have gone so deeply into the significance of physical embodiment. "The body is the first proselyte the Soul makes," he wrote in his journal in 1840, "Our life is but the Soul made known by its fruits, the body. The whole duty of man may be expressed in one line, – Make to yourself a perfect body."[36] A few years later, while hiking in Maine, he had a revelation of the sheer physicality of existence:

> I stand in awe of my body, this matter to which I am bound has become so strange to me. ... What is this Titan that has possession of me? Talk of mysteries! – Think of our life in nature, – daily to be shown matter, to come in contact with it, – rocks, trees, wind on our cheeks! The *solid* earth! the *actual* world! the *common sense! Contact! Contact! Who* are we? *where* are we?

The enlightened scholar, he wrote in 1853, "will confine the observations of his mind as closely as possible to the experience or life of his senses. His thought must live with and be inspired with the life of the body."[37]

Thoreau's "I" is present throughout the journal, but it is rarely an "I" looking in. Usually it is absorbed in "the experience or life of his senses," as in these examples from January 1858: "I see one of those fuzzy winter caterpillars, black at the two ends and brown-red in middle, crawling on a rock by the Hunt's Bridge causeway." "I see some tree sparrows feeding on the fine grass seed above the snow, near the road on the hillside below the Dutch house." "My attention was caught by a snowflake on my coat-sleeve. It was one of those perfect, crystalline, star-shaped ones, six-rayed, like a flat wheel with six spokes, only the spokes were perfect little pine-trees in shape, arranged around a central spangle." His psychological observations were rarely as fine-grained, and when they were the result was often gloomy. He considered friendship a sacred thing but had trouble holding on to his friends. After one disappointing meeting, which he analyzed at length, he wrote with bitter irony: "I leave my friends early; I go away to cherish my idea of friendship." Yet in his hours of solitude, he reflected long and deeply on the mysteries of the self. "We are constantly invited to be what we are; as to something worthy and noble," he wrote in 1841, adding: "I never waited but for myself to come round; none ever detained me, but I lagged or tagged after myself."[38] This self-critical attitude, which at its worst drove him to compare the flow of his thoughts to "the very gutters," must have made it difficult for him to set down the results of his self-examination.

Toward the end of his short life (he died of tuberculosis at the age of forty-four) Thoreau began to identify his self with his physical surroundings: "Now I am ice, now I am sorrel. Each experience reduces itself to a mood of the mind," he wrote in 1857. Eventually he went so far as "to feel that he *was* Concord in human form," as scholar Odell Shepard put it, and "from that belief it seemed to follow that studying Concord in its full sweep of time and place would amount to a close self-examination." Shepard sometimes found this identification with nature excessive, as when Thoreau wrote: "Almost I believe the Concord [River] would not rise and overflow its banks again, were I not here."[39] But it may have been a logical consequence of his intense awareness of himself as a conscious body on the earth.

The Separate Person and the Word En-Masse: Walt Whitman

Walt Whitman considered himself a "born democrat" and he bestowed the same title on Emerson; but he rebuked Thoreau for his "disdain, contempt, for average human beings: for the masses of men." His admiration for Emerson's writings (and gratitude for his endorsement of *Leaves of Grass*) may have made him go easy on Emerson's evident distain for "the unintelligent brute force that lies at the bottom of society." But there was another side to Emerson's attitude: he believed in the fundamental equality of human beings and in their ability to lift themselves higher. "As to what we call the masses, and common men," he wrote in *Representative Men*, "there are no common men. All men are at last of a size; and true art is only possible, on the conviction that every talent has its apotheosis somewhere."[40] It was this side of Emerson that responded to the inclusiveness of Whitman's poetry, as in these lines the poet placed at the beginning of *Leaves of Grass*:

> One's-Self I sing, a simple, separate person,
> Yet utter the word Democratic, the word En-Masse.[41]

The two lines must be read together. Whitman's boundless fascination with himself was balanced by an equally boundless fascination with the selves of others:

> Trippers and askers surround me,
> People I meet, the effect upon me of my early life or the ward and city I
>   live in, or the nation, …
> These come to me days and nights and go from me again,
> But they are not the Me myself.
> Apart from the pulling and hauling stands what I am,
> Stands amused, complacent, compasssionating, idle, unitary, …
> Both in and out of the game and watching and wondering at it.

He might, as he wrote elsewhere, "contain multitudes," but behind these multitudes was a unitary self, which was not fundamentally different from the selves of those around him, because (as he told his readers): "every atom belonging to me as good belongs to you."[42]

Whitman was born on Long Island in 1819. The habit of identifying himself with the world seems to have come to him early:

> There was a child went forth every day,
> And the first object he look'd upon, that object he became,
> And that object became part of him for the day or a certain part of the
>   day,
> Or for many years or stretching cycles of years.[43]

Quitting school at the age of eleven, he worked briefly as an office boy before entering the printing trade, first as an apprentice, later as a compositor, and still later as a writer and editor. In 1855 he published the first edition of *Leaves of Grass*, a collection of free-verse poems unlike anything ever seen in Western literature. But it was not without precedents. Wordsworth's *Prelude* (published posthumously in 1850 though perhaps never read by Whitman) explored the possibilities of the poetic autobiography. Earlier in time but closer in spirit, the Puritan and Evangelical conversion narrative created a template for secular confessional literature. Whitman, who was never religious, transformed the duty of godly self-scrutiny into an exuberant celebration of self, with the positions of God and self reversed:

> And I say to mankind, Be not curious about God,
> For I who am curious about each am not curious about God,
> (No array of terms can say how much I am at peace about God, and
>   about death.)
> I hear and behold God in every object, yet understand God not in the
>   least,
> Nor do I understand who there can be more wonderful than myself.[44]

Whitman's confessions were rarely confidential; he spoke of himself for hundreds of pages yet revealed little about himself as a discrete individual. A key poem begins with a reference to his birthplace, but soon moves on to lands never visited and professions never practiced:

> Starting from fish-shape Paumanok where I was born,
> Well-begotten, and rais'd by a perfect mother,
> After roaming many lands, lover of populous pavements,
> Dweller in Mannahatta my city, or on southern savannas,
> Or a soldier camp'd or carrying my knapsack and gun, or a miner in
>   California,
> Or rude in my home in Dakota's woods, my diet meat, my drink from
>   the spring; ...

Even when he speaks of a certain "Walt Whitman," the qualities are those of a rough-and-tumble mythical hero:

> Walt Whitman, a kosmos, of Manhattan the son,
> Turbulent, fleshy, sensual, eating, drinking and breeding,
> No sentimentalist, no stander above men and women or apart from them,
> No more modest than immodest.[45]

This mythical "Walt Whitman" was a product of the American nineteenth century but it became the model for a new sort of self that would colonize the world in the twentieth and twenty-first.

It is hard to list all the attributes of a "kosmos," but it may be possible to isolate a few characteristics of the Whitmanian self. First, it is simultaneously and equally physical and spiritual:

> I have said that the soul is not more than the body,
> And I have said that the body is not more than the soul,
> And nothing, not God, is greater to one than one's self is, ...

And I say to any man or woman, Let your soul stand cool and composed
before a million universes.

This self is permeable and moves toward fusion, through pulsations of the
"body electric":

The armies of those I love engirth me and I engirth them,
They will not let me off till I go with them, respond to them,
And discorrupt them, and charge them full with the charge of the soul.

Or through imaginative identification:

I am the actor, the actress, the voter, the politician,
The emigrant and the exile, the criminal that stood in the box,
He who has been famous and he who shall be famous after to-day,
The stammerer, the well-form'd person, the wasted or feeble person.

Or emotional empathy:

Not a cholera patient lies at the last gasp but I also lie at the last gasp,
My face is ash-color'd, my sinews gnarl, away from me people retreat.

At its highest reach, the Whitmanian self finds its identity with the universal
and divine:

Swiftly arose and spread around me the peace and knowledge that pass
all the argument of the earth,
And I know that the hand of God is the promise of my own,
And I know that the spirit of God is the brother of my own,
And that all the men ever born are also my brothers, and the women
my sisters and lovers,
And that a kelson of the creation is love.[46]

Whitman's prose works, including those written in the first person, reveal
comparatively little about his idea of the self. The entries in *Specimen Days*
are those of a keen observer of nature, a curious onlooker in cities and towns,
and a compassionate wound-dresser in Civil War hospitals. But occasionally
he paused to reflect on the miracle of the self and its place in democratic
America. In the "Thoughts and Jottings" of 1882, he pondered "the most
profound theme that can occupy the mind of man," namely, "the relation
between the (radical, democratic) Me, the human identity of understanding,
emotions, spirit, &c., on the one side," and on the other "the (conservative)
Not Me, the whole of the material objective universe and laws, with what is
behind them in time and space." This was a problem that had occupied him
since the days when a child "went forth" and identified himself with "the first

object he look'd upon." More than sixty years later, the man who was the boy was still fascinated by the relations of the Me and Not Me, and he turned to German philosophy to help formulate a response. Schelling, Whitman wrote, made a valuable and important contribution when he wrote that the qualities that "exist in a conscious and formulated state" in the human being "exist in an unconscious state" in the external universe, "thus making the impalpable human mind, and concrete Nature ... convertible, and in centrality and essence one." Hegel was even more suggestive when he wrote that the "contrarieties" of the world are "necessary sides and unfoldings, different steps or links, in the endless process of Creative thought, which, amid numberless apparent failures and contradictions, is held together by central and never-broken unity."[47]

The intellectual history of nineteenth century America began with imported theological debates, came to maturity in the essays of Emerson and reached a sort of apotheosis in the works of Whitman. His great themes were Democracy and the individual Self, two sides of a single subject. Democracy was a word he often had used, he wrote in *Democratic Vistas*, but its true sense was still obscure. As far as he could see, "the tendencies of our day, in the States ... are toward those vast and sweeping movements, influences, moral and physical, of humanity, now and always current over the planet." At the same time, it was necessary to view things from the point of view "of a single self, a man, a woman, on permanent grounds. Even for the treatment of the universal, in politics, metaphysics, or anything, sooner or later we come down to one single, solitary soul." For "only in the perfect uncontamination and solitariness of individuality may the spirituality of religion positively come forth. ... Bibles may convey, and priests expound, but it is exclusively for the noiseless operation of one's isolated Self, to enter the pure ether of veneration, reach the divine levels, and commune with the unutterable."[48]

Doubting the Soul and Discovering the Body

"Body am I and soul" – thus talks the child. And why should one not talk like children?
But the awakened one, the one who knows, says: Body am I through and through, and nothing besides; and soul is merely a word for something about the body.

– Friedrich Nietzsche

In 1819, when Walt Whitman was born, most people in the United States and Europe took it for granted that they were souls created by God for his purposes. By 1892, when Whitman died, a large and growing number had rejected this idea or had serious reservations about it. The change came about partly through the influence of creative writers who increasingly took the place of religious experts as interpreters of life. People looking for answers to the great moral questions turned to Goethe, Dostoyevsky, and Whitman rather than the now-forgotten theologians of the period. Philosophers like Kant and Hegel remained influential, but their ideas reached the public through the writings of popular essayists such as Emerson and Carlyle. It was Carlyle's *Sartor Resartus* that showed Thomas Henry Huxley that "a deep sense of religion was compatible with the entire absence of theology." Absorbed in his scientific research, Huxley took no interest in theological questions such as whether the soul was immortal, but this did not make him morally insensitive. "Love opened up to me a view of the sanctity of human nature," he wrote to a clergyman, "and impressed me with a deep sense of responsibility." For him as for many others, science provided "a resting-place independent of authority and tradition."[1]

By the middle of the century, there were, roughly speaking, three principal ways of looking at the relationship between the soul (or mind or self) and the world: dualism, idealism, and materialism. Dualism held that mind and matter were completely different substances. Based on religious teachings and given philosophical form by Descartes, it appealed to people who thought the soul was immaterial but left them with the problem of explaining how this substance was related to the material world and body. Idealism held that reality is fundamentally mental or spiritual. It took several forms, the most extreme being the absolute idealism of Hegel, which viewed Nature as not different from Spirit. At the opposite end of the spectrum was materialism, which held that matter was the primary if not the only component of reality.

Harking back to the ideas of ancient Greek atomistic thinkers, materialism was reformulated by the natural philosophers of the seventeenth century, and adopted by Enlightenment thinkers such as Holbach and Laplace during the eighteenth. The rise of Idealism during the early nineteenth century put materialism in the shadow again. Schopenhauer, a Kantian idealist, declared: "materialism is the philosophy of the subject who forgets to take account of himself."[2] But Idealism could not long withstand the continuing impact of science. By end of the century many philosophers joined scientists in affirming the materiality of the universe and the corporeality of the self. This provided a theoretical basis for an increasingly materialistic view of life. Poets, novelists, artists, and thousands of ordinary people looked without guilt on the physical world and the body as valuable ends in themselves.

A Machine for Grinding General Laws: Charles Darwin

In August 1831, Charles Darwin, a young gentleman from Shropshire who had recently graduated from Cambridge, came home from a rock-hunting trip in Wales to find a letter inviting him to join a round-the-world scientific expedition. He was all for it, but his father put his foot down. Disappointed by his son's lack of interest in medicine, Robert Darwin had sent him to Cambridge to become a clergyman. While there, Charles spent most of his time shooting and collecting beetles, but he still managed to earn his degree. Now he wanted to go off to the South Seas to indulge his passion for natural history! In the end, the elder Darwin agreed to let Charles go, and he sailed on *H.M.S. Beagle* in December 1831.

The expedition lasted almost five years. From the beginning Darwin kept notes in personal and scientific diaries, using them later to write an account of the voyage. His *Journal of Researches*, generally known as *The Voyage of the Beagle*, became a bestseller, and remains one of the great narratives of exploration. Besides presenting heaps of geological, botanical, and zoological data, it detailed the young man's experiences and impressions, all in excellent prose. Of the giant tortoises of the Galápagos Islands, Darwin wrote:

> I was always amused, when overtaking one of these great monsters as it was quietly pacing along, to see how suddenly, the instant I passed,

it would draw in its head and legs, and uttering a deep hiss fall to the ground with a heavy sound, as if struck dead. I frequently got on their backs, and then, upon giving a few raps on the hinder part of the shell, they would rise up and walk away; but I found it very difficult to keep my balance.

This is certainly more engaging than the corresponding passage in one of his notebooks: "In my walk I met two very large Tortoises (circumference of shell about 7 ft). One was eating a Cactus & then quietly walked away. – The other gave a deep & loud hiss & then drew back his head." But the notebooks contain a number of observations that Darwin omitted from the book. Here he is, part naturalist, part sailor on leave, checking out the ladies of Lima: "'They wear a black silk veil, which is fixed round the waist behind, is brought over the head, & held by the hands before the face, allowing only one eye to remain uncovered. – But then that one eye is so black & brilliant & has such powers of motion & expression, that its effect is very powerful."[3]

Darwin's powers of description were remarkable but such as any intelligent graduate might have developed. What was unusual about this particular young naturalist was his ability to arrive at far-reaching conclusions after reflecting carefully on his data. In an autobiographical note, written late in life, he referred to his mind as "a kind of machine for grinding general laws out of large collections of facts."[4] This machine started working during the *Beagle* expedition. A year after leaving the Galápagos Archipelago, he wrote in one of his notebooks that he had noticed that the finches found on several of the islands showed interesting differences as well as similarities. "I must suspect they are only varieties," he wrote, adding: "If there is the slightest foundation for these remarks, the Zoology of Archipelagoes will be well worth examining, for such facts would undermine the stability of species." It was a dogma of zoology that species were immutable, each one a special creation of God. When an English ornithologist classified Darwin's finches in 1837, it became clear that they were species that had diverged from one another while isolated on their different islands. Darwin saw the explosive effect this conclusion might have and did not mention it in the 1839 edition of the *Voyage*. Five years later, in the second edition, he tossed out a hint of what he was thinking: "Seeing this gradation and diversity of structure in one small, intimately related group of birds, one might really fancy that from an original paucity of birds in this archipelago, one species had been taken and modified for different ends."[5] But he waited another fifteen years before publishing his complete theory of descent with modification – called by others the theory of evolution – in the pages of *The Origin of Species by Means of Natural Selection*.

There was nothing new in the idea that species could be arranged in an ascending hierarchy: this was part of the concept of the Great Chain of Being, which had been prevalent since classical times. The idea that species developed over time was also not without precedent. Among those who flirted with this notion was the physician and poet Erasmus Darwin (Charles's paternal grandfather), who wrote in a poem published posthumously in 1803:

> These, as successive generations bloom,
> New powers acquire, and larger limbs assume;
> Whence countless groups of vegetation spring,
> And breathing realms of fin, and feet, and wing.[6]

What was different about Charles Darwin's theory was that he put forward natural selection as the mechanism of evolutionary change. Species possessing the most favorable traits tend to survive and reproduce with greater success than others. To hit on this idea, Darwin had to synthesize the results of several different lines of research: Malthusian population theory, Lamarkian inheritance, current ideas about genetics. Putting it all together caused him some torment. In a letter to a colleague of 1844, he wrote that

> I have been now ever since my return engaged in a very presumptuous work & which I know no one individual who w^d not say a very foolish one. – I was so struck with distribution of Galapagos organisms &c &c & with the character of the American fossil mammifers, &c &c that I determined to collect blindly every sort of fact, which c^d bear any way on what are species. ... At last gleams of light have come, & I am almost convinced (quite contrary to opinion I started with) that species are not (it is like confessing a murder) immutable. ... I think I have found out (here's presumption!) the simple way by which species become exquisitely adapted to various ends.[7]

He knew his conclusions flew in the teeth of religious belief and scientific opinion, but he persisted in spite of ill health until he worked out his theory completely.

Darwin had received a conventional religious upbringing, and before going to Cambridge, as he wrote in his autobiography, he "did not then in the least doubt the strict & literal truth of every word in the Bible." At Cambridge he read and was impressed by William Paley's *Natural Theology*, but empirical observations made him doubt Paley's argument from design. Still, the feeling that God was present in His creation remained with him for some time. After exploring the forests of Brazil, he wrote in his journal "it is not possible to give an adequate idea of the higher feelings of wonder, admiration, & devotion which fill & elevate the mind" while contemplating the grandeur of nature. Such feelings reinforced his inner conviction that "there is more in man than the mere breath of his body." Reflecting on this many years later, he had to admit: "Now the grandest scenes would not cause any such convictions & feelings to rise in my mind." Disciplined reasoning about his empirical data had turned him into a materialist.[8]

Darwin never denied the existence of God or the immortality of the soul. Indeed he acknowledged "the extreme difficulty or rather impossibility of conceiving this immense & wonderful universe, including man with his capacity of looking far backwards & far into futurity, as the result of blind chance of necessity"; all this seemed to support the idea of "a First Cause having an intelligent mind in some degree analogous to that of man." But every time he started thinking on such lines, a doubt arose: "can the mind of man, which has, as I fully believe, been developed from a mind as low as that possessed by the lowest animal, be trusted when it draws such grand conclusions?" Finally, he concluded, "the mystery of the beginning of things is insoluble to us," so he was content "to remain an Agnostic."[9]

The word "agnostic" was coined by Darwin's friend and supporter Huxley in 1870, and it encapsulated an important intellectual trend. Huxley and hundreds of others did not deny that God exists or that the soul is immortal; they simply said that the human mind was incapable of knowing such things. Along with this intellectual incertitude came a sense of resignation, if not despair, searingly expressed by Matthew Arnold in his 1867 poem "Dover Beach." After remarking that "the Sea of Faith" was once "at the full," the first-person narrator says:

> But now I only hear
> Its melancholy, long, withdrawing roar.

Turning to his companion, he cries:

> Ah, love, let us be true
> To one another! for the world, which seems
> To lie before us like a land of dreams,
> So various, so beautiful, so new,
> Hath really neither joy, nor love, nor light,
> Nor certitude, nor peace, nor help for pain,

but was as if a "darkling plain ... Where ignorant armies clash by night."[10]

Naturalizing the "I": Nineteenth-Century Psychology and Sociology

At the beginning of the scientific revolution, the key discoveries were in the fields of astronomy and physics. During the eighteenth and nineteenth centuries, science drew closer to the human scale by investigating chemical, biological, and eventually psychological and social phenomena. After 1859, the shadow of Darwin hung over all these fields. By including the human being within the scope of evolution, Darwin opened himself to attacks by clergymen, philosophers, and others who feared that his theory called into question the special place of humanity in God's creation. The anti-Darwin forces did not limit themselves to arguments from scripture; they turned to the new science of psychology for confirmation of the Christian and Cartesian assumption that humans were fundamentally different than animals. The creators of psychology "did not assume that the new discipline was materialist in its inspiration or goals," wrote philosopher of science Edward S. Reed, but by the end of the century, most practicing psychologists had abandoned the God-friendly "science of the soul" in favor of naturalistic if not materialistic theories of the mind.[11]

The philosophical psychology of the early nineteenth century arrived at its results through reasoning based on data obtained by introspection. But from the start, investigators were troubled by the irregularity of treating a single mind as the subject and object of the same act of perception. Meanwhile, practitioners of self-observation – diarists and memoirists, for example – were finding that they could no longer take the idea of a coherent self for granted. Delacroix's cry "What is this *I?* What is *a man?*" (1824), Coleridge's question "*What* ... am I to call my *Self?*" (1829), Stendhal's "What have I been? What am I?" (1835) and Thoreau's "*Who* are we? *where* are we?" (1846) had few precedents in Western literary history. Personal identity was becoming a *problem*. Creative as well as academic writers struggled with the notion that there were corners of the mind that were inacces-sible to self-observation. In 1853 the physiologist W. B. Carpenter coined the term "unconscious cerebration" to designate cerebral activities that produced mental effects without the benefit of consciousness. Within a few decades, "the unconscious" had established itself as an indispensable term in psychology, philosophy, and literature. Eduard von Hartmann made it the centerpiece of his *Philosophy of the Unconscious* (1869), which attempted to harmonize the rationalism of Hegel and the irrationalism of Schopenhauer. Scientists like Huxley were unimpressed by von Hartmann's metaphysics but they found the distinction between the conscious and the unconscious useful in their studies of human and animal volition. The so-called consciousness of animals, Huxley wrote in 1874, was just a "collateral product" of the body's working, something like "the steam-whistle which accompanies the work of a locomotive engine." Humans were not much better: "the feeling we call volition is not the cause of a voluntary act, but the symbol of that state of the brain which is the immediate cause of that act."[12] This way of looking at mental events became known as epiphenomenalism. In its most extreme form, it turned consciousness into a side effect of psycho-physical activities.

In 1879 the German William Wundt opened the world's first laboratory of experimental psychology. A few years later, Théodule-Armand Ribot was appointed professor of experimental psychology in Paris. From the start he distanced himself from what he called "metaphysical psychology." There was no need, he insisted, to assume *a priori* the existence of "a self, utterly one, simple and identical." The nature of the self, whatever it might be, had to be determined by empirical investigation. This scientific approach to the study of the self trickled down into popular culture. Oscar Wilde's character Dorian Gray "used to wonder at the shallow psychology of those who conceive the ego in man as a thing simple, permanent, reliable and of one essence." To Dorian, "man was a being with myriad lives and myriad sensations, a complex multiform creature that bore within itself strange legacies of thought and passion."[13]

While psychologists were undermining the idea of a coherent I, sociologists were demonstrating that the individual self was always and inescapably involved in a network of social relations. Writing a half-century before Huxley and Ribot, Auguste Comte disparaged metaphysicians for insisting on the distinction between humans and animals in order to preserve "the unity of what they called the *I*." The I of the philosophers was just a carryover from the soul of the theologians, and under either name designated "a purely fictitious state." Far from being unified, human nature was "eminently multiple," driven one way or another by "distinct and independent powers."[14] Karl Marx agreed with Comte that the individual was subordinate to society, writing in *Theses on Feuerbach* (1845): "The essence of man is no abstraction inherent in each single individual. In reality, it is the ensemble of the social relations."[15]

Like Huxley and Comte, Marx had no time for metaphysics or metaphysicians. He began his career as a radical Hegelian but later declared that Hegel had turned the dialectic on its head. "It must be turned right side up again," Marx wrote, "if you would discover the rational kernel within the mystical shell." This meant viewing history not as a dialectic of ideas but as a struggle between social classes. In setting forth what became known as dialectical materialism, he was concerned with individuals "only in so far as they are the personifications of economic categories, embodiments of particular class-relations and class-interests."[16]

Émile Durkheim was interested less in the conditions of social change than the nature of social cohesion. Central to his view were what he called "social facts," modes of behavior that exert coercive power on individuals. Such facts – laws, beliefs, institutions, demographic patterns – could not be reduced to psychology but existed in their own right and had to be studied in relation to one another. "The determining cause of a social fact," Durkheim wrote in 1894, "has to be sought among the social facts that precede it and not among states of individual consciousness."[17] In traditional societies, a strong collective consciousness smothered the expression of individual differences. In modern societies, individualism became possible but the results were not all happy. Modern individuals suffered from what Durkheim called anomie, a lack of consistent social norms leading to confusion, despair, and suicide.

Diary as *Document Humain*: the Goncourt Brothers and Marie Bashkirtseff

By the middle of the nineteenth century, sociology, psychology, and even physiology had begun to make their influence felt in fiction and poetry, particularly in France. In 1842 the leading novelist of the era, Honoré de Balzac, wrote a preface to his enormous cycle of novels, *La Comédie humaine*, in which he tried to explain what he was up to. Briefly, he wanted to make a catalogue of "social species" to rival the catalogues of zoological species compiled by taxonomists. Earlier novelists had been content to depict a few typical figures. He and other writers of the Realist school would provide a photographic documentation of the whole of human society.[18]

Despite his quasi-scientific claims, Balzac remained a literary demiurge, creating larger-than-life characters with confident strokes of his pen. This troubled the novelists of the next generation, in particular Émile Zola, the leader of the Naturalist school. The problem with Balzac, he said, was "the exaggerated size of his heroes." The greatness of a novel should not be measured by the scale of its characters but founded "in the unquestionable truth of the human document [*document humain*]." In writing this, he borrowed a term introduced a few years earlier by another Naturalist writer, Edmond de Goncourt, who declared that the novels he wrote with his brother Jules showed from the start the tendency "to introduce the reality of the *document humain* into [literary] invention, to bring into the novel a little of that individual history that, in History, does not have a historian."[19] By insisting on the sometimes sordid uniqueness of the particular human being, the Naturalists delivered the *coup de grâce* to literary Romanticism and also challenged the philosophical historicism of Hegel and Marx.

Document humain, according to a contemporary dictionary, meant a piece of evidence about an aspect of human life recorded or collected on the spot. Moving around Paris, the Goncourts amassed a mountain of material that captured the habits and social interactions of the men and women of the metropolis. They used this data in writing their novels and also included it in their multi-volume *Journal*, still remembered as one of the great French diaries. A series of entries from 1860 gives a glimpse of how they worked: "To write our novel *Soeur Philomène*," they wrote, "we need to take notes in hospital, studies from life made on the spot." This proved to be more difficult than they imagined. Their legs buckled as they followed a doctor on his rounds and they were haunted by "those pale women's faces, glimpsed on their pillows, almost bluish in color and transformed by suffering and immobility." Their detailed observations found their way into the novel but also survive, more vividly, in the *Journal*.[20]

Like their older contemporary Thoreau, the Goncourts were masters of observation but the nature they studied was urban rather than rural. Returning to Paris after a spell in the country, they went for dinner to a tavern where they watched "the setting sun shed a golden light on the big, gilded placards over the Passage des Panoramas," more thrilled by "the sight of that slice of plaster covered with huge letters, scribbled on and dirtied" than by anything the country had to offer. Again like Thoreau, they were slow to record the results of introspection, though they were capable of sharp self-criticism. "I am left with a craving which, in drunkenness, outlasts love and copulation," one of them wrote after a night of debauchery. "The pity of it is that the soul outlives the body, or in other words that impression judges sensation and that one thinks about and finds fault with the pleasure one has taken." Staunch atheists, they did not care about their souls in the traditional sense of the term. What mattered was "the facts," because "worship of the facts leads to everything, to happiness first of all and then to wealth."[21]

The brothers' relaxed acceptance of materialism made it possible for them to enjoy pleasure when it came and to reflect without religious preconceptions on the fact of embodiment. Lying in bed beside a transient lover, one of them felt something close to terror "bending over that body, in which everything seemed to be extinct and only an animal life lingered on." When she spoke in her sleep, he reflected on the "mystery of unconscious thought, that voice in a darkened bedroom, all that was as frightening as a corpse possessed by a dream." Edmond had a similar experience standing by the bed of his dead brother in 1870: "How frightful is the immobility of this body under the sheets, no longer rising and falling with the gentle movements of respiration, no longer living the life of sleep." He felt that he had literally lost a part of himself.[22]

After Jules's death, Edmond's primary concern was the postmortem survival of traces of his and his brother's physical existence. "Only that which contributes to the survival of my personality can afford me a little pleasure," he wrote in June 1884, and by "survival of personality" he meant mainly the survival of material artifacts: "the engraving of a portrait, the republishing of a book." As his own death approached this desire became an obsession: "My constant preoccupation is to save the name of Goncourt from oblivion in the future by every sort of survival: survival through works of literature, survival through foundations, survival through the application of my monogram to all the *objets d'art* which have belonged to my brother and myself."[23] The foundation he set up proved to be his winning bet: it perpetuates the name "Goncourt" in France's most coveted literary prize.

Aware of its importance as a social and literary monument, Edmond published a first volume of his and his brother's journal in 1887. The frankness of their record did not please everyone. The critic Ernest Renan, who was mentioned several times, called Edmond an "indiscrete individual" for divulging the contents of private conversations. Edmond accepted the reproach but felt no shame, insisting that "since the world began, the only memoirs of any interest have been written by 'indiscreet individuals', and my only crime is to be still alive twenty years after these were written – something for which, humanly speaking, I cannot feel any remorse."[24] Up to that point few memoirs and no diaries had been published during the lifetime of their authors. Even the posthumous publication of diaries was comparatively new: extracts from Maine de Biran's journal were published as "Pensées" in 1857, thirty-three years after his death. Extracts from other literary diaries followed, but it was not until 1887 that the diary as *document humain* made its public debut in the Goncourts' journal and, almost simultaneously, in *The Journal of Marie Bashkirtseff.*

A young Russian artist who studied and exhibited in Paris and died there in 1884, Bashkirtseff kept a private diary from her fourteenth year. Early entries differ little from those in other girls' diaries, telling of her family, her travels, and her crushes, but as she grew older she gave evidence of unusual talent and intelligence as well as a burning desire for fame. Realizing in her last year that the paintings she had produced were not enough to assure postmortem survival, she hoped that her journal, which now filled a hundred notebooks, would be her monument. In a preface written in May 1884 for the proposed publication, she did not conceal her motives for offering it to the public: "What use is there in posing and deceiving? Well, then, it is clear that I have the desire, if not the hope, to remain on the earth, through whatever means." The woman of twenty-five experienced the same yearning for physical survival that Edmond de Goncourt, who was then sixty-two, would write about in June of the same year. Bashkirtseff realized that she "as the subject of interest may possibly appear slight" to her readers, but she asked them to think of her as another human being who was displaying herself "*at full length*," in a spirit of "*exact, absolute, strict* truth." If nothing else, her journal would "prove very interesting as a human document." A few weeks earlier she had written a letter to Goncourt in which she offered to bequeath her journal to him, "laying herself bare" for the sake of art. Goncourt did not reply (he received a lot of such offers from female fans), so she made her mother swear that she would get it published. This was the only way, Marie thought, that she could escape oblivion. What she feared was not death but to be "as if I had never existed."[25]

Bashkirtseff was raised as a Christian but clearly did not have much confidence in the afterlife. The diary is filled with conventional references to God and the soul, but she showed more concern for her body. In a remarkable entry written when she was just seventeen, Bashkirtseff took as her starting point the Christian-Cartesian dichotomy of body and soul, but soon found reason to question it: "Since the soul exists; since it is the soul which animates the body; since it is that vaporous substance which alone feels, loves, hates, desires; since, finally, it is the soul which gives us life, how does it happen, then, that any wound in this vile body, or any internal disorder … can put the soul to flight." It simply did not make sense: "The soul, which sets in motion the various portions of our body, ought not to be driven away, it, the essence of reason, by a hole in the head, or an indigestion caused by eating lobster." Thus "the conclusion must be drawn that the soul is a pure invention." If the existence of the soul was doubtful at best, that of the body was sure. Bashkirtseff found her own to be tolerably pretty, though she remained sensitive to others' remarks about it: "Marie Sapogenikoff says, with reason, that, for such a body, a much more beautiful face is required, and bear in mind that I am far from being homely. When I think of what I shall be when I am twenty, I am filled with delight."[26] A year earlier she had given herself a thorough inspection, and was not dissatisfied with the result. Here is part of her lengthy self-portrait:

> I am of average height. I have golden hair that falls to my waist, curly at the ends and wavy above. A broad forehead, white and noble, which I cover with a fringe of hair. … Dark eyebrows, thick and well formed. Grey eyes – or rather of all colors and all expressions. Eyelashes as dark or almost as dark as the eyebrows but otherwise unremarkable. A nose quite straight and rounded at the end, nostrils somewhat

large, always moving but not ugly – in short a pretty nose. A pretty, small ruby-colored mouth, with corners that are remarkably fresh, soft, well-formed, and nice. ... A pretty neck, gorgeous shoulders and arms, beauty marks on the left shoulder. ... Firm, well-formed breasts, glowing white and pink where it counts. The place I dare not name is so ample that people always think I am wearing a big bustle. ... In short I may say without boasting that I am marvelously well made.[27]

Bashkirtseff was certainly not the first teenage girl to examine herself in front of a mirror, but she may have been the first to write a description of her body that was so long, so detailed, and so unembarrassed.

She went on in the same entry to describe her mental and moral qualities, giving herself equally good marks. Other people found her high-strung and egoistic, an assessment she would probably not have disputed. But along with her ordinary ego she was sometimes aware of a second "that remains always the passionless spectator of the first." This sense of detachment gave her the ability to view herself in the midst of confusion and suffering as if she was someone else. "In this state of stupefaction and incessant pain," she wrote during a period of illness, "I do not curse life; on the contrary I love it, and I find it good to live. ... I find everything agreeable, and while demanding happiness, I find happiness in being miserable. I am no longer myself; my body weeps and laments, yet something within me, which is stronger than I am, rejoices at it all." The psychologist William James found this passage so remarkable that he quoted it in *The Varieties of Religious Experience* as an example of the "religion of healthy mindedness." Bashkirtseff would have been pleased. She wrote in her preface: "If I should not live long enough to win renown, this journal will interest the psychologists; for it is curious, at least."[28]

The Revaluation of All Values: Friedrich Nietzsche

Realism and naturalism became the dominant modes of fiction throughout Europe and America during the 1870s. Writers strove to document the conditions of societies that were struggling with the breakdown of tradition and the resultant anomie. One symptom of the prevailing confusion was nihilism, the negation or rejection of mental and moral standards. Prevalent to the point of faddishness in Russia, it was part of the intellectual makeup of some of Dostoyevsky's most memorable characters – Raskolnikov in *Crime and Punishment*, Stavrogin in *The Possessed*, Ivan in *The Brothers Karamazov*. The nihilist attitude was epitomized by a phrase attributed to Ivan: if there is no God and the soul is not immortal, then "everything is permitted."[29]

In 1888 the German philosopher Friedrich Nietzsche wrote in one of his notebooks under the heading "Nihilism – for the preface": "Until now I have endured a torture: all of the laws by which life unfolds appeared to me to be in opposition to the values for the sake of which we endure life." This was "the really tragic problem of our modern world," and it had "become conscious in me." More than anyone else in the nineteenth century, he grappled with the consequences of the loss of fixed standards of belief and conduct. Nihilism meant "that there is no truth, that there is no absolute nature of things," thus no reality on which to base values, thus "no meaning at all." The result was social pathology and moral breakdown. Christian morality had served as an antidote against this pathological condition, but the antidote no longer worked, and "mediocrity, wretchedness, dishonesty, etc." had taken over. The only way out was to treat nihilism as a "transitional stage" and move beyond it. After experiencing the general collapse of values, people had to make a heroic "Attempt at a Revaluation of All Values."[30]

Nietzsche believed that all philosophical systems could be reduced "to the personal records of their originators."[31] Whether or not this approach would work with someone like Kant, it could easily be applied to Nietzsche himself. All his works are personal, some frankly autobiographical, and they reveal a man in constant revolt against conventionality and hypocrisy. Born in a small town near Leipzig in 1844, he showed unusual brilliance at school and university. Abandoning theology after a semester, he concentrated on classical philology and when he was only twenty-four was named Professor of Philology at the University of Basel. By this time he had begun to read widely in philosophy. Going through Schopenhauer's *The World as Will and Representation*, he caught a glimpse of the "terrifying grandeur" of the world, of life, and of his own character, and was filled with "the need for self-knowledge."[32] He adopted Schopenhauer's concept of Will but rejected his pessimism and life-denial. In his first important work, *The Birth of Tragedy* (1872), he wrote that early Greek tragedy was the supreme form of art because it combined the organic, instinctive and irrational (the Dionysian) and the separative and rational (the Apollonian). Later Greek culture, Christianity, and the European Enlightenment had turned their back on Dionysian ecstasy. The end result was nihilism, which could only be overcome by the affirmation of life in all its complexity.

In June 1879 Nietzsche retired from his post in Basel because of persistent ill health. For the next ten years he led a wanderer's life in Italy and Switzerland, writing in occasional bursts of inspiration the works that would win him posthumous fame. We get an idea of the way his thoughts were moving in an aphorism published in 1879: "Active, successful natures act, not according to the dictum 'know thyself', but as if there hovered before them the commandment: *will* a self and thou shalt *become a* self."[33] This intuition marked a dramatic break with the Socratic tradition of self-knowledge, and Nietzsche remained true to it throughout his life. In the four great works he published between 1882 and 1887 – *The Gay Science, Thus Spoke Zarathustra, Beyond Good and Evil* and *On the Genealogy of Morality* – he rejected the established certitudes of religion and the modern gospel of progress in favor of a revolutionary doctrine of self-overcoming.

In *The Gay Science*, Nietzsche announced: "God is dead. God remains dead. And we have killed him." People had to face up to the fact that they had murdered the ancient ground of truth and morality – and then "become gods" themselves. They had to affirm life even if this meant experiencing again and again everything that had ever happened "in the same succession and sequence." This myth of the eternal return, which became a major theme of *Thus Spoke Zarathustra*, was the opposite of the myth of eternal progress, which philosophers and other thinkers were building on the foundations of Darwin's theories. Nietzsche rejected Darwinism because it meant not the triumph of "the more highly developed types" but "the inevitable dominion of the average, even the *sub-average* types." He offered instead a gospel of transcendence: the coming of the *Übermensch* or Overhuman. "The human is a rope, fastened between beast and Overhuman," he had Zarathustra say. "What is great in the human is that it is a bridge and not a goal." [34]

After announcing the advent of the Overhuman, Zarathustra had a message for the "despisers of the body": it was childish to speak in Christian or Cartesian terms of "body and soul." The human being is nothing but body, soul simply a word "for something about the body." He continued: " 'I' you say, and are proud of this word. But the greater thing – in which you do not want to believe – is your body and its great reason: it does not say I, but does I." Senses and spirit are mere "tools and toys"; behind them lies the Self. "In your body it dwells, he is your body." The prophet concluded: "There is more reason in the body than in your finest wisdom." The despisers of the body miss out on these truths and Zarathustra rejects them: "You are for me no bridges to the Overhuman!"[35]

It is not altogether clear what Nietzsche meant by the Self that dwells in the body and at the same time *is* the body. He may not have been sure himself: in a fragment from the same period he wrote that the body and the self in the body are the *terra incognita* or unknown land.[36] He did not find it strange to say that the body and the self, those most familiar of friends, were in fact the least well known. He began *The Genealogy of Morality* with an exposition of this paradox: "We are unknown to ourselves, we knowers: and with good reason. We have never looked for ourselves, – so how are we ever supposed to *find* ourselves?" We are like people who are awakened by the town clock and say "Who *are* we, in fact?" Not understanding ourselves, "we *must* confusedly mistake who we are." In brief, we "are not 'knowers' when it comes to ourselves." The *Genealogy* was Nietzsche's most rigorous attempt to understand "the *descent* of our moral prejudices." Since early adolescence he had been "preoccupied with the problem of the origin of evil." Although raised as a Lutheran, he learned "to separate theological from moral prejudice," and did not search "for the origin of evil *beyond* the world." Rather he began to ask himself: "under what conditions did man invent the moral judgments good and evil?" In the *Genealogy* he approached this and related questions from several different angles. Here we will examine his treatment of one problem: the origin of the inner world and the soul. His view, in brief, was that the soul is a deformation of physical instinct:

> All instincts which are not discharged outwardly *turn inwards* – this is
> what I call the *internalization* of man: with it there now evolves in man
> what will later be called his "soul". The whole inner world, originally
> stretched thinly as though between two layers of skin, was expanded and
> extended itself and gained depth, breadth and height in proportion to
> the degree that the external discharge of man's instincts was *obstructed*.

The obstruction was due to social compulsion, in particular the fear of punishment. The result was that "those instincts of the wild, free, roving man were turned backwards, *against man himself.*" Obliged to conform to custom, "man impatiently ripped himself apart."[37]

Nietzsche was even more explicit about the harmful effects of the concepts of God, the other world, and the soul in *Ecce Homo: How to Become What You Are*. "The concept 'God' invented as a counter-concept to life," he wrote in this autobiographical work. "The concept 'hereafter', 'true world' invented in order to devalue the *only* world there is – so as to leave no goal, no reason, no task for our earthly reality! The concepts 'soul', 'spirit', ultimately even 'immortal soul' invented so as to despise the body, to make it sick. ... Instead of health the 'salvation of the soul.'" It is hard to imagine a more thoroughgoing dismissal of the intellectual and moral absolutes that had supported European culture for two millennia, whether as religious dogmas or philosophical postulates. Nietzsche was not reticent about the role he thought he was playing in announcing the end of these so-called eternal verities. "I am," he wrote, "by far the most terrifying human being there has ever been." His role as revaluator of all values was like that of Moses or Christ and his destined end would be Christlike: "they crucify him who writes *new* values on new tablets, they sacrifice the future *to themselves*, they crucify all human future!"[38]

Ecce Homo was the last book Nietzsche wrote before his health collapsed in 1889 and it gives evidence of the insanity that overtook him during the last ten years of his life. But his conviction that society would not tolerate an individual who opposed the norms of truth and morality had been with him for several years. "When I was younger I worried about what a philosopher really was," he wrote in a notebook of 1885, "for I believed I saw contradictory features in the famous philosophers." He eventually realized that there were two kinds of thinkers: "those who have to hold fast some large body of valuations" – Kant for example – and "those who themselves are legislators of valuations," who say "this is how it *shall* be!" Clearly he included himself in the latter category. He added that philosophers of the second sort rarely turn out well, "indeed their situation and danger is tremendous," because they failed to see "the narrow margin that separates them from the abyss."[39]

Nietzsche's works were little read while he was alive and well, but by the time of his death in 1900 they had begun to exert an influence on intellectuals and artists who were fed up with the mediocrity and hypocrisy of early twentieth-century Europe and America. Many of Nietzsche's ideas anticipated those of Sigmund Freud, for example the "internalization" of undischarged instinct, which has obvious similarities to Freud's ideas of repression and sublimation. Freud never acknowledged his predecessor's influence, but he once told a friend that Nietzsche "had a more penetrating knowledge of himself than any other man who ever lived or was ever likely to live."[40] Nietzsche's reputation took a blow during the middle years of the twentieth century when he was illegitimately appropriated by the Nazis, but after the Second World War he emerged as a major influence on several important Continental philosophers: Heidegger, Sartre, Camus, Foucault, Derrida, and others.

During the late nineteenth century, the advances of the physical and social sciences encouraged writers, artists, and philosophers to affirm the importance of the universe of matter and the human body. For the first time since the early Roman Empire, the intellectual elite of the West could speak openly about the facts of embodiment without taking religious dogmas into account. For some, this freedom from ancient assumptions was exhilarating. But for most it was, as Nietzsche observed, the start of an era of confusion and anxiety.

Evolution and Affirmation

*Evolution is not finished; reason is not the last word nor the reasoning
animal the supreme figure of Nature. As man emerged out of the animal,
so out of man the superman emerges.*

– Sri Aurobindo

At the turn of the nineteenth century, it was possible for people to look on
science, philosophy, and religion as different but complementary approaches
to a single truth. By the middle of the century, especially after the publication
of Darwin's *Origin*, this peaceful coexistence had broken down. Scientists,
philosophers, and theologians felt obliged to tell the others to keep off their
turf. Huxley, Ribot, Durkheim, and other physical and social scientists
insisted that their studies, based on empirical research, invalidated the
claims of religion and metaphysics. Philosophers of various sorts – Idealists,
Marxists, Utilitarians, loners like Nietzsche – subordinated religion and
science to whatever principle or critical stance they preferred. Apologists for
religion defended sacred scripture by insisting that its dogmas lay beyond
the scrutiny of science and philosophy. "Natural science is welcome to its
conjectures, so long as it does not lay them as the foundation of unbelief in a
province not its own," declared Anglican theologian E. B. Pusey in a sermon
of 1878. "The thought of a First Cause belongs to Theology, or in its degree,
to Philosophy, not to the natural sciences."[1] Yet it was futile to try to keep
the inhabitants of one "province" out of the others' territories. When Darwin
read Pusey's sermon he wrote to the local vicar:

> I hardly see how religion & science can be kept as distinct as he desires,
> as geology has to treat of the history of the Earth & Biology that of
> man. – But I most wholly agree with you that there is no reason why
> the disciples of either school should attack each other with bitterness,
> though each upholding strictly their beliefs.[2]

But as Darwin well knew, it was difficult for most people to uphold their own
beliefs without attacking those of others.

The conflict was especially bitter in questions where science, philosophy,
and religion each had a stake but offered incompatible answers. Was the
primordial substance Matter or the Idea or God? Was the human self an

epiphenomenon of nervous activity or a self-existent ego or an immortal soul? Hardliners believed that accepting one answer meant denying all the others. But there were also synthetic thinkers who sought common ground between the scientific, philosophical, and religious approaches, generally by giving a novel twist to the ruling idea of the day: the theory of evolution.

Writing at the turn of the twentieth century, the American psychologist and philosopher William James said that evolutionism offered ways of thinking and acting that rendered conventional religion obsolete: "In that 'theory of evolution' which, gathering momentum for a century, has within the past twenty-five years swept so rapidly over Europe and America, we see the ground laid for a new sort of religion of Nature, which has entirely displaced Christianity from the thought of a large part of our generation." James went on to say that "the idea of a universal evolution" lent itself "to a doctrine of general meliorism and progress" that fit "the religious needs of the healthy-minded so well that it seems almost as if it might have been created for their use."[3] The "idea of universal evolution" to which he referred was not something Darwin had proposed. It was the brainchild primarily of British philosopher Herbert Spencer, who began to develop his synthetic philosophy of evolution from 1857 – two years before the publication of the *Origin of Species*. To Spencer, the evolutionary process began with the creation of matter and continued up to the development of human societies, encompassing everything that has existed, exists and will exist. The ultimate simplicity of the original germ of matter will give rise, inevitably, to the ultimate complexity of a perfect human society. Spencer formulated his central insight in a famous sentence of *First Principles* (1862): "Evolution is an integration of matter and concomitant dissipation of motion; during which the matter passes from an indefinite, incoherent homogeneity to a definite, coherent heterogeneity."[4] Ideas like this, once reduced to ordinary language, had great appeal to people struggling with the breakdown of faith and the dizzying speed of social change during the industrial age. A quasi-scientific belief in the inevitability of progress made it possible for people who had lost faith in God to look forward to what the poet Alfred Tennyson called the "one far-off divine event, / To which the whole creation moves."[5]

The Most Puzzling Puzzle: William James

James began his career as a psychologist with a strong foundation in science and became a philosopher whose distrust of metaphysics and theology did not prevent him from taking an active interest in religion. His father, Henry James, Sr., was a Swedenborgian theologian who knew many of the leading thinkers of the day, including Emerson, who became William's godfather. Henry provided his children with a cosmopolitan education in the United States and Europe, hoping that this would give them intellectual independence, but he disapproved when William decided to become an artist and was only slightly less dissatisfied when he entered Harvard Medical School. Before and during his college career, William suffered from physical and psychological problems, sometimes wondering whether he would go insane. He received his degree in 1869 but did not become a doctor, preferring to sit at home brooding and studying philosophy and psychology. In 1870, he had a sort of conversion experience after reading an essay by the French philosopher Charles Renouvier, which gave him a way to deal with the problem of free will. "I think that yesterday was a crisis in my life," he wrote in his diary that April. He could see no reason why Renouvier's "definition of Free Will – 'the sustaining of a thought *because I choose to* when I might have other thoughts' – need be the definition of an illusion. ... My first act of free will shall be to believe in free will." Abandoning metaphysical speculation, he would "voluntarily cultivate the feeling of moral freedom." Asserting his "individual reality and creative power," he would "posit life (the real, the good) in the self-governing *resistance* of the ego to the world." Hereafter his life would be defined by "doing and suffering and creating."[6]

In 1872 James accepted the position of instructor of anatomy and physiology at Harvard. Three years later he began to teach physiological psychology, and in 1878 signed a contract to write a book on the subject. The result, *Principles of Psychology*, became the dominant work in the field after it was published in 1890. It was at once a review of the professional literature in English, French, and German, and an exposition of the author's own ideas, arrived at through introspection and presented in a highly personal, at times almost autobiographical style. James began, like Wundt, Ribot, and other proponents of the "new psychology," by insisting that his approach would be scientific. "Attempts to *explain* our phenomenally given thoughts as products of deeper-lying entities (whether the latter be named 'Soul,' 'Transcendental Ego,' 'Ideas,' or 'Elementary Units of Consciousness')" were metaphysical and had to be rejected. He devoted the first eight chapters of the book to a survey of current theories on the brain and mental functioning. Only then did he turn to the "study of the mind from within." His starting point was not sensation but thought: "The first fact for us, then, as psychologists, is that thinking of some sort goes on." But this thinking "does not appear to itself chopped up in bits." It is "nothing jointed; it flows." To describe it he invented the metaphor "stream of thought, of consciousness, or of subjective life." This and not the self was "the immediate datum in psychology." Still, the self was of interest because "it is, and must remain, true that the thoughts which psychology studies do continually tend to appear as parts of personal selves."[7]

In the next chapter, "The Consciousness of Self," James looked first at the empirical Ego or "Me," putting off consideration of the pure Ego or "I" until later. *"A man's Self,"* he wrote, *"is the sum total of all that he* CAN *call his,* not only his body and his psychic powers, but his clothes and his house, his wife and children, his ancestors and friends, his reputation and works, his lands and horses, and yacht and bank-account." This empirical self could be broken down into three parts: the physical self, the social self, and the spiritual self. The physical self was not just the body but also family, clothes, and possessions. The social self consisted of recognition given by others. Taking a page from social scientists and philosophers, James wrote that *"a man has as many social selves as there are individuals who recognize him and* carry an image of him in their mind." The spiritual self, "so far as it belongs to the Empirical Me" (as opposed to the pure Ego), was "a man's inner or subjective being, his psychic [i.e., mental] faculties or dispositions." For most of us, these "dispositions are the most enduring and intimate part of the self, that which we most verily seem to be."[8]

Having cleared the ground to some extent, James turned his attention to what he called "the most puzzling puzzle with which psychology has to deal," namely the problem of the Pure Ego or Self. The traditional religio-philosophical idea was that the self was a substantial being: a soul or transcendent "I." But according to Hume and Kant and contemporary psychologists as well, this self was something that could not be observed, and therefore had been excluded from scientific psychology. James found this unjustifiable, since "belief in a distinct principle of selfhood" was part of the "commonsense of mankind." His own observations convinced him that the sense of self arose from the continuity of the stream of consciousness: *"Resemblance among the parts of a continuum of feelings* (especially bodily feelings) experienced along with things widely different in all other regards," was the basis of *"the real and verifiable 'personal identity' which we feel."*[9]

From the mid-1890s, James gave more attention to philosophy than psychology. Still turned off by metaphysics, particularly German Idealism, he developed an approach he called "radical empiricism," which rejected all final answers, viewing order as something "gradually won and always in the making."[10] Three casualties of this approach were pure being, essential consciousness, and absolute truth. In the 1904 essay "Does Consciousness Exist?" James argued that consciousness was not an entity but a function. In answer to the objection that all of us feel that we are conscious beings, he asserted that "in myself, the stream of thinking ... is only a careless name for what, when scrutinized, reveals itself to consist chiefly of the stream of my breathing."[11] As for truth, it was just a relation between our ideas and the rest of experience. "The truth of an idea is not a stagnant property inherent in it," he wrote in his 1907 classic *Pragmatism*. "Truth HAPPENS to an idea. It BECOMES true, is MADE true by events."[12]

There is a lot of similarity between the ideas of James and those of his contemporary Nietzsche. Both denied that truth was absolute, gave formative power to the will, and put the body at the center of the question of identity. But they differed in several respects, notably in their attitude toward religion. Nietzsche attacked it in all its forms, James believed it had pragmatic value. The religion he defended in *The Varieties of Religious Experience* (1902) was not a social institution but "the feelings, acts, and experiences of individual men [and women] in their solitude, so far as they apprehend themselves to stand in relation to whatever they may consider the divine."[13] To illustrate this individual side of religion he turned to "documents humains," in particular memoirs, diaries, and other first-person writings by well-known figures (Augustine, George Fox, Jonathan Edwards) and anonymous contemporaries (one of whom was himself in disguised form). Without affirming or denying the existence of God, James concluded: "We and God have business with each other; and in opening ourselves to his influence our deepest destiny is fulfilled. ... God is real since he produces real effects."[14]

Elsewhere, in a modernization of Pascal's Wager, James wrote that religion made two affirmations: (1) "the best things are the more eternal things"; and (2) "we are better off even now if we believe [the] first affirmation to be true."[15] By putting his bet on the positive side of religion, James aligned himself with contemporary writers who were making a distinction between "religion" (institutional, creedal, static) and "spirituality" (personal, experiential, transformative). The "spirituality of religion" that Whitman had spoken of in 1871 was familiar enough by 1905 for James's colleague George Santayana to write epigrammatically: "This aspiring side of religion may be called Spirituality."[16] James did not use the term in that sense in his writings, but his whole approach was (to use the modern cliché) "spiritual but not religious." He also was involved in a related trend: the study of paranormal phenomena. The first president of the American Society for Psychical Research, he published articles on parapsychology and performed experiments that convinced him that "our normal waking consciousness ... is but one special type of consciousness, whilst all about it, parted from it by the filmiest of screens, there lie potential forms of consciousness entirely different."[17] Even if consciousness was a function and not an entity, its full range – and thus the full amplitude of the human self – had yet to be explored.

Supramental Evolution: Sri Aurobindo

Darwin rarely wrote about the future course of evolution. Such matters lay beyond his scope and he was content to leave them to speculative philosophers like Spencer. But occasionally he indulged in speculations of his own. In his 1837 notebook on transmutation of species, he jotted down this cryptic remark: "If all men were dead, then monkeys make men. – Men make angels – " Three decades later he closed the *Descent of Man* by observing that the human being, who had risen "to the very summit of the organic scale," might yet hope "for a still higher destiny in the distant future." He felt obliged to add, however, that man's rise had not come about "through his own exertions" and that he still bore "in his bodily frame the indelible stamp of his lowly origin."[18]

Other writers were more upbeat about the human being's potentialities. From the 1860s dozens of books were published that tried to incorporate evolution into larger philosophical and religious systems. Some of them followed lines laid down by Schelling, Comte, Spencer, and other thinkers. Others were attempts by Christian theologians to appropriate Darwin's insights and prestige. Still others tried to synthesize science, philosophy, and religion, and even include the findings of psychical research. The most unusual of these was *The Secret Doctrine* (1888), an attempt by H. P. Blavatsky, co-founder of the Theosophical Society, to integrate science, Eastern religion, Neoplatonic philosophy, and esoteric traditions. This enjoyed some vogue at the turn of the century but was undone by what James called Blavatsky's unsustainable "claims to physical mediumship."[19] In the decades that followed, Henri Bergson and Pierre Teilhard de Chardin in France, Samuel Alexander in England, and Sri Aurobindo and Muhammad Iqbal in India developed evolutionary philosophies that gave different degrees of importance to science, philosophy, religion, and inner experience.

When the British rulers of India made English the medium of instruction, they gave students the key not only to the poetry of Wordsworth, but also the philosophy of Spencer, the sociology of Comte, and the political thought of Mill. Soon young Indians were writing sonnets, discussing evolution, and wondering why Mill's *On Liberty* didn't apply to them. The result was a cultural renaissance that became the basis of an independence movement. Aurobindo's father, an early beneficiary of English education, studied medicine in Calcutta and Aberdeen, where he became a Darwinian atheist. He took his sons to England in 1879, when Aurobindo was seven. Aurobindo returned to India fourteen years later with a mastery of Greek, Latin, French and English literature and a general knowledge of contemporary philosophy and science. An opponent of British colonialism, he became a leader of the independence movement in 1907. A year later he was arrested and put on trial for "waging war against the Government."[20]

While in jail Aurobindo devoted himself to meditation and had a series of inner experiences that transformed his life. Released in 1909, he resumed his political work but also continued his spiritual practices. During a speaking tour that July, he began to keep a record of his visions and experiences in a small pocket notebook. The visions were of ordinary as well as otherworldly objects, for instance "Glass jug with napkin on top" followed by "Nil Surya [blue sun] with blue black rays." The experiences included alterations of the kinesthetic sense ("All liberty of bodily movement being steadily taken away") as well as classic spiritual states such as *samadhi* or yogic trance.[21] A few months later he retired from politics and settled in Pondicherry, a French colony on the southeast coast of India. There he resumed his diary, recording his inner experiences using an arcane terminology drawn from various spiritual and philosophical traditions. For example, on January 16, 1912, he wrote: "The morning has been chiefly devoted to the taking entire possession by the personality of the Ishwara [Lord] of the thought-expression and the removal of all restraints or government of the thought by the Shakti [Power]." He used the same impersonal form of expression when speaking about his physical condition: "Arogya [health] is reasserting itself but not yet reestablished in possession of the body."[22]

Aurobindo's concept of personal identity was based on the Upanishadic idea of *atman*, the individual Self that is also "the one Self of all beings." *Atman*, as he wrote in a manuscript of 1914, is

> my Self as well as the self of all others, friend and enemy, saint and sinner, man, bird and beast, tree & stone, and all things in the manifestation are the forms and activities of my Self. Moreover, this Self is again the Lord of the Cosmos ... of whom every individual soul is a conscious centre, aware of its unity with Him in being and also of its difference in the universe.[23]

This Self had to be distinguished from the *ahankara* or ego-sense, "the illusion ... which makes each being conceive of itself as an independent personality." Aurobindo viewed the *ahankara* as a lower or false self that had to be overcome before a person could become conscious of his or her higher self. He also spoke of physical, vital, mental, and gnostic selves and of an evolutionary soul, or "psychic being," which "gathers the essence of all our mental, vital and bodily experience and assimilates it for the farther evolution of our existence in Nature." All this made for an extremely complex idea of the self, incorporating concepts from different Indian and Western traditions. But to Aurobindo it was a unity in diversity, since behind the various presentations of the self there was a single "central being."[24]

Evolution had two meanings for Aurobindo. First, it was a cosmic process in which the divine in the universe manifested matter, life, mind, and higher principles on its way to multiple unity. Second, it was a journey of individual psychic beings toward perfection. The next stage of universal evolution would be the manifestation of gnosis or "supermind"; the corresponding stage of personal evolution would be the "superman." These terms first appeared in his diary in 1914: "Transfer the centre of the active consciousness from the mind to the supermind. The supermind is the seat of the superman."[25] Soon they became recurrent themes in his philosophical writings, as in this passage from a notebook:

> Man is a transitional being, he is not final; for in him and high beyond him ascend the radiant degrees which climb to a divine supermanhood.
>
> The step from man towards superman is the next approaching achievement in the earth's evolution. There lies our destiny and the liberating key to our aspiring, but troubled and limited human existence – inevitable because it is at once the intention of the inner Spirit and the logic of Nature's process."[26]

Aurobindo was familiar with Nietzsche, regarding him as "the most vivid, concrete and suggestive of modern thinkers."[27] But his superman – despite the occasional verbal echo – differed greatly from the German philosopher's *Übermensch*. Nietzsche was an opponent of the theory of evolution and contemptuous of those who saw the hand of God in human affairs. Aurobindo believed that the superman would be "the last product of that progressive self-manifestation of God in world, Spirit out of matter, which is now called the principle of evolution." The two agreed on one point, however: the superman would not abandon life but would affirm it in all its variety. For Nietzsche this meant a rejection of the pessimism and asceticism of Schopenhauer, Buddhism, and Christianity, for Aurobindo a rejection of the post-Upanishadic idea that the world was *maya* or illusion. Nietzsche found the "highest attainable formula of affirmation" in the idea of eternal recurrence. Aurobindo endorsed this, writing in a notebook that the strong soul contemplating eternal recurrence "is seized by it with the thrill of an inconceivable rapture. It hears behind the thought the childlike laughter and ecstasy of the Infinite." Around the same time he noted in his diary: "The principle of Affirmation to replace the principle of rejection & denial."[28]

Aurobindo kept his diary sporadically from 1909 to the end of 1912, and regularly from then until 1920. During the first period, he occasionally referred to himself in the first person as a physical actor ("As I was walking ...") or thinker ("I take it that ...") or experiencer ("I see the ahankara only as a play ..."). During the second he did not use the pronoun "I" even once although he wrote almost exclusively about himself. He presented the movements of his inner and outer life as though they were events that he was watching but not participating in. A typical entry is this one of April 1914: "There is an attempt to break the violently pronounced tamas [inertia] of the body which has prevented all work recently," followed by "Ananda Brahma [*brahman* in the form of delight] is now an established element of the Brahmabodha [realization of *brahman*], but it is not perfectly manifest in the mortal object, only as something possessing & enjoying it." This impersonal form of expression was characteristic of what he called the "witness consciousness," a way of looking on "the whole action of the universe" and even one's own action as though one were "watching a play or a drama."[29] The witness (*sakshi*) consciousness had been described centuries earlier by philosophers of the Sankhya and Vedanta schools, but it was not unknown to European writers, including some discussed earlier in this book. Wordsworth wrote in *The Prelude*, "my theme has been / What *passed* within me"; Maine de Biran wrote similarly: "I can truthfully say that no other man has seen or *watched himself go by* as I have." Constant and Amiel and Bashkirtseff all wrote of a part of themselves that was a "spectator."[30]

In Aurobindo, the passivity of the witness was combined with a drive for transformation, as if a Wordsworthian mystic had been touched by the Nietzschean will to power. He devoted the second half of his life to what he called the "supramentalization" of his being, viewing this as an ascent into the gnostic levels of consciousness and the descent of the powers of those levels into his body. He resumed his diary in 1926 in an effort to keep track of this process. A typical entry is this one from January 1927: "Mark that the dependence on the critical verifying mind decreases. Verification is becoming automatic, criticism also automatic. Both will soon be entirely gnostic."[31] He spent the last two decades of his life secluded in his room, practicing meditation and writing thousands of letters to the men and women who had gathered around him. He told them that he was seeking the supermind not for himself but because its attainment would serve as "a key for opening the gates of the supramental to the earth consciousness." He meant by this that if the supermind descended it would become available to those who were ready for it just as mind had become available to hominids during the course of evolution. People could aspire for supramentalization so long as they did "not make too personal or egoistic an affair of it turning it into a Nietzschean or other ambition to be a superman." But the basic aim of yoga remained what it had been since the time of the Upanishads: "an inner self-development by which each one who follows it can in time discover the one Self in all and evolve a higher consciousness than the mental, a spiritual and supramental consciousness which will transform and divinise human nature."[32]

Secrets of the Self: Muhammad Iqbal

In 1908, the year Aurobindo was arrested for waging war against the British government, another brilliant scholar who had done his undergraduate work at Cambridge, Muhammad Iqbal, returned to India and began working as a professor and lawyer in Lahore. Like Aurobindo, Iqbal was well versed in Western literature but repelled by the materialism of European life. He too felt his homeland was superior to Western countries but came to believe that his true homeland was the global Muslim community and in 1930 he proposed that the northwestern provinces of India should band together as a separate Muslim country. Seventeen years later his wish was fulfilled when British India was divided into two separate nations, secular India and Islamic Pakistan, an outcome Aurobindo deplored.

For all his disapproval of European life, Iqbal recognized that the West had made enormous progress since the start of the modern age, while Islamic civilization, once the pacesetter, had fallen behind. The difference between the two, he decided, was the way they looked on the self. The East, under the influence of Vedantic, Platonic, and Sufic "pantheism," had adopted self-negation as its watchword; yet "the moral and religious ideal of man is not self-negation but self-affirmation," and ironically it was the godless West that understood this.[33]

There is nothing intrinsically Western about the self, Iqbal insisted. It is, metaphysically, "the central fact of the universe," and psychologically, "the central fact in the constitution of man." Iqbal used the Persian term *khudi* for this "indescribable feeling of 'I,' which forms the basis of the uniqueness of each individual," and also for its ethical expression: "self-reliance, self-respect, self-confidence, self-preservation, even self-assertion."[34] He made this the subject of his first major work, *Asrar-i-Khudi* or *Secrets of the Self*, a long philosophical poem published in 1915. Inspired by the poetry of the Persian Sufi Rumi, the writer "rose like music from the string" of a heavenly lute. Whereupon, he declared,

> I unveiled the mystery of the self
> And disclosed its wondrous secret.

All we see around us, he said, "is an effect of the self":

> When the self awoke to consciousness,
> It revealed the universe of Thought.

But this act of cosmic self-affirmation brought "*not-self* to light":

> By the self the seed of opposition is sown in the world:
> It imagines itself to be other than itself
> It makes from itself the forms of others
> In order to multiply the pleasure of strife.

This clash of self and other was necessary for the fulfillment of God's purpose. In the end, "When the self is made strong by Love," its power will rule the world. The poet's final message to his audience was this:

> Save thyself by affirmation of self.[35]

Affirmation implied action, action implied ethics, and the basis of ethics was personality, which provided a universal standard of value. Stated simply: "That which fortifies personality is good, that which weakens it is bad."[36]

According to Iqbal, God, the "Ultimate Ego," is the creator of the individual egos that make up the universe: "From the Ultimate Ego only egos proceed. ... The world, in all its details, from the mechanical movement of what we call the atom of matter to the free movement of thought in the human ego, is the self-revelation of the 'Great I am.'" This self-revelation takes the form of an evolutionary movement in which human egos play a vital role. The universal order "is not eternally achieved and complete in itself." Human beings "are gradually travelling from chaos to cosmos and are helpers in this achievement." Creation was not a one-shot deal: it "is still going on and man too takes his share in it."[37] Borrowing an idea from contemporary philosophers such as Henri Bergson and Samuel Alexander, Iqbal asserted that new qualities "emerge" during the process of evolution: lifeless matter is "a colony of egos of a low order out of which emerges the ego of a higher order," namely "soul-life." It does not follow that the emergent entity "can be resolved into what has conditioned its birth and growth"; as it grows in power it shakes off the hold of matter and "may eventually rise to a position of complete independence."[38]

In order to achieve the self-affirmation that is humanity's moral and religious ideal, each of us must become "more and more individual, more and more unique," that is, "more and more like the most unique Individual," which is God. To do this, we must pass through three stages: "obedience to the Law," "self-control, which is the highest form of self-consciousness or ego-hood," and finally the state of perfection that Iqbal called "divine vicege-rency." The vicegerent or Perfect Man is "the completest ego" and "the last fruit of the tree of humanity," in whom "all the trials of a painful evolution are justified because he is to come at the end."[39]

Secrets of the Self took the Muslim youth of India by storm. They responded enthusiastically to Iqbal's summons to stand up and take their place in the modern world. But to some his *khudi* smacked too much of European individualism, even of the Nietzschean superman. He angrily denied that his Perfect Man had anything to do with Nietzsche; the idea came, he said, from Islamic mysticism and was firmly based on the Quran. In his next long poem, *Mysteries of Selflessness*, he explained that the development of the individual self was a necessary stage in the evolution of an ideal society. And the model of such a society already existed: it was the *ummah* or global Muslim community. During the last decade of his life, he became more and more involved in politics. As the president of the All-India Muslim League in 1930, he asserted that the "religious ideal of Islam" was "organically related to the social order" such that the one could not exist without the other. Accordingly "the construction of a polity on national lines, if it means a displacement of the Islamic principle of solidarity, is simply unthinkable to a Muslim." This was, as writer V. S. Naipaul later observed, "an extraordinary speech for a thinking man to have made in the twentieth century," implying that Muslim India would always stand apart as a theocratic state, in which "the mullahs would always hold the ring, would limit inquiry."[40]

The Human Phenomenon: Pierre Teilhard de Chardin

As a student in England and Germany, Iqbal recognized that the West had gained predominance over Asia through the power of science. At the same time he believed that Western scientists were blind to the secret of selfhood and the aim of evolution. As he wrote in *Asrar-i-Khudi*:

> Science is an instrument for the preservation of Life,
> Science is a means of invigorating the self.
> Science and art are servants of Life.[41]

Iqbal was not the only religious figure of his time who longed to make science a servant of cosmic Life and to reveal the spiritual nature of the evolutionary process. The year he published his poem, a scientifically minded priest who was serving as a stretcher-bearer during World War I began to keep a journal in order "to relieve the boredom of barracks life and to oblige" himself "to think, observe and be precise." The periods of boredom never lasted long, and Pierre Teilhard de Chardin was cited more than once for bravery in the face of danger; yet he never mentioned military events in his journal. His purpose in writing was to trace the lines of the evolutionary advance he believed was underway. "If I write something, if I act intellectually," he noted in January 1916, "it seems to me that it must be *in order to* bring about a conciliation, a reconciliation (in one sense) of God and the World."[42]

Born in central France in 1881, Teilhard became a priest at the age of thirty after years of study in Jesuit schools and seminaries. Fascinated by physical science from his boyhood, he took courses in geology, chemistry, and physics, along with the theological curriculum. Around 1912 he read Henri Bergson's *Creative Evolution*, which helped him harmonize his religious and scientific interests. The central idea of Bergson's book is that evolution is driven toward increasing complexity by a life force or *élan vital*. Analytic thought cannot grasp the nature of this force or of anything that persists in time; intuition alone can do that. Bergson did not invoke God in so many words but it seemed to Teilhard and others that he provided an opening to a religious understanding of evolution.

Throughout the war years, Teilhard crammed his diary with speculations (complete with diagrams and tables) on the development of life and mind on earth and the possibility of a future "man-god" or "super-humanity." During this period he frequently felt himself in touch with the spirit of the universe. Later he wrote: "It was not I who laboriously discovered the All; it was the All which showed itself to me, imposed itself on me through a kind of 'cosmic consciousness'. It is the attraction of the All that has set everything in motion in me, brought it to life and given it organic form." His mission, he wrote in his journal in 1916, would be "to contribute very humbly but tirelessly to the *sanctification of the progress of Nature, Evolution,* by revealing ... its sacred end and its subjection to the realization of the Reign of God." For this he had to cut himself loose from religious as well as scientific orthodoxy. "*The real way to measure and follow [human] evolution* is not to measure the variations of brain or teeth but to appreciate the development, the awakening of mental powers," he wrote in 1915. This went against accepted paleontological practice. "We are crossing a *threshold* in the history of Dogma," he wrote two years later, "we must break a shell, the shell of our complacent belief that we possess a universal explanation of the World." This flew in the face of ecclesiastical authority. The Church, he wrote, had to see that humanity, the universe and God were linked together by love, and that "man, *by turning back upon himself* (upon his *integral* being)" could transform himself into God.[43]

Teilhard was aware that many of his ideas came close to pantheism, the belief, condemned by the Church, that God and the universe are one. "The great *attraction* of pantheism," he wrote in his journal, "is to make us *touch the divine* ... in what *attracts us naturally.*" Pantheists yearned "to go out of themselves, to give themselves to the All in which they hope to lose themselves. But this gesture," Teilhard said, was "a supreme *egoism*, that tries in an obscure way to put itself at the center of things, *to divinize itself by integrating itself*" with the All. While it was clear to Teilhard that this "pagan" conception had to be avoided, he moved toward it "instinctively" and so "had to react, to correct it." The solution, he found, was to generalize the pantheistic impulse and integrate it with the teachings of the Church: "Every man is undeniably *one body* with the Cosmos. Therefore the mystic Body of Christ (organic Sum of all the elect) is one body with the Cosmos. ... The mystic body of Christ is thus *necessarily* a Cosmic Body." But pantheism continued to be a problem for Teilhard, forcing him to renounce in print what he felt drawn to in his inner life: "Pantheism seduces us by its vistas of perfect universal union," he wrote in *The Divine Milieu*. "But ultimately, if it were true, it would give us only fusion and unconsciousness; for, at the end of the evolution it claims to reveal, the elements of the world vanish in the God they create or by whom they are absorbed. Our God, on the contrary, pushes to its furthest possible limit the differentiation among the creatures he concentrates within himself. ... Christianity alone therefore saves."[44] Like Maine de Biran a hundred years earlier, Teilhard let dogma determine how far his speculations could go.

In July and August 1918 French forces took part in the Second Battle of the Marne, one of the bloodiest of the war, which left more than 300,000 dead or wounded. On September 8, after a long period of duty at the front, Teilhard made a rare personal entry in his diary, resolving "to use this renewal to attain a clearer consciousness of myself, the World and God":

> By the inner development of my thought, and by external necessity (days passed at death's door), – I have above all been occupied with the Future, with its inexorable and ever-renewed mystery, – with its identification with the living and creative action of God, – and above all, perhaps, with the effective action that confidence exerts on the individual future of each of us.

The future was the unknown; confidence helped "to consolidate, clarify, animate all this chaos and incertitude," giving a "heart and a face to blind chance." Looking forward with confidence, he examined the future's "Structure or Pre-formation." Seven points arose in this connection, of which the second was: "The indeterminacy of the higher *orders* of existence (the higher Terms of the Evolution). There is a tendency toward an Ω [omega] that is created (*in relation* to us) as needed. ..."[45]

Teilhard's Omega is the pre-existing point of supreme consciousness that draws the evolution in the direction of ever-increasing complexity. He mentioned it first in diary entries of 1917–18 and developed it in the years that followed. Eventually it became the distinguishing term of his philosophy, an evolutionary endpoint that he identified with the cosmic Christ. In *The Human Phenomenon*, his main philosophical work, he defined it as "a supremely autonomous focus of union." To understand what this meant for the human self, he made a distinction between the individual and the person. The drive of any element to individualize itself leads back toward dissolution, he wrote. "To be fully ourselves" we must move "in the direction of convergence with all the rest," for "the peak of ourselves, the acme of our originality, is not our individuality but our person." Giving a scientific spin to the Christian idea of the true and false self, he concluded: "The true ego grows in inverse proportion to 'egoism'. Like the Omega which attracts it, the element only becomes personal when it universalizes itself."[46]

In May 1918, Teilhard took solemn vows, binding himself to a life of obedience to the Church. After the armistice he resumed his scientific studies, earning a doctorate for his geological and paleontological research and spending a year and a half doing fieldwork in China. He also continued to elaborate his evolutionary philosophy. In an essay of 1923 he proposed that the emergence of the human being was "of the same order of zoological magnitude" as the emergence of the biosphere, the realm of life, from the lithosphere and atmosphere. Humans were not just markedly developed animals but representatives of a higher order, superior to but still rooted in the animal order. Together they constituted a "noosphere" or realm of mind-and-spirit, a "sphere of reflection, of conscious invention, of the conscious unity of souls." In theological writings of the same period, Teilhard offered an evolutionary explanation of the doctrine of original sin. Returning to France in 1924, he was stunned to learn that Church authorities objected to some of his statements on this topic. He was forced to withdraw them and to agree to stick to scientific subjects in what he published. Back in China, he resumed his teaching and research but also continued to work out his evolutionary ideas in his notebooks. One of the most important concepts he introduced was "planetization," the process by which "the different races and civilizations of *Homo sapiens sapiens* become synthesized to form a linked organic whole in which different spiritual elements converge and the ultra-human develops."[47] For Teilhard the superhuman was not an individual but a global phenomenon, a spiritual synthesis with a high-tech underpinning.

In 1948 Teilhard sought permission to publish *The Human Phenomenon* and to accept an invitation to lecture at the Collège de France. Church officials refused both requests. Two years later the pope condemned some of his ideas in an encyclical letter. Teilhard remained outwardly obedient but privately continued his work. "Obviously I cannot abandon my own personal search," he wrote to the head of his order, for "that would involve me in an interior catastrophe and in disloyalty to my most cherished vocation."[48] After his death in 1955, his colleagues published *The Divine Milieu* and *The Human Phenomenon,* and they have remained in print ever since.

Dare to Be Yourself: André Gide

On January 30, 1916, while Teilhard was billeted behind the lines in Flanders, the French writer André Gide, who was working at a center for Belgian refugees, made an entry in his journal that might almost have been written by Teilhard:

> If I had to formulate a credo, I should say: God is not behind us. He is to come. He must be sought, not at the beginning, but at the end of the evolution. He is terminal and not initial. He is the supreme and final point toward which all nature tends in time. And since time does not exist for Him, it is a matter of indifference to Him whether that evolution of which He is the summit follows or precedes, and whether He determines it by propulsion or attraction.

The next sentence, however, is far from Teilhardian: "It is through man that God is molded."[49] For Gide, the human always takes precedence over the divine, if indeed there is such a thing as divinity.

Born in Paris in 1869 to an austere Protestant family, Gide struggled to reconcile the teachings of the Bible with his strong sexual urgings and a desire for personal freedom. He began to keep a journal in 1889 and continued it for almost sixty years, producing a text that is both a literary masterpiece and a significant document in the history of the self. An early entry set the tone for the whole: "Dare to be yourself. I must underline that in my head too." For some years he remained a believing Christian, asking God to guide him "in thy paths of light," but he was torn "by a conflict between the rules of morality and the rules of sincerity."[50] His literary life got off to a good start in 1891 when his work came to the attention of Stéphane Mallarmé, Oscar Wilde, and other famous writers. His personal life was less satisfactory, as he continued to suffer from emotional and sexual frustration and persistent ill health. The year 1893 was a turning point. "It is a duty to make oneself happy," he wrote that April, "We shall no longer ask God to raise us up to happiness." Later in the year he and a friend went to North Africa, where Gide experienced sexual fulfillment for the first time. Refusing to accept the burden of guilt, he wrote on his return to Europe: "I am unwilling to understand a rule of conduct which does not permit and even teach the greatest, the finest, and the freest use and development of all our powers." He wrote of his sexual experiences in the novel *The Immoralist* and later in his memoirs. About the latter, the novelist Marcel Proust told him: "You can tell anything" but only "on condition that you never say: 'I.'" Gide's response: "But that won't suit me." For him, sincerity was a necessity but at the same time a will-o'-the-wisp. As he wrote in *The Immoralist*, "One cannot both be sincere and seem so."[51]

Gide felt that most Western novelists "were concerned only with the relations of men [and women] among themselves, relations of passion, intellect, family, society, social classes." Only the rarest of writers, Dostoyevsky and a few others, "were concerned with the relations of the individual with himself or with God."[52] Gide tried to illuminate this personal domain in his own fiction. In *The Immoralist*, Ménalque (a character based on Wilde) advises Michel (representing a part of Gide) to rise above moral conventions. Michel claims his freedom but neglects his wife, who dies of tuberculosis. In the end he tells his friends: "To know how to free oneself is nothing; the arduous thing is to know what to do with one's freedom." In a companion novel, *Strait is the Gate,* the beautiful Alissa refuses to marry the man she loves, telling him "We were born for a happiness other than that," but she dies without tasting either heavenly or earthly bliss. Gide himself, looking back to when his own beliefs were as inflexible as Alissa's, wrote that he regretted "not having taken better advantage of my youth. When pleasure invited me, I used to refuse my body to harmony; it was only much later, only too late, that I understood what a reliable guide is desire. I used to localize God in a certain suprasensual region, inaccessible or almost, toward which I tended with an Alpinist's ambition, and grace was not vouchsafed me."[53]

Gide affirmed life in a Nietzschean rather than a Teilhardian way; but he was not afraid to turn to the Bible for moral examples. The story of Noah's sacrifice after the flood restored to him the confidence "that everything progresses toward the best," for "it is in the negation of self that springs up and takes shelter the highest affirmation of self." Thirty years later, toward the end of his life and after a devastating war, he could still write: "I shall be able to say: 'So be it' to whatever happens to me, were it even ceasing to exist, disappearing after having been. But," he added, "just now I am and I do not know exactly what that means. I should like to try to understand." Then he wrote a remarkable passage on the meaning of being, nothingness, and evolutionary change:

> There might very well be nothing; nor anyone. No one to notice that there is nothing, and to consider that natural.
>
> But there is something, and, whatever it may be, the strange thing! I shall never cease being amazed at this.

Something and not complete nonexistence. It required centuries of centuries to produce that something, to get that, whatever it may be, from chaos. Even more centuries to obtain the least life. And even more for that to achieve consciousness. ...

Faced with the mystery of the simple fact of being, it was natural for people to turn to God, but Gide rejected that move:

Get along without God. ... I mean: get along without the idea of God, without a belief in an attentive, tutelary, and retributive Providence ... not everyone can achieve this.

Despite his refusal of otherworldly certitude, he was able to affirm the value of life and selfhood:

Take things, not for what they claim to be, but for what they are.
Play the game with the hand one has.
Insist upon oneself as one is.[54]

This passage clearly is colored by the thought of the French existentialist thinkers such as Jean-Paul Sartre, whose *Being and Nothingness* was published in 1943. Sartre, for whom Gide was the model of the engaged writer, provided an apt summary of his predecessor's work after his death in 1951: "In a word, he *lived* his ideas, and one, above all – the death of God. ... Chosen in the abstract, at twenty, his atheism would have been false. Slowly earned, crowning the quest of half a century, this atheism becomes his concrete truth and our own."[55]

Aurobindo, Iqbal, and Teilhard all anchored their views about the self on a spiritual or religious tradition. But unlike most earlier Vedantic, Islamic, and Catholic thinkers, they believed that the self was revealed in evolution and affirmed the value of the world. Gide, too, affirmed life and found meaning in evolution, but he rejected God and religion. His atheism was seconded by many later thinkers, who found no reason to accept a cosmic theory of evolution or to affirm the spiritual value of a world that seemed to be in terminal decline.

The Search for Authenticity

The only drama that really interests me and that I should always be willing to depict anew is the debate of the individual with whatever keeps him from being authentic, with whatever is opposed to his integrity, to his integration.

– André Gide

By the turn of the twentieth century, the idea of the unconscious had spread from psychology and philosophy to creative literature and general culture but had not had much impact on popular ideas of the self. In 1912 two leading psychiatrists, Sigmund Freud and Carl Gustav Jung, published works that tried to bring the unconscious from the realm of speculation to the forefront of clinical practice. In "A Note on the Unconscious in Psycho-Analysis," Freud wrote: "The term *unconscious*, which was used in the purely descriptive sense before, now comes to imply something more. It designates not only latent ideas in general, but especially ideas with a certain dynamic character, ideas keeping apart from consciousness in spite of their intensity and activity."[1] According to Freud, people repress impulses, emotions, ideas and other mental contents that are too painful or too threatening to assimilate. The repressed contents enter the unconscious and lie beyond the reach of memory but make themselves known through indirect means such as dreams and verbal slips. Conflict between the repressed contents and the person's conscious mind is the source of neurosis and insanity. Freudian psychiatrists or psychoanalysts treat these conditions by means of dream analysis, verbal free association, and other methods that bring the repressed contents to the surface, where they can be dealt with. The details of Freud's theory have always been controversial and are not generally accepted by psychiatric professionals today, but there is broad agreement about his central insight: people are unaware of much that goes on within them and these unconscious activities have important effects on their conscious minds and bodies.

During the late 1910s and early 1920s, Freud developed a theory of the structure of the mind that went beyond the simple conscious-unconscious dichotomy of his earlier work. He proposed in *The Ego and the Id* that the mind consists of an *Ich* ("I" or *ego*), "derived from bodily sensations" and partly conscious, and an *Es* ("it" or *id*), made up of impulses and entirely unconscious. There is, in addition, a "modification of the ego" representing social authority that Freud called the *Über-Ich* (*super-ego*). These three are in constant conflict, with most of the strain falling on the ego. As Freud explained graphically in a later work: "the ego, driven by the id, confined by the super-ego, repulsed by reality, struggles to master its economic task of bringing about harmony among the forces and influences working in and upon it." Sometimes it succeeds but more often it "reacts by generating anxiety." Here too, the details of Freud's theory are no longer widely accepted, but his insight that the human self is not unitary, harmonious, and transparent but multiple, conflicted, and wrapped in obscurity has spread throughout Western culture and forever changed the way that people view themselves. Freud wrote that his theory was as damaging to humanity's "naïve self love" as the discoveries of Copernicus and Darwin, since it demonstrated "to the 'ego' of each of us that he is not even master of his own house, but that he must remain content with the veriest scraps of information about what is going on unconsciously in his own mind." He added that the discovery of the dynamics of the unconscious was the result of "present-day psychological research," primarily his own.[2] This was an exaggeration: dozens of thinkers from Augustine to Nietzsche had analyzed mental conflict and speculated about regions of the mind that are beyond our ken. But Freud and his followers were among the first to bring these ideas to the general public, which at the beginning of the twentieth century was ready to receive them.

The other work of 1912 that enlarged the idea of the unconscious was Jung's *Psychology of the Unconscious*, in which he presented a theory of the *libido* that differed considerably from Freud's.[3] In Freudian psychoanalysis *libido*, or sexual energy, is not just the drive to reproduce but the energy behind all human activity and indeed all civilization, since even cultural activities such as religion and art are at root transformed sexuality. Jung redefined *libido* as psychic energy in general, saying that it took different forms at different stages of life. Sucking, for instance, was better explained as an expression of the nutritive instinct than as a form of infant sexuality. Jung dealt at some length with religious mythology, which he called "one of the greatest and most significant human institutions," not, as in Freud, an "unconscious recasting of the erotic into something religious."[4]

In subsequent works, Jung gave special attention to three ideas that are present in seed form in the *Psychology*: the collective unconscious, the archetypes, and individuation. He theorized that "in addition to our immediate consciousness" and the "personal unconscious" that it creates, there is "a second psychic system of a collective, universal, and impersonal nature which is identical in all individuals." This collective unconscious, unlike the personal unconscious, "does not develop individually but is inherited." Its contents are "pre-existent forms, the archetypes," which are present in the oral and written literature of the world and emerge in our dreams.[5] Examples are the Child, the Hero, and the Great Mother, along with the five primary archetypes: the Self, the Shadow, the Anima, the Animus, and the Persona. Here we will concern ourselves with Jung's Self, "the principle and archetype of orientation and meaning." He believed that "the goal of psychic development" was to realize the Self through a process he called individuation. This was, he clarified, not the same as "individualism," which was just "deliberately stressing and giving prominence to some supposed particularity rather than collective considerations and obligations." Individuation meant "becoming an 'in-dividual' [i.e., undivided being], and, in so far as 'individuality' embraces our innermost, last and incomparable uniqueness, it also implies becoming one's own self." This was an arduous process, requiring the subject to integrate the contents of the personal and collective unconscious. It also was a process that was never really complete, since "there will always exist an indeterminate and indeterminable amount of unconscious material" that has to be assimilated. Best undertaken during the second half of life, integration was "a gathering together of what is scattered, of all things in us that have never been properly related, and a coming to terms with oneself with a view of achieving full consciousness." The true individual had to be sought through an "uncommonly difficult" process of "profound reflection."[6]

Jung's speculations on authenticity, integration, and the self paralleled similar developments in other schools of psychiatry as well as in philosophy and literature. Freud took little interest in such matters, giving most of his attention to the sources of psychic conflict, in particular repressed sexuality; but from the 1920s a few psychoanalysts began to study the role of non-sexual factors in personality formation, and this led to a renewed interest in the idea of the self. Melanie Kline, an Austrian working in England, stressed the importance of "object relations," that is, the relations of young children with other people, especially their mothers, or with internalized images of them. The self, she thought, took form in relation to these objects. Ronald Fairbairn, another object-relations theorist, asserted in 1946 that "libido is not primarily pleasure-seeking, but object-seeking" and that "the real libidinal aim is the establishment of satisfactory relationships with objects." Like Jung, he developed "a psychology of individuation and thus of the identity of the self essentially based on meaning and value rather than on instinctual gratification."[7]

Fairbairn's colleague Donald Winnicott drew on extensive clinical experience in writing "Ego Distortion in Terms of True and False Self" (1960), the most important contribution to the study of the self from a modified Freudian perspective. According to Winnicott, an infant's "True Self does not become a living reality except as a result of the mother's repeated success in meeting the infant's spontaneous gesture or sensory hallucination." If maternal care is inadequate, a defensive false self takes form that conceals the true self, preventing it from making "the spontaneous gesture and the personal idea." If this condition is not corrected, the false self becomes entrenched and the person goes through life "feeling unreal" or burdened with a "sense of futility," because "only the True Self can be creative and only the True Self can feel real." Winnicott admitted that the idea of a true and false self was not new, since it had appeared already "in certain religions and philosophical systems" – an acknowledgement of the contribution of thinkers such as Augustine, Rousseau, and Heidegger – but he felt that its acceptance by psychiatry would have "an important effect on psycho-analytic work."[8]

A Self of One's Own: Marion Milner

Fairbairn and Winnicott were members of the independent group of British psychiatrists, aligned neither with the orthodox school headed by Freud's daughter Anna nor with the object-relations group of Melanie Klein. Another member of the independent group was Marion Milner, an Englishwoman who came to psychiatry after years of work as a practical psychologist and more than fifteen years of self-study aided by diary keeping. Born in 1900, she earned a degree in psychology and physiology from the University of London and in 1924 began work as an industrial psychologist. Two years later she was bowled over by a reading of Montaigne's *Essays* and around the same time took a self-help mental training course. The essays and the course inspired her to start a diary. Her aim was to discover what she really wanted and what sort of experiences made her happy. With this in mind, she would note down what she did and thought and felt and afterwards go over her notes to see if she could "discover any rules about the conditions in which happiness occurred." The experiment, she supposed, might last "a few weeks or months," after which she would be able to say: "These are the facts of my life. Now I'm going to take it in hand for myself."[9] As it turned out, the experiment lasted for more than seventy years. Along the way she published three books based on her diaries along with a number of professional monographs.

Early on, Milner found that the best way to proceed was to record "not carefully considered aims, but just the first thing that came into my head." This was a very Montaignian way to proceed, but unlike her predecessor she had few literary ambitions: "fine words" would not get her where she wanted to go. Better, she thought, to let the pen run on:

> Oh, I want to let go, to lose myself, my soul, what does it mean, to feel life pulsing through me, the big tides sweeping in, till I'm one with the immense surging fullness of the sea: and when it ebbs I would be clear and cool, washed free from stinking garbage and stagnant fetid water. What does all that mean?[10]

Montaigne discovered that the idle mind generated chimeras and monsters; Milner found that her mind "had a host of thoughts I never knew about," some of which were rather embarrassing. Eventually she learned to impose order on the chaos by making what she called an "internal gesture of the mind. It was as if one's self-awareness had a central point of intensest being, the very core of one's I-ness."[11] Continuing her research, she found that she had "two quite different selves, one which answered when I thought deliberately, another which answered when I let my thought be automatic." The right way to understand the automatic self and bring it under control was neither to "push my thought nor let it drift. I must simply make an internal gesture of standing back and watching." The act of self-observation "was somehow a force in itself which changed my whole being." Likewise, "the effort of recording my experiences" had "an influence upon their nature."[12]

After four years of observing herself and noting the results, Milner began work on a book she published in 1934 as *A Life of One's Own*. In the course of writing it she observed that it "was not so easy to know just what one's self was" and to act in accordance with that knowledge. "It was far easier to want what other people seemed to want and then imagine that the choice was one's own." Her diaries and the book helped her "see through my own eyes instead of at second hand" but they also convinced her that her own self-consciousness – by which she meant her automatic self – was an "imprisoning island" from which she had to escape.[13]

A few years later, Milner went to Spain on a sabbatical and began what she called "an experiment in leisure." As before, she kept a diary and reflected on her experiences but she also followed suggestions that came from the books she read, the places she visited, and the concerts she attended. One of the discoveries she had made while working on *A Life* was that by taking the mental attitude "I want nothing" she could bring about a remarkable change in her state of consciousness. She decided to try this out again while exploring the idea of sacrifice. When she became anxious, she wrote, "I tried a ritual sacrifice of all my plans and strivings. Instead of straining harder. … I said: 'I am nothing, I know nothing, I want nothing,' and with a momentary gesture wiped away all sense of my own existence."[14] One result of this self-emptying was the discovery of an "other" that could be "a guiding force in one's life." This was "not one's self, in the ordinary sense of the word self"; on the other hand she felt "it would be insolent to call this God" even though it was characterized by an extraordinary knowledge that had nothing to do with her. She finally decided to call it "Answering Activity" without trying to pin down its nature.[15]

Milner devoted many pages of *An Experiment in Leisure* to an analysis of symbols that emerged in dream or idle thought or were found in ancient and modern literature. She knew this was the sort of material "that the psycho-analyst would claim was only his to interpret." People in the psychiatric profession had always given her "the feeling that they considered the unconscious mind as a sort of special preserve which no layman must tamper with." She refused to go along with this. Not only did she decline to pay for "a daily hour of help from the psycho-analyst," she also refused "to force psycho-analytic interpretations upon what I observed if the spontaneous wanderings of my mind did not seem to lead me to them." She did, however, "borrow one guiding principle from psycho-analysis, the principle that when you give your mind the reins and let it rove freely, there is no such thing as irrelevance" and that "whatever thought pops up is in some way important, however far-fetched it may appear."[16]

Before she began her experiment in leisure, Milner had found "much of Freudian theory so difficult to grasp" that she gave up trying to understand it. Afterwards she made another try and found she could relate it to her own experience because it helped explain the spontaneous images she had been observing in herself.[17] Intrigued, she began psychoanalysis under Sylvia Payne, a member of the independent group, and in 1943 was admitted to the British Psycho-Analytical Society. In the years that followed she became professionally and personally close to Winnicott; one of his biographers wrote that she was "his only intellectual and imaginative peer in the British Society."[18] Their views on growth and creativity were similar but she differed from him in regard to the formation of the self and the relation of the self to the body. Winnicott held that the self was not observable or communicable, while she believed that "in the right setting" the self could "be related to by the conscious ego discovering that it can turn in upon itself, make contact with the core of its own being, and find there a renewal, a rebirth." She also came to feel that the discovery of the self was closely related to "the discovery of one's own body."[19]

As a psychoanalyst, Milner worked with patients and published in professional journals but she also continued her personal investigations. One result of this was *On Not Knowing How to Paint* (1950), her best-known book. Another was *Eternity's Sunrise: A Way of Keeping a Diary* (1987), which she saw as a continuation of the work she had begun in *An Experiment*. Her method in *Eternity's Sunrise* was to concentrate on "beads" of memory to see where they led her. It seemed clear that "what the beads were about was the idea of making contact with an inner something, something that can apparently be reached by various kinds of attention to the inside of the body, contacted rather than thought about, and combined with an inner silence." She had to learn to let go of ordinary aims and desires, to "sink right down inside to the bottom of things," in order to be able "to come up truly refreshed." The attitude of letting go brought her back to the Answering Activity she had noticed in her earlier experiments. As before, it seemed to be connected with what people called "God," but she still wasn't ready to call it that. As she wrote in her diary:

> This word God, how my heart sinks when people hold forth about Him, him. Would it be better if they said "She"? Or is "It" better? Who said, "He, she or it living its own life through each of us"? That sounds better. "The Tao of which we speak is not the real Tao". That sounds better still. Yes, of course, the other day I found myself saying: "God is all right if no one says anything about him."

She had received an Anglican upbringing but found that "routine praying, Church praying, isn't any good, for me at least." What was lacking in such prayer was the bodily side of things; for her, opening to the Answering Activity was "a kind of concentration of the body." Reflecting on the Christian term "incarnation," she realized that this was something that happens "every morning when one wakes," when the imaginative body descends "to indwelling in its own flesh and bones."[20] She came around to an insight she had had some years earlier:

> I had suspected often before, and this confirmed my suspicion, that for me at least, there was no method for salvation, richness came only when I faced experience naked of expectancy or hope – "the readiness is all".
> It seemed then, that all these years I had apparently been trying to reach after, grasp, comprehend, this mysterious and astonishing fact of simply being alive."[21]

Milner's colleagues sometimes referred to her – sometimes dismissively – as a "mystic." She always got annoyed when people said that: "To me," she said, "it's just living."[22]

Letting Go: Thomas Merton

Milner may not have been a mystic, but there were a number of parallels between her approach and the teachings of various spiritual traditions. She often spoke of "letting go" and of discovering "emptiness." These ideas are present in some Hindu and Buddhist traditions and also in the apophatic or negative path of Christian mysticism. She was aware of these parallels and tried meditation and yoga but never became a mystic because, she wrote, "I don't feel I want to give up everything for union with God."[23] A younger contemporary of hers, the American Thomas Merton, did choose to give up everything in his pursuit of God, following the path of apophatic mysticism as a Catholic monk of the Cistercian order. He was born in France in 1915 to an American mother and a New Zealander father, both of them artists who died before he finished school. In 1933 he went to Cambridge on a scholarship but spent more time drinking than studying and fathered an out-of-wedlock child. Expelled, he went to New York, enrolled in Columbia University and became a student of literature and a writer. Attracted by Catholicism, he was received into the Church in 1938 and three years later entered a Cistercian monastery in Kentucky.

The Cistercians or Trappists follow a very strict rule, rising at two in the morning for a day of prayer, ritual, study, and work. Despite his struggles as a novice, Merton was content with his lot, finding the "atmosphere of the cloister" to be "charged with supernatural happiness and radiant with an indefinable sense of vision which belongs to all." In the mid-1940s, he began to do literary work for the order, published two collections of poetry and gave serious attention to a diary he had begun before entering the monastery. "What was painfully artificial in that [earlier] diary," he wrote in January 1948, "was that I was trying so much to write it like every other pious diary that was ever written: 'I resolve this' – 'I pray that.' Well, I am very slow to learn what is useless in my life!" He realized he had to stop conforming "to a lot of artificial standards, to things external and fragmentary that tend to keep my interior life on the surface." His journal became a self-revealing testament of a seeker of truth who was also, and perhaps primarily, a writer. "It is possible to doubt whether I have become a monk (a doubt I have to live with)," he wrote in 1962, "but it is not possible to doubt that I am a writer, that I was born one and will most probably die as one."[24]

Merton's spiritual autobiography *The Seven Storey Mountain* was published in 1948 and became an immediate bestseller. Enclosed in his monastery, bound by a vow of silence, he became a world-famous literary figure, corresponding with Nobel laureates and ordinary readers and writing dozens of books, most of them based in one way or another on his journal. At the same time he carried out his religious duties, becoming a priest, then a guide of students for the priesthood and finally a master of novices. But as the years passed, he began to chafe against the restrictions of his order and to yearn for more personal freedom. Between 1965 and 1968 he lived as a hermit on the grounds of the monastery, praying, meditating, and writing books and articles on religion and politics, reading Pasternak and Miłosz and Basho, corresponding with Zen scholar D. T. Suzuki and psychologist Reza Arasteh and listening to Bob Dylan and Joan Baez. In 1968 he was allowed to leave the monastery to visit India, Ceylon, and Thailand. The trip began on a high note:

> Joy. We left the ground – I with Christian mantras and a great sense of destiny, of being at last on my true way after years of waiting and wondering and fooling around.
>
> May I not come back without having settled the great affair. Without having found also the great compassion, *mahakaruna*. …
>
> I am going home, to the home where I have never been in this body.[25]

It ended tragically, when Merton electrocuted himself while getting out of the bath in a Bangkok hotel room.

From the beginning of his monastic life, Merton was drawn to the negative path, the path of Gregory of Nyssa, Meister Eckhart, and John of the Cross. "The way to contemplation," he wrote in 1948, "is the way of emptiness and night." It meant, as Eckhart wrote, making oneself utterly empty, for "to be naked, poor, empty of all created things lifts the soul up to God." Staying up one night in 1952, Merton addressed his God:

> With You there is no longer any dialogue, any contest, any opposition. You are found in communion! Thou in me and I in Thee and Thou in them and they in me: dispossession within dispossession, dispassion within dispassion, emptiness within emptiness, freedom within freedom. I am alone. The Father and I are One.

Later he found that the way of the Christian mystics was not very different from certain forms of Buddhism and that both paths were arduous and long. In 1968 he sat with a Tibetan lama comparing fine points of Christian and Buddhist doctrine: "*dharmakaya* – the Risen Christ, suffering, compassion for all creatures, motives for 'helping others,' all leading back to *dzogchen*, the ultimate emptiness, the unity of *sunyata* and *karuna*, going 'beyond the *dharmakaya*' and 'beyond God' to the ultimate perfect emptiness." The lama told him he "had meditated in solitude for thirty years or more and had not attained to perfect emptiness." Merton said he hadn't either.[26]

Mystics of the negative path try to reach the unnamable God by means of detachment, what Eckhart called *Gelassenheit*. "The man who has attained this complete detachment," the German mystic wrote, "is so carried into eternity that no transient thing can move him." Merton reflected on this concept in his journal:

> *Gelassenheit* – letting go – not being encumbered by systems, words, projects. And yet being free *in* systems, projects. ... Error of self-conscious contemplatives: to get hung up in a certain kind of non-action which is an imprisonment, a stupor, the opposite of *Gelassenheit*. Actually quietism is incompatible with true inner freedom. The burden of this stupid and enforced "quiet" – the self sitting heavily on its own head.

Letting go meant abandoning one's personal identity in order to find a greater self. He expressed this in Christian terms in *The Wisdom of the Desert* (1960): "What the Fathers sought most of all was their own true self, in Christ. And in order to do this, they had to reject completely the false, formal self, fabricated under social compulsion in 'the world.'" He expressed it again in *Zen and the Birds of Appetite* (1968): "The man who has truly found his spiritual nakedness, who has realized he is empty, is not a self that has *acquired* emptiness or *become* empty. He just 'is empty from the beginning.' ... He loves with a purity and freedom that spring spontaneously and directly from the fact that he has fully recovered the divine likeness, and is now fully his true self because he is lost in God."[27]

The idea of the true and false self is a feature of various Eastern and Western religions, a recurrent theme in modern literature, and a category in the psychiatric thought of Winnicott and others. In early discussions of this subject, Merton appealed to Christian authorities, sometimes putting modern language into the mouths of the Doctors of the Church. "After all, what *is* your personal identity?" he wrote in *The Waters of Siloe*. "It is what you really are, your real self. ... We do not generally know what is good for us. That is because, in [Cistercian founder] St. Bernard's language, our true personality has been concealed under the 'disguise' of a false self, the *ego* whom we tend to worship in place of God." Later, while remaining orthodox in inspiration, he drew on his personal experience as a monk to give an original turn to his expression: "We must be saved above all from that abyss of confusion and absurdity which is our own worldly self. The person must be rescued from the individual. ... The creative and mysterious inner self must be delivered from the wasteful, hedonistic and destructive ego that seeks only to cover itself with disguises." In answer to the question "What is the inner self?" he said there was no point trying to define it since it was "first of all, a spontaneity" and that it was "nothing if not free." Alluding to the philosophy of Jean-Paul Sartre, he explained that the inner self could not be boiled down to an essence that could be used to bring it under our control. "Such an idea," he wrote, "would imply a complete misapprehension of the *existential* reality we are talking about. The inner self is not a part of our being, like a motor in a car. It is our entire substantial reality itself, on its highest and most personal and most existential level."[28]

In trying to rise above his lower or false self, Merton was following in the footsteps of Augustine, Bernard, John of the Cross, and dozens of other saints. In trying to manifest his higher or true self, he was emulating not only these Christian exemplars but also modern writers such as Lawrence, Gide, Sartre, and Camus, secular priests of the cult of authenticity. The two inspirations sometimes sat rather uncomfortably together. He wrote in his journal in 1958, using language no modernist would have rejected: "Finally I am coming to the conclusion that my highest ambition is to be what I already am. That I will never fulfill my obligation to surpass myself unless I first accept myself, and if I accept myself fully in the right way, I will already have surpassed myself." Yet around the same time he wrote: "You can never be sure whether you are being true to your true self or only building up a defense for the false personality that is the creature of your own appetite for esteem." Examining the dangers of the spiritual path, he noted: "So much more than mere 'prudence' is needed – and infinitely more than simple 'personal responsibility – autonomy – authenticity,' etc. A superficial existentialism can be a disaster." He summed up the difficulties in a brilliant entry of 1965, which shows his ability to see a problem from different sides without trying to force a premature conclusion:

> The time has probably come to go back on all that I have said about one's "real self," etc. etc., and show that there is after all no hidden mysterious "real self" *other than* or "hiding behind" the self that one is. The "real self" is not an object, but I have betrayed it by seeming to promise a possibility of knowing it somewhere, sometimes as a reward for astuteness, fidelity, and a quick-witted ability to stay one jump ahead of reality. However, the empirical self is not to be taken as fully "real" either. Here is where the illusion begins.[29]

Living and Dying Authentically: Phenomenology and Existentialism

Authenticity has been a theme in Western literature since the Renaissance. It is evident in the works of Montaigne and Shakespeare, whose "To thine own self be true" remains a classic formulation of this attitude.[30] It came to the forefront in the writings of Rousseau, whose *Confessions* and *Reveries* inaugurated the tradition of the self-revealing memoir. The writers of the Romantic movement championed the integrity of the individual in the face of political and religious oppression and the impersonality of industrial society. Later writers such as Stendhal, Tocqueville, Emerson, and Thoreau stressed the need of the individual to resist the withering effects of the crowd, while sociologists such as Marx and Durkheim showed how modern society produced alienation and anomie in its members. Reacting against the conceit of systematic philosophy and the hypocrisy of established religion, Kierkegaard asserted the primacy of "the single individual," while Nietzsche attacked the hypocrisy of Christian morality and looked forward to the advent of the Overhuman. The writings of Kierkegaard and Nietzsche as well as Dostoyevsky were inspirations to the phenomenological and existential philosophers who dominated European thought during the middle of the twentieth century, presenting the struggle for freedom and authenticity as the purpose of human life.

The most influential of these philosophers was the German Martin Heidegger, whose *Being and Time* (1927) deals at great and difficult length with the fundamental questions of existence. One of his insights is that the human being in the world, which he called *Dasein* ("being-there"), always finds itself embedded in a preexisting web of culture and cannot be conceived without reference to that. As a result of this embeddedness, most individuals follow the dictates of the crowd, which Heidegger referred to by the neologism *das Man*, "the one" or "the they," that is, everyone and no one in particular. His description of this situation in *Being and Time* is a tortuous but (once one gets the hang of the jargon) devastating account of the absorption of the individual by the mass: "The 'they' is there alongside everywhere, but in such a manner that it has always stolen away whenever Dasein presses for a decision. Yet because the 'they' presents every judgment and decision as its own, it deprives the particular Dasein of its answerability." As a result "the particular Dasein in its everydayness is *disburdened* by the 'they.'" In ordinary language: as a result of the pressure of the crowd, most people lead lives that are inauthentic and irresponsible. The "they" watches over "everything exceptional that thrusts itself to the fore. Every kind of priority gets noiselessly suppressed." There is a general "levelling down," a socially enforced "averageness," in which everything authentic "gets glossed over as something that has long been well known."[31]

A being not answerable to anything that happens is spared the *Angst* or anxiety that is the lot of those who face up to the necessity of choice and the inevitability of death. This angst is the mark of authenticity. Reverting again to Heidegger's difficult but illuminating jargon: "*Authentic* Being-towards-death" cannot "*give a new explanation* for it to accord with the common sense of the 'they.'" Nor should the possibility of death be actualized in suicide; it "must be cultivated *as a possibility*, and we must *put up with* it *as a possibility*." In this way a particular Dasein is freed from the grip of the "they" and becomes an authentic individual.[32]

Heidegger's "existence philosophy" developed out of the phenomenology of Edmund Husserl, under whom Heidegger studied between 1919 and 1923. Phenomenology is an approach to philosophical enquiry that gives its attention to consciousness and the appearances of the objects of consciousness without regard to their ultimate reality. It influenced not only Heidegger but also Sartre and his colleagues Simone de Beauvoir and Maurice Merleau-Ponty, who emerged during the 1940s as the leaders of a school of philosophy that they called existentialism. In his first major work, *The Transcendence of the Ego*, Sartre argued against the so-called transcendental ego, which according to Husserl (as well as Descartes and the German idealists) was the subject of consciousness but not its object. When there is no transcendental ego, Sartre concluded,

> there is no longer an "inner life" … because there is no longer anything which is an *object* and which can at the same time partake of the intimacy of consciousness. Doubts, remorse, the so-called "mental crises of consciousness," etc. – in short, all the content of intimate diaries [*journaux intimes*] – become sheer *performance*.

But this denial of subjective existence did not rule out personal engagement. "The phenomenologists have plunged man back into the world," he insisted in this 1937 essay, "they have given full measure to man's agonies and sufferings, and also to his rebellions."[33]

A year after publishing *The Transcendence of the Ego*, Sartre brought out the first of his literary works, a novel in the form of a diary entitled *Nausea*. He later made it clear that he used this book "to show, without complacency, the texture of my life," describing "the bitter unjustified existence of my fellowmen" in an effort to exonerate his own. In the novel, Roquentin, a scholar living in a city like Le Havre (where Sartre was posted during the 1930s), is tormented by the notion that he is not free, that he has no inner life: "Never have I felt as strongly as today that I was devoid of secret dimensions, limited to my body," he writes in one entry. Like a phenomenologist he attends to the surfaces of things: "as my eyes fell on the pad of white sheets, I was struck by its appearance, and I stayed there, my pen raised, gazing at that dazzling paper: how hard and brilliant it was, how present it was. There was nothing in it that wasn't present." The objects of consciousness exist, but what about the subject? Eventually he realizes that no purpose is served by "this sort of painful rumination: I *exist*. It is I. The body lives all by itself, once it has started." The problem lies not with the body but the mind: "when it comes to thought, it is I who continue it, I who unwind it. I exist. I think I exist. Oh, how long and serpentine this feeling of existing is." When he attends to his senses, listening to a record for example, "everything is full, existence everywhere, dense and heavy and sweet." But beyond this sweetness is something rigid and unbearable: mere existence and the nausea it brings.[34]

In the novel's climactic scene, Roquentin has a revelation while sitting under a spreading chestnut tree: "And then, all of a sudden, there it was, as clear as day: existence had suddenly unveiled itself. It had lost its harmless appearance as an abstract category: it was the very stuff of things, that root was steeped in existence. Or rather the root, the park gates, the bench, the sparse grass on the lawn, all that had vanished; the diversity of things, their individuality, was only an appearance, a veneer." It comes to him that "existence is not necessary. To exist is simply *to be there*; what exists appears, lets itself be *encountered*, but you can never *deduce* it." But this new understanding does not help him take control of his disintegrating life. In the end he realizes the only way he could justify himself would be to write a novel, something "beautiful and hard as steel," that would "make people ashamed of their existence."[35]

Sartre was mobilized in 1939 and spent a number of months working in the meteorology department in eastern France, where he passed most of his time filling notebooks with observations and reflections. He found this an excellent exercise, helping him "to think spontaneously." As a writer he was too systematic, he thought: "I might easily have worked out a theory of war starting from first principles and ending with final conclusions."[36] This period ended abruptly in June 1940 when he was captured and sent to a prison camp in Germany. Released after a few months on the strength of a false medical certificate, he returned to Paris, where he wrote a few resistance pamphlets and an enormous philosophical treatise, *Being and Nothingness*. Based in large measure on Heidegger's *Being and Time*, which he read while in Germany, *Being and Nothingness* was his answer to the problems of authenticity and freedom. "Authenticity and individuality have to be earned," he wrote. "I shall be my own authenticity only if under the call of conscience I launch out toward death with a resolute-decision as toward my own most particular possibility." I am "condemned to be free," which means I am "condemned to be wholly responsible for myself." The result of this is anguish, "but most of the time," Sartre wrote, "we flee anguish in bad faith" – his term for self-deception.[37]

After the war, Sartre's pronouncements on freedom and responsibility struck a nerve in a country where the indignity of the German occupation still rankled. Sartre became France's reigning public intellectual and his 1945 lecture "Existentialism is a Humanism" became the manifesto of a new philosophical movement. Its catchphrase "existence precedes essence" was on everybody's lips. By this Sartre meant that there is no essential human nature (which could only be the case if there was a God to uphold it) and that therefore human beings had to be ready at every moment to define themselves afresh. "We have neither behind us, nor before us in a luminous realm of values, any means of justification or excuse. We are left alone, without excuse. That is what I mean when I say that man is condemned to be free."[38]

At that time Beauvoir was known primarily as a collaborator of Sartre who helped popularize existentialism in less portentous prose. "The supreme end at which man must aim is his freedom, which alone is capable of establishing the value of every end," she wrote. Through the exercise of freedom, men and woman must "fashion the world by giving it a meaning" and must do without the benefit of pre-existing standards of truth and morality. Citing Montaigne, she affirmed that "Life is in itself neither good nor evil; it is the place of good or evil as you make them." Recalling Kierkegaard, who struggled with the problem of moral choice within a Christian framework, she observed that the problem the Existentialists were posing was different but that their solution was basically the same: that "morality resides in the painfulness of an indefinite questioning."[39]

After the publication of *The Second Sex* in 1949 Beauvoir emerged as a pioneering theorist of feminism, drawing attention to the effects of gender ideas on the concept of the self. She approached this question from the point of view of "existentialist morality," writing (in the gender-specific language of the day) that "every individual concerned with justifying his existence experiences his existence as an infinite need to transcend himself." Woman, although in principle autonomous, finds herself "in a world where men force her to assume herself as Other." Labeled inessential and dependent, she is doomed to be "forever transcended" by man's "essential and sovereign consciousness."[40]

Part of Beauvoir's strategy was to show that there was nothing in woman's physiological or psychological makeup that condemned her to eternal subordination. In this she drew on, and sometimes disagreed with, the work of her existentialist colleague Merleau-Ponty, who more than any other philosopher of the twentieth century made an inquiry into the nature of the body a necessary part of the study of the self. In *The Phenomenology of Perception* (1945) he showed that the so-called higher functions of the mind are rooted in bodily existence and cannot be considered apart from that. The animate body has the remarkable characteristic of being at the same time subject and object of sensation, as shown by the fact that the hand can touch and be touched, the eye can see and be seen. The body, he wrote, "unites these two properties within itself, and its double belongingness to the order of the 'object' and to the order of the 'subject' reveals to us quite unexpected relations between the two orders."[41] Erasing the boundary between body and soul laid down by Plato, Augustine, and Descartes, Merleau-Ponty argued that the human being is equally mental and physical.

In an essay of 1948, Beauvoir distinguished the idea of "ambiguity" from that of "absurdity." To say that existence is ambiguous, she wrote, "is to assert that its meaning is never fixed, that it must be constantly won," while to say "that existence is absurd is to deny that it can ever be given a meaning."[42] This was meant as a critique of the work of Albert Camus, who gave central importance to the idea of the absurd in two works published in 1942: the essay *The Myth of Sisyphus* and the novel *The Stranger*. To Camus, the absurd is a relation between the human being, who cries out for rationality and justice, and an indifferent universe that does not give an answer. The universe is simply unreasonable; "what is absurd is the confrontation of this irrational and the wild longing for clarity whose call echoes in the human heart." Faced with the absurd, the human being can make the deliberate choice to inhabit a body and act, saying in effect "the flesh is my only certainty" and therefore "I have chosen this absurd and ineffectual effort," because "the struggle itself toward the heights is enough to fill a man's heart."[43] To Camus, the idea of God was not so much false as irrelevant. Like Meursault, the will-less protagonist of *The Stranger*, he was content to lay himself open to the "gentle indifference of the world."[44]

The middle years of the twentieth century were characterized by a search for authenticity in literature, art, psychology, philosophy, and life. The idea of the true self, earlier an element of religious discourse, was taken up by psychiatrists, novelists, and philosophers, and then reclaimed by religious thinkers such as Merton. The votaries of authenticity condemned the groupthink of the masses, but it was the masses who had the last word. The defining event of the era, the Second World War, was precipitated by leaders who knew how to manipulate feelings of national identity. In their hands, the search for personal authenticity became the assertion of collective self-interest. During the post-war era many thinkers discarded the hopes of earlier generations for secure truth, assured knowledge, and evolutionary progress, and questioned the very reality of the idea of the self.

The Death of the Subject

Even if the person is, for special speculative purposes, momentarily concentrating on the Problem of the Self, he has failed and knows that he has failed to catch more than the flying coat-tails of that which he was pursuing. His quarry was the hunter.

– Gilbert Ryle

Throughout the history of the concept of the self in the post-classical world, people have always assumed that there was such a thing as the self or soul or mind. During the early nineteenth century, some of the writers discussed in this book expressed puzzlement over what the self might be, but few went so far as to question its very existence. Psychologists, with their ideas of epiphenomenalism and the unconscious, began to do so during the 1860s and 1870s. Before long poets and novelists (our culture's canaries in the coal mine) began to toss off lines that made it evident that the concept of self was under stress. "It is a mistake to say: I think. One ought to say: I am thought," wrote French poet Arthur Rimbaud in 1871, adding: "*I* is someone else." "If I say that *I am*, this is false and evil. I am not," wrote British novelist D. H. Lawrence in 1915, continuing: "Our ready-made individuality, our identity, is no more than an accidental cohesion in the flux of time."[1] A more sinister challenge to the idea of the self came from the totalistic ideologies that arose during the first part of the twentieth century. To Russian Communists and German National Socialists, the human being was just an ephemeral bubble in the inexorable river of Society. "If we examine each individual in his development, we shall find that at bottom he is filled with the influences of his environment, as the skin of a sausage is filled with sausage-meat," wrote Soviet politician Nikolai Bukharin in 1921, "The individual himself is a collection of concentrated social influences, united in a small unit." This attitude opened the way to the Great Purge of the late 1930s, in which Bukharin himself perished. A similar outlook is found in Joseph Goebbels's semi-autobiographical novel *Michael* (1929): "Being a [national] socialist means subordinating the *I* to the *you*, sacrificing the individual personality to the totality."[2] Pushed to its extreme by the Nazi party, this contempt for individual dignity prepared the way for Adolf Hitler's total war and the Holocaust of the Jews. The existential philosophies of Heidegger and Sartre, with their valorization of individual choice, were in part responses to the stranglehold of social organization that made itself felt during these years. It is an irony of the history of this confused period that Heidegger became a member of the Nazi party and Sartre a tireless defender of Communism.

While phenomenology and existentialism ruled the roost in Germany and France, philosophers in Britain and the United States turned to analytic philosophy, which was characterized by a hostility to metaphysics and a belief that the body was central to an understanding of what was meant by the self. In *Language, Truth and Logic* (1936), logical positivist A. J. Ayer insisted that the self, "if it is not to be treated as a metaphysical entity, must be held to be a logical construction out of sense experiences," and that sense-experiences could only be regarded as belonging to a specific self if they contained "organic sense-contents which are elements of the same body." Gilbert Ryle wrote about what he called "the 'systematic elusiveness' of the concept of 'I,'" using the example of a diarist to illustrate his idea that "a higher order action cannot be the action upon which it is performed." Every thought of a diarist cannot "be the topic of a record in his diary," Ryle observed, "for the last entry made in his diary still demands that the making of it should in its turn be chronicled," and so on infinitely. Ryle dismissed the mind-body dualism of Descartes as a logical confusion. Mind and body belong to different, incompatible orders of being and it is pointless to try to link them together. Those who did – picturing the person as a "ghost" in the physical "machine" – were just talking nonsense. Ludwig Wittgenstein believed that it made sense to picture the person, but maintained that "the human body is the best picture of the human soul."[3]

To Dissolve Man: Claude Lévi-Strauss

While mid-century Anglo-American philosophers viewed the self as an individual construct, postwar French thinkers gave most of their attention to the social matrix in which the self arose. Phenomenologists and existentialists held that the self was constituted by its interactions with "the other" and achieved authenticity through the exercise of freedom. Claude Lévi-Strauss, an anthropologist, rebuked phenomenologists for thinking that conscious experience could be relied on and existentialists for succumbing to "the illusion of subjectivity." It was not through the practice of "shop-girl metaphysics" that humans could discover the truth of what they were. The right way to do this was to collect and analyze data – languages, myths, marriage practices, and so forth – in search of the "invariants beyond the empirical diversity of human societies." And the aim of all this was "not to constitute, but to dissolve man,"[4] that is, to discover the invariable unconscious structures beneath our ephemeral lives.

Lévi-Strauss did his fieldwork in Brazil during the late 1930s. Fifteen years later he published a memoir entitled *Tristes Tropiques* (Unhappy Tropics), in which he gave an account of his years as an anthropologist and put down his reflections on the imperiled cultures that he studied and on human life in general. He began ironically: "Travel and travellers are two things I loathe – and yet here I am, all set to tell the story of my expeditions." He mocked the modern craze for travelogues, knowing full well he was adding another to the shelves. But his book had little in common with the typical expedition chronicle. It invited comparison with *The Voyage of the Beagle* both in the quality of the writing and in the author's ability to deduce "general laws out of large collections of facts." The facts that interested Lévi-Strauss were those of exotic cultures, but there was nothing romantic about how he collected them. "It may be that we shall have spent six months of travel, privation, and sickening physical weariness merely in order to record – in a few days, it may be, or even a few hours – an unpublished myth, a new marriage-rule, or a complete list of names of clans."[5] From such material, he and his colleagues tried to find out what makes human beings human.

Tristes Tropiques is full of the writer's observations on traditional cultures in Amazonia and other remote places; but wherever he went, he found it was impossible to escape the detritus of Western civilization: "What travel has now to show us is the filth, *our* filth, that we have thrown in the face of humanity." Culture was "no longer a fragile flower, to be carefully preserved and reared with great difficulty here and there in sheltered corners of a territory rich in natural resources"; it was something produced "in bulk, as if it were sugar-beet" on a factory farm. The result has been a general impoverishment of the human world, carried out in the name of progress – but was it really? "The zealots of progress," Levi-Strauss complained, "run the risk of underestimating, and thus of knowing too little about, the immense riches which our race has accumulated to one side and the other of the narrow furrow on which they keep their eyes fixed."[6]

Lévi-Strauss was no believer in the myth of the noble savage but at the same time no champion of Western rationalism and Western institutions. Comparing the systems of punishment of American Indians and modern Europeans, he noted sardonically: "It is grotesque to believe that we have made a 'great spiritual advance' simply because, instead of eating our fellow human beings, we prefer to mutilate them, both physically and morally."[7] He dealt with this theme at greater length in the concluding chapter of his book. The setting was a village in the Chittagong Hill Tracts, a Buddhist region in what is now Bangladesh. Leading him into a shrine, Levi-Strauss's host bowed before the altar. The anthropologist thought the gestures "no more than conventions," but wouldn't have minded following his host's example: "It was not a question of bowing down to idols," he thought, "or of adoring a supposedly supernatural order of things, but simply of paying homage to decisive reflections which had been formed twenty-five centuries earlier by a thinker, or by the society which created his legend." Thoughts on the Buddhist idea of Nothingness led him to reflect on the nature and future of humanity:

> The world began without the human race and it will end without it. The institutions, manners, and customs which I shall have spent my life in cataloguing and trying to understand are an ephemeral efflorescence of a creative process in relation to which they are meaningless, unless it be that they allow humanity to play its destined role. That role does not, however, assign to our race a position of independence. ... As for the creations of the human mind, they are meaningful only in relation to that mind and will fall into nothingness as soon as it ceases to exist.[8]

Going Pascal one better, he wrote: "Not only is the 'I' hateful: there is no room for it between the 'we' and nothingness." Still, he opted for the "we" – human society – even though he knew it was a mere appearance. "Let us," he concluded, "grasp the essence of what our species has been and still is, beyond thought and beneath society."[9]

Lévi-Strauss called his school "structural anthropology" and it was associated, at least in the public mind, with related developments in psychology, sociology, and literary criticism that dominated cultural analysis in France during the 1960s. Structuralism began with the work of Ferdinand de Saussure, who showed that the relation between the elements of language was arbitrary, their significance being determined by their place in the structure and not by their history. Structural anthropologists, sociologists, and psychoanalysts applied this insight to other aspects of human culture. Common to these approaches was the belief that beneath surface phenomena were constant laws of structure unaffected by historical developments. Another idea shared by structuralists of all stripes was that the autonomous individual of the West was a simple illusion.

The Death of the Author: Roland Barthes

Lévi-Strauss and other structuralist anthropologists gave a great deal of attention to the analysis of myths, reducing them to their basic elements and showing how these elements interacted according to a fixed set of rules.

In this process, there was no room for personal creativity. Myths have no authors; they are the products of cultures, not individuals. During the 1960s, linguists and literary critics began to apply structuralist methods to the study of modern literature. The leading figure in this trend was the French literary theorist Roland Barthes. In a much-discussed essay of 1968, Barthes compared the mythic narratives of preliterate societies to the literatures of the modern West: "The responsibility for a [mythic] narrative is never assumed by a person but by a mediator," who is a performer, not a creative genius. The "author" was an invention of the Renaissance, an age that "discovered the prestige of the individual." But since the start of literary modernism, "it is language which speaks, not the author," it is language which "acts, 'performs', and not 'me.'" Falling back on linguistic terminology, Barthes said that "the author is never more than the instance writing, just as *I* is nothing other than the instance saying *I*." Texts are made up of "multiple writings, drawn from many cultures." What gives them unity "is the reader, not, as was hitherto said, the author." Barthes closed with one of those oracular pronouncements that French theorists of the sixties and seventies became famous for: "the birth of the reader must be at the cost of the death of the Author."[10]

Barthes admitted that the author was still with us, lurking in literary histories and biographies, featured in magazine interviews and present "in the very consciousness of men of letters anxious to unite their person and their work through diaries and memoirs." In writing this he was thinking primarily of Gide, who was, as he put it, "my original language." Barthes's first published article was entitled "On Gide and his Journal" (1942), and it marked the beginning of his conflicted relationship with the *journal intime*. He had many good things to say about his idol's journal: "silences – exquisite instances of wit – trivial avowals which make him man par excellence, another Montaigne." But it was not Gide the man that interested Barthes so much as Gide the maker of a text. His keeping of a journal, Barthes wrote, was "valid only because of its reflective force, turning back on Gide himself." This self-reflexivity was the hallmark of a new type of literature, in which "the artist himself dismantles the procedures of creation and is interested in them almost as much as in his work itself."[11] It was this dismantling of the text that Barthes would attempt in his own works.

Barthes's field of academic specialization was semiology, the science of signs. As a structuralist, he held that signs do not have natural meanings. There was no inevitable relationship between the word "apple" (the signifier) and the concept "apple" (the signified), or between these and a physical apple (the referent). Signs acquired their meaning through relations of difference and these relations were always in flux. If a meaning became fixed it was because of external pressure. In *Mythologies* (1957) Barthes applied these ideas to the "myths" of bourgeois French life – wrestling matches, wine drinking, and so forth – to show that what people took for granted (the "*what-goes-without-saying*") gained its naturalness by means of ideological coercion. Meanings, instead of being fluid, were frozen in the service of the existing social order. "Every day and everywhere," Barthes concluded, "man is stopped by myths, referred by them to this motionless prototype [that is, a fixed conception of man] which lives in his place." Emerson spoke of "the mob," Kierkegaard of "the crowd," Heidegger of "the they"; Barthes inveighed against "the *doxa*," by which he meant "Public Opinion, the mind of the majority, petit bourgeois Consensus, the Voice of Nature, the Violence of Prejudice."[12]

Where in the midst of all this social conditioning was the true, unconditioned self? Barthes was skeptical of its existence and didn't think that psychology could help us find it. In his study of the "mythical" French dramatist Racine, he wrote: "Of all the approaches to man, psychology is the most unprovable [*improbable*], the most marked by its time. This is because, in fact, *knowledge* of the profound self is illusory: there are only different ways of articulating it. … But to acknowledge this incapacity to *tell the truth* about Racine is precisely to acknowledge, at last, the special status of literature." Sartre had said two decades earlier: "The genius of Proust is the totality of the works of Proust; the genius of Racine is the series of his tragedies, outside of which there is nothing."[13] Barthes took this one step further. Racine, the author, had no essential self, no existence outside the texts that make up his corpus.

Barthes was suspicious of writing that presented itself as factual, such as history and biography, and of realistic novels that were modeled on historical discourse. All of these genres used detailed descriptions to create a "reality effect" that lulled readers into thinking that they were dealing with unadulterated truth. In fact the meaning of such writings depended not on conformity "to the model," that is, the thing depicted, "but to the cultural rules of representation," that is, the underlying laws governing symbolic communication, from primitive myths to the daily newspaper. Modern men and women had developed a taste for so-called objective genres "such as the realistic novel, the private diary, documentary literature, the news item, the historical museum, the exhibition of ancient objects, and, above all, the massive development of photography." Writers in the age of the death of the author had to avoid the snare of realism. Passing through "a perquisite impersonality (not at all to be confused with the castrating objectivity of the realist novelist)," they aimed to reach the point where language itself spoke and the subject or self was recognized as "*merely an effect of language*."[14]

Barthes saw himself as a post-death-of-the-author writer but he remained fascinated by two authorial genres he claimed to despise, the memoir and the diary, and eventually tried his hand at both. His American champion Susan Sontag explained the inconsistency by saying that his "commitment to impersonality does not preclude the avowal of the self; it is only another variation on the project of self-examination: the noblest project of French literature." When Barthes undertook to write a memoir, he became "the latest major participant in the great national literary project, inaugurated by Montaigne: the self as vocation, life as a reading of the self."[15] But, given his stand on the illusoriness of the self, he had to approach the task ironically. He wrote *Roland Barthes on Roland Barthes* (1975) as a contribution to a series of books on French authors, to which he had already contributed the volume on Jules Michelet. He didn't say much about his days on earth but did reproduce a series of family photographs that were saved from bourgeois obviousness by the irony of their inclusion. The verbal contents of the book were a mélange of thoughts on writing, reflections on a variety of other topics, and scattered reminiscences. The overall effect was that of a writer's notebook, as even he had to admit:

> With the alibi of a pulverized discourse, a dissertation destroyed, one arrives at the regular practice of the fragment; then from the fragment one slips to the "journal." At which point, is not the point of all this to entitle oneself to write a "journal"? Am I not justified in considering everything I have written as a clandestine and stubborn effort to bring to light again, someday, quite freely, the theme of the Gidean "journal"?

In *Roland Barthes* he referred to himself sometimes as "I," sometimes as "he," sometimes even as "you," but he left the signified of these signifiers up in the air:

> I do not strive to put my present expression in the service of my previous truth (in the classical system, such an effort would have been sanctified under the name of *authenticity*), I abandon the exhausting pursuit of an old piece of myself, I do not try to *restore* myself (as we say of a monument). I do not say: "I am going to describe myself" but: "I am writing a text, and I call it R. B." ... The fact (whether biographical or textual) is abolished in the signifier, because it immediately *coincides* with it. ... I myself am my own symbol, I am the story which happens to me.

"To write on oneself," he concluded, "may seem a pretentious idea; but it is also a simple idea: simple as the idea of suicide."[16] From one point of view, *Roland Barthes* is the Montaignian essay collection pushed to its self-referential extreme; from another, it is the form the memoir must take in the age of the death of the self.

In *Roland Barthes* Barthes declared that the autobiographical diary was discredited, by which he meant that he did not think it an interesting form of writing. He had tried, from time to time, to keep a diary but, after an initial spurt of pleasure ("this is simple, this is easy"), he had always become discouraged by "the artifice of 'sincerity,' the artistic mediocrity of the 'spontaneous,'" and disgusted "to find a 'pose' I certainly hadn't intended." These quotations are from an essay on diaries called "Deliberation," which he published in 1979. The point under deliberation was whether it was worthwhile to "keep a journal *with a view to publication*." He concluded that it was not. The aims of the *journal intime* were "all connected to the advantages and the prestige of 'sincerity,'" but it was hard to take any of that seriously now that "psychoanalysis, the Sartrean critique of bad faith, and the Marxist critique of ideologies" had "made 'confession' futile."[17] The journal, he concluded, was necessarily inessential and inauthentic. Nevertheless he came up with four motives for keeping one and, with that justification, quoted some passages from journals he had kept.

As it turned out, "Deliberation" was the last piece of writing Barthes published. He died unexpectedly in 1980 after being knocked down by a delivery van. In the years that followed, his executors brought out several diaries that were discovered among his papers. The most moving of them was *Mourning Diary*, which he wrote after his mother's death. Whatever he might have said about the inauthenticity of the *journal intime*, it was impossible for him to hide the sincerity of his emotion, as when he wrote: "bereavement (depression) is different from sickness. What should I be cured of? To find what condition, what life?" Three weeks later, he added this Heideggarian observation: "Now, everywhere, in the street, the café, I see each individual under the aspect of ineluctably *having-to-die*, which is exactly what it means to be *mortal*. – And no less obviously, I see them as *not knowing this to be so*."[18]

To Free Oneself of the Inner Life: Alain Robbe-Grillet

In his first major work, *Writing Degree Zero* (1953), Barthes made much of "neutral writing" – writing that was devoid of style, flat, impersonal. Sartre earlier gave the name *écriture blanche* (colorless writing) to this sort of prose, holding up Camus's *The Stranger* as its prime exemplar. That novel's monotonous style was a perfect match for the thoughts and acts of its protagonist, who drifted through life without reacting in any way to what was going on around him. Barthes agreed that Camus's book was remarkable for achieving "a style of absence which is almost an ideal absence of style" (a good example of his portentous word-play) but he disagreed with Sartre about the role of the author and the function of literature. Sartre was an advocate of social engagement, Barthes wanted writers to work "in the midst of all those ejaculations and judgments, without becoming involved in any of them."[19] Sartre's author was an agent creating meaning through freely chosen action, Barthes's writer was an impersonal element in the shifting web of language.

The same year that Barthes published *Writing Degree Zero* he began to promote the work of the novelist Alain Robbe-Grillet, whose prose, he said, was remarkable for having "no alibis, no resonance, no depth." It kept to the surface, examining objects without emphasis, "favoring no one quality at the expense of another." Robbe-Grillet studiously avoided "poetic" language and also shunned "the painstaking artistry of the naturalistic novelist," who tried to plumb the depths of the individual and society, looking for a non-existent "human essence *at the bottom of things*." His aim was to record "man's direct experience of what surrounds him without his being able to shield himself with a psychology, a metaphysic, or a psychoanalytic method." In so doing, wrote philosopher Bernard-Henri Lévy, Robbe-Grillet was fulfilling an ambition conceived by Sartre in his phenomenological days: "To free oneself of the inner life! That was Sartre's great desire. To free oneself of that French malady that is the cult of the inner life, that was Robbe-Grillet's."[20]

Jealousy (1957), like Robbe-Grillet's other novels, is made up mostly of descriptions, with no hint of the characters' reactions to the situation that develops around them. The unnamed narrator reports what he sees and hears without ever using the word "I." Columns cast shadows; his wife, called "A," comes and goes; sounds "can be heard." This relentless objectivity forces the reader to see the world through the narrator's eyes, in effect becoming the otherwise absent subject. The narrator describes the scene in geometrical terms: "the sixth row [of banana trees] gives the following numbers: twenty-two, twenty-one, twenty, nineteen – which represent respectively the rectangle, the true trapezoid, the trapezoid with a curved edge. ..." Yet even in this world of lines and planes, there are hints of human intention: "When do you think you'll be going down?" A asks Franck, a visiting neighbor. He replies, "I don't know," then, "Maybe next week." The narrator reports: "They look at each other, their glances meeting above the platter Franck is holding in one hand six inches above the table top," but it is left to the reader to connect the dots.[21] All this was in accord with the theory of the *nouveau roman* (new novel), as promoted by Barthes and Robbe-Grillet. The aim of such writing, Barthes explained, was "to make the reader no longer a consumer but a producer of the text." Readers of *Jealousy* rarely fail to produce a story of real or imagined betrayal but they do so without much help from the author. When A and Franck return from their trip, the narrator watches them through a window whose irregularities "obscure the details of their actions." As they walk toward the house "the distance between them is at least a yard. Under the precise noonday sun, they cast no shadows."[22] There is a certain fascination in this novel of concealed action and blank surfaces but most of its readers have found it deadly boring. Barthes put the blame for this squarely on their own shoulders: "The reduction of reading to a consumption is clearly responsible for the 'boredom' experienced by many in the face of the modern ('unreadable') text, the avant-garde film or painting: to be bored means that one cannot produce the text, open it out, *set it going*."[23]

It is easier to do this with Robbe-Grillet's best-known work, the 1961 film *Last Year at Marienbad*. As in *Jealousy* there is no clear-cut plot or well-developed characters, but the succession of images creates a dreamlike continuity. The film opens with a man walking through the opulent halls of a European resort hotel, sometimes alone, sometimes passing others. A disembodied voice adds to the atmosphere of mystery but it is a mystery without event or resolution. The man is drawn to a beautiful woman he sees at social gatherings. Getting her alone, he tells her that they met the year before, that they agreed to meet again and to go off together. She resists him, her husband becomes involved, the tension rises, but nothing decisive happens. Giving a clue to his intentions in a note to the screenplay, Robbe-Grillet wrote that viewers can either force what they see into a rigid logical scheme, in which case the film won't make sense, or let themselves be carried along by the images, voices, music, situations, in which case it will begin to correspond to the flow of their "daily emotional life," a field of perception and sensation, undisturbed by ready-made systems of interpretation or psychological analysis.[24]

In the late 1970s, after a quarter-century of writing avant-garde novels and screenplays, Robbe-Grillet decided that he had had enough. The revolutionary forms he and others had developed had begun to lose their edge, becoming platitudes suitable for treatment in literary guidebooks. It was time to try something new, he thought, and he began work on an autobiography that was published in 1985 as *Le miroir qui revient* (The Returning Mirror). He began with a surprising declaration: "I have never spoken about anything but myself. From within, so it was hardly noticed." In writing these sentences, he was, he admitted, using three terms that were supposed to be taboo: "self," "within," and "speaking about." "Within" brought to life again the "humanist myth of depth." "Speaking about" opened the door to representational language and "as for self, always hateful [another nod to Pascal], it doubtless is getting ready to make another appearance in a still more frivolous scene: that of biography-writing." Yet Robbe-Grillet's book is hardly a conventional autobiography. In places like a memoir, in places like a novel, it frequently gives the impression of someone moving through a dream, and this was just how he approached the act of writing. His aim, he wrote, was "to destroy the nocturnal monsters that threatened to invade my waking life by describing them precisely."[25]

The Disappearance of Man: Michel Foucault

In the introduction of a book published in 1984, the year of his death, Michel Foucault looked back on two decades of thinking differently. "After all," he wrote,

> what would be the value of the passion for knowledge if it resulted only in a certain amount of knowledgeableness and not, in one way or another and to the extent possible, in the knower's straying afield of himself? … What is philosophy today – philosophical activity, I mean – if it is not the critical work that thought brings to bear on itself? In what does it consist, if not in the endeavor to know how and to what extent it might be possible to think differently, instead of legitimating what is already known?[26]

Over the years, Foucault's thinking underwent three theoretical shifts, each marking the beginning of a new phase of his writings. The first shift, he wrote, "seemed necessary in order to analyze what was often designated as the advancement of learning." In his works of this phase, such as *The Order of Things* (1966), he analyzed the "games of truth" of various scientific disciplines, arguing that truth was a function of discourse, by which he meant, roughly speaking, that what counts as truth in a given epoch depends on the epistemological assumptions and practices that prevail in that epoch. His second shift was "required in order to analyze what is often described as the manifestations of 'power.'" In the works of this phase, notably *Discipline and Punish* (1975), he examined the interactions of games of truth "with power relations, as exemplified by punitive practices." One of the main points he made was that the so-called humane forms of discipline that came into practice during the late eighteenth century were actually more coercive than the brutal forms of punishment that preceded them. He also argued that the Enlightenment individual, far from being autonomous, was brought into being by the state and its institutions as part of its mechanism of control. Finally, toward the end of the 1970s, Foucault realized he "had to undertake a third shift, in order to analyze what is termed 'the subject,'" and so he began a study of "the games of truth in the relationship of self with self and the forming of oneself as a subject." The whole three-stage process was a continual challenge because he had to learn how far "the effort to think one's own thought can free thought from what it silently thinks, and so enable it to think differently."[27] In his attempts to undermine the restrictive discourse of his time, he had to alter his own patterns of thought, which were themselves expressions of that discourse.

When he wrote the above passages, Foucault was the most famous intellectual in the world and he remains the most-cited author in the humanities and social sciences as well as a staple of undergraduate rap sessions. There is some irony in this in that he, along with Lévi-Strauss and Barthes, was a believer in the death of the author and a critic of dominant discourses. In "What Is an Author?" (1969) he acknowledged that he had cited dozens of authors in his works but still insisted that the "disappearance of the author" was "an event of our times." Analyzing the rise of the "author-function" in modern Europe, he argued that it was "tied to the legal and institutional systems that circumscribe, determine, and articulate the realm of discourses." The underlying problem was that of the subject or self. "Under what conditions and through what forms," he asked, "can an entity like the subject appear in the order of discourse?" It was time to stop treating the subject as anything but "a complex and variable function of discourse," since it was quite possible "to imagine a culture where discourse would circulate without any need for an author."[28]

Foucault became interested in the question of the subject during the first phase of his work and it became increasingly important as he went along. In *The Order of Things* he argued that "man" – that is, the universal category "man" understood as having a fixed, essential nature – was a creation of the last hundred fifty years or so and would cease to be when the current epistemological epoch came to an end. Man was "an invention of recent date," he wrote in the last chapter of the book, "and one perhaps nearing its end." The emergence of man was not "the entry into objectivity of something that had remained trapped within beliefs and philosophies." It was simply "the effect of a change in the fundamental arrangements of knowledge," which happened without the aid of individual effort. And "if those arrangements were to disappear" as the result of an event "of which we can at the moment do no more than sense the possibility," then we could "certainly wager that man would be erased, like a face drawn in sand at the edge of the sea."[29]

The Order of Things was one of two books in which Foucault took an "archeological" approach to knowledge, unearthing layers belonging to different eras without trying to link them together. Later he adopted

Nietzsche's genealogical approach as a way to come to grips with historical change without reintroducing the idea of the self. "The true historical sense," he wrote in 1971, "confirms our existence among countless lost events, without a landmark or a point of reference." Such an approach deprived "the self of the reassuring stability of life and nature" and this was necessary because "nothing in man – not even his body – is sufficiently stable to serve as the basis for self-recognition or for understanding other men." A few years later he spelled out more clearly what genealogy meant in relation to the subject. It was "a form of history which can account for the constitution of knowledges, discourses, domains of objects etc., without having to make reference to a subject which is either transcendental in relation to the field of events" – that is, enjoying a godlike freedom from contingency – "or runs in its empty sameness," impervious to change, "throughout the course of history." It was necessary, he said, "to dispense with the constituent subject, to get rid of the subject itself" by finding a way to account for its constitution "within a historical framework."[30]

Foucault's genealogical studies convinced him that human subjectivity has not always been the same and that therefore it was an error to think that there was an essential, unchanging subject that could be experienced by means of introspection. During the second phase of his work he concentrated on the role played by power relations – confiner and confined, for example – in the constitution of the subject in different eras. But during his final period he began to give his attention to something he previously had ignored: the ways that human beings turn *themselves* into subjects. He found that there exist in all societies "techniques which permit individuals to effect, by their own means, a certain number of operations on their own bodies, on their own souls, on their own thoughts, on their own conduct, and this in a manner so as to transform themselves." This insight provided him with a whole new way of approaching the study and experience of the self, opening the way to what he called "the politics of ourselves."[31]

To some it seemed as if Foucault was moving back to a conventional idea of the subject. In an interview given in January 1984, he made it clear that this was not the case. Although he was interested "in the way in which the subject constitutes himself in an active fashion, by the practices of the self," he insisted that "these practices are nevertheless not something that the individual invents by himself. They are patterns that he finds in his culture and which are proposed, suggested and imposed on him by his culture." Three months later, in one of his last interviews, he stressed that he remained hostile to the idea of a "sovereign, founding subject." The subject, he maintained, was "constituted through practices of subjection." Yet, he went on, it could be constituted in more autonomous ways as well: "through practices of liberation, of liberty, as in Antiquity, on the basis, of course, of a number of rules, styles, inventions to be found in the cultural environment." Such practices, traced out by Socrates and the Stoics and reaffirmed by Nietzsche, offered the possibility that one could elaborate "one's own life as a personal work of art, even if it obeyed certain collective canons." This would mean affirming one's liberty in an effort "to give one's own life a certain form in which one could recognize oneself, be recognized by others, and which even posterity might take as an example."[32]

The Myth of the Subjective: Anglo-American Philosophy and Neuroscience

Philosophers in the English-speaking world paid comparatively little attention to the structuralists of the 1950s and 1960s and to the so-called poststructuralists and postmodernists who followed. But while they had fundamental differences with thinkers such as Lévi-Strauss, Barthes, and Foucault, most Anglo-American philosophers agreed with them that the self was not a freestanding entity but a mental construct rooted in bodily existence. In *Individuals* (1959), English philosopher P. F. Strawson observed that we speak of ourselves as having physical characteristics, such as height, weight, position, and color, and also of having feelings, thoughts, and other conscious states that we would never think of ascribing to material objects. This led him to inquire why states of consciousness "are ascribed to anything at all" and why they are ascribed "to the very same thing as certain corporeal characteristics." He gave the name "persons" to entities that could be described in physical as well as mental terms, and he believed the "concept of a person is logically prior to that of an individual consciousness." In other words, there had to be persons (in his technical sense) before there could be conscious individuals. It followed that "the concept of the pure individual consciousness – the pure ego – is a concept that cannot exist," or at any rate cannot explain what it is to be a person. The word "I," whatever else it might mean, can never refer to a pure subject.[33] Thirty years later, American philosopher Donald Davidson made a similar point in an essay called "The Myth of the Subjective." Human minds exist and so does the rest of nature, but the line between the two is much less distinct than people think. Davidson admitted that "thoughts are private" and that "the person who has a thought generally knows he has it in a way in which others cannot," but that, he concluded, "is all there is to the subjective."[34]

Another American, Thomas Nagel, was one of the few contemporary philosophers who had anything positive to say about the embattled idea of subjectivity. In a much-discussed essay of 1974, he insisted that the experience of any conscious organism is irreducibly subjective: "there is something that it is like to *be* that organism – something it is like *for* the organism," and that something cannot be accounted for by purely physical explanations. But while writing about the persistence of the self in time, Nagel was careful not to fall back on the idea of a metaphysical ego. "The ego," he said, "if it is a continuing individual with its own identity over time, would be just one more thing about which the same problem [of continuity] could be raised." The idealism of the phenomenologists and the physicalism of the scientists both failed to provide a convincing account of conscious experience. Their error was to think that "a single world cannot contain both irreducible [subjective] points of view and irreducible objective reality." For his part, he was willing to accept both ends of the objective-subjective polarity "without allowing either of its terms to swallow the other."[35]

With this acceptance, Nagel placed himself with the small minority of philosophers who were willing to accept methodological dualism. Most philosophers, along with virtually all cognitive scientists and neuroscientists, stood – and still stand – on the side of physical reductionism, confident that all aspects of experience can be explained with reference to the brain alone. A high-profile representative of this point of view is the philosopher Daniel Dennett, who in *Consciousness Explained* (1991) wrote that "if dualism is the best we can do, then we can't understand human consciousness." Consistent with his physicalist approach, Dennett described the self as the leading character in a story the brain tells itself. This character is fictional though extraordinarily useful to the human organism. Dennett called it a "center of narrative gravity," comparing it to the physical concept of center of gravity, which is useful for making computations even though it doesn't exist in its own right. Waxing poetic, Dennett wrote: "Our tales are spun, but for the most part we don't spin them; they spin us. Our human consciousness, and our narrative selfhood, is their product, not their source."[36] It made no sense to look for the self in the brain or anywhere else; it just wasn't something that had independent existence.

Just as Dennett looked down on dualistic philosophers, so neuroscientists looked down on philosophers in general and Dennett in particular; but most of them agree with his view that there is no such thing as a freestanding self. Two books of the early 1990s by Nobel Prize-winning biologists gave differing accounts of the neurological basis of the self or soul. Francis Crick, in *The Astonishing Hypothesis*, was frankly reductionist: "'You,' your joys and your sorrows, your memories and your ambitions, your sense of personal identity and free will, are in fact no more than the behavior of a vast assembly of nerve cells and their associated molecules," he affirmed. The aim of his book was to bring consciousness, including the "special case" of self-consciousness, into the ambit of neuroscience. He gave most of his attention to visual awareness and admitted at the end that many of his readers "might justifiably complain that what has been discussed in this book has very little to do with the human soul as they understand it." Still he did not doubt that further research along the same lines would end up proving that our sense of self was a purely biological phenomenon.[37] The approach of Gerald Edelman in *Bright Air, Brilliant Fire* was more sophisticated and more modest. He was as committed as Crick to a physical explanation of the phenomenon of consciousness but allowed that physical science, by definition objective, could never provide a complete explanation of the subjective, qualitative aspects of consciousness. This was not, he felt, a retreat into dualism but simply an acceptance of the limits of scientific enquiry. His plan was to "explain how primary consciousness evolved, and then explain how it was followed by higher-order consciousness," the "consciousness of consciousness" that permitted the development of the sense of past and future and the idea of the self. Edelman also laid stress on the role of society in the development of self-consciousness. Even though the self had "been selected for during evolution to realize mainly the aims and satisfactions of each biological individual," it was constructed "by social interactions."[38] As Hegel and Durkheim and Lévi-Strauss had said in the language of their own disciplines, the self, however it might be conceived, always develops within a social matrix.

Long Live the Self

The old ego dies hard. Such as it was, a minister of dulness, it was also an agent of security.

– Samuel Beckett

Summing up the situation at the beginning of the twenty-first century, the consensus of opinion among philosophers, social scientists, cultural theorists, and neuroscientists is that the self is not a substance but a construct, not an entity existing in its own right but the product of corporeal and social operations that will cease when its physical support dissolves. The impersonality of modern life – anonymous cities, bureaucratic governments, manipulative corporations, factory-like hospitals – has undermined the sense of individuality that had prevailed since the Renaissance. The sheer number of people alive – seven billion and counting – makes each of us seem like a particle of dust. Yet in spite of all this, everyone – at any rate everyone who is not in a coma or suffering from a serious neurological or psychological disorder – feels herself or himself as having a self or simply *being* a self. Call it fact or commonsense or illusion, the sense of self has never gone out of style.

Most people in modern society take selfhood for granted and don't bother theorizing about it. If somebody did a survey on contemporary conceptions of the self, many respondents would cobble together an answer based on what they could remember of what they had been taught about the soul or *nafs* or *atman* according to the Bible or Quran or Upanishads. Others might refer to philosophical ideas of autonomy or psychological theories of personality formation. But the majority would just say, "The self? That's *me*." The self, in other words, is not something to reflect on but to be, to express, to affirm. And affirm it we do. The age in which the self has been authoritatively declared dead is also the age when human beings spend more of their time than ever before affirming their personal identities. Hundreds of millions of people have accounts on social networking services; tens of millions have blogs, many of which are personal diaries. Millions add comments below content on the Web and post reviews of books, music, gadgets, and accessories. Their selections from these products and the ways that they arrange them (libraries, playlists, wardrobes) are meant to tell others that they are unique. Turning from commodities to the literary genres that have been the main focus of this book, the memoir has become one of the most admired and most profitable forms of literary expression. Millions of people keep diaries in physical notebooks, using this "journaling" (as it is now called) as a way to say "I exist. I am me." The self is dead; long live the self.

Technologies of the Self, Then and Now

Before looking in more detail at personal identity in the age of the Internet, it will be good to glance back quickly over the history of the idea of the self and of the means that have been used to express it (if it is a substance) or create it (if it is a work in progress). Michel Foucault, who endorsed the second of these alternatives, coined the term "technologies of the self" for the methods people use "to transform themselves in order to attain a certain state of happiness, purity, wisdom, perfection or immortality." In his research of the 1980s, he focused on the development of such techniques in classical Greece and the early Roman Empire, but he also looked at the seventeenth century, when the methods of the Stoics and early Christians were taken up "in a different context by the so-called human sciences in order to use them without renunciation of the self but to constitute, positively, a new self." His aim was to explore the relationship between the idea of the self prevailing in a given era and the technologies of self practiced in that era, because he believed that "the self is nothing else than the historical correlation of the technology built in our history."[1] That conclusion followed naturally from his ideas about self-consciousness, which he reached at the end of a singular intellectual journey. I will not try to follow his lead but will borrow his term "technologies of the self" and pay attention to the correlation between technology and concept as I summarize the history sketched in the preceding chapters.

People in most ancient cultures believed that a spirit or soul survived the death of the body but did not regard this spirit as the bearer of personal identity. The knowledge of spirits and the techniques for entering the spirit-world were transmitted by shamans and priests, either orally or by means of esoteric texts that were not available to the public. During the Axial Age, thinkers in India, Greece, and other places developed the idea of a substantial self or soul superior to the body and unaffected by death. Elite teachers – Brahmins in India, philosophers in Greece – formulated doctrines and techniques of self-knowledge; other teachers, such as Mahavira and the Buddha and the Stoics and Epicureans, taught methods of self-mastery but no elaborate theories of selfhood. These teachings, popular as well as elite, were transmitted orally for centuries before being written down. During the first millennium CE, clerics of the monotheistic religions codified doctrines and techniques of the self, recording them in texts that were widely disseminated. State patronage, ecclesiastical coercion and proselytism helped spread the idea of the substantial soul throughout the Western world.

Between around 400 and 1400 CE, a few people, among them Augustine, Hildegard of Bingen, and Ruzbihan Baqli, wrote first-person texts – memoirs and visionary narratives – that were intended to promote the doctrines they believed in but that marked, in addition, the beginning of the literature of self-expression. Such teachings were preserved in handwritten manuscripts that had to be copied one by one. The development of printing in the fifteenth century made it possible for priests such as Luther and Ignatius and humanistic scholars such as Erasmus and Montaigne to propagate their thoughts with a speed that would have been unthinkable a century earlier. Protestant churches encouraged self-examination in place of auricular confession, and this personal self-scrutiny found an outlet in diaries and memoirs. More and more, people viewed themselves as separate individuals, and this attitude found its way into the works of philosophers like Descartes and Locke, who arrived at their ideas using reasoning and introspection without reference to religious teachings. Their treatises, many of them written in modern languages, were discussed all over Europe.

From the mid-eighteenth century, thinkers like Rousseau, Goethe, and Blake used fiction and poetry as well as prose treatises to present new ways of looking at the human being. They encouraged men and women to follow the promptings of their hearts even if it meant ignoring the counsels of reason. Everything taken for granted was questioned, including the political order. The French Revolution was followed by a period of reaction, during which orthodox ideas made a comeback, but writers like Stendhal, Kierkegaard, and Emerson attacked the crowd-mentality of their era and chronicled their personal development in diaries. Around the same time Hegel and the pioneers of sociology re-emphasized the role of society in the formation of the self. They were opposed by Schopenhauer and Nietzsche, who spurned systematic philosophy and stressed the importance of the body in the process of self-formation. The works of all these writers competed with one another in the marketplace of ideas; readers were free to pick and choose from various viewpoints.

During the nineteenth and twentieth centuries, scientific writing replaced philosophical and religious speculation as the most prestigious form of discourse. Philosophers and psychologists tried to emulate the exact sciences, while evolutionary theorists tried to harmonize the scientific and spiritual approaches to the self. Poets, novelists, and dramatists invented new literary forms to give voice to the personal and social disintegration they saw around them. Critics and philosophers announced the death of the self, while neuroscientists viewed it as at best a biological construct.

We see that over the last two millennia, the prevailing idea of the self has changed from a ghostly spirit to a substantial soul to an autonomous individual to a center of expression to a fiction constructed by social or biological forces. The authorities of self-knowledge have been, in succession, shamans, clerics, philosophers, poets and novelists, and social and physical scientists. The techniques of self-cultivation have changed from ritual to religious austerities to written reflection to scientific experimentation, as transmitted by oral tradition, handwritten texts, printed literature and online journals. In each case the movement has been from the realm of the spirits through the temples of religion and the colloquia of philosophers to the laboratories of science. The texts and technologies became more easily available to a wider and wider public. And the movement accelerated as it went along. Ideas invented in the Axial Age persisted almost unchanged into the medieval era. The fifteenth and sixteenth centuries saw enormous development, quickly surpassed by that of the seventeenth. During the late eighteenth and early nineteenth centuries everything that preceded was turned upside down, and by the twentieth the rate of change was so great that people started speaking of decades the way they used to speak of centuries.

Toward the middle of the twentieth century, concepts and technologies from around the world and from all preceding ages were brought together in a single market, where they were offered on a come-one-come-all basis. Consumers did not need to belong to a particular tradition in order to sample the wares: Jews could practice Zen, Muslims try psychoanalysis, Japanese plow through *Being and Time*. Methods that were more than two thousand years old jostled with techniques patented the day before. Eclectic combinations abounded: Christian yoga, existential psychology, Tantric couples therapy. At the center of it all was a vague idea that the self was something to be discovered or realized or expressed or constituted. The weirdness of some of the expressions of this movement made it an easy target for social critics. Tom Wolfe, in "The 'Me' Decade and the Third Great Awakening" (1976), wrote mockingly of encounter groups, Primal Therapy, and so on, but he also pointed out that for perhaps the first time in history the masses were able to indulge in something that previously only the wealthiest could afford: "The old alchemical dream was changing base metals into gold. The new alchemical dream is: changing one's personality – remaking, remodeling, elevating, and polishing one's very *self.*"[2]

Diaries and Memoirs on the Eve of the Internet Revolution

In the 1980s five million people a year bought blank diaries in the United States. Others made entries on odd pieces of paper, on typed sheets, or in word-processing files. The most assiduous chronicler of this or perhaps of any period was the Reverend Robert W. Shields of Dayton, Washington, who in the twenty-five years preceding 1997 devoted four hours a day to a diary that in the end amounted to 37.5 million words. This is thirty times longer than the diary of Samuel Pepys but it does not seem likely that future scholars will find Shields's diary as vibrant or useful as the seventeenth-century Englishman's. He obsessively recorded his daily activities, from changing light bulbs to urination, together with his thoughts on God and existence and reflections on the weather and the news.[3] His toil resembles that of the protagonist of Jorge Luis Borges's story "Funes, His Memory": "Two or three times he had reconstructed an entire day; he had never once erred or faltered, but each reconstruction had itself taken an entire day." Funes explained to the narrator: "I, myself, alone, have more memories than all mankind since the world began," and again: "My memory, sir, is like a garbage heap."[4]

From the very beginnings of the personal diary, its practitioners have been concerned with self-improvement. Rogers and Ward, Shepard and Wigglesworth all found that the act of recording their thoughts and feelings helped bring them under control. During the second half of the twentieth century, psychologists and self-help gurus popularized and monetized the therapeutic diary, offering workshops, how-to guides, and specialized notebooks for the practice of journaling. Their methods were and are by and large the same. Subjects are encouraged to write in a systematic way and to avoid holding back painful thoughts or feelings. Later they review what they have written, either on their own or with the help of a therapist. Benefits are said to include mental and emotional clarity and the ability to confront and deal with problems. Some therapists make more ambitious claims, one insisting that "when people write about emotionally difficult events or feelings for just 20 minutes at a time over three or four days, their immune system functioning increases."[5] There is of course nothing new in the idea of using personal writing to help one deal with one's inner demons. Montaigne pioneered the technique four centuries ago, and Edwards, Swedenborg,

Maine de Biran, Kierkegaard, Emerson, Milner, Merton, and Barthes, among many others, used their journals for therapeutic purposes. Which leads one to the conclusion that it may be possible to get the benefits of diary writing without signing up for a journaling workshop.

In 1841, after reading a disappointing work of fiction, Emerson wrote in his journal: "These novels will give way, by and by, to diaries or autobiographies; – captivating books, if only a man knew how to choose among what he calls his experiences that which is really his experience, and how to record truth truly!"[6] Autobiographical writing saw an upswing during the twentieth century but the problems of selection and presentation remained. Modernist writers, haunted by the specter of the unconscious, felt obliged to record the totality of their lives without trying to filter out the commonplace. The novelist Virginia Woolf, in a posthumously published memoir, wrote of her struggles to describe the "nondescript cotton wool" of experience in which "moments of being" were embedded. "Every day includes much more non-being than being," she wrote, and in her memoir as well as her novels she tried to bring out both.[7] Other prose artists – James Joyce, Samuel Beckett, Alain Robbe-Grillet – tried to do the same thing in their own ways. So did the writers of the innumerable memoirs that began to crowd novels from bookstore shelves toward the end of the twentieth century.

Before the 1980s, the term "memoirs" (in the plural) was generally reserved for an account of a historical figure or period by someone with direct knowledge of the facts. One of the first to apply "memoir" (in the singular) to an incomplete autobiographical work was the American writer Tobias Wolff, whose *This Boy's Life: A Memoir* (1989) remains one of the best examples of the genre. Wolff began his career as a short-story writer, and his memoir, though based on the facts of his life, resembles a work of fiction, with carefully drawn characters, dramatic tension, and symbolic themes. It also has a plot, that of the "self-inventing man," which according to Wolff is "the central motif of American literature." The American literary hero uses "individual will and imagination in forging an identity." In this act of self-creation, imagination plays a crucial role: "You can't become what you can't imagine becoming," Wolff said, "You imagine who you are." And imagination draws upon and at the same time alters memory. "The very act of remembering is bending experience," Wolff told an interviewer. "The faculty of your memory is doing this even before you get to it." Thus the memoir is "not a documentary, it's not a work of history. It is something else; it's the story that memory tells you about yourself and who you are."[8]

All this is in line with the findings of psychologists who at the end of the twentieth century began to focus on the role of narrative in the making of what we are. Psychologist Jerome Bruner wrote in 1991: "We organize our experience and our memory of human happenings mainly in the form of narrative," but these narratives are not straightforward retellings of objective events. They are creations, like novels or literary biographies. Each narrative is "a version of reality whose acceptability is governed by convention and 'narrative necessity' rather than by empirical verification and logical requiredness."[9] This means that a factually defective narrative can be as true as a painstakingly footnoted one. Even in our everyday thoughts and daydreams, we choose fragments from the past that agree with our current self-understanding and piece them together to make the mosaic we call ourselves. Literary craftsmen like Wolff do the same in a more deliberate way. The "Jack" Wolff who emerges from the pages of his book is what the author wanted the reader to accept of what he could remember of what he used to be. The Tobias Wolff who narrates the story is an ironic observer of his younger self and at the same time the outcome of his struggles.

Wolff frequently explored the ill-lit territory between verbal truth and falsehood. Jack, he tells us, had a habit of telling lies he ended up believing himself. But this was not a case of simple self-deception. While forging a bunch of recommendation letters he needed to enter a private school, Jack "felt full of things that had to be said, full of stifled truth." The lying letters were part of this truth: "It was truth known only to me, but I believed in it more than I believed in the facts arrayed against it. I believed that in some sense not factually verifiable I was a straight-A student. In the same way I felt that I was an Eagle Scout, and a powerful swimmer, and a boy of integrity." He wrote the letters "without heat or hyperbole, in the words my teachers would have used if they had known me as I knew myself."[10] Confessions of youthful peccadilloes have been a regular feature of the Western memoir from its origins. Augustine, Fox, and Rousseau sought absolution by turning to God or discovering their true self within. Wolff had no interest in religion and did not see the self as a static truth. Rather it was something to be created through existential struggle.

The success of books like *This Boy's Life* encouraged many others to try their hands at works of self-discovery. Like other literary fashions, this one was shaped by the marketplace. The public wanted unhappy childhoods. Memoirists obliged. The public wanted down-and-dirty details. Soon readers were swimming in them. Writers found they had to up the ante to get the payoff they wanted. It was not enough to be recovered addicts, they had to have plumbed the depths of degradation before reascending to the light of day. As a literary strategy, all this was hardly new. Saint Paul invented the "worst of sinners" figure and Fox, Edwards and many others developed it. The power of such narratives rested on the assumption that the sins and sufferings depicted were real. James Frey broke the rules in *A Million*

Little Pieces (2003) when he put fabricated incidents in a book published as a "memoir." Readers objected not just because they had been lied to but because Frey extorted their sympathy without deserving it.

The Self in the Age of Digital Reproduction

In 1928, the French poet and essayist Paul Valéry wrote that "for the last twenty years neither matter nor space nor time has been what it was from time immemorial." The incredible growth of technology made it certain that "profound changes are impending." One of his predictions was eerily on the mark: "Just as water, gas, and electricity are brought into our houses from far off to satisfy our needs in response to a minimal effort, so we shall be supplied with visual or auditory images, which will appear and disappear at a simple movement of the hand, hardly more than a sign."[11] This must have seemed over-the-top in the age of the gramophone and black and white photography. Seventy years later it was a matter of daily experience.

Building on Valéry's ideas, German critic Walter Benjamin wrote in "The Work of Art in the Age of Mechanical Reproduction" (1936) that "the greatly increased mass of participants [in literary and artistic activities] has produced a change in the mode of participation." For one thing, "the distinction between author and public" had begun to lose its sharpness, with readers becoming writers at the drop of a hat.[12] In the seventy-seven years since Benjamin wrote, the "mode of participation" has gone through a few major and many minor transformations. Broadcast television replaced radio as the medium of choice in the late 1940s. Cable services became dominant during the 1970s, and in the 1980s the popularization of the Internet and wireless telephony set the stage for a proliferation of new technologies that shows no sign of abating. There has been an exponential increase in the number of participants, ease of access, variety of choices, and amount of interactivity, and this has brought about huge changes in the old technologies of the self along with the invention of new ones.

Internet bulletin boards and email lists, popular during the 1980s and 1990s, were fairly limited in scope. The development of the Web and graphical browsers opened up a multitude of new possibilities. During the mid-1990s a few individuals began to post to online diaries. This was the first time in the history of the genre that entries were published immediately after being written. Formerly a repository for secrets that the writers hardly dared to admit to themselves, the diary became a public confessional with the whole world as potential witnesses. Those who were disgusted by this airing of dirty laundry were outnumbered by those who wanted to try it out and those who wanted to observe. In 1887, the publication of the diaries of Marie Bashkirtseff and the Goncourt brothers sparked off a debate over the negative effects of self-absorption. A century later, after decades of published diaries, tell-all memoirs, advice columns, and daytime television, the public confession of personal hang-ups became an everyday matter. Pioneer blogger The Misanthropic Bitch noted in a post of 1999:

> Sitting in psychology class, I found myself questioning my normalcy. The discussion had turned to psychological disorders and their causes (sexual and physical abuse being the most popular). My classmates told sob stories deserving of violins and extended stays at Bellevue. I was the lone hold-out; I refused to participate.
>
> The class assumed I was holding back because the truth was too horrible to unload on a class full of strangers. Perhaps a Satanic ritual involving the dismemberment of a younger brother was eating at my psyche. (Why *is* she an only child?) The sad truth is I had nothing to tell.
>
> Why has it become so trendy to be fucked-up? When did normal become abnormal? Where was I when this shift occurred?[13]

The blogs of the late 1990s were generally focused on a particular theme; the blogs of the 2000s and after are multi-purpose or purposeless, competing for attention in a gigantic blogosphere that is said to include ten percent of American Internet users.

By 2005 social networking services had replaced standalone blogs as the main electronic technology of self. By creating a profile and uploading text and pictures, users define who they are or rather create an online identity that they offer to others as themselves. The simulacrum is reinforced by visitors through sharing, discussions, and so forth. The result has been a blurring of the line between the user's "actual" identity and his or her online persona, together with an undermining of traditional ideas about responsibility and privacy. Users of Facebook and Twitter express surprise that anything said or done online should have repercussions "out in the real world."[14] To post details of an intimate encounter, or set up a live webcam feed of one, seems to many the most natural thing in the world. It's only older people who don't get it. Speaking about the difference between her generation and the slightly younger Facebook Generation, the novelist Zadie Smith wrote in 2010: "We have different ideas about what a person is, or should be. I often worry that my idea of personhood is nostalgic, irrational, inaccurate." The sort of person she had always taken for granted – "a private person, a person who is a mystery, to the world and – which is more important – to herself" – might no longer exist: "Personhood is certainly changing," she concluded, "perhaps has already changed."[15]

For all her reservations about the Facebook Generation, Smith agreed with Mark Zuckerberg about one thing: "selves evolve."[16] That they do – or at any rate that the idea of the self has changed across history – has been the main theme of this book. It is clear that the ideas of self available to an Axial Age worshipper in a culture of iron tools differed greatly from those of a twenty-first-century atheistic computer programmer. Even if we grant that each had a similar sense of physical and mental apartness, the way they conceived of themselves *as selves* was vastly different.

In tracing the path between the self in the age of the shaman and the self in the age of Facebook, I have given special attention to some salient turning points: the rise of monotheism, the Renaissance and Reformation, the Enlightenment, the revolutionary period, the Romantic movement, modernity and late modernity. These of course are the periods that are always used for structuring histories of Western society. I have followed the convention but avoided the word "evolution" while speaking of changes between periods. Instead I have shown how the writers I focused on were influenced by the available fund of knowledge as well as by specific predecessors. Inheriting or selecting a body of ideas, they subjected it to a process of appropriation, transformation, or reaction, producing something original that could be added to the general fund and taken up by their successors. If not evolutionary, the process has at least been developmental.

Evolutionary ideas of cultural development arose during the nineteenth century but declined after the Second World War. There were a number of reasons for this. First, the idea of evolution was usually associated with an idea of progress, and often with the idea of a Spirit that guided the course of history. Even Darwin, who tried to get away from teleology, felt that the increasing complexity of organisms pointed to an overall progress that might continue in the future. Spencer and others took up this idea and developed it into a philosophy of progressive evolution that accorded well with the optimism of the late nineteenth century. That optimism took a hit during the First World War and perished in the death camps of Auschwitz. In philosophy, the Hegelian and Bergsonian versions of evolution, with their foundational ideas of Spirit or *élan vital*, were replaced by ideas of historical discontinuity and the death of the subject. These ideas still reign in intellectual circles around the world despite the efforts of neo-evolutionary thinkers.

Yet evolutionary thinkers foresaw a few things that postmodern theorists missed. Teilhard de Chardin, for example, wrote in *The Human Phenomenon* of how technological advances were bringing the human family together in ways that earlier generations could never have conceived. "Thanks to the prodigious biological event represented by the discovery of electro-magnetic waves," he wrote, every individual is now "simultaneously present" in every corner of the globe. In another book he suggested that millions of scientific researchers, making use of electronic calculating machines, would soon be linked together in a "vast organic system that will remain in future indispensable to the life of the community."[17] Within a few decades, the crude calculators of his era had been replaced by supercomputers and the organic system he foresaw had taken form as the World Wide Web.

The Web was developed by scientists for scientists but by 2005 most bandwidth was being used for streaming and downloading music and films, not to mention online shopping and spam. Still, the Web remains an unimaginably powerful tool for exchanging information and linking together an enormous number of people in an incalculable number of ways. It certainly is the extant technology of the self that will have the most impact on the future development of the idea of the human person. Increasingly, personhood is being defined by the mode of technology we use to connect with one another. And this is changing very fast. "People two, three or four years apart are having completely different experiences with technology," said the director of the Pew Research Center's Internet and American Life Project in the beginning of 2010. "College students scratch their heads at what their high school siblings are doing, and they scratch their heads at their younger siblings. It has sped up generational differences."[18] This evolving relationship with technological devices has become grist for the academic mill. "There is no more reason, from the perspective of evolution or learning, to favor use of a brain-only cognitive strategy" than to favor "combinations of brain, body and world," wrote philosopher Andy Clark in December 2010. Brains "play a major role, of course," but one can't forget the various "task-related bursts of energy" taking place in muscles and organs and "even outside the physical body – in the iPhones, BlackBerries, laptops and organizers which transform and extend the reach of bare biological processing."[19]

There is of course nothing new in using handheld devices to extend the range of our bodies and minds. We've been scratching and painting and inscribing marks and lines and letters on stones and walls and papers for tens of thousands of years. Most of this work has been done to facilitate the business of life: recording the delivery of a bushel of grain or marketing a new microprocessor. But some of us have grabbed whatever tool came to hand and used it to express – or to create – our selves. The history of this creative self-expression is far from over.

Notes

Chapter One

Epigraph: Descartes, *Meditations*, in *Philosophical Writings*, vol. 2, 18.

1   Mauss, "Une catégorie," 265.
2   See for instance Snell, *Discovery of the Mind*, and Jaynes, *Origin of Consciousness*. Both of these books are controversial but even scholars who disagree with them concede that the mentality of the ancient Greeks was radically different from ours.
3   Augustine, *Of True Religion*, 69.
4   Montaigne, *Complete Works*, 606.
5   Locke, *Essay* (2.11.17), 146.
6   Nietzsche, *Genealogy* (essay 2, section 16), 57.
7   Geertz, "Native's Point of View," 31.
8   Girard, *Journal intime*, xix.
9   See Mulligan, "Self Scrutiny," 316; Brown, "Postrevolutionary Self," 240; De Man, "Autobiography as Defacement"; Foucault, *Technologies of the Self* and "Hermeneutics of the Self."
10 Dostoyevsky, *Notes*, 122; Orwell, "Notes on Dali," http://www.k-1.com/Orwell/site/work/essays/dali.html [accessed September 2012].
11 UK statistics: "Rank frequency list for the whole corpus (not lemmatized)," http://ucrel.lancs.ac.uk/bncfreq/samples/120.pdf [accessed September 2012]; US statistics: "Word frequency lists and dictionary," http://www.wordfrequency.info/free.asp?s=y [accessed September 2012].
12 Sontag, "Writing Itself," vii.
13 Lejeune and Bogaert, *Journal à soi*, 25.
14 Shakespeare, *Hamlet* (I. 5), in *Complete Works*, 300.
15 Lejeune and Bogaert, *Journal à soi*, 41.
16 North, *General Preface & Life*, 78; Amiel, *Journal*, March 23, 1879, quoted in Girard, *Journal intime*, 472.
17 Keene, *Travelers*, 31, 28.
18 Keene, *Travelers*, 129.
19 Basho, *Narrow Road*, 85.
20 Merton, *Intimate Merton*, 316.

Chapter Two

Epigraph: Plato, *Republic* 10.608d, in *Republic of Plato*, 315.

1 Taylor, *Sources*, 112–13.
2 Scurlock, "Soul Emplacements," 1.
3 Confucius, *Analects* 5.12, http://www.wright-house.com/religions/confucius/ Analects.html [accessed September 2012]; *Leviticus* 19.18, in *New Revised Standard Bible*, http://www.biblestudytools.com/nrs/leviticus/19-18.html [accessed September 2012].
4 *Majjima Nikaya* 109.16, in Nanamoli and Bodhi, trans., *Middle Length Discourses*, 891.
5 Berkson, "Conceptions of Self/No-Self," 308.
6 Plato, *Phaedrus* 229d–230a, in Plato, *Phaedrus and Letters*, 25.
7 Lorenz, "Ancient Theories of Soul," http://plato.stanford.edu/entries/ ancient-soul/#4 [accessed September 2012].
8 Lucretius, *On the Nature of the Universe*, 88.
9 Seneca, *Moral Epistles*, Epistle 31, http://en.wikisource.org/wiki/Moral_ letters_to_Lucilius/Letter_31 [accessed September 2012].
10 Plotinus, *Enneads* 6.5–7, quoted in Cary, *Augustine's Invention*, 29.
11 *Isaiah* 49:6, in *New Revised Standard Bible*, http://www.biblestudytools.com/ nrs/isaiah/49-6.html [accessed September 2012].
12 *Mark* 1:15, in *New Revised Standard Bible*, http://www.biblestudytools.com/ nrs/mark/1-15.html [accessed September 2012].
13 Justin Martyr, *On the Resurrection*, http://www.newadvent.org/fathers/0131. htm [accessed September 2012].
14 Epictetus, quoted in Marcus Aurelius, *Meditations* (4.41), 46.
15 Seneca, *On the Shortness of Life*, chapter 7, http://en.wikisource.org/wiki/ On_the_shortness_of_life/Chapter_VII [accessed September 2012].
16 Marcus Aurelius to Fronto, quoted in Foucault, *Technologies of the Self*, 28.
17 Hampl, "Augustine's Passionate Quest," http://articles.latimes.com/1999/ jan/24/books/bk-986 [accessed September 2012].
18 Augustine, *Confessions*, 22, 24, 35, 145.
19 Augustine, *Confessions*, 54.
20 Augustine, *Confessions*, 123.
21 Augustine, *Confessions*, 147–8.
22 Augustine, *Confessions*, 152–3.
23 Augustine, *Confessions*, 180–1, 186–7, 194.
24 Cary, *Augustine's Invention*, 128, 77.
25 Augustine, *Confessions*, 43.
26 Augustine, *Sermons* 348.2, quoted in Brown, *Augustine of Hippo*, 436.
27 Augustine, *Confessions*, 148.
28 Ovid, *Metamorphosis*, 7.20, translation in *Oxford Dictionary of Quotations*, 366.
29 James, *Varieties*, lecture 8, http://ebooks.adelaide.edu.au/j/james/william/ varieties/chapter6.html [accessed September 2012].
30 Chandrakirti, *Madhyamakavatara* 150, in Chandrakirti, *Introduction*, 89.
31 Shantideva, *Way of the Bodhisattva*, 43, 60, 148, 115, 135–6.

32 Hildegard, *Secrets of God,* 175–6.
33 *Vita Sanctae Hildegardis,* in Maddocks, *Hildegard,* 55.
34 Hildegard, *Scivias,* 1.2.1–2, in Hildegard, *Secrets of God,* 12–13.
35 Makdisi, *Diary in Islamic Historiography.*
36 Ruzbihan Baqli, *Unveiling of Secrets,* 10–11.
37 Ruzbihan Baqli, *Unveiling of Secrets,* 58.
38 Ruzbihan Baqli, *Unveiling of Secrets,* 73.
39 Ruzbihan Baqli, *Unveiling of Secrets,* 94.
40 Ernst, *Ruzbihan Baqli,* xiv, 146.
41 Ernst, *Ruzbihan Baqli,* 85–6.
42 Attar, quoted in Happold, *Mysticism,* 227.

Chapter Three

Epigraph: Montaigne, *Complete Works,* 754.
1 Albertus Magnus, *Summa Theologica,* quoted in Martin and Barresi, *Rise and Fall,* 97.
2 Julian of Norwich, *Revelations,* 7.
3 Julian of Norwich, *Revelations,* 132–3.
4 Kempe, *Book of Margery Kempe,* 77–8.
5 Pico della Mirandola, *Oration on the Dignity of Man,* http://cscs.umich. edu/~crshalizi/Mirandola/ [accessed September 2012].
6 Burckhardt, *Civilization,* 52.
7 Greenblatt, *Renaissance Self-Fashioning,* 162.
8 Burckhardt, *Civilization,* 134.
9 Luther, "The Tower Experience, 1519," http://www.fordham.edu/halsall/ mod/1519luther-tower.html [accessed September 2012].
10 Bartoli-Michel, *Vie de Saint Ignace de Loyola,* cited in James, *Varieties,* lectures 16 and 17, http://ebooks.adelaide.edu.au/j/james/william/varieties/ chapter11.html [accessed September 2012].
11 Ignatius of Loyola, *Personal Writings,* 63.
12 Ignatius of Loyola, *Personal Writings,* 283.
13 Ignatius of Loyola, *Personal Writings,* 289.
14 Ignatius of Loyola, *Personal Writings,* 348–50.
15 Ignatius of Loyola, *Personal Writings,* 356–8.
16 Ignatius of Loyola, *Personal Writings,* 73.
17 Ignatius of Loyola, *Personal Writings,* 90–1.
18 Ignatius of Loyola, *Personal Writings,* 103.
19 Teresa of Avila, *Life,* 62, 69.
20 Teresa of Avila, *Life,* 63, 90.
21 Teresa of Avila, *Life,* 203; Weber, "Counter-Reformation Misogyny," 144.
22 Montaigne, *Complete Works,* 962.

23 Montaigne, text inscribed on the wall of his study, cited in *Complete Works*, xvi.

24 Montaigne, *Complete Works*, 25.

25 Montaigne, *Complete Works*, 331.

26 Montaigne, *Complete Works*, 2.

27 Montaigne, *Complete Works*, 333–4, 611, 740.

28 Montaigne, *Complete Works*, 602.

29 Montaigne, *Complete Works*, 337.

30 Montaigne, *Complete Works*, 331.

31 Montaigne, *Complete Works*, 612.

32 Montaigne, *Complete Works*, 78.

33 Montaigne, *Complete Works*, 513, 552.

34 Montaigne, *Complete Works*, 992–3, 1044, 1001, 1037, 1044.

35 Montaigne, *Complete Works*, 740.

36 Frame, "Montaigne," xxvii.

37 Ong, *Orality and Literacy*, 103.

38 Montaigne, *Complete Works*, 1078.

39 Montaigne, *Complete Works*, 1096–7.

40 Montaigne, *Complete Works*, 1210.

41 Montaigne, *Complete Works*, 1229, 1224.

42 Montaigne, *Complete Works*, 741.

43 Babur, *Baburnama*, 393.

44 Babur, *Baburnama*, 115–17.

45 Babur, *Baburnama*, 89, 241.

46 Terzioglu, "Man in the Image of God," 142–3.

47 Jahanara, *The Confidant of Spirits*, in Ernst, *Teachings*, 196, 198.

48 Dara Shikoh, *Hasanat-ul-'Arifin*, in Hazrat, *Dara Shikuh*, 107, 242–3.

49 Dara Shikoh, preface to *Sirr-i-Akbar*, in Hazrat, *Dara Shikuh*, 267.

50 Kafadar, "Self and Others," 148.

51 Terzioglu, "Man in the Image of God," 160, 163.

Chapter Four

Epigraph: Bunyan, *Grace Abounding*, paragraph 255.

1 Calvin, quoted in Ozment, *Age of Reform*, 355. I follow Ozment in dating Calvin's conversion to May 1534.

2 Calvin, *Institutes* (3.2.10, 3.16.1, 3.2.29), vol. 2: 23, 281, 45.

3 Erasmus and Luther, in Ross and McLaughlin (eds), *Renaissance Reader*, 686, 703, 726.

4 Calvin, *Institutes* (3.21.1), vol. 2: 415.

5 Weber, *The Protestant Ethic and the Spirit of Capitalism*, Chapter 4, http://www.marxists.org/reference/archive/weber/protestant-ethic/ch04.htm [accessed September 2012].

6 Hamilton, quoted in Botonaki, "Spiritual Diaries," 19–20.
7 Rogers, in Knappen (ed.), *Two Elizabethan Puritan Diaries*, 64 (modernized).
8 Rogers, in Knappen (ed.), *Two Elizabethan Puritan Diaries*, 62 (modernized).
9 Rogers, in Knappen (ed.), *Two Elizabethan Puritan Diaries*, 88 (modernized).
10 Ward, in Knappen (ed.), *Two Elizabethan Puritan Diaries*, 106, 108 (modernized).
11 Todd, *Puritan Self-Fashioning*, 236–7.
12 Ward, in Knappen (ed.), *Two Elizabethan Puritan Diaries*, 104 (modernized).
13 Rogers, in Knappen (ed.), *Two Elizabethan Puritan Diaries*, 88–9 (modernized).
14 John Beadle, quoted in Webster, "Writing to Redundancy," 47–8.
15 Shakespeare, *Julius Caesar* (I. 2), in *Complete Works*, 336.
16 Spenser, *Fairie Queene*, book 2, 158 (modernized).
17 Traherne, "Nature," in *Poetical Works*, 52.
18 Bunyan, *Grace Abounding*, paragraph 22.
19 Bunyan, *Grace Abounding*, paragraphs 58–9.
20 Bunyan, *Grace Abounding*, paragraphs 204, 229, 262.
21 Bunyan, *Pilgrim's Progress,* http://www.gutenberg.org/ebooks/131 [accessed September 2012].
22 Fox, *Journal*, chapter 1, http://www.strecorsoc.org/gfox/ch01.html [accessed September 2012].
23 Fox, *Journal*, chapter 1, http://www.strecorsoc.org/gfox/ch01.html [accessed September 2012].
24 Fox, *Journal*, chapter 2, http://www.strecorsoc.org/gfox/ch02.html [accessed September 2012].
25 Fox, *Journal*, chapter 2, http://www.strecorsoc.org/gfox/ch02.html [accessed September 2012].
26 Fox, *Journal*, chapter 4, http://www.strecorsoc.org/gfox/ch04.html [accessed September 2012].
27 Royce, "George Fox as a Mystic," 53.
28 "Mayflower Compact, 1620," Plymouth Colony Archive Project, http://www.histarch.uiuc.edu/plymouth/compact.html (modernized) [accessed September 2012]; Winthrop, "A Model of Christian Charity," Religious Freedom Page, http://religiousfreedom.lib.virginia.edu/sacred/charity.html [accessed September 2012].
29 Winthrop, *Experiencia*, http://tucnak.fsv.cuni.cz/~calda/Winthrop_Experiencia.doc [accessed September 2012].
30 Quotations from Maclear, "Heart of New England Rent," 642–3 (modernized).
31 Shepard, quoted in Miller, *New England Mind: From Colony*, 123; Shepard, quoted in Brekus, "A Place to Go," 6; Shepard, quoted in Rosenwald, "Sewall's Diary," 340.
32 Shepard, quoted in Tipson, "Routinized Piety," 65.

33 Shepard, quoted in Tipson, "Religious Experience of the Past," 700; Miller, *New England Mind: Seventeenth*, 53.

34 Wigglesworth, *Diary*, 21, 4, 5 (modernized).

35 Anthony, quoted in Brekus, "A Place to Go," 5; Brekus, "A Place to Go," 6; Shepard in Brekus, "A Place to Go," 6.

36 Dummer, quoted in Cohen, "Diary of Jeremiah Dummer," 401, 413, 409 (modernized).

37 Cohen, "Diary of Jeremiah Dummer," 397–8.

38 Sewall, quoted in Hilmer, "The Other Diary," 354.

39 Pepys, *Diary*, http://www.pepysdiary.com/archive/1667/03/ [accessed September 2012]; http://www.pepysdiary.com/archive/1667/05/ [accessed September 2012].

40 Pepys, *Diary*, http://www.pepysdiary.com/archive/1666/09/ [accessed September 2012].

41 Stevenson, Robert Louis. "Samuel Pepys," http://www.bartleby.com/28/12.html [accessed September 2012].

42 Pepys, *Diary*, http://www.pepysdiary.com/archive/1663/01/09/ [accessed September 2012].

43 Pepys, *Diary*, http://www.pepysdiary.com/archive/1666/02/ [accessed September 2012] (modernized).

44 Stevenson, "Samuel Pepys," http://www.bartleby.com/28/12.html [accessed September 2012].

45 Pepys, *Diary*, http://www.pepysdiary.com/archive/1662/06/ [accessed September 2012] (modernized).

46 Pepys, *Diary*, http://www.pepysdiary.com/archive/1668/11/13/ [accessed September 2012].

47 Hooke, quoted in Mulligan, "Self-Scrutiny," 321, 340 [accessed September 2012] (modernized).

48 Hooke, quoted in Mulligan, "Self-Scrutiny," 338.

Chapter Five

Epigraphs: Descartes, *Meditations*, in *Philosophical Writings,* vol. 2, 18; Pascal, *Pensées*, 158.

1 Luther to Erasmus, in *Renaissance Reader*, 701; Calvin, *Institutes* (3.2.10), vol. 2, 23.

2 Descartes to Mersenne, November 1633, reproduced in Descartes, *Principles of Philosophy*, 83.

3 Descartes, *Discours*, Part One, http://www.columbia.edu/cu/tat/core/descartes.htm [accessed September 2012].

4 Montaigne, *Complete Works*, 437.

5 Descartes to Beckman, quoted in Clarke, *Descartes*, 45.

6 Descartes, quoted in Seigel, *Idea of the Self*, 66.

7 Descartes, *Discours*, Part Two, http://www.columbia.edu/cu/tat/core/descartes.htm [accessed September 2012].

8 Descartes, *Discours*, Part Four, http://www.columbia.edu/cu/tat/core/descartes.htm [accessed September 2012].

9 Descartes to Andreas Colvius, November 14, 1640, in *Philosophical Letters*, 84.

10 Pascal, *Memorial*, http://www.users.csbsju.edu/~eknuth/pascal.html [accessed September 2012].

11 Pascal, *Lettres provinciales*, translation in *Oxford Dictionary of Quotations*, 369.

12 Pascal, *Pensées*, 153.

13 Pascal, *Pensées*, 131, 139, 118.

14 Pascal, *Pensées*, 44, 131.

15 Hobbes, *English Works*, vol. 1, 137–8.

16 Dacome, "Noting the Mind," 603.

17 Locke, quoted in Pinto, Review of *Locke's Travels in France*, 70–1 (modernized).

18 Locke, *Essay*, 10.

19 Locke, *Essay*, 13, 83.

20 Descartes to Gibieuf, January 19, 1642, quoted in Taylor, *Sources*, 144.

21 Locke, *Essay*, 87.

22 Locke, *Essay*, 330.

23 Locke, *Essay*, 318, 331.

24 Locke, *Essay*, 325, 331.

25 Locke, *Essay*, 614.

26 Moody, quoted in Carroll, "I Indulged," 168.

27 Edwards, "Personal Narrative," in *Letters and Personal Writings*, 791–2.

28 Edwards, "Personal Narrative," 792–3.

29 Edwards, "Personal Narrative," 795.

30 Edwards, "Diary," in *Letters and Personal Writings*, 753, 759, 764, 765, 776.

31 Edwards, "God Glorified in Man's Dependence," in *Sermons and Discourses 1730–1733*, 200, 211, 213.

32 Weddle, "Image of the Self," 70, 76.

33 Edwards, "Personal Narrative," 803.

34 Edwards, "Sinners in the Hands of an Angry God," in *Sermons and Discourses 1739–1742*, 411–12.

Chapter Six

Epigraph: Hume, "An Abstract of A Book Lately Published entitled, A Treatise of Human Nature," paragraph 28, http://web.mnstate.edu/gracyk/courses/web%20publishing/hume%27sabstract.htm [accessed September 2012].

1 Kant, "An Answer to the Question: What is Enlightenment?" http://
theliterarylink.com/kant.html [accessed September 2012].

2 Kant, "An Answer to the Question: What is Enlightenment?" http://
theliterarylink.com/kant.html [accessed September 2012].

3 Taylor, *Sources*, 185.

4 Hume, "My Own Life," http://ebooks.adelaide.edu.au/h/hume/david/h92my/
[accessed September 2012].

5 Hume, *Letters*, vol. 1, 154 (modernized).

6 Hume, *Treatise* (1.4.1), http://ebooks.adelaide.edu.au/h/hume/david/h92t/
B1.4.1.html [accessed September 2012].

7 Hume, *Treatise*, title page, http://ebooks.adelaide.edu.au/h/hume/david/
h92t/index.html [accessed September 2012].

8 Hume, *Treatise*, "Introduction," http://ebooks.adelaide.edu.au/h/hume/
david/h92t/introduction.html [accessed September 2012].

9 Hume, *Treatise* (1.4.2), http://ebooks.adelaide.edu.au/h/hume/david/h92t/
B1.4.2.html [accessed September 2012].

10 Hume, *Treatise* (1.4.6), http://ebooks.adelaide.edu.au/h/hume/david/h92t/
B1.4.6.html [accessed September 2012].

11 Hume, *Treatise* (1.4.6), http://ebooks.adelaide.edu.au/h/hume/david/h92t/
B1.4.6.html [accessed September 2012].

12 Hume, *Treatise* (1.4.6), http://ebooks.adelaide.edu.au/h/hume/david/h92t/
B1.4.6.html [accessed September 2012].

13 Hume, *Treatise*, Appendix, http://ebooks.adelaide.edu.au/h/hume/david/
h92t/appendix.html [accessed September 2012].

14 Hume, "An Abstract of A Book Lately Published entitled, A Treatise of
Human Nature," paragraph 28, http://web.mnstate.edu/gracyk/courses/
web%20publishing/hume%27sabstract.htm [accessed September 2012].

15 Hume, *Treatise* (2.3.3), http://ebooks.adelaide.edu.au/h/hume/david/h92t/
B2.3.3.html [accessed September 2012].

16 Hume, *Treatise* (3.1.1), http://ebooks.adelaide.edu.au/h/hume/david/h92t/
B3.1.1.html [accessed September 2012].

17 Hume, "On the Immortality of the Soul," in *Essays on Suicide and
Immortality,* http://www.anselm.edu/homepage/dbanach/suicide.htm#A2
[accessed September 2012].

18 Smith, letter to William Strahan, November 9, 1776, in Hume, "My Own
Life," http://ebooks.adelaide.edu.au/h/hume/david/h92my/#smith [accessed
September 2012].

19 Hume, "My Own Life," http://ebooks.adelaide.edu.au/h/hume/david/h92my/
[accessed September 2012].

20 Diderot, quoted in "The Encyclopedia of Diderot & D'Alembert," http://
quod.lib.umich.edu/d/did/intro.html [accessed September 2012].

21 "Système Figuré des Connoissances Humaines," reproduced graphically in
Wikipedia, "Figurative System of Human Knowledge," http://en.wikipedia.
org/wiki/Figurative_system_of_human_knowledge

22 Diderot, quoted in Wilson, *Diderot*, 210, 237.

23 Diderot, *Les Eleuthéromanes*, quoted in French by Strugnell, *Diderot's Politics*, 196. The text is "Et ses mains ourdiraient les entrailles du prêtre/ Au défaut d'un cordon pour étrangler les rois." It is usually cited in English in the form: "Man will never be free until the last king is strangled with the entrails of the last priest."

24 Holbach, *System of Nature*, trans. Taylor, *Sources*, 326.

25 Diderot, "Éloge de Richardson," http://graduate.engl.virginia.edu/enec981/ dictionary/25diderotC1.html [accessed September 2012].

26 Richardson, *Clarissa*, 35, 721.

27 Richardson, *Pamela*, 89, 102, 214.

28 Richardson, *Pamela*, 493.

29 Richardson, *Pamela II* in *Pamela* (1816 edition), 556.

30 Sterne, *Tristram Shandy*, 51, 50, 132–3. For Locke's equation of mental association and madness, see *Essay*, 379.

31 Sterne, *Tristram Shandy*, 380.

32 Sterne, *Tristram Shandy*, 367.

33 Brown, "Postrevolutionary Self," 240.

34 Boswell, *Corsica*, preface to third edition, http://www.gutenberg.org/ files/20263/20263-h/20263-h.htm [accessed September 2012].

35 Boswell, *Journal*, 8–9.

36 Boswell, *Journal*, 2, 81, 17–18.

37 Boswell, *Journal*, 38–9.

38 Hume, *Treatise* (1.4.6), http://ebooks.adelaide.edu.au/h/hume/david/h92t/ B1.4.6.html [accessed September 2012].

39 Boswell, *Journal*, 141.

40 Boswell, *Journal*, 73–4.

41 Boswell, *Journal*, 78.

42 Boswell, *Journal*, 247–51.

43 Kant, *Prolegomena to Any Future Metaphysics*, http://web.mnstate.edu/ gracyk/courses/phil%20306/kant_materials/prolegomena2.htm [accessed September 2012].

44 Kant, *Kant's Inaugural Dissertation* (paragraphs 8–12), 54–7.

45 Kant to Lambert, September 2, 1770, in *Kant's Inaugural Dissertation*, 34–5.

46 Kant, *Anthropology*, 20–22.

47 Kant, *Critique*, 22.

48 Kant, *Critique*, 168.

49 Kant, *Critique*, 380.

Chapter Seven

Epigraph: Rousseau, *Émile*, Book 4, paragraph 958.

1 Kant, Fragment, trans. Beck, quoted in Dent, *Rousseau*, v.

2 Rousseau, letter to Malesherbes, January 12, 1762, trans. Hendel, reproduced in Dent, *Rousseau*, 183.

3 Rousseau, *Émile*, Book 1, paragraphs 28 and 42.

4 Rousseau, *Émile*, Book 2, paragraph 223.

5 Rousseau, *Émile*, Book 3, paragraph 714.

6 Rousseau, *Émile*, Book 4, paragraph 756.

7 Rousseau, *Émile*, Book 4, paragraphs 989, 1025, 1038, 1051, 1093.

8 Hume, letter to Mme de Boufflers, quoted in Mossner, *Life of David Hume*, 508.

9 Hume, letters to Charlemont and Blair, quoted in Mossner, *Life of David Hume*, 429 (normalized).

10 Rousseau, *Confessions*, 5.

11 Rousseau, *Confessions*, 84–5, 505, 170.

12 Rousseau, *Confessions*, 270.

13 Dent, *Rousseau*, 197.

14 Rousseau, *Rousseau Judge of Jean-Jacques* (2.176), quoted in Dent, *Rousseau*, 201.

15 Rousseau, *Reveries*, 33–4.

16 Rousseau, *Reveries*, 88–9, 91.

17 Bloom, "Rousseau's Critique," 145.

18 Swedenborg, *Dream Diary*, 91, 120–1.

19 Swedenborg, *Dream Diary*, 160–1, 173.

20 Swedenborg, *Arcana Coelestia*, paragraph 68.

21 Swedenborg, *Heaven and Hell* paragraphs 89, 547.

22 Kant, letter to Charlotte von Knobloch, August 10 [?1863], http://en.wikisource.org/wiki/Dreams_of_a_Spirit-Seer/Appendix_2 [accessed September 2012].

23 Emerson, *Representative Men*, chapter 4, http://www.online-literature.com/emerson/representative-men/4/ [accessed September 2012].

24 Swedenborg, *Dream Diary*, 136.

25 Hamann, *Sämtliche Werke,* volumes I and II, quoted in Abrams, *Natural Supernaturalism*, 400–1.

26 Hamann, *Sämtliche Werke,* volume I, quoted in Abrams, *Natural Supernaturalism*, 401.

27 Hamann, letter quoted in Dickson, *Relational Metacriticism*, 351.

28 Hume, *Enquiry Concerning Human Understanding*, section 8, http://ebooks.adelaide.edu.au/h/hume/david/h92e/chapter8.html [accessed September 2012].

29 Herder, *Philosophical Writings*, 167–8.

30 Herder, *Ideen zur Philosophie der Geschichte der Menschheit* 8.1, trans. Taylor, *Sources*, 375.

31 Goethe, *Wilhelm Meister's Apprenticeship*, 174.

32 Blake, *The Marriage of Heaven and Hell*, in *Complete Poetry & Prose*, 34, http://www.blakearchive.org/exist/blake/archive/erdgen.xq?id=b1.7

33 Blake, *Vala*, in *Complete Poetry & Prose*, 301, http://www.blakearchive.org/exist/blake/archive/erdman.xq?id=b2.3.1 [accessed September 2012]; The Urizen Books of William Blake, Glossary, http://facstaff.uww.edu/hoganj/gloss.htm [accessed September 2012].

34 Blake, *Milton*, in *Complete Poetry & Prose*, 132, 142, http://www.blakearchive.org/exist/blake/archive/erdman.xq?id=b1.15.3 [accessed September 2012].

35 Coleridge, "Religious Musings," in *Poetical Works*, 181.

36 Coleridge, *Notebooks*, vol. 5, 564 (modernized).

37 Coleridge, letter to C.A. Tulk, January 12, 1818, in *Collected Letters*, vol. 4, 807.

38 Keats, letter to George and Georgiana Keats, in *Poetical Works and Letters*, 369.

39 Keats, *The Fall of Hyperion*, in *Poetical Works and Letters*, 235.

40 Shelley, *A Defence of Poetry*, paragraph 48, http://www.bartleby.com/27/23.html [accessed September 2012].

41 Wordsworth, *The Recluse* I.1.675-99, http://www.bartleby.com/145/ww301.html [accessed September 2012].

42 Wordsworth, "Fenwick Notes" (MS page 152), in *The Fenwick Notes,* 188. Written between 1799 and 1805, the poem was published three months after the author's death under the editorial title *The Prelude, or Growth of a Poet's Mind.*

43 Wordsworth, *Prelude* 1: 301–2, 340–4, 401–7, http://www.gutenberg.org/files/12383/12383-h/Wordsworth3c.html [accessed September 2012].

44 Sontag, "Writing Itself," xiv.

45 Taylor, *Sources*, 376.

46 Berlin, *Sense of Reality*, 168.

Chapter Eight

Epigraph: Constant, *Mélanges*, 337.

1 Southey, letter reproduced in *Correspondence with Caroline Bowles*, 52.

2 Wordsworth, *Prelude* 6. 339–41, http://www.gutenberg.org/files/12383/12383-h/Wordsworth3c.html [accessed September 2012].

3 Blake, *The French Revolution*, 236–7, in *Complete Poetry & Prose*, 296. http://www.blakearchive.org/exist/blake/archive/erdgen.xq?page=296 [accessed September 2012].

4 Wordsworth, letter to Coleridge, 1799, quoted in Holmes, *Coleridge*, 242; Shelley, letter to Byron, September 8, 1816, in Byron, *Lord Byron's Correspondence*, Part 2, 15.

5 "Declaration of the Rights of Man and of the Citizen," articles 1, 3, 6, 10, http://hrcr.law.columbia.edu/docs/frenchdec.html [accessed September 2012].

6 Rousseau, *Social Contract*, book 1, http://www.constitution.org/jjr/socon_01. htm [accessed September 2012].

7 Rousseau, *Social Contract*, book 3, http://www.constitution.org/jjr/socon_03. htm [accessed September 2012].

8 Robespierre, "Dedication to Jean-Jacques Rousseau," reproduced in Blum, *Rousseau*, 156.

9 McNeil, "The Cult of Rousseau," 201.

10 Robespierre, "Dedication to Jean-Jacques Rousseau," reproduced in Blum, *Rousseau*, 156–7.

11 Maine de Biran, *Nouveaux essais*, Introduction, reproduced in Cresson (ed.), *Maine de Biran*, 103.

12 Maine de Biran, in Naville (ed.), *Sa vie et ses pensées*, 119 (translation by Huxley, *Themes*, 57).

13 Maine de Biran, *Sa vie et ses pensées*, 121.

14 Maine de Biran, *Sa vie et ses pensées*, 123, 128.

15 Condillac, *Essai sur l'origine des connaissances humanines* (1. 2. 1. 15), 37.

16 Maine de Biran, *Influence de l'habitude* (Introduction, 2), 71.

17 Amiel, *Journal*, June 17, 1857, http://www.gutenberg.org/ebooks/8545 [accessed September 2012].

18 Mlle Maurice, quoted in Frogneux and Thirion, "Pour penser," 105 (cf. Huxley, *Themes*, 18).

19 Maine de Biran, *Sa vie et ses pensées*, 253, 252.

20 Maine de Biran, *Sa vie et ses pensées*, 292–3.

21 Maine de Biran, *Sa vie et ses pensées*, 399–401.

22 Maine de Biran, *Nouveaux essais*, Introduction, reproduced in Cresson (ed.), *Maine de Biran*, 122–3; *Sa vie et ses pensées*, 402–3; *Nouveaux essais*, in Cresson (ed.), 123; *Sa vie et ses pensées*, 362.

23 Biran, *Journal*, July 24, 1816, quoted in Girard, *Journal Intime*, 239–40; Constant, *Adolphe*, 77.

24 Constant, *Mélanges*, i–ii (translation by Wood, "Life and Work," 3).

25 Constant, *Adolphe*, 42.

26 Constant, *Journaux intimes*, 72, 76.

27 Constant, *Adolphe*, 16.

28 Constant, *Journaux intimes*, 178, 216, 246–7, 269.

29 Constant, *Adolphe*, 11.

30 Constant, *De la religion*, 27.

31 Constant, *Journaux intimes*, 208.

32 E.-J. Delécluze, *Journal*, May 8, 1825, quoted in Girard, *Journal intime*, 289.

33 Stendhal, *Journal*, 1, 24, 51.

34 Lemaître, *Les contemporains*, http://www.green-ebook-shop.com/ ebooks/2/9/9/1/29918/29918.html [accessed September 2012].

35 Stendhal, journal entry of October 10, 1808, cited by Girard, *Journal intime*, 317.

36 Stendhal, journal entry of June 1, 1810, in Sage (ed.), *Private Diaries*, 324.

37 Stendhal, *Journal*, 421, 111.
38 Stendhal, *Journal*, 368, 52.
39 Letter to Édouard Mounier, December 15, 1803, in *Souvenirs d'égotisme*, 167.
40 Stendhal, *The Red and the Black*, Book 2, chapter 13, http://ebooks.adelaide.
edu.au/s/stendhal/red/book2.13.html [accessed September 2012].
41 Stendhal, *The Red and the Black*, Book 1, chapter 13, http://ebooks.adelaide.
edu.au/s/stendhal/red/book1.13.html [accessed September 2012].
42 Stendhal, *The Red and the Black*, Book 2, chapter 26, http://ebooks.adelaide.
edu.au/s/stendhal/red/book2.26.html [accessed September 2012].
43 Stendhal, *The Red and the Black*, Book 2, chapter 41, http://ebooks.adelaide.
edu.au/s/stendhal/red/book2.41.html [accessed September 2012].
44 Stendhal, *The Red and the Black*, Book 2, chapter 45, http://ebooks.adelaide.
edu.au/s/stendhal/red/book2.45.html [accessed September 2012].
45 Stendhal, *Lucien Leuwen*, 61, 212.
46 Stendhal, *Henry Brulard*, 5.
47 Delacroix, *Journal*, 411.
48 Delacroix, *Journal*, 1, 316.
49 Delacroix, *Journal*, 62.
50 Renan, "Henri Frédéric Amiel," quoted in Girard, *Journal intime*, 580.
51 Vigny, *Oeuvres*, 1341, 1284; journal entries quoted in Girard, *Journal intime*,
364.
52 Vigny, "L'esprit pur," http://poesie.webnet.fr/lesgrandsclassiques/poemes/
alfred_de_vigny/l_esprit_pur.html [accessed September 2012].
53 Amiel, *Amiel's Journal*, http://www.gutenberg.org/ebooks/8545 [accessed
September 2012].
54 Amiel, journal entry, September 20, 1864. In Jaccard, (ed.), *Du journal
intime* 4: 74–5.
55 Amiel, *Amiel's Journal*, http://www.gutenberg.org/ebooks/8545 [accessed
September 2012].
56 Siegel, *Idea of the Self*, 290.

Chapter Nine

Epigraphs: Fichte, *Science of Knowledge*, 97; Kierkegaard, *Papers and Journals*, 51.
1 Locke, *Second Discourse*, chapter 2, section 6, http://www.constitution.org/
jl/2ndtr02.htm [accessed September 2012]; Kant, *Lectures on Ethics*, 193.
2 Fichte, *Foundations of Natural Right*, 9–11.
3 Fichte, "To the German Nation," in Modern History Sourcebook, http://
www.fordham.edu/Halsall/mod/1806fichte.asp [accessed September 2012].
4 Schelling, *System of Transcendental Philosophy*, "Introduction," section 3,
http://www.cddc.vt.edu/marxists/reference/subject/philosophy/works/ge/
schellin.htm [accessed September 2012].
5 Schelling, quoted in Reardon, *Religion*, 113.

6   Schelling, *On University Studies*, and Schelling, *Complete Works* 6:573, both quoted in Williamson, *Longing for Myth*, 69; Williamson, *Longing for Myth*, 69.

7   Hegel, *Phenomenology of Mind*, Preface, http://www.class.uidaho.edu/mickelsen/texts/Hegel%20Phen/hegel_phen_preface.htm [accessed September 2012].

8   Hegel, *Philosophy of History*, Introduction, http://www.class.uidaho.edu/mickelsen/texts/Hegel%20-%20Philosophy%20of%20History.htm [accessed September 2012].

9   Hegel, *Phenomenology of Mind*, chapter 4A, http://www.class.uidaho.edu/mickelsen/texts/Hegel%20Phen/hegel%20phen%20ch%204%20A.htm [accessed September 2012].

10 Hegel, *Phenomenology of Mind*, Preface, http://www.class.uidaho.edu/mickelsen/texts/Hegel%20Phen/hegel_phen_preface.htm [accessed September 2012].

11 Hegel, *Philosophy of History*, Introduction, http://www.class.uidaho.edu/mickelsen/texts/Hegel%20-%20Philosophy%20of%20History.htm [accessed September 2012].

12 Hegel, *Lectures on the History of Philosophy*, Final Result, http://www.class.uidaho.edu/mickelsen/texts/Hegel%20-%20Hist%20Phil/final.htm [accessed September 2012].

13 Schopenhauer, *On the Basis of Morality*, 15.

14 Schopenhauer, *Will and Representation*, vol. 1, 3.

15 Schopenhauer, *Will and Representation*, vol. 1, 165; vol. 2, 358.

16 Schopenhauer, *Will and Representation*, vol. 1, 100.

17 Schopenhauer, *Will and Representation*, vol. 1, 352–3.

18 Schopenhauer, *Will and Representation*, vol. 1, 253.

19 Schopenhauer, *Will and Representation*, vol. 1, 185.

20 Schopenhauer, *Will and Representation*, vol. 1, 411.

21 Kierkegaard, *Papers and Journals*, 117–18, 341.

22 Kierkegaard, *Papers and Journals*, 50, 97.

23 Kierkegaard, *Papers and Journals*, 32, 98.

24 Kierkegaard, *Papers and Journals*, 159–60.

25 Kierkegaard, *Fear and Trembling; Repetition*, 222.

26 Kierkegaard, *Papers and Journals*, 175–6, 195; *The Point of View for my Work as an Author*, trans. Walter Lowrie, in Kierkegaard, *Kierkegaard Anthology*, 326, 328.

27 Kierkegaard, *Concept of Anxiety*, 42.

28 Kierkegaard, *Papers and Journals*, 204.

29 Kierkegaard, *Postscript*, 189, 203–5, 242, 256.

30 Kierkegaard, *Papers and Journals*, 277–8, 245, 254, 465, 513.

31 Kierkegaard, *Sickness Unto Death*, 13.

32 Kierkegaard, *Sickness Unto Death*, 13, 20–1, 14.

33 Kierkegaard, *Papers and Journals*, 641.

34 Dostoyevsky, *Notes*, 112.
35 Dostoyevsky, *Karamazov*, 101.
36 Dostoyevsky, *Notes*, 110, 112–13, 203.
37 Dostoyevsky, *Karamazov*, 317.
38 Dostoyevsky, *Karamazov*, 275.
39 Dostoyevsky, *Karamazov*, 304–9.
40 Nietzsche, *Twilight of the Idols*, section 45, http://www.lexido.com/EBOOK_
   TEXTS/TWILIGHT_OF_THE_IDOLS_.aspx?S=10 [accessed September
   2012].
41 Dostoyevsky, quoted in Mochulsky, "Dostoyevsky," xii.

Chapter Ten

Epigraph: Thoreau, *Journal*, vol. 2, 390.
1 Tocqueville, *Democracy* (2.2.2), http://xroads.virginia.edu/~HYPER/
   DETOC/ch2_02.htm [accessed September 2012].
2 Tocqueville, *Democracy* (2.1.2), http://xroads.virginia.edu/~HYPER/
   DETOC/ch1_02.htm [accessed September 2012].
3 Tocqueville, *Democracy* (1.17), http://xroads.virginia.edu/~HYPER/
   DETOC/1_ch17.htm [accessed September 2012].
4 Tocqueville, *Democracy* (2.1.5), http://xroads.virginia.edu/~HYPER/
   DETOC/ch1_05.htm [accessed September 2012].
5 Tocqueville and Channing quoted in Pierson, *Tocqueville in America*, 156,
   422.
6 Channing, "Likeness to God," "Unitarian Christianity," and "The Moral
   Argument against Calvinism." History Tools.org, http://www.historytools.
   org/sources/channing-unitarianism.pdf [accessed September 2012].
7 Emerson, *Journal*, vol. 1, 10, 362–3.
8 Emerson, *Representative Men*, "Montaigne; or, the Skeptic," http://www.
   online-literature.com/emerson/representative-men/5/ [accessed September
   2012].
9 Emerson, *Journals*, vol. 2, 164.
10 Emerson, letter to William Emerson, in *Letters*, vol. 1, 176.
11 Emerson, *Journals*, vol. 3, 163.
12 Emerson, *Journals*, vol. 3, 270–1.
13 Emerson, "Nature," chapter 1, http://www.online-literature.com/emerson/
   nature/1/ [accessed September 2012]. Several phrases in this passage come
   straight from the journal entry of March 19, 1835 (*Journals*, vol. 3, 451–2),
   but the famous "transparent eye-ball" owes more to the Mount Auburn
   experience.
14 Emerson, *Journals*, vol. 3, 267, 272, 274.
15 Emerson, *Essays: First Series*, "Self-Reliance," http://www.online-literature.
   com/emerson/essays-first-series/2/ [accessed September 2012].

16 Carlyle, *Sartor Resartus*, book 3, chapter 8, http://www.gutenberg.org/dirs/1/0/5/1051/1051-h/1051-h.htm#2HCH0029 [accessed September 2012].

17 Emerson, "The American Scholar," http://www.online-literature.com/emerson/3780/ [accessed September 2012].

18 Emerson, "Divinity School Address," http://www.online-literature.com/emerson/3778/ [accessed September 2012].

19 *Biblical Repertory and Princeton Review*, 97; Norton, "A Discourse on the Latest Form of Infidelity," History Tools.org, http://www.historytools.org/sources/norton.html [accessed September 2012].

20 Emerson, *Essays: First Series*, "Self-Reliance," http://www.online-literature.com/emerson/essays-first-series/2/ [accessed September 2012].

21 Emerson, *Journals*, vol. 2, 290, 294–5; vol. 4, 247–9.

22 Emerson, *Essays: First Series*, "The Over-Soul," http://www.online-literature.com/emerson/essays-first-series/9/ [accessed September 2012].

23 Emerson, *Journals and Miscellaneous Notebooks*, vol. 8, 98–9. The passage is incorporated in the 1842 essay "The Transcendentalist."

24 Emerson, *Journals*, vol. 7, 122; vol. 8, 46; vol. 5, 380–1.

25 Emerson, *Journals*, vol. 10, 191.

26 Harding, *Days*, 51.

27 Thoreau, *Journals*, vol. 1, 3.

28 Richardson, *Emerson*, 283. Richardson was also the author of *Henry Thoreau: A Life of the Mind*.

29 Emerson, *Journals*, vol. 6, 74.

30 Thoreau, *A Week*, "Friday," http://etext.virginia.edu/toc/modeng/public/ThoWeek.html [accessed September 2012].

31 Thoreau, *Journal*, vol. 3, 99.

32 Thoreau, *Journal*, vol. 1, 36; vol. 3, 293; vol. 4, 258–9.

33 Thoreau, *Journal*, vol. 10, 169; vol. 4, 263.

34 Emerson, *Journals*, vol. 9, 43; Thoreau, *Journal*, vol. 2, 406; vol. 5, 4.

35 Thoreau, Journal, vol. 3, 250; Hawthorne, from *American Notebooks*, entry of September 1, 1842. http://www.eldritchpress.org/nh/nhhdt1.html [accessed September 2012].

36 Thoreau, *Journal*, vol. 1, 147.

37 Thoreau, *Maine Woods*, "Ktaadn," part 6, http://thoreau.eserver.org/ktaadn06.html [accessed September 2012]; *Journal*, vol. 5, 16–17.

38 Thoreau, *Journal*, vol. 10, 237–41; vol. 4, 314; vol. 1, 191.

39 Thoreau, *Journal*, vol. 9, 407; Shepard, *Heart*, 140, 186; Thoreau, *Journal*, vol. 10, 127.

40 Whitman, quoted in Traubel, *With Walt Whitman in Camden*, 23, 285; Emerson, *Representative Men*, "Uses of Great Men," http://www.online-literature.com/emerson/representative-men/1/ [accessed September 2012].

41 Whitman, *Leaves of Grass*, 9.

42 Whitman, *Leaves of Grass*, 31–2, 78, 29.

43　Whitman, *Leaves of Grass*, 282.

44　Whitman, *Leaves of Grass*, 76.

45　Whitman, *Leaves of Grass*, 18, 48.

46　Whitman, *Leaves of Grass*, 76, 81, 326, 64, 32.

47　Whitman, *Complete Prose Works*, 175–6.

48　Whitman, *Complete Prose Works*, 229–34.

Chapter Eleven

Epigraph: Nietzsche, *Thus Spoke Zarathustra* (1. 4), 30.

1　T. H. Huxley, letter to Charles Kingsley, reproduced in Leonard Huxley (ed.), *Life and Letters of Thomas Henry Huxley*, vol. 1, 191–2.

2　Schopenhauer, *Will and Representation*, vol. 1, 13.

3　Darwin, *Voyage*, 278–9; Darwin, *Beagle Diary*, 354, 350.

4　Darwin, "Recollections," 116.

5　Darwin, notebook entry quoted in note to *Beagle Diary*, 357; Darwin, second edition of *Journal of Researches*, quoted in note to *Beagle Diary*, 360.

6　Erasmus Darwin, *The Temple of Nature*, quoted in Bowler, *Evolution*, 86.

7　Darwin, letter to J. D. Hooker, January 11, 1844. Darwin Correspondence Project, http://www.darwinproject.ac.uk/entry-729 [accessed September 2012].

8　Darwin, "Recollections," 26, 70–1.

9　Darwin, "Recollections," 72–3.

10　Arnold, "Dover Beach." The Victorian Web, http://www.victorianweb.org/authors/arnold/writings/doverbeach.html [accessed September 2012].

11　Reed, *Soul to Mind*, 1–8.

12　Huxley, *Method and Results*, 240, 244.

13　Ribot, *Maladies*, 1; Wilde, *Dorian Gray*, chapter 11, http://etc.usf.edu/lit2go/contents/2100/2185/2185_txt.html [accessed September 2012].

14　Comte, *Positive Philosophy*, vol. 1, 385.

15　Marx, *Theses on Feuerbach*, thesis 6, http://www.marxists.org/archive/marx/works/1845/theses/index.htm [accessed September 2012].

16　Marx, *Capital*, vol. 1, "Afterword to the Second German Edition," http://www.marxists.org/archive/marx/works/1867-c1/p3.htm [accessed September 2012]; *Capital*, vol. 1, "Preface to the First German Edition," http://www.marxists.org/archive/marx/works/1867-c1/p1.htm [accessed September 2012].

17　Durkheim, *Régles*, 64.

18　Balzac, "Avant-propos" to the 1842 edition of *La Comédie humaine*, http://port-lingua.pdx.edu/psu-svp/fr427/avantPro.pdf [accessed September 2012].

19　Zola, "Les romanciers naturalistes," http://www.lettres.ac-versailles.fr/spip.php?article187 [accessed September 2012]; Goncourt, Preface, dated

August 1876, to the 1878 edition of *Quelques créatures de ce temps,* http://
www.gutenberg.ca/ebooks/goncourtej-quelquescreatures/goncourtej-
quelquescreatures-00-u.txt [accessed September 2012].

20 Goncourt and Goncourt, *Journals,* 54.
21 Goncourt and Goncourt, *Journals,* 19, 61.
22 Goncourt and Goncourt, *Journals,* 42, 165.
23 Goncourt and Goncourt, *Journals,* 297, 309.
24 Goncourt and Goncourt, *Journals,* 358.
25 Bashkirtseff, *Journal,* 9; *Lettres,* 88–9; *Journal,* 14.
26 Bashkirtseff, *Journal,* 118, 213.
27 Bashkirtseff, journal entry of May 6, 1875, reproduced in Lejeune and
   Bogaert, *Journal à soi,* 142.
28 Bashkirtseff, *Journal,* 657, 55; James, *Varieties,* Lectures 4 and 5,
   http://ebooks.adelaide.edu.au/j/james/william/varieties/chapter4.html
   [accessed September 2012]; Bashkirtseff, *Journal,* 14.
29 The famous phrase "everything is permitted [or allowed]" occurs at least
   ten times in *Karamazov.* Each time it is attributed by another to Ivan or (in
   one instance) is heard by him in a dream. He never pronounces the phrase
   himself. See *Karamazov,* 80, 95, 317, 713, 726, 751, 760 (twice), 782, 839.
30 Nietzsche, fragment of 1888, in *Kritische Studienausgabe* 12: 7 [8],
   reproduced in Carr, *Banalization,* 25; *Will to Power* (sections 13, 1, Preface),
   14, 8, 3.
31 Nietzsche, letter to Lou Andreas-Salomé, in Andreas-Salomé, *Nietzsche,* 3.
32 Nietzsche, *Nachgelassene Aufzeichnungen,* 513.
33 Nietzsche, *Assorted Opinions and Maxims* (366), in Hollingdale, ed. and
   trans., *Nietzsche Reader,* 232.
34 Nietzsche, *Gay Science* (sections 125 and 341), 181, 273; *Will to Power*
   (section 685), 364; *Zarathustra* (Prologue 4), 13.
35 Nietzsche, *Zarathustra* (1. 4), 30–1.
36 Nietzsche, *Nachgelassene Fragmente* (item 5 [31]), 229.
37 Nietzsche, *Genealogy* ("Preface," sections 1–3; essay 2, section 16), 3–5, 57.
38 Nietzsche, *Ecce Homo* (4.8, 2, 4), 95, 89, 91.
39 Nietzsche, *Writings from the Late Notebooks* (section 38 [13]), 39.
40 Freud, oral remark recorded by Ernest Jones in *Sigmund Freud: Life and
   Work,* reproduced in Hergenhahn, *Introduction,* 206.

Chapter Twelve

Epigraph: Aurobindo, *Essays Divine and Human,* 443.
1 Pusey, "Un-Science, not Science, Adverse to Faith," Anglicanhistory.org,
   www.anglicanhistory.org/pusey/unscience.pdf [accessed September 2012].
2 Darwin, letter to J. B. Innes, November 27, 1878, http://www.darwinproject.
   ac.uk/entry-11763 [accessed September 2012].

3   James, *Varieties*, Lectures 4 and 5, http://ebooks.adelaide.edu.au/j/james/william/varieties/chapter4.html [accessed September 2012].

4   Spencer, *First Principles*, chapter 17, http://etext.virginia.edu/etcbin/toccer-new2?id=SpeFirs.xml&images=images/modeng&data=/texts/english/modeng/parsed&tag=public&part=23&division=div2 [accessed September 2012].

5   Tennyson, *In Memoriam*, Epilogue, http://www.poets.org/viewmedia.php/prmMID/20265 [accessed September 2012].

6   James, diary entry of April 30, 1870, reproduced in James, *Letters*, vol. 1, 147–8.

7   James, *Principles*, Preface, http://ebooks.adelaide.edu.au/j/james/william/principles/preface.html; *Principles*, chapter 9, http://ebooks.adelaide.edu.au/j/james/william/principles/chapter9.html#fn215 [accessed September 2012].

8   James, *Principles*, chapter 10, http://ebooks.adelaide.edu.au/j/james/william/principles/chapter10.html#fn258 [accessed September 2012].

9   James, *Principles*, chapter 10, http://ebooks.adelaide.edu.au/j/james/william/principles/chapter10.html#fn258 [accessed September 2012].

10 James, *Letters*, vol. 2, 204.

11 James, "Does Consciousness Exist?" http://psychclassics.yorku.ca/James/consciousness.htm [accessed September 2012].

12 James, *Pragmatism*, lecture 6, http://ebooks.adelaide.edu.au/j/james/william/pragmatism/lecture6.html [accessed September 2012].

13 James, *Varieties*, Lecture 2, http://ebooks.adelaide.edu.au/j/james/william/varieties/chapter2.html [accessed September 2012]. In the text the entire phrase is in caps.

14 James, *Varieties*, Lecture 1, http://ebooks.adelaide.edu.au/j/james/william/varieties/chapter1.html [accessed September 2012]; James, *Varieties*, Lecture 20, http://ebooks.adelaide.edu.au/j/james/william/varieties/chapter14.html#fn360 [accessed September 2012].

15 James, "The Will to Believe," http://ebooks.adelaide.edu.au/j/james/william/will/index.html [accessed September 2012].

16 Santayana, *Reason in Religion,* 193.

17 James, *Varieties*, Lectures 16 and 17, http://ebooks.adelaide.edu.au/j/james/william/varieties/chapter11.html [accessed September 2012].

18 Darwin, Notebook B, page 167, http://darwin-online.org.uk/content/frameset?viewtype=text&itemID=CUL-DAR121.-&pageseq=1 [accessed September 2012]; Darwin, *Descent of Man*, chapter 21, http://www.darwin-literature.com/The_Descent_Of_Man/23.html [accessed September 2012].

19 James, "What Psychical Research Has Accomplished," in *Writings 1878–1899*, 690.

20 Heehs, *Lives*, 165.

21 Aurobindo, *Record*, 34.

22 Aurobindo, *Record*, 57.

23 Aurobindo, *Record*, 28.

24 Aurobindo, *Isha Upanishad*, 18; *Life Divine*, 925–6; 931.

25 Aurobindo, *Record*, 520.

26 Aurobindo, *Essays Divine and Human*, 157. Compare this passage to Nietzsche's "What is great in man is that he is a bridge and not a goal: what can be loved in man is that he is a transition and a destruction" (*Zarathustra* 1.4, Tille's 1896 translation, http://en.wikisource.org/wiki/Page:Thus_Spake_Zarathustra_-_Alexander_Tille_-_1896.djvu/42 [accessed September 2012]). The English term "superman" was coined by George Bernard Shaw in 1903 with reference to Nietzsche and used in many early translations of *Zarathustra*.

27 Aurobindo, *Essays in Philosophy and Yoga*, 224.

28 Aurobindo, *Essays Divine and Human*, 102, 141; Nietzsche, *Ecce Homo* (4), 65; Aurobindo, *Record*, 484.

29 Aurobindo, *Record*, 38, 39, 100, 429, 29.

30 Wordsworth, *Prelude*, book 3: 175–6, http://www.gutenberg.org/files/12383/12383-h/Wordsworth3c.html (my emphasis) [accessed September 2012]; for Maine de Biran, Constant, and Amiel, see Chapter 8; for Bashkirtseff see Chapter 11.

31 Aurobindo, *Record*, 1251.

32 Aurobindo, *Letters on Himself and the Ashram*, 283–4; *Autobiographical Notes*, 549–50.

33 Iqbal, introduction to *Secrets of the Self*, 3.

34 Iqbal, *Thoughts and Reflections*, 238, 243–4.

35 Iqbal, *Secrets of the Self*, 8, 9, 13, 23.

36 Iqbal, introduction to *Secrets of the Self*, 4.

37 Iqbal, *Reconstruction*, 51; introduction to *Secrets of the Self*, 3.

38 Iqbal, *Reconstruction*, 72.

39 Iqbal, introduction to *Secrets of the Self*, 3, 5.

40 Iqbal, "Presidential Address," 3; Naipaul, *Beyond Belief*, 269, 329.

41 Iqbal, *Secrets of the Self*, 10.

42 Teilhard, *Journal*, 19, 27.

43 Teilhard, *Science et Christ*, quoted in English translation in Zaehner, *Evolution in Religion*, 7; Teilhard, *Journal*, 95, 61, 243.

44 Teilhard, *Journal*, 35, 172, 215–16; Teilhard, *Divine Milieu*, 116.

45 Teilhard, *Journal*, 330–1.

46 Teilhard, *Phenomenon*, 263.

47 Teilhard, *Hominization*, quoted in Cowell, *Teilhard Lexicon*, 131; Cowell, *Teilhard Lexicon*, 156.

48 Teilhard, letter of October 1951, reproduced in biographical note to *Divine Milieu*, 39.

49 Gide, *Journals*, vol. 1, 220–1.

50 Gide, *Journals*, vol. 1, 8, 10, 12.

51 Gide, *Journals 1889–1913* (Illinois edition), vol. 1, 23; *Journals*, vol. 1, 24, 304; *Immoralist*, 77.

52 Gide, quoted in Stoltzfus, "Voices," 80.

53 Gide, *Immoralist*, 13; *Strait*, 95; *Journals*, vol. 2, 218.

54 Gide, *Journals*, vol. 1, 245; vol. 2, 348, 351–4.

55 Sartre, "The Living Gide," reproduced from *Gide: A Collection of Critical Essays* (1970) http://www.andregide.org/remembrance/sagide.html [accessed September 2012].

Chapter Thirteen

Epigraph: Gide, *Journals*, vol. 2, 96.

1 Freud, *Case of Schreber*, 262.

2 Freud, *Ego and the Id*, 20, 30; Freud, *New Introductory Lectures*, 97; Freud, *Introductory Lectures* (trans. J. Riviere), reproduced in Cunningham (ed.), *Western Philosophy: An Anthology*, 208.

3 The book was published in German in 1912 under the title *Wandlungen und Symbole der Libido*. An English translation, entitled *Psychology of the Unconscious*, came out in 1916. A revised version, published in German in 1952, was brought out in English in 1956 as *Symbols of Transformation*.

4 Jung, *Psychology of the Unconscious*, 262, 82.

5 Jung, *Archetypes and Collective Unconscious*, 43.

6 Jung, *Memories, Dreams*, 224, 222; *Two Essays*, 173, 177; "Transformation Symbolism," 327; *Two Essays*, 155.

7 Fairbairn, *Psychoanalytic Studies*, 137–8; Scharff and Birtles, "Introduction," in Fairbairn, *Psychoanalytic Studies*, xii.

8 Winnicott, *Maturational Process*, 140–52.

9 Milner [Field], *Life*, 11, 34–5.

10 Milner [Field], *Life*, 21, 22.

11 Milner [Field], *Life*, 70, 71.

12 Milner [Field], *Life*, 62, 104, 197, 38.

13 Milner [Field], *Life*, 97, 207.

14 Milner [Field], *Life*, 109; *Experiment*, 40.

15 Milner [Field], *Experiment*, 185.

16 Milner [Field], *Experiment*, xxi; *Life*, 202.

17 Milner [Field], *Experiment*, 229–30.

18 Rodman, *Winnicott*, 139.

19 Milner, *Suppressed Madness*, 250.

20 Milner, *Eternity's Sunrise*, 42, 49, 52, 67.

21 Milner [Field], *Experiment*, 187.

22 Milner, oral remark quoted in Dragstedt, *Creative Illusions*, 522.

23 Milner, *Eternity's Sunrise*, 114.

24 Merton, *Waters of Siloe*, 347; *Intimate Merton*, 48; "First and Last Thoughts," in *Reader*, 17.

25 Merton, *Intimate Merton*, 340.

26 Merton, *Cistercian Contemplatives*, 55, quoted in Teahan, "Dark and Empty Way," 266; Eckhart, *Meister Eckhart Sermons*, 221; Merton, *Intimate Merton*, 101, 354.

27 Eckhart, *Meister Eckhart Sermons*, 288; Merton, *Intimate Merton*, 304; Merton, *Reader*, 476; Merton, *Zen*, 129.

28 Merton, *Waters of Siloe*, 349; *New Seeds*, 38; *Inner Experience*, 6.

29 Merton, *Intimate Merton*, 130; *New Seeds*, 100; *Intimate Merton*, 261, 218.

30 Shakespeare, *Hamlet* (I. 3), in *Complete Works*, 298.

31 Heidegger, *Being and Time* (1. 4), 164–5.

32 Heidegger, *Being and Time* (2. 1), 304–6.

33 Sartre, *Transcendence of the Ego*, 93–4, 105.

34 Sartre, *The Words*, 251; *Nausea*, 53, 139, 145, 149.

35 Sartre, *Nausea*, 183, 188, 252.

36 Sartre, diary entry from *Journal de Guerre,* September–October 1939, reproduced in Lejeune and Bogaert, *Journal à soi*, 19.

37 Sartre, *Being and Nothingness*, 332, 707, 711.

38 Sartre, "Existentialism is a Humanism" (trans. Philip Mairet), in Kaufmann, ed., *Existentialism*, 353.

39 Beauvoir, *Ethics of Ambiguity*, section 3, http://www.webster.edu/~corbetre/philosophy/existentialism/debeauvoir/ambiguity-3.html [accessed September 2012]; "What is Existentialism," in *Philosophical Writings*, 325–6; *Ethics of Ambiguity*, section 3, http://www.webster.edu/~corbetre/philosophy/existentialism/debeauvoir/ambiguity-3.html [accessed September 2012].

40 Beauvoir, *Second Sex*, 16–17.

41 Merleau-Ponty, *Visible and Invisible*, chapter 4, in *Basic Writings*, 254.

42 Beauvoir, *Ethics of Ambiguity*, section 3, http://www.webster.edu/~corbetre/philosophy/existentialism/debeauvoir/ambiguity-3.html [accessed September 2012].

43 Camus, *Myth*, 16, 64, 91.

44 Camus, *Stranger*, 122.

Chapter Fourteen

Epigraph: Ryle, *Concept*, 177.

1 Rimbaud, letter to Georges Izambard, May 1871, in *Collected Poems*, 6; Lawrence, *Reflections*, 272.

2 Buhkarin, *Historical Materialism*, chapter 4, http://www.marxists.org/archive/bukharin/works/1921/histmat/4.htm [accessed September 2012]; Goebbels, *Michael*, 18.

3 Ayer, *Language, Truth, and Logic*, 125; Ryle, *Concept*, 166, 175–6, 11; Wittgenstein, *Philosophical Investigations*, iv.25 (pages unnumbered).

4 Lévi-Strauss, *Tristes Tropiques*, 62 (translation emended); *Savage Mind*, 247.
5 Lévi-Strauss, *Tristes Tropiques*, 17.
6 Lévi-Strauss, *Tristes Tropiques*, 39, 392.
7 Lévi-Strauss, *Tristes Tropiques*, 387.
8 Lévi-Strauss, *Tristes Tropiques*, 394, 397.
9 Lévi-Strauss, *Tristes Tropiques*, 398 (translation emended).
10 Barthes, *Image-Music-Text*, 142–8.
11 Barthes, *Image-Music-Text*, 143; *Roland Barthes by Roland Barthes*, 99; "On Gide and his Journal," in *Barthes Reader*, 3, 4, 13.
12 Barthes, *Mythologies*, 10, 156; *Roland Barthes by Roland Barthes*, 47.
13 Barthes, *On Racine*, in Culler, *Barthes*, 64; Sartre, "Existentialism is a Humanism," in Kaufmann (ed.), *Existentialism*, 359.
14 Barthes, *Rustle*, 145, 139; *Image-Music-Text*, 143; *Roland Barthes on Roland Barthes*, 79.
15 Sontag, "Writing Itself," xxviii–xxix.
16 Barthes, *Roland Barthes by Roland Barthes*, 95, 56.
17 Barthes, *Rustle*, 359–60.
18 Barthes, *Mourning Diary*, 8, 52.
19 Barthes, *Writing Degree Zero*, 77.
20 Barthes, "Objective Literature," 12–13, 25; Lévy, email quoted in Donadio, "He was Nouveau when it was New," http://www.nytimes.com/2008/02/24/weekinreview/24donadio.html?pagewanted=all [accessed September 2012].
21 Robbe-Grillet, *Jealousy*, in *Two Novels*, 42, 52, 64.
22 Barthes, *S/Z*, 4; Robbe-Grillet, *Jealousy*, in *Two Novels*, 131–2.
23 Barthes, *Image-Music-Text*, 163.
24 Robbe-Grillet, "Introduction to the Screenplay," 33.
25 Robbe-Grillet, *Mirroir*, 10, 17.
26 Foucault, *Use of Pleasure*, 8–9.
27 Foucault, *Use of Pleasure*, 6, 9.
28 Foucault, "What Is an Author," in *Language, Counter-Memory, Practice*, 120, 130, 137–8.
29 Foucault, *Order of Things*, 386–7.
30 Foucault, "Nietzsche, Genealogy, History" in *Language, Counter-Memory, Practice*, 155, 154, 153; "Truth and Power," in *Power/Knowledge*, 117.
31 Foucault, "Hermeneutics of the Self," 203, 223.
32 Foucault, "The Ethic of Care for the Self" (trans. J. D. Gauthier), in *Final Foucault*, 11; "Aesthetics of Existence" (trans. Alan Sheridan), in *Politics, Philosophy, Culture*, 50–1, 49.
33 Strawson, *Individuals*, 90, 103.102.
34 Davidson, "Myth of the Subjective," 171.
35 Nagel, *Mortal Questions*, 166, 200, 212–13.
36 Dennett, *Consciousness Explained*, 39, 418.
37 Crick, *Astonishing Hypothesis*, 3, 21, 259.
38 Edelman, *Bright Air*, 116, 132, 139.

Chapter Fifteen

Epigraph: Beckett, *Proust*, 10.

1 Foucault, *Technologies of the Self*, 18, 49; "Hermeneutics of the Self," 222.

2 Wolfe, "The 'Me' Decade," http://nymag.com/news/features/45938/ [accessed September 2012].

3 Martin, "Robert Shields, Wordy Diarist, Dies at 89," http://www.nytimes. com/2007/10/29/us/29shields.html [accessed September 2012].

4 Borges, *Collected Fictions*, 135.

5 Dr. James Pennebaker, in Adams, "Brief History," http://journaltherapy.com/ journaltherapy/journal-cafe/journal-writing-history [accessed September 2012].

6 Emerson, *Journal* vol. 5, 516.

7 Woolf, *Moments of Being*, 79.

8 Wolff, quoted in Haven, "Life as Invention," http://www.stanfordalumni. org/news/magazine/2004/julaug/show/wolff.html [accessed September 2012]; quoted in Peterson (ed.), "Talking with Tobias Wolff," http://www. continuum.utah.edu/summer98/finally.html [accessed September 2012].

9 Bruner, "Narrative Construction," 4.

10 Wolff, *This Boy's Life*, 213–14.

11 Valéry, "The Conquest of Ubiquity," in *Aesthetics*, 225, 226.

12 Benjamin, "The Work of Art in the Age of Mechanical Reproduction," http://www.marxists.org/reference/subject/philosophy/works/ge/benjamin. htm [accessed September 2012].

13 The Misanthropic Bitch, post of February 3, 1999, captured by the Internet Archive Wayback Machine, http://web.archive.org/web/19990203030717/ bitch.shutdown.com/normal.html [accessed September 2012]; for background see http://en.wikipedia.org/wiki/The_Misanthropic_Bitch [accessed September 2012].

14 Mike Turk, quoted in Jadhav and Graber, "Student's Sex Story on Web Backfires."

15 Smith, "Generation Why?" http://www.nybooks.com/articles/archives/2010/ nov/25/generation-why/ [accessed September 2012].

16 Smith, "Generation Why?" http://www.nybooks.com/articles/archives/2010/ nov/25/generation-why/ [accessed September 2012].

17 Teilhard, *Phenomenon*, 240; Teilhard, *Man's Place in Nature*, 106.

18 Lee Rainie, quoted in Stone, "Children of Cyberspace," http://www.nytimes. com/2010/01/10/weekinreview/10stone.html [accessed September 2012].

19 Clark, "Out of our Brains," http://opinionator.blogs.nytimes. com/2010/12/12/out-of-our-brains/ [accessed September 2012].

Bibliography

Abrams, M. H. *Natural Supernaturalism*. New York: W. W. Norton, 2002.

Adams, Kathleen. "A Brief History of Journal Writing." Center for Journal Therapy. http://journaltherapy.com/journaltherapy/journal-cafe/journal-writing-history [accessed September 2012].

Amiel, Henri-Frédéric. *Amiel's Journal*. Trans. by Mrs Humphrey Ward. Project Gutenberg. http://www.gutenberg.org/ebooks/8545 [accessed September 2012].

—*Du journal intime*. Roland Jaccard (ed.), vol. 4. Brussels: Éditions complexe, 1987.

Andreas-Salomé, Lou. *Nietzsche*. Trans. by Siegfried Mandel. Urbana, IL: University of Illinois Press, 2001.

Arnold, Matthew. "Dover Beach." The Victorian Web. http://www.victorianweb.org/authors/arnold/writings/doverbeach.html [accessed September 2012].

Augustine, Saint. *Confessions*. Trans. by Henry Chadwick. Oxford: Oxford University Press, 1998.

—*Of True Religion*. Trans. by J. H. S. Burleigh. Chicago: Henry Regnery Co, 1959.

Aurobindo, Sri. *Autobiographical Notes and Other Writings of Historical Interest*. Pondicherry: Sri Aurobindo Ashram, 2006.

—*Essays Divine and Human*. Pondicherry: Sri Aurobindo Ashram, 1997.

—*Essays in Philosophy and Yoga*. Pondicherry: Sri Aurobindo Ashram, 1998.

—*Isha Upanishad*. Pondicherry: Sri Aurobindo Ashram, 2003.

—*Letters on Himself and the Ashram*. Pondicherry: Sri Aurobindo Ashram, 2011.

—*The Life Divine*. Pondicherry: Sri Aurobindo Ashram, 2005.

—*Record of Yoga*. Pondicherry: Sri Aurobindo Ashram, 2001.

Ayer, Alfred Jules. *Language, Truth, and Logic*. New York: Dover Publications, 1952.

Babur. *The Baburnama: Memoirs of Babur, Prince and Emperor*. Trans. by Wheeler M. Thackston (ed.). New York: Modern Library, 2002.

Balzac, Honoré de. *La comédie humaine*: Avant-propos (1842). Port-lingua, Portland State University. http://port-lingua.pdx.edu/psu-svp/fr427/avantPro.pdf [accessed September 2012].

Barthes, Roland. *A Barthes Reader*. Susan Sontag (ed.). New York: Barnes & Noble, 2009.

—*Image–Music–Text*. Trans. by Stephen Heath. London: Fontana Press, 1990.

—*Mourning Diary*. Trans. by Richard Howard. New York: Hill and Wang, 2010.

—*Mythologies*. Trans. by Annette Lavers. New York: Noonday Press, 1991.

—"Objective Literature: Alain Robbe-Grillet." Trans. by Richard Howard. In *Alain Robbe-Grillet, Two Novels by Robbe-Grillet*, 11–25. New York: Grove Press, 1965.

—*Roland Barthes by Roland Barthes*. Trans. by Richard Howard. Berkeley: University of California Press, 1994.

—*The Rustle of Language*. Trans. by Richard Howard. New York: Hill and Wang, 1986.

—*S/Z: An Essay*. Trans. by Richard Miller. New York: Hill and Wang, 1975.

—*Writing Degree Zero*. Trans. by Annette Lavers and Colin Smith. New York: Hill and Wang, 1977.

Bashkirtseff, Marie. *Journal of Marie Bashkirtseff*. Trans. by A. D. Hall and G. B. Heckel. Chicago and New York: Rand McNally & Co., 1890.

—*Lettres de Marie Bashkirtseff*. Fairford: Echo Library, 2008.

Basho, Matsuo. *The Narrow Road to the Deep North and Other Travel Sketches*. Trans. by Nobuyuki Yuasa. Harmondsworth: Penguin, 1966.

Beauvoir, Simone de. *The Ethics of Ambiguity*. Trans. by Bernard Frechtman. Webster University Philosophy Department. http://www.webster.edu/~corbetre/philosophy/existentialism/debeauvoir/ambiguity.html [accessed September 2012].

—*Philosophical Writings*. Trans. by Marybeth Timmermann. Urbana, IL: University of Illinois Press, 2004.

—*The Second Sex*. Trans. by Constance Borde and Sheila Malovany-Chevallier. New York: Vintage, 2011.

Beckett, Samuel. *Proust*. New York: Grove Press, 1970.

Benjamin, Walter. "The Work of Art in the Age of Mechanical Reproduction." Philosophy Archive @ marxists.org. http://www.marxists.org/reference/subject/philosophy/works/ge/benjamin.htm [accessed September 2012].

Berkson, Mark A. "Conceptions of Self/No-Self and Modes of Connection: Comparative Soteriological Structures in Classical Chinese Thought." *Journal of Religious Ethics* 33 (2005), 293–331.

Berlin, Isaiah. *The Sense of Reality*. New York: Farrar, Straus and Giroux, 1997.

Biblical Repertory and Princeton Review, vol. 11 (1839).

Blake, William. *The Complete Poetry & Prose*. Electronic Edition. Charlottesville, VA: Institute for Advanced Technology in the Humanities, 2001. http://www.blakearchive.org/exist/blake/archive/erdgen.xq?id=a2 et seq [accessed September 2012].

Bloom, Allan. "Rousseau's Critique of Liberal Constitutionalism." In *The Legacy of Rousseau*. Clifford Orwin and Nathan Tarcov (eds), 143–67. Chicago: University of Chicago Press, 1997.

Blum, Carol. *Rousseau and the Republic of Virtue*. Ithaca, NY: Cornell University Press, 1989.

Borges, Jorge Luis. *Collected Fictions*. Trans. by Andrew Hurley. New York: Penguin, 1998.

Boswell, James. *Bosewll's Correspondence with the Honourable Andrew Erskine, and His Journal of a Tour to Corsica*. George Birkbeck Hill (ed.). Project

Gutenberg. http://www.gutenberg.org/files/20263/20263-h/20263-h.htm [accessed September 2012].

—*The Journals of James Boswell 1762–1795*. New Haven and London: Yale University Press, 1991.

Botonaki, Effie. "Seventeenth-Century Englishwomen's Spiritual Diaries: Self-Examination, Covenanting, and Account-Keeping." *Sixteenth Century Journal* 30 (1999), 3–21.

Bowler, Peter J. *Evolution: The History of an Idea*. Berkeley: University of California Press, 1984.

Brekus, Catherine A. "'A Place to Go to Connect with Yourself': A Historical Perspective on Journaling." Chicago: Marty Center Religion and Culture Web Forum, 2004. http://divinity.uchicago.edu/martycenter/publications/webforum/022004/Brekus%20Essay.pdf [accessed September 2012].

Brown, Gregory S. "Am 'I' a Postrevolutionary Self?" *History and Theory* 47 (2008), 229–48.

Brown, Peter. *Augustine of Hippo: A Biography*. Berkeley: University of California Press, 2000.

Bruner, Jerome. "The Narrative Construction of Reality." *Critical Inquiry* 18 (1991), 1–21.

Bukharin, Nikolai. *Historical Materialism*. Nikolai Bukharin Internet Archive. http://www.marxists.org/archive/bukharin/works/1921/histmat/index.htm [accessed September 2012].

Bunyan, John. *Grace Abounding to the Chief of Sinners*. Grand Rapids, MI: Christian Classics Ethereal Library. http://www.ccel.org/ccel/bunyan/grace.html [accessed September 2012].

—*The Pilgrim's Progress from this World to that which Is To Come*. Project Gutenberg. http://www.gutenberg.org/ebooks/131 [accessed September 2012].

Burckhardt, Jacob. *The Civilization of the Renaissance in Italy*. Trans. by S. G. C. Middlemore. Project Gutenberg. http://paduan.dk/Kunsthistorie%202008/Tekster/The%20Civilization%20of%20the%20Renaissance%20in%20Italy%20-%20Burckhardt.pdf [accessed September 2012].

Byron, George Gordon, Lord. *Lord Byron's Correspondence*, Part Two. Whitefish, MT: Kessinger Publishing, 2005.

Calvin, John. *Institutes of the Christian Religion*. Trans. by John Allen, vol. 2. Philadelphia: Philip H. Nicklin, 1816.

Camus, Albert. *The Myth of Sisyphus and Other Essays*. Trans. by Justin O'Brian. New York: Vintage, 1955.

—*The Stranger*. Trans. by Matthew Ward. New York: Vintage, 1989.

Carlyle, Thomas. *Sartor Resartus: The Life and Opinions of Herr Teufelsdrockh*. Project Gutenberg. http://www.gutenberg.org/files/1051/1051-h/1051-h.htm [accessed September 2012].

Carr, Karen Leslie. *The Banalization of Nihilism*. Albany, NY: SUNY Press, 1992.

Carroll, Brian D. "'I Indulged My Desire Too Freely': Sexuality, Spirituality, and the Sin of Self-Pollution in the Diary of William Moody, 1720–24." *William and Mary Quarterly.* 3rd series, vol. 60 (2003), 155–70.

Cary, Philip. *Augustine's Invention of the Inner Self.* Oxford: Oxford University Press, 2000.

Chandrakirti. *Introduction to the Middle Way.* Trans. by Padmakara Translation Group. Boston: Shambhala, 2005.

Channing, William Ellery. "Excerpts from 'Unitarian Christianity' (1819), 'The Moral Argument against Calvinism' (1820) and 'Likeness to God' (1828)." History Tools.org. http://www.historytools.org/sources/channing-unitarianism.pdf [accessed September 2012].

Clark, Andy. "Out of Our Brains." *New York Times,* December 12, 2010. http://opinionator.blogs.nytimes.com/2010/12/12/out-of-our-brains/ [accessed September 2012].

Clarke, Desmond. *Descartes: A Biography.* New York: Cambridge University Press, 2006.

Cohen, Sheldon S. "The Diary of Jeremiah Dummer." *William and Mary Quarterly,* 3rd series, vol. 24 (1967), 397–422.

Coleridge, Samuel Taylor. *Collected Letters of Samuel Taylor Coleridge,* vol. 4. Oxford: Oxford University Press, 2002.

—*The Notebooks of Samuel Taylor Coleridge,* vol. 5, part 1. Princeton: Princeton University Press, 2002.

—*Poetical Works.* Princeton: Princeton University Press, 2001.

Comte, Auguste. *The Positive Philosophy of Auguste Comte.* Trans. by Harriet Martineau. Two volumes. n.p. Cosimo, 2010.

Condillac, Étienne. *Essai sur l'origine des connaissances humaines.* Paris: Ch. Houel, 1798. Les classiques des sciences sociales. http://classiques.uqac.ca/classiques/condillac_etienne_bonnot_de/essai_origine_des_connaissances/origine_des_connaissances.html [accessed September 2012].

Confucius. *The Analects.* The Wright House. http://www.wright-house.com/religions/confucius/Analects.html [accessed September 2012].

Constant, Benjamin. *Adolphe.* Trans. by Margaret Mauldon. Oxford: Oxford University Press, 2001.

—*De la religion.* Book One. Paris: Bosange, 1824.

—*Journaux intimes: Édition intégrale des manuscrits autographes.* Paris: Gallimard, 1952.

—*Mélanges de littérature et de politique.* Brussels: Société Belge de Librarie, 1838.

Cottingham, John. *Western Philosophy: An Anthology.* Malden, MA: Blackwell, 1996.

Cowell, Siôn. *The Teilhard Lexicon.* Brighton: Sussex Academic Press, 2001.

Cresson, André (ed.). *Maine de Biran: Sa vie, son oeuvre.* Paris: Presses universitaires de France, 1950.

Crick, Francis. *The Astonishing Hypothesis.* New York: Scribner, 1994.

Culler, Jonathan. *Barthes*. London: Fontana, 1990.

Dacome, Lucia. "Noting the Mind: Commonplace Books and the Pursuit of the Self in Eighteenth-Century Britain." *Journal of the History of Ideas* 65 (2004), 603–25.

Darwin, Charles. *The Autobiography of Charles Darwin*. Nora Barlow (ed.). London: Collins, 1958. The Complete Work of Charles Darwin Online. http://darwin-online.org.uk/content/frameset?viewtype=side&itemID=F149 7&pageseq=4 [accessed September 2012].

—*Charles Darwin's Beagle Diary*. R. D. Keynes (ed.). Cambridge: Cambridge University Press, 2001. The Complete Work of Charles Darwin Online. http://darwin-online.org.uk/content/frameset?itemID=F1925&viewtype=tex t&pageseq=1 [accessed September 2012].

—*The Descent of Man*. Darwin-literature.com, 2008. http://www.darwin-literature.com/The_Descent_Of_Man/index.html [accessed September 2012].

—Letter to J. B. Innes, November 27, 1878. Darwin Correspondence Project. http://www.darwinproject.ac.uk/entry-11763 [accessed September 2012].

—*Notebook B*. The Complete Work of Charles Darwin Online. http://darwin-online.org.uk/content/frameset?viewtype=text&itemID=CUL-DAR121.-&pageseq=1 [accessed September 2012].

—"Recollections of the development of my mind & character" [Autobiography]. The Complete Work of Charles Darwin Online. http://darwin-online.org.uk/content/frameset?viewtype=side&itemID=CUL-DAR26.1-121&pageseq=195 [accessed September 2012].

—*Voyage of the* Beagle: *Charles Darwin's* Journal of Researches. London: Penguin, 1989.

Davidson, Donald. "The Myth of the Subjective." In *Relativism: Interpretation and Confrontation*. Michael Krausz (ed.), 159–72. Notre Dame, IN: University of Notre Dame Press, 1989.

"Declaration of the Rights of Man and of the Citizen." Human and Constitutional Rights Resource Page. http://hrcr.law.columbia.edu/docs/frenchdec.html [accessed September 2012].

Delacroix, Eugène. *Journal de Eugène Delacroix*. Tome premier, 1823–1850. Paris: Plon, 1926. The Internet Archive. http://openlibrary.org/books/OL24191300M/Journal_de_Eug%C3%A8ne_Delacroix [accessed September 2012].

De Man, Paul. "Autobiography as De-facement." *MLN* 94 (1979), 919–30.

Dennett, Daniel. *Consciousness Explained*. Boston: Back Bay Books, 1992.

Dent, Nicholas. *Rousseau*. Abingdon: Routledge, 2005.

Descartes, René. *Le Discours de la Méthode*. Columbia University, Graduate School of Arts & Sciences Teaching Center. http://www.columbia.edu/cu/tat/core/descartes.htm [accessed September 2012].

—*Philosophical Letters*. Trans. by Anthony Kenny. Oxford: Clarendon Press, 1970.

—*The Philosophical Writings of Descartes*, vol. 2. Trans. by John Cottingham, Robert Stoothoff, and Dugald Murdoch. Cambridge: Cambridge University Press, 1985.

—*Principles of Philosophy*. Trans. by V. R. Miller and R. P. Miller. Dordrecht: Kluwer Academic Publishers, 1983.

Dickson, Gwen Griffith. *Johann Georg Hamann's Relational Metacriticism*. Berlin and New York: Walter de Gruyter, 1995.

Diderot, Denis. "Éloge de Richardson." University of Virginia, Department of English, Graduate Program. http://graduate.engl.virginia.edu/enec981/ dictionary/25diderotC1.html [accessed September 2012].

Donadio, Rachel. "He was Nouveau when it was New." *New York Times*, February 24, 2008. http://www.nytimes.com/2008/02/24/ weekinreview/24donadio.html?pagewanted=all [accessed September 2012].

Dostoyevsky, Fyodor. *The Brothers Karamazov*. Trans. by Andrew H. MacAndrew. New York: Bantam Books, 1981.

—*Notes from Underground*. Trans. by Andrew R. MacAndrew. New York: New American Library, 1961.

Dragstedt, Naome Rader. "Creative Illusions: The Theoretical and Clinical Work of Marion Milner." *Journal of Melanie Klein and Object Relations* 16 (1998), 425–536.

Durkheim, Émile. *Les règles de la méthode sociologique*. Chicoutimi, Québec: Les classiques des sciences sociales, 2002. http://classiques.uqac.ca/ classiques/Durkheim_emile/regles_methode/durkheim_regles_methode.pdf [accessed September 2012].

Eckhart, Meister. *Meister Eckhart Sermons*. Mahwah, NJ: Paulist Press, 1981.

Edelman, Gerald. *Bright Air, Brilliant Fire: On the Matter of the Mind*. New York: Basic Books, 1993.

Edwards, Jonathan. *Letters and Personal Writings*. George S. Claghorn (ed.). Vol. 16 of *The Works of Jonathan Edwards*. New Haven, CT: Yale University Press, 1998.

—*Sermons and Discourses 1730–1733*. Mark Valeri (ed.). Vol. 17 of *The Works of Jonathan Edwards*. New Haven, CT: Yale University Press, 1999.

—*Sermons and Discourses 1739–1742*. Harry S. Stout and Nathan O. Hatch (eds). Vol. 22 of *The Works of Jonathan Edwards*. New Haven, CT: Yale University Press, 2003.

Emerson, Ralph Waldo. "The American Scholar," The Literature Network. http://www.online-literature.com/emerson/3780/ [accessed September 2012].

—"Divinity School Address." The Literature Network. http://www.online-literature.com/emerson/3778/ [accessed September 2012].

—*Essays: First Series*. The Literature Network. http://www.online-literature. com/emerson/essays-first-series/ [accessed September 2012].

—*Journals of Ralph Waldo Emerson.* Ten volumes. Boston and New York: Houghton Mifflin Co., 1909–14.

—*The Journals and Miscellaneous Notebooks of Ralph Waldo Emerson*, vol. 8. Cambridge, MA: Harvard University Press, 1970.

—*The Letters of Ralph Waldo Emerson*, vol. 1. New York: Columbia University Press, 1939.

—*Nature.* The Literature Network. http://www.online-literature.com/emerson/nature/ [accessed September 2012].

—*Representative Men.* The Literature Network. http://www.online-literature.com/emerson/representative-men/ [accessed September 2012].

"The Encyclopedia of Diderot & D'Alembert: Collaborative Translation Project." University of Michigan Library: MPublishing. http://quod.lib.umich.edu/d/did/intro.html [accessed September 2012].

Ernst, Carl W. *Ruzbihan Baqli: Mysticism and the Rhetoric of Sainthood in Persian Sufism.* Richmond, Surrey: Curzon Press, 1996.

—(ed. and trans.), *Teachings of Sufism.* Boston: Shambhala, 1999.

Fairbairn, W. R. D. *Psychoanalytic Studies of the Personality.* With an introduction by David E. Schaff and Ellinor Faibairn Birtles. New York: Taylor & Francis e-Library, 2001.

Fichte, Johann Gottlieb. *Foundations of Natural Right.* Trans. by Michael Baur. Cambridge: Cambridge University Press, 2000.

—*Science of Knowledge.* Trans. by Peter Heath and John Lachs. Cambridge: Cambridge University Press, 1982.

—"To the German Nation." The Modern History Sourcebook, Fordham University. http://www.fordham.edu/Halsall/mod/1806fichte.asp [accessed September 2012].

Foucault, Michel. "About the Beginning of the Hermeneutics of the Self." *Political Theory* 21 (1993), 198–227.

—*The Final Foucault.* Cambridge, MA: MIT Press, 1988.

—*Language, Counter-Memory, Practice: Selected Essays and Interviews.* Ithaca, NY: Cornell University Press, 1984.

—*The Order of Things.* (Translator not stated). New York: Vintage, 1994.

—*Politics, Philosophy, Culture: Interviews and Other Writings.* Lawrence D. Kritzman (ed.). New York: Routledge, 1990.

—*Power/Knowledge: Selected Interviews & Other Writings.* Trans. by Colin Gordon. New York: Pantheon, 1980.

—*Technologies of the Self: A Seminar with Michel Foucault.* L. H. Martin, Huck Gutman, and Patrick Hutton (eds). London: Tavistock, 1988.

—*The Use of Pleasure.* Trans. by Robert Hurley. New York: Vintage, 1990.

Fox, George. *An Autobiography* [The *Journal*]. Rufus M. Jones (ed.). Christian Classics Ethereal Library. http://www.strecorsoc.org/gfox/title.html#contents [accessed September 2012].

Frame, Donald M. "Montaigne." In *Selected Essays.* Trans. by Donald M. Frame, xiii–xxx. Roslyn, NY: Walter J. Black, 1943.

Freud, Sigmund. *The Case of Schreber, Papers on Technique, and Other Works.* Trans. by James Strachey. London: Hogarth Press and the Institute of Psycho-Analysis, 1974.

—*The Ego and the Id.* Trans. by James Strachey. New York: W. W. Norton & Company, 1990.

—*New Introductory Lectures on Psycho-Analysis.* Trans. by James Strachey. New York: W. W. Norton & Company, 1990.

Frogneux, Nathalie, and Benoît Thirion. "Pour penser la condition de moi: Maine de Biran." *Revue philosophique de Louvain* 103 (2005), 1–5.

Geertz, Clifford. " 'From the Native's Point of View': On the Nature of Anthropological Understanding." *Bulletin of the American Academy of Arts and Sciences* 28 (1974), 26–45.

Gide, André. *The Immoralist.* Trans. by Dorothy Bussy. New York: Vintage Books, 1960.

—*Journals 1889–1913,* vol. 1. Trans. by Justin O'Brian. Urbana, IL: University of Illinois Press, 2000.

—*The Journals of André Gide 1889–1949.* Trans. by Justin O'Brian. Two volumes. New York: Vintage Books, 1956.

—*Strait is the Gate.* Trans. by Dorothy Bussy. New York: Vintage Books, 1952.

Girard, Alain. *Le journal intime.* Paris: Presses universitaires de France, 1963.

Goebbels, Joseph. *Michael: A Novel.* Trans. by Joachim Neugroschel. New York: Amok Press, 1987.

Goethe, Johann Wolfgang von. *Wilhelm Meister's Apprenticeship.* Trans. by Eric A. Blackall and Victor Lange. Princeton: Princeton University Press, 1995.

Goncourt, Edmond de, and Jules de Goncourt. *Pages from the Goncourt Journals.* Trans. by Robert Baldick. New York: New York Review Books, 2007.

—*Quelques créatures de ce temps.* Project Gutenberg Canada. http://www.gutenberg.ca/ebooks/goncourtej-quelquescreatures/goncourtej-quelquescreatures-00-u.txt [accessed September 2012].

Greenblatt, Stephen. *Renaissance Self-Fashioning: From More to Shakespeare.* Chicago: University of Chicago Press, 2005.

Hampl, Patricia. "Why Augustine's Passionate Quest to Know Himself and Praise God Still Matters." *Los Angeles Times,* January 24, 1999. http://articles.latimes.com/1999/jan/24/books/bk-986 [accessed September 2012].

Happold, F. C. *Mysticism: A Study and an Anthology.* Baltimore: Penguin, 1964.

Harding, Walter. *The Days of Henry Thoreau: A Biography.* New York: Dover Publications, 1982.

Hasrat, Bikrama Jit. *Dara Shikuh: Life and Works.* New Delhi: Munshiram Manoharlal, 1982.

Haven, Cynthia. "Life as Invention." *Stanford Magazine.* July/August 2004. http://www.stanfordalumni.org/news/magazine/2004/julaug/show/wolff.html [accessed September 2012].

Hawthorne, Nathaniel. *American Notebooks,* entry of September 1, 1842. Eldrich Press. http://www.eldritchpress.org/nh/nhhdt1.html [accessed September 2012].

Heehs, Peter. *The Lives of Sri Aurobindo.* New York: Columbia University Press, 2008.

Hegel, G. W. F. *Lectures on the History of Philosophy* (Selections). Trans. by E. S. Haldane. University of Idaho. http://www.class.uidaho.edu/mickelsen/Phil%20310/ToC/Hegel-Hist%20of%20Phil.htm [accessed September 2012].

—*The Phenomenology of Mind.* Trans. by J. B. Baillie. University of Idaho. http://www.class.uidaho.edu/mickelsen/Phil%20310/ToC/Hegel%20 Phen%20ToC.htm [accessed September 2012].

—*The Philosophy of History.* Trans. by J. Sibree. University of Idaho. http://www.class.uidaho.edu/mickelsen/texts/Hegel%20-%20Philosophy%20of%20 History.htm [accessed September 2012].

Heidegger, Martin. *Being and Time.* Translated by John Macquarrie and Edward Robinson. Malden, MA: Blackwell, 1962.

Herder, Johann Gottfried. *Philosophical Writings.* Trans. by Michael N. Forster. Cambridge: Cambridge University Press: 2002.

Hergenhahn, B. R. *Introduction to the History of Philosophy.* Belmont, CA: Wadsworth, 2005.

Hildegard of Bingen. *Secrets of God: Writings of Hildegard of Bingen.* Trans. by Sabina Flanagan. Boston and London: Shambhala, 1996.

Hilmer, Mary Adams. "The Other Diary of Samuel Sewall." *The New England Quarterly* 55 (1982): 354–67.

Hobbes, Thomas. *The English Works of Thomas Hobbes of Malmesbury,* vol. 1. London: J. Bohn, 1839.

Hollingdale, R. J. (ed. and trans.), *A Nietzsche Reader.* Harmondsworth, Middlesex: Penguin, 1979.

Holmes, Richard. *Coleridge: Early Visions.* New York: Penguin, 1990.

Hume, David. "An Abstract of a Book Lately Published, entitled A Treatise of Human Nature &c." Minnesota State University– Moorhead. http://web.mnstate.edu/gracyk/courses/web%20publishing/hume%27sabstract.htm [accessed September 2012].

—*Essays on Suicide and the Immortality of the Soul.* Philosophy Department, St. Anselm College. http://www.anselm.edu/homepage/dbanach/suicide.htm [accessed September 2012].

—*The Letters of David Hume,* vol. 1. J. Y. T. Greig (ed.). New York: Oxford University Press, 2011.

—"My Own Life." Adelaide, South Australia: eBooks@adelaide, 2009. http://ebooks.adelaide.edu.au/h/hume/david/h92my/ [accessed September 2012].

—*A Treatise of Human Nature.* Adelaide, South Australia: eBooks@adelaide, 2006 http://ebooks.adelaide.edu.au/h/hume/david/h92t/index.html [accessed September 2012].

Huxley, Aldous. *Themes and Variations.* London: Chatto & Windus, 1950.

Huxley, Leonard (ed.). *The Life and Letters of Thomas Henry Huxley*, vol. 1. Fairford, Gloucestershire: Echo Library, 2007.

Huxley, Thomas H. *Method and Results: Essays*. New York: D. Appleton & Co., 1898.

Ignatius of Loyola, Saint. *Personal Writings*. London: Penguin, 1996.

Iqbal, Muhammad, *The Reconstruction of Religious Thought in Islam*. http://www.islamicsearchcenter.com/library/Iqbal/The%20Reconstruction%20of%20Religious%20Thought%20in%20Islam.pdf [accessed September 2012].

—*Secrets of the Self*. Trans. by Reynold A. Nicholson. http://www.allamaiqbal.com/works/poetry/persian/asrar/translation/01secretsoftheself.pdf [accessed September 2012].

—"Sir Muhammad Iqbal's 1930 Presidential Address to the 25th Session of the All-India Muslim League." Footprintsonsand.com. http://www.footprintsonsand.com/files/Iqbal_1930_Allahabad.pdf [accessed September 2012].

—*Thoughts and Reflections of Iqbal*, Syed Abdul Vahid (ed.). Lahore: Sh. Muhammad Ashraf, 1964.

Jadhav, Adam, and Shane Graber. "Student's Sex Story on Web Backfires: SIUE undergrad may face expulsion after subject of posting goes to authorities." *St. Louis Post Dispatch*, September 27, 2006.

James, William. "Does Consciousness Exist?" Classics in the History of Psychology. Toronto: York University. http://psychclassics.yorku.ca/James/consciousness.htm [accessed September 2012].

—*The Letters of William James*. Two volumes combined. New York: Cosimo Classics, 2008.

—*Pragmatism*. Adelaide, South Australia: eBooks@Adelaide, 2009. http://ebooks.adelaide.edu.au/j/james/william/pragmatism/index.html [accessed September 2012].

—*Principles of Psychology*. Adelaide, South Australia: eBooks@Adelaide, 2009. http://ebooks.adelaide.edu.au/j/james/william/principles/index.html [accessed September 2012].

—*The Varieties of Religious Experience*. Adelaide, South Australia: eBooks@Adelaide, 2009. http://ebooks.adelaide.edu.au/j/james/william/varieties/index.html [accessed September 2012].

—"The Will to Believe." Adelaide, South Australia: eBooks@Adelaide, 2009. http://ebooks.adelaide.edu.au/j/james/william/will/index.html [accessed September 2012].

—*Writings 1878–1899*. New York: Library of America, 1992.

Jaynes, Julian. *The Origin of Consciousness in the Breakdown of the Bicameral Mind*. Boston: Houghton Mifflin: 1976.

Julian of Norwich. *Revelations of Divine Love*. Trans. by Elizabeth Spearing and A. C. Spearing. London: Penguin, 1998.

Jung, Carl Gustav. *The Archetypes and the Collective Unconscious*. Trans. by R. F. C. Hull. Princeton: Princeton University Press, 1990.

—*Memories, Dreams, Reflections*. Trans. by Richard Winston and Clara Winston. London: Fontana Press, 1995.

—*The Psychology of the Unconscious*. Trans. by Beatrice M. Hinkle. New York: Dodd Mead, 1949.

—"Transformation Symbolism in the Mass." In *The Mysteries: Papers from the Eranos Yearbooks*, vol. 2, Joseph Campbell (ed.). London: Routledge & Kegan Paul, 1955.

—*Two Essays on Analytical Philosophy*. Trans. by Gerhard Adler and R. F. C. Hull. London: Routledge, 1990.

Justin Martyr. *On the Resurrection*. New Advent. http://www.newadvent.org/fathers/0131.htm [accessed September 2012].

Kafadar, Cemal. "Self and Others: The Diary of a Dervish in Seventeenth Century Istanbul and First-Person Narratives in Ottoman Literature." *Studia Islamica* 69 (1989), 121–50.

Kant, Immanuel. "An Answer to the Question: What is Enlightenment?" The Literary Link. http://theliterarylink.com/kant.html [accessed September 2012].

—*Anthropology from a Pragmatic Point of View*. Trans. by Robert B. Louden. Cambridge: Cambridge University Press, 2006.

—*Dreams of a Spirit-Seer*. Trans. by Emanuel F. Goerwitz. Wikisource. http://en.wikisource.org/wiki/Dreams_of_a_Spirit-Seer [accessed September 2012].

—*Immanuel Kant's Critique of Pure Reason*. Trans. by Norman Kemp Smith. London: Macmillan, 1929. http://www.hkbu.edu.hk/~ppp/cpr/toc.html [accessed September 2012].

—*Kant's Inaugural Dissertation of 1770*. Trans. by William J. Eckoff. Whitefish, MT: Kessinger Publishing, 2004.

—*Lectures on Ethics*. Trans. by Louis Infield. London: Methuen and Co., 1930.

—*Prolegomena to Any Future Metaphysics*. Minnesota State University–Moorhead. http://web.mnstate.edu/gracyk/courses/phil%20306/kant_materials/prolegomena2.htm [accessed September 2012].

Kaufmann, Walter (ed.). *Existentialism From Dostoyevsky to Sartre*. New York: Plume, 1975.

Keats, John. *The Complete Poetical Works and Letters of John Keats*. Forgotten Books. http://www.forgottenbooks.org/ [accessed September 2012].

Keene, Donald. *Travelers of a Hundred Ages*. New York: Columbia University Press, 1999.

Kempe, Margery. *The Book of Margery Kempe*. Trans. by B. A. Windeatt. London: Penguin, 1985.

Kierkegaard, Søren. *The Concept of Anxiety*. Trans. by Reidar Thomte and Albert B. Anderson. Princeton: Princeton University Press, 1981.

—*Concluding Unscientific Postscript to Philosophical Fragments*. Trans. by Howard Vincent Hong and Edna Hatlestad Hong. Princeton: Princeton University Press, 1992.

—*Fear and Trembling; Repetition.* Trans. by Howard Vincent Hong and Edna Hatlestad Hong. Princeton: Princeton University Press, 1983.

—*A Kierkegaard Anthology.* Robert Bretall (ed.). New York: The Modern Library, 1973.

—*Papers and Journals: A Selection.* Trans. by Alastair Hannay. New York: Penguin, 1996.

—*The Sickness Unto Death.* Trans. by Howard Vincent Hong and Edna Hatlestad Hong. Princeton: Princeton University Press, 1980.

Knappen, M. M. (ed.). *Two Elizabethan Puritan Diaries.* Chicago: American Society of Church History, 1933.

Lawrence, D. H. *Reflections on the Death of a Porcupine and Other Essays.* Cambridge: Cambridge University Press, 1988.

Lejeune, Philippe and Catherine Bogaert. *Un journal à soi: Histoire d'une practique.* Paris: Éditions textuel, 2003.

Lemaître, Jules. *Les contemporains.* The Green eBook Shop. http://www.green-ebook-shop.com/ebooks/2/9/9/1/29918/29918.html [accessed September 2012].

Lévi-Strauss, Claude. *The Savage Mind.* (Translator not stated.) Chicago: University of Chicago Press, 1966.

—*Tristes Tropiques.* Trans. by John Russell. New York: Criterion Books, 1961.

Locke, John. *An Essay Concerning Human Understanding.* University Park, PA: Pennsylvania State University, 1999. http://www.dca.fee.unicamp. br/~gudwin/ftp/ia005/humanund.pdf [accessed September 2012].

—*The Second Treatise of Civil Government.* The Constitution Society. http:// www.constitution.org/jl/2ndtreat.htm [accessed September 2012].

Lorenz, Hendrik. "Ancient Theories of Soul." *Stanford Encyclopedia of Philosophy.* http://plato.stanford.edu/entries/ancient-soul/ [accessed September 2012].

Lucretius. *On the Nature of the Universe.* Trans. by Ronald E. Latham. Harmondsworth, Middlesex: Penguin, 1951.

Luther, Martin. "The Tower Experience, 1519." The Modern History Sourcebook, Fordham University. http://www.fordham.edu/halsall/ mod/1519luther-tower.html [accessed September 2012].

Maclear, James Fulton. "'The Heart of New England Rent': The Mystical Element in Early Puritan History." *Mississippi Valley Historical Review* 42 (1956), 621–52.

Maddocks, Fiona. *Hildegard of Bingen: The Woman of Her Age.* New York: Doubleday, 2001.

Maine de Biran, Pierre. *Influence de l'habitude sur la faculté de penser.* Paris: Presses Universitaires de France, 1954. Les classiques des sciences sociales. http://classiques.uqac.ca/classiques/maine_de_biran/influence_habitude/ influence_habitude.html [accessed September 2012].

—*Maine de Biran: Sa vie et ses pensées.* Ernest Naville (ed.). Paris: Joël Cherbuleiz, 1857. The Internet Archive. http://www.archive.org/details/ mainedebiransav01biragoog [accessed September 2012].

Makdisi, George. "The Diary in Islamic Historiography: Some Notes." *History and Theory* 25 (1986), 173–85.

Marcus Aurelius, *Meditations*. Trans. by Gregory Hays. New York: Modern Library, 2002.

Marx, Karl. *Capital: A Critique of Political Economy*, vol. 1. Reprint of first English edition (1887). Marxists.org. http://www.marxists.org/archive/marx/works/1867-c1/index.htm [accessed September 2012].

—*Theses on Feuerbach*. Marxists.org. http://www.marxists.org/archive/marx/works/1845/theses/index.htm [accessed September 2012].

Martin, Douglas. "Robert Shields, Wordy Diarist, Dies at 89." *New York Times*, October 29, 2007. http://www.nytimes.com/2007/10/29/us/29shields.html [accessed September 2012].

Martin, Raymond, and John Barresi. *The Rise and Fall of Soul and Self: An Intellectual History of Personal Identity*. New York: Columbia University Press, 2006.

Mauss, Marcel. "Une catégorie de l'esprit humain: la notion de personne celle de 'moi.'" *Journal of the Royal Anthropological Institute of Great Britain and Ireland* 68 (1938), 263–81.

"Mayflower Compact, 1620." Plymouth Colony Archive Project. http://www.histarch.uiuc.edu/plymouth/compact.html [accessed September 2012].

McNeil, Gordon H. "The Cult of Rousseau and the French Revolution." *Journal of the History of Ideas* 6 (1945), 197–212.

Merleau-Ponty, Maurice. *Basic Writings*. New York: Routledge, 2003.

Merton, Thomas. *The Inner Experience*. New York: HarperSanFrancisco, 2004.

—*The Intimate Merton: His Life from His Journals*. Patrick Hart and Jonathan Montaldo (eds). New York: HarperSanFrancisco, 1999.

—*New Seeds of Contemplation*. New York: New Directions, 2007.

—*A Thomas Merton Reader*. Thomas P. McDonnell (ed.). New York: Doubleday, 1989.

—*The Waters of Siloe*. Boston: Houghton Mifflin Harcourt, 1979.

—*Zen and the Birds of Appetite*. New York: New Directions, 1968.

Miller, Perry. *The New England Mind: From Colony to Province*. Cambridge, MA: Harvard University Press, 1983.

—*The New England Mind: The Seventeenth Century*. Cambridge, MA: Harvard University Press, 1983.

Milner, Marion. *Eternity's Sunrise: A Way of Keeping a Diary*. London: Virago Press, 1987.

—[as Joanna Field]. *An Experiment in Leisure*. Los Angeles: J. P. Tarcher, 1987.

—[as Joanna Field]. *A Life of One's Own*. Los Angeles: J. P. Tarcher, 1981.

—*The Suppressed Madness of Sane Men*. Hove, East Sussex: Routledge-Brunner, 2002.

Misanthropic Bitch. The, post of February 3, 1999, captured by the Internet Archive Wayback Machine. http://web.archive.org/web/19990203030717/bitch.shutdown.com/normal.html [accessed September 2012].

Mochulsky, Konstantin. "Dostoevsky and the Brothers Karamazov." In *The Brothers Karamazov*, by Fyodor Dostoevsky, xi–xx. New York: Bantam Books, 1981.

Montaigne, Michel de. *The Complete Works*. Trans. by Donald M. Frame. New York: Alfred A. Knopf, 2003.

Mosner, Ernest Campbell. *The Life of David Hume*. Oxford: Oxford University Press, 2001.

Mulligan, Lotte. "Self Scrutiny and the Study of Nature: Robert Hooke's Diary as Natural History." *Journal of British Studies* 35 (1996), 311–42.

Nagel, Thomas. *Mortal Questions*. Cambridge: Cambridge University Press, 1979.

Naipaul, V. S. *Beyond Belief: Islamic Excursions among the Converted Peoples*. New Delhi: Viking, 1998.

Nanamoli, Bikkhu, and Bikkhu Bodhi (trans.). *The Middle Length Discourses of the Buddha*, Somerville, MA: Wisdom Publications, 1995.

New Revised Standard Bible. BibleStudyTools.com. http://www.biblestudytools. com/nrs/ [accessed September 2012].

Nietzsche, Friedrich. *Ecce Homo: How to Become What You Are*. Trans. by Duncan Large. Oxford: Oxford University Press, 2007.

—*The Gay Science*. Trans. by Walter Kaufmann. New York: Vintage, 1974.

—*Nachgelassene Aufzeichnungen: Herbst 1864–Frühjahr 1868*. Berlin: Walter de Gruyter, 1999.

—*Nachgelassene Fragmente: Juli 1882–Winter 1883/84*. Berlin: Walter de Gruyter, 1977.

—*On the Genealogy of Morality*. Trans. by Carol Diethe. New York: Cambridge University Press, 2008.

—*Thus Spoke Zarathustra*. Trans. by Graham Parkes. Oxford: Oxford University Press, 2005.

—*Twilight of the Idols*. Lexido, the Full and Free Nietzsche Portal. http://www. lexido.com/EBOOK_TEXTS/TWILIGHT_OF_THE_IDOLS_.aspx?S=10 [accessed September 2012].

—*The Will to Power*. Trans. by Walter Kaufmann and R. J. Hollingdale. New York: Random House, 1967.

—*Writings from the Late Notebooks*. Trans. by Kate Sturge. Cambridge: Cambridge University Press, 2003.

North, Roger. *General Preface & Life of Dr John North*. Peter Milard (ed.). Toronto: University of Toronto Press, 1984.

Norton, Andrews. "A Discourse on the Latest Form of Infidelity." History Tools.org. http://www.historytools.org/sources/norton.html [accessed September 2012].

Ong, Walter J. *Orality and Literacy*. New York: Routledge, 2002.

Orwell, George. "Notes on Dali." George Orwell 1903–1950. http://www.k-1. com/Orwell/site/work/essays/dali.html [accessed September 2012].

Oxford Dictionary of Quotations, The. Oxford: Oxford University Press, 1980.

Ozment, Steven. *The Age of Reform 1250–1550: An Intellectual and Religious History of Late Medieval and Reformation Europe*. New Haven and London: Yale University Press, 1980.

Pascal, Blaise. *Pensées and Other Writings*. Trans. by Honor Levi and Anthony Levi. Oxford: Oxford University Press, 1999.

Pepys, Samuel. *The Diary of Samuel Pepys*. Project Gutenberg. http://www. pepysdiary.com/ [accessed September 2012].

Peterson, Anne Palmer (ed.). "And Finally... Talking with Tobias Wolff." *Continuum: The Magazine of the University of Utah*, vol. 8, no. 1 (Summer 1998). http://www.continuum.utah.edu/summer98/finally.html [accessed September 2012].

Pico della Mirandola, Giovanni. *Oration on the Dignity of Man*. University of Michigan, Center for the Study of Complex Systems. http://cscs.umich. edu/~crshalizi/Mirandola/ [accessed September 2012].

Pierson, George Wilson, *Tocqueville in America*. Baltimore: JHU Press, 1996.

Pinto, V. de S. Review of *Locke's Travels in France 1675–1679*. *The Modern Language Review* 50 (1955), 70–1.

Plato. *Phaedrus and the Seventh and Eighth Letters*. Trans. by Walter Hamilton. Harmondsworth: Penguin, 1977.

—*The Republic of Plato: An Ideal Commonwealth*. Trans. by Benjamin Jowett. New York: The Colonial Press, 1901.

Pusey, E. B. "Un-Science, not Science, Adverse to Faith." Anglicanhistory.org. www.anglicanhistory.org/pusey/unscience.pdf [accessed September 2012].

"Rank frequency list for the whole corpus (not lemmatized)." University Centre for Computer Corpus Research on Language, Lancaster University. http:// ucrel.lancs.ac.uk/bncfreq/samples/120.pdf [accessed September 2012].

Reardon, Bernard. *Religion in the Age of Romanticism*. Cambridge: Cambridge University Press, 1985.

Reed, Edward S. *From Soul to Mind: The Emergence of Psychology from Erasmus Darwin to William James*. New Haven and London: Yale University Press, 1997.

Ribot, Théodule-Armand. *Les maladies de la personnalité*. Paris: Felix Alcan, 1885.

Richardson, Robert D., Jr. *Emerson: The Mind on Fire*. Berkeley, CA: University of California Press, 1995.

Richardson, Samuel. *Clarissa, or The History of a Young Lady*. New York: Penguin, 1985.

—*Pamela, or Virtue Rewarded*. London: T. Kinnersley, 1816.

—*Pamela, or Virtue Rewarded*. New York: Penguin, 1985.

Rimbaud, Arthur. Collected Poems. Trans. by Olivier Bernard. London: Penguin, 1987.

Robbe-Grillet, Alain. "Introduction to the Screenplay." In untitled booklet accompanying the Criterion Collection DVD of *Last Year at Marienbad*, 20–33. 2009.

—*Le miroir qui revient*. Paris: Les éditions de minuit, 1984.

—*Two Novels by Robbe-Grillet*. New York: Grove Press, 1965.

Rodman, F. Robert. *Winnicott: His Life and Work*. Cambridge, MA: Da Capo Press, 2003.

Rosenwald, Lawrence. "Sewall's Diary and the Margins of Puritan Literature." *American Literature* 58 (1986), 325–41.

Ross, James Bruce, and Mary Martin McLaughlin (eds). *The Portable Renaissance Reader*. New York: Penguin, 1977.

Rousseau, Jean-Jacques. *Confessions*. Trans. by Angela Scholar. Oxford: Oxford University Press, 2008.

—*Emile, or On Education*. Trans. by Barbara Foxley and Grace Roosevelt. Institute for Learning Technologies, Columbia University. http://www.ilt.columbia.edu/pedagogies/rousseau/index.html [accessed September 2012].

—*Reveries of the Solitary Walker*. London: Penguin, 2004.

—*The Social Contract*. Trans. by G. D. H. Cole. The Constitution Society. http://www.constitution.org/jjr/socon.htm [accessed September 2012].

Royce, Josiah. "George Fox as a Mystic." *The Harvard Theological Review* 6 (1913), 31–59.

Ruzbihan Baqli, *The Unveiling of Secrets: Diary of a Sufi Master*. Trans. by Carl W. Ernst. Chapel Hill, NC: Parvardigar Press, 1997.

Ryle, Gilbert. *The Concept of Mind*. New York and London: Routledge, 2009.

Santayana, George. *The Life of Reason: Reason in Religion*. New York: C. Scribner's Sons, 1905.

Sartre, Jean-Paul. *Being and Nothingness*. Trans. by Hazel E. Barnes. New York: Washington Square Press, 1993.

—"The Living Gide," reproduced from *Gide: A Collection of Critical Essays* (1970). Andregide.org. http://www.andregide.org/remembrance/sagide.html [accessed September 2012].

—*Nausea*. Trans. by Robert Baldick. Harmondsworth, Middlesex: Penguin, 1967.

—*The Transcendence of the Ego*. New York: Hill and Wang, 1991.

—*The Words: The Autobiography of Jean-Paul Sartre*. Trans. by Bernard Frechtman. New York: Vintage, 1981.

Schelling, Friedrich Wilhelm Joseph. *System of Transcendental Philosophy*. Philosophy Archive @ marxists.org. http://www.cddc.vt.edu/marxists/reference/subject/philosophy/works/ge/schellin.htm [accessed September 2012].

Schopenhauer, Arthur. *On the Basis of Morality*. Trans. by E. F. J. Payne. Indianapolis, IN: Hackett, 1998.

—*The World as Will and Representation*. Trans. by E. F. J. Payne. Two volumes. Mineola, NY: Dover Publications, 1958.

Scurlock, JoAnn. "Soul Emplacements in Ancient Mesopotamian Funerary Rituals." In *Magic and Divination in the Ancient World*. Leda Jean Ciralo and Jonathan Lee Seidel (eds), 1–6. Leiden: Brill, 2002.

Seigel, Jerrold. *The Idea of the Self*. Cambridge: Cambridge University Press, 2005.

Seneca. "Epistle 31." In *Moral Epistles*. Trans. by Richard M. Gummere. Wikisource. http://en.wikisource.org/wiki/Moral_letters_to_Lucilius/Letter_31 [accessed September 2012].

—*On the Shortness of Life*. Trans. by John W. Basore. Wikisource. http://en.wikisource.org/wiki/On_the_shortness_of_life [accessed September 2012].

Shakespeare, William. *The Arden Shakespeare Complete Works*. Richard Proudfoot, Ann Thompson, and David Scott Kastan (eds). Walton-on-Thames, Surrey: Thomas Nelson and Sons, 1998.

Shantideva, *The Way of the Bodhisattva: A Translation of the Bodhicaryavatara*. Trans. by Padmakara Translation Group, Boston: Shambhala, 1999.

Shelley, Percy Bysshe. "A Defence of Poetry." Bartleby.com. http://www.bartleby.com/27/23.html [accessed September 2012].

Shepard, Odell (ed.). *The Heart of Thoreau's Journals*. New York: Dover Publications, 1961.

Smith, Zadie. "Generation Why?" *New York Review of Books*, November 25, 2010. http://www.nybooks.com/articles/archives/2010/nov/25/generation-why/ [accessed September 2012].

Snell, Bruno. *The Discovery of the Mind*. Trans. by T. G. Rosenmeyer. Mineola, NY: Dover Publications, 1982.

Sontag, Susan. "Writing Itself: On Roland Barthes." In *A Barthes Reader*. Susan Sontag (ed.), vii–xxxi. New York: Barnes & Noble, 2009.

Southey, Robert and Caroline Bowles Southey. *The Correspondence of Robert Southey with Caroline Bowles*. Dublin: Hodges, Figgis & Co., 1881.

Spencer, Herbert. *First Principles*. Electronic Text Center: University of Virginia Library. http://etext.virginia.edu/toc/modeng/public/SpeFirs.html [accessed September 2012].

Spenser, Edmund. *The Faerie Queene*. London: William Ponsonbie, 1596. Renaissance Editions. https://scholarsbank.uoregon.edu/xmlui/bitstream/handle/1794/784/faeriequeene.pdf?sequence=1 [accessed September 2012].

Stendhal [Henri Beyle]. *Journal de Stendhal*. Paris: Charpantier, 1888. The Internet Archive. http://ia700301.us.archive.org/9/items/journaldestendha00stenuoft/journaldestendha00stenuoft.pdf [accessed September 2012].

—*The Life of Henry Brulard*. Trans. by John Sturrock. New York: NYRB Classics, 2001.

—*Lucien Leuwen*. n.p.: Elibron Classics, 2001.

—*The Private Diaries of Stendhal*. Trans. by Robert Sage (ed.). New York: Doubleday, 1954.

—*The Red and the Black*. Trans. by C. K. Scott Moncrieff. Adelaide, South Australia: eBooks@Adelaide, 2009. http://ebooks.adelaide.edu.au/s/stendhal/red/index.html [accessed September 2012].

—*Souvenirs d'égotisme*. Paris: Charpantier, 1892.

Sterne, Laurence. *Tristram Shandy*. Ware, Hertfordshire: Wordsworth, 1999.

Stevenson, Robert Lewis. "Samuel Pepys." Bartleby.com. http://www.bartleby.com/28/12.html [accessed September 2012].

Stoltzfus, Ben. "Andre Gide and the Voices of Rebellion." *Contemporary Literature* 19 (1978): 80–98.

Stone, Brad. "Children of Cyberspace: Old Fogies by Their 20s." *New York Times*, January 9, 2010. http://www.nytimes.com/2010/01/10/weekinreview/10stone.html [accessed September 2012].

Strawson, P. F. *Individuals*. London: Routledge, 1996.

Strugnell, Anthony. *Diderot's Politics: A Study of the Evolution of Diderot's Political Thought*. The Hague: Springer, 1973.

Swedenborg, Emanuel. *Arcana Coelestia*. Trans. by John F. Potts. Internet Sacred Text Archives. http://www.sacred-texts.com/swd/ac/index.htm [accessed September 2012].

—*Heaven and Its Wonders and Hell*. Trans. by John Ager. Project Gutenberg. http://www.gutenberg.org/cache/epub/17368/pg17368.html [accessed September 2012].

—*Swedenborg's Dream Diary*. Trans. by Anders Hallengren. West Chester, PA: Swedenborg Foundation Publishers, 2001.

"Système Figuré des Connoissances Humaines." In Wikipedia, "Figurative System of Human Knowledge." http://en.wikipedia.org/wiki/Figurative_system_of_human_knowledge [accessed September 2012].

Taylor, Charles. *Sources of the Self: The Making of the Modern Identity*. Cambridge, MA: Harvard University Press, 1989.

Teahan, John F. "A Dark and Empty Way: Thomas Merton and the Apophatic Tradition." *The Journal of Religion* 58 (1978), 263–87.

Teilhard de Chardin, Pierre. *The Divine Milieu*. New York: Harper and Row, 1960.

—*Journal: 26 août 1915–4 janvier 1919*. Paris: Fayard, 1975.

—*Man's Place in Nature: The Human Zoological Group*. New York: Harper and Row, 1966.

—*The Phenomenon of Man*. New York: Harper and Row, 1965.

Tennyson, Alfred. *In Memoriam*, Epilogue. Academy of American Poets, Poets.org. http://www.poets.org/viewmedia.php/prmMID/20265 [accessed September 2012].

Teresa of Avila, Saint. *The Life of Saint Teresa of Avila by Herself*. London: Penguin, 1957.

Terzioglu, Derin. "Man in the Image of God in the Image of the Times: Sufi Self-Narratives and the Diary of Niyazi-i Misri (1618–94)." *Studia Islamica* 94 (2002), 139–65.

Thoreau, Henry David. *The Journal of Henry David Thoreau*, Fourteen volumes. Boston: Houghton Mifflin Co., 1906.

—*The Maine Woods*. Thoreau Reader. http://thoreau.eserver.org/mewoods.html [accessed September 2012].

—*A Week on the Concord and Merrimack Rivers*. Electronic Text Center, University of Virginia Library. http://etext.virginia.edu/toc/modeng/public/ ThoWeek.html [accessed September 2012].

Tipson, Baird. "How Can the Religious Experience of the Past Be Recovered? The Examples of Puritanism and Pietism." *Journal of the American Academy of Religion* 43 (1975), 695–707.

—"The Routinized Piety of Thomas Shepard's Diary." *Early American Literature* 13 (1978), 64–80.

Tocqueville, Alexis de. *Democracy in America*. Trans. by Henry Reeve. University of Virginia, American Studies Program. http://xroads.virginia. edu/~HYPER/DETOC/toc_indx.html [accessed September 2012].

Todd, Margo. "Puritan Self-Fashioning: The Diary of Samuel Ward." *The Journal of British Studies* 31 (1992), 236–64.

Traherne, Thomas. *The Poetical Works of Thomas Traherne*. London: Bertram Dobell, 1906. The Internet Archive. http://www.archive.org/stream/ poeticalworksoft00trah/poeticalworksoft00trah_djvu.txt [accessed September 2012].

Traubel, Horace. *With Walt Whitman in Camden*, vol. 1. New York: Rowman and Littlefield, 1961.

Valéry, Paul. *Aesthetics*. Trans. by Ralph Manheim. Princeton: Princeton University Press, 1964.

Vigny, Alfred de. "L'esprit pur." Les grands classiques. http://poesie.webnet.fr/ lesgrandsclassiques/poemes/alfred_de_vigny/l_esprit_pur.html [accessed September 2012].

—*Oeuvres complètes*, vol. 2. Paris: Gallimard, 1948.

Weber, Alison. "Little Women: Counter-Reformation Misogyny." In *The Counter Reformation*. David M. Luebke (ed.), 143–62. Malden, MA: Blackwell, 1999.

Weber, Max. *The Protestant Ethic and the Spirit of Capitalism*. Trans. by Talcott Parsons and Anthony Giddens. London and Boston: Unwin Hyman, 1930. Max Weber Reference library. http://www.marxists.org/reference/archive/ weber/protestant-ethic/index.htm [accessed September 2012].

Webster, Tom. "Writing to Redundancy: Approaches to Spiritual Journals and Early Modern Spirituality." *The Historical Journal* 39 (1996), 33–56.

Weddle, David L. "The Image of the Self in Jonathan Edwards: A Study of Autobiography and Theology." *Journal of the American Academy of Religion* 43 (1975), 70–83.

Whitman, Walt. *Complete Prose Works*. Philadelphia: David McKay, 1892. The Walt Whitman Archive. http://www.whitmanarchive.org/published/other/ CompleteProse.html [accessed September 2012].

—*Leaves of Grass*. Philadelphia: David McKay, 1891–2. The Walt Whitman Archive. http://whitmanarchive.org/published/LG/1891/whole.html [accessed September 2012].

Wigglesworth, Michael. *The Diary of Michael Wigglesworth 1653–1657*. Edmund S. Morgan (ed.). New York: Harper & Row, 1965.

Wilde, Oscar. *The Picture of Dorian Gray*, chapter 11. Lit2Go. http://etc.usf.edu/
lit2go/contents/2100/2185/2185_txt.html [accessed September 2012].

Williamson, George S. *The Longing for Myth in Germany*. Chicago: University
of Chicago Press, 2004.

Wilson, Arthur. *Diderot*. Oxford: Oxford University Press, 1972.

Winnicott, D. W. *The Maturational Process and the Facilitating Environment*.
London: Karnac Books, 1990.

Winthrop, John. *Experiencia*. Charles University, Prague, Department of
American Studies. http://tucnak.fsv.cuni.cz/~calda/Winthrop_Experiencia.
doc [accessed September 2012].

—"A Model of Christian Charity." Religious Freedom Page. http://religiousfreedom.
lib.virginia.edu/sacred/charity.html [accessed September 2012].

Wittgenstein, Ludwig. *Philosophical Investigations*. Trans. by G. E. M.
Anscombe, P. M. S. Hacker and Joachim Schulte. Chichester: Wiley-
Blackwell, 2009.

Wolfe, Tom. "The 'Me' Decade and the Third Great Awakening." *New York*, August
23, 1976: 26–40, http://nymag.com/news/features/45938/ [accessed September
2012].

Wolff, Tobias. *This Boy's Life: A Memoir*. New York: Grove Press, 1989.

Wood, Dennis. "Benjamin Constant: Life and Work." In *The Cambridge
Companion to Constant*. Helena Rosenblatt (ed.), 3–22. Cambridge:
Cambridge University Press, 2009.

Woolf, Virginia. *Moments of Being*. London: Grafton Books, 1989.

"Word frequency lists and dictionary from the Corpus of Contemporary
American English." http://www.wordfrequency.info/free.asp?s=y [accessed
September 2012].

Wordsworth, William. *The Fenwick Notes of William Wordsworth*. Tirril:
Humanities-Ebooks, 2007.

—*Poetical Works*, vol. 3, *The Prelude*. Project Gutenberg. http://www.gutenberg.
org/files/12383/12383-h/Wordsworth3c.html [accessed September 2012].

—*The Recluse*. Bartleby.com. http://www.bartleby.com/145/ww301.html
[accessed September 2012].

Zaehner, R. C. *Evolution in Religion: A Study in Sri Aurobindo and Pierre
Teilhard de Chardin*. Oxford: Clarendon Press, 1971.

Zola, Émile. "Les romanciers naturalistes." La Page des Lettres. http://www.
lettres.ac-versailles.fr/spip.php?article187 [accessed September 2012].

Index